Yosemite, Sequoia
& Kings Canyon
National Parks

Yosemite
National Park
p44

Around Yosemite
National Park
p134

Sequoia &
Kings Canyon
National Parks
p165

Michael Grosberg, Jade Bremner

PLAN YOUR TRIP

ON THE ROAD

NIGHT SKY, GLACIER POINT P104

HORSETAIL FALL P103

VIEW FROM TUNNEL VIEW P45

Contents

VIEW OF HALF DOME FROM GLACIER POINT P104

TAHA RAJA/500PX ©

SUMMIT OF CLOUDS REST P59

OWEN REISER/SHUTTERSTOCK ©

Welcome to Yosemite, Sequoia & Kings Canyon

With fierce granite mountains brooding over high-altitude lakes, the Sierra Nevada is an exquisite topographic barrier enclosing magnificent natural landscapes and an adventurer's wonderland.

Backcountry Bonanza

Spanning central California, the Sierra Nevada encompasses dazzling mountain canyons and some of the highest peaks in the country. Trails lure visitors to valleys of wildflowers and desolate pinnacles. Bears tear open logs, marmots whistle in warning, and crickets and frogs harmonize to a nightly fever pitch. Spending time in the wilderness resets your brain. Maybe it has something to do with the timelessness of the landscape – the ancient glaciers or the glow of the lakes at dusk and dawn.

Time Warps

This region has a past both wide and deep. Glaciers, though receding, gnaw at granite shoulders as they have for millennia. Prehistoric forests loom within the parks and at inhospitable heights beyond them. The volcanic forces that moved these mountains to life still rumble underfoot and in simmering hot springs. Humans have left their mark as well. Trails show the routes taken by indigenous Californians – the Sierra Miwok, the Paiute and the Shoshone – who traded between the western foothills and the Eastern Sierra. Pioneers abandoned mining camps to the elements, creating desolate ghost towns and the remains of forgotten railway lines.

Winter Wonderland

Summer may be high season, but after you've seen snow in the Sierra you might well question why. The peaks are some of the highest in the US, occasionally bursting to 14,000ft, and are blanketed by snow for much of the year. There are full-moon snowshoeing and cross-country adventures, plus the chance to camp under giant sequoias. Go swooshing across the hushed backcountry, barrel down powdery slopes, or just stay inside and warm your toes by a roaring wood fire.

High Peaks

Punctuated with fairy-tale spires, knobby domes and talus-encrusted mountaintops, the scenery in the national parks of Yosemite, Sequoia and Kings Canyon might just put a crick in your neck as you gaze at it all. A jaunt through Yosemite Valley is a ticker-tape parade of granite skyscrapers, with Half Dome taking a deep bow. Tempestuous Mt Whitney lords over the far-eastern reaches of Sequoia National Park. With wild rock formations, groves of the planet's largest trees, astonishing waterfalls, deep canyons, unimaginably vast swaths of granite, humbling peaks and a four-season dance card, Yosemite, Sequoia and Kings Canyon are no less than perfect.

Why I Love Yosemite, Sequoia & Kings Canyon

By Michael Grosberg, Writer

When city life gets claustrophobic, the Sierra Nevada national parks beckon me. Whether driving down Kings Canyon Scenic Byway or hiking a mountain trail, the scale appears other-worldly, like being in an Albert Bierstadt painting or a CGI version of the American West. On the eastern side, where the desert meets snowcapped peaks, the road and the landscape seem endless and the contrast feels liberating. Being in the backcountry, whether in a national park or other wilderness area, my thoughts become effortlessly meditative as the rhythm of my pace and the challenge of the terrain are the only concerns.

For more about our writers, see p264.

Above: Paddling in Yosemite Valley (p48)

Yosemite, Sequoia & Kings Canyon

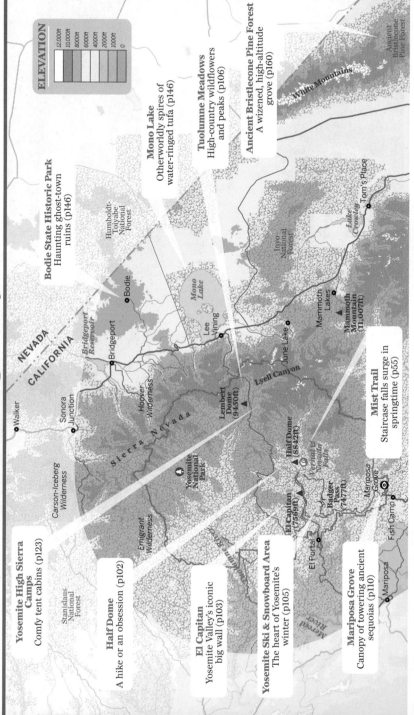

Bodie State Historic Park
Haunting ghost-town ruins (p146)

Mono Lake
Otherworldly spires of water-ringed tufa (p146)

Tuolumne Meadows
High-country wildflowers and peaks (p106)

Ancient Bristlecone Pine Forest
A wizened, high-altitude grove (p160)

Yosemite High Sierra Camps
Comfy tent cabins (p123)

Half Dome
A hike or an obsession (p102)

El Capitan
Yosemite Valley's iconic big wall (p103)

Yosemite Ski & Snowboard Area
The heart of Yosemite's winter (p105)

Mariposa Grove
Canopy of towering ancient sequoias (p110)

Mist Trail
Staircase falls surge in springtime (p55)

ELEVATION

12,000ft
10,000ft
8000ft
6000ft
4000ft
2000ft
1000ft
0

20 miles
40 km

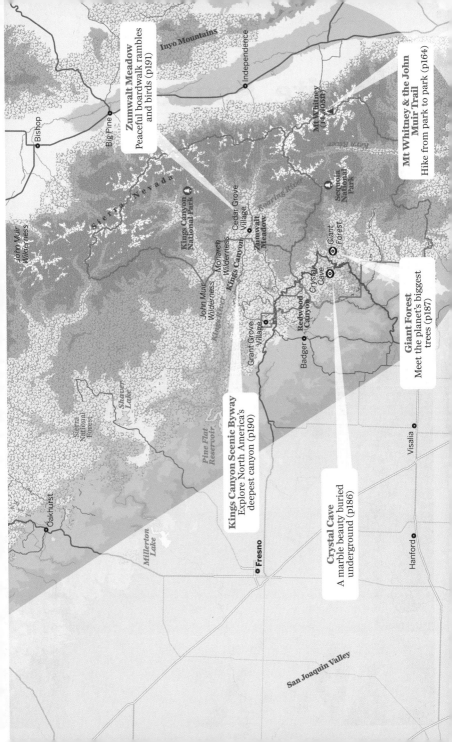

Zumwalt Meadow
Peaceful boardwalk rambles and birds (p191)

Mt Whitney & the John Muir Trail
Hike from park to park (p164)

Giant Forest
Meet the planet's biggest trees (p187)

Kings Canyon Scenic Byway
Explore North America's deepest canyon (p190)

Crystal Cave
A marble beauty buried underground (p186)

Inyo Mountains

Independence

Bishop

Big Pine

Sierra Nevada

John Muir
Wilderness

Kings Canyon
National Park

Cedar Grove
Village

Zumwalt
Meadow

Monarch
Wilderness

John Muir
Wilderness

Kings Canyon

Mt Whitney
(4,405m)

Kern River

Sequoia
National
Park

Giant
Forest

Crystal
Cave

Redwood
Canyon

Grant Grove
Village

Badger

Shaver
Lake

Sierra
National
Forest

Pine Flat
Reservoir

Oakhurst

Millerton
Lake

Fresno

Visalia

Hanford

San Joaquin Valley

Yosemite, Sequoia & Kings Canyon's
Top 16

1

Spring Waterfalls

1 Nothing can strike you speechless like water plunging off a cliff. Standing at the base of a massive waterfall, hearing its roar and reveling in its drenching mist is simultaneously invigorating and humbling. Yosemite holds one of the world's greatest collections of waterfalls and, in springtime, Yosemite Valley is spray central. In addition to the seasonal creeks tumbling over the valley's walls, the iconic cataracts of Yosemite Falls (pictured; p102) and Bridalveil Fall (p103) will satisfy any falls fanatic.

Tuolumne Meadows & Tioga Road

2 Winter makes you wait to take in the beauty of Tuolumne (p106), but it's so worth it. In summer, after Tioga Rd has been plowed and the roadside walls of snow recede, make a beeline for Yosemite's high country for carpets of outrageous wildflowers and a cornucopia of alpine lakes. Climbers clip in to tackle the park's high peaks, backpackers lace their eager boots and mules plod the trails to stock the High Sierra camps. Explore the granite eye candy at one of the Cathedral Lakes (pictured; p109) or just roam Tuolumne's creek-laced main meadow.

JASON FINN/SHUTTERSTOCK ©

ADONIS VILLANUEVA/SHUTTERSTOCK ©

CHRISTOPHER FAIRFAX/SHUTTERSTOCK ©

DRIENDL GROUP/GETTY IMAGES ©

Climbing Half Dome

3 Just hold on, don't forget to breathe and – whatever you do – don't look down. A pinnacle so popular that hikers need a permit to scale it, Half Dome (p74) lives on as Yosemite Valley's coveted jewel and a must-reach-it obsession for millions. It's a day hike longer than an average work day, an elevation gain equivalent to almost 480 flights of stairs, and a final stretch of near-vertical steps that melts even the strongest legs and arms to masses of quivering jelly.

Giant Forest

4 When it's time to pay your respects to the most massive trees on the planet, there's nowhere better to go than Sequoia National Park. Giant sequoias (*Sequoiadendron giganteum*) can live for almost 3000 years, and some of the ancient ones standing in the Giant Forest have been around since the fall of the Roman Empire. There the world's largest living specimen, the General Sherman Tree (p187), is taller than a 27-story building and measures over 100ft around its massive trunk – crane your neck as you stare in awe at its leafy crown.

El Capitan

5 A pale fortress rising abruptly from the Yosemite Valley floor, El Capitan (p103) is a majestic spectacle in the glow of dusk. Summiting the sheer granite and splintering cracks of this monolith is the vertigo-conquering achievement of a lifetime. Now the world standard for big-wall climbs, it was once deemed impossible to ascend. Strain your eyes to find the glowing, moth-like bivuoac shelters dangling from its face at night, and bite your nails tracking the climbers' progress by day.

LYNN YEH/SHUTTERSTOCK ©

Mt Whitney & the John Muir Trail

6 In for the long haul? Load up that pack and connect the dots from the heart of Yosemite to the pinnacle of Mt Whitney (p164), the highest peak in the contiguous USA. A true adventure, the physically demanding, 211-mile John Muir Trail goes step by step up and over six Sierra passes topping 11,000ft. Join other blister-footed obsessives crossing chilly rivers and streams between bumper-to-bumper Yosemite Valley, the roadless backcountry of Kings Canyon and Sequoia and the oxygen-scarce Whitney summit. Hikers on the Mt Whitney trail

DANITA DELIMONT/GETTY IMAGES ©

Kings Canyon Scenic Byway

7 Marvel at soaring granite walls and river-carved clefts deeper than the Grand Canyon on this scenic drive (p190), which connects Grant Grove and Cedar Grove in Kings Canyon National Park. Pull into Junction View just before sunset or dawn to truly appreciate the glacier-smoothed canyon, which John Muir called 'a rival to the Yosemite.' Twisting hairpin turns, sheer drop-offs and mile-high cliffs are all part of the thrill as you wind down to the bottom alongside the rushing Kings River.

Bodie State Historic Park

8 Hopscotch back in time to the era of the lawless Wild West, and imagine the quick-draw barroom brawls and frenzied gold strikes of the former boom town of Bodie (p146). One of the West's most authentic and best-preserved ghost towns, it's accessed via a long road that bumps toward a desolate high valley. Now a serene landscape dotted with weather-battered wooden buildings, in its heyday it was renowned for its opium dens and more than 60 saloons.

BJORN ALBERTS/GETTY IMAGES ©

CURTIS/SHUTTERSTOCK ©

Mariposa Grove

9 Pace the needle-carpeted trails in a cathedral of ancient trees (p110), where almost 500 hardy sequoias rocket to the sky. In the early evening, after the crowds have gone, you can explore in solitude and contemplate the thousands of years the trees have witnessed. Fire scars blaze the trunks, and you can walk through the heart of the still-living California Tunnel Tree and wonder at the girth of the Grizzly Giant. Snowshoe or ski here after the road closes for winter to see its yearly hibernation, and snow camp beneath a giant.

Yosemite High Sierra Camps

10 Who said you had to bust your back to trek overnight in the mountains? In the tradition of European hut-to-hut hikes, each of Yosemite's five tent-cabin camps (p123) sits in the spectacular high country, spaced one day's walk apart in a splendid alpine loop. Spend each day bouncing almost weightlessly down the trail, and then end with a hot meal – prepared by someone else – and the possibility of a hot shower. Warning: this may be addictive.
Merced Lake High Sierra Camp

Hiking the Mist Trail

11 This hike (p55) was made for springtime, when the thundering waters of the Merced River form the Giant Staircase, ricocheting 594ft from Nevada Fall and then 317ft down from Vernal Fall on the way to meet Yosemite Valley. Views of Illilouette Fall in the distance complete a stunning panorama of granite, forest and gushing water. Pack your lunch, and maybe a rain jacket for the trail's namesake mist, and take your time on the steep granite steps, pausing to catch your breath and contemplate the scenery. Vernal Fall

Zumwalt Meadow

12 There's something magical about Zumwalt Meadow (p191), secreted deep inside Kings Canyon and ranged against soaring granite walls. Here abundant birdlife peacefully flits between trees, and you'll have an excellent chance of spotting mule deer or even a black bear and her cubs munching on sweet grasses and berries. Zumwalt Meadow is a living geology lesson, wildlife primer and Zen meditation all rolled into one. Traipse across the footbridge and out onto the wooden boardwalks (pictured below) for wide-angle views of its lushness.

Majestic Yosemite Hotel

13 The soaring ceilings and tapestried walls of the 1927 Majestic Yosemite Hotel (p100) epitomize luxury – in a dignified, Old West, National Historic Landmark kind of way. The muted elegance of the iconic lodging in the nation's most iconic park is on view for all to see, not just the lucky overnighters lounging on its stuffed sofas. Dress up for dinner in its grand, high-beamed dining room, stop in for evening drinks at the piano bar, or grab afternoon tea or coffee at the outdoor patio.

AMIN TANG/GETTY IMAGES ©

KIT LEONG/SHUTTERSTOCK ©

Crystal Cave

14 Step through the creepy Spider Gate to explore the subterranean tunnels and cool passageways of this rare marble cave (p186). Among hundreds of caves that have been discovered in Sequoia and Kings Canyon National Parks, this is the only one open to the public. A hot spot for biodiversity, the marble karst cave is full of stalagmites and stalactites that appear frozen in time, as well as even more impressive hanging curtains and flowstone formations. Guided tours are given daily during summer – don't forget to dodge the bats!

Yosemite Ski & Snowboard Area

15 Play like a puppy dog at California's oldest ski resort (p105), where fun is paramount and the hills are gentle. It's the center of winter activity in Yosemite, so bring the kids to get them started on skis, or send them tubing down an easy slope. With a convenient shuttle from the valley, it's also an easy-to-reach terminus for ranger-led snowshoe walks to Dewey Point (pictured) and overnight cross-country trips to Glacier Point Ski Hut. At the end of the day, don't forget to treat everyone to hot chocolate piled high with whipped cream.

Mono Lake

16 Brought back from the brink of extinction by local conservationists battling the might of Los Angeles, the enormous Mono Basin (p146) – the second-oldest lake in North America – is truly a sight to ponder. Salty tufa castles rise from subterranean springs, standing watch where mountains meet the desert. Migrating birds feast on clouds of lake flies once relished by local Native American tribes, and bubbly volcanic craters and deep rock fissures buffer this vast blue bowl.

Need to Know

For more information, see Survival Guide (p231).

Entrance Fees
Yosemite: $35/30/20 per car/motorcycle/person on foot or bicycle.
Sequoia & Kings Canyon: $35/30/20 per car/motorcycle/ person on foot or bicycle; admits to both parks.

Annual Visitors
Yosemite: 4.3 million
Sequoia & Kings Canyon: 1.98 million

Year Founded
1890 (all parks)

Money
If you need to change money, do so at the airport or in a major city.

Cell Phones
Cell-phone reception can be patchy through the Sierra region. See p242 for details.

Transportation
Sealed roads throughout parks. Ample parking in Yosemite Valley and shuttle buses stop throughout Yosemite. Summer shuttles in Kings Canyon and Sequoia National Parks.

When to Go

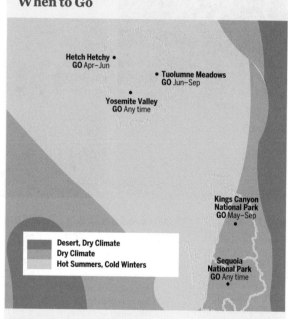

Hetch Hetchy
GO Apr–Jun

Tuolumne Meadows
GO Jun–Sep

Yosemite Valley
GO Any time

Kings Canyon
National Park
GO May–Sep

Sequoia
National Park
GO Any time

Desert, Dry Climate
Dry Climate
Hot Summers, Cold Winters

High Season (Jun–Aug)
➡ Temperatures in Yosemite Valley and lower areas of Sequoia and Kings Canyon soar above 90°F (32°C), but higher altitudes are sublime.

➡ Head to the mountains for wilderness adventures and glorious sunshine.

Shoulder (Apr, May, Sep & Oct)
➡ Splendid fall foliage.

➡ Temperatures drop in late October.

➡ Spectacular Yosemite waterfalls in the spring.

➡ Crowds usually at weekends only.

➡ High-country and Sierra mountain passes inaccessible.

Low Season (Nov–Mar)
➡ Take a wintertime romp through snowy forests, but snows close the high-elevation roads.

➡ Most facilities shut down in and around the parks.

➡ Crowds disappear.

Useful Websites

Yosemite National Park
(www.nps.gov/yose) Official park website.

Sequoia & Kings Canyon National Parks (www.nps.gov/seki) Official parks website.

Sierra Web (www.thesierraweb.com) Eastern Sierra events and links to local visitor information.

Sierra Wave (www.sierrawave.net) Regional news site.

High Sierra Topix (www.highsierratopix.com) Excellent Sierra Nevada forums.

Yosemitenews.info (www.yosemitenews.info) Forums with deep Yosemite knowledge.

Lonely Planet (www.lonelyplanet.com/usa/california) Destination information, hotel bookings, traveler forum and more.

Important Numbers

Yosemite National Park	209-372-0200
Sequoia & Kings Canyon National Parks	559-565-3341
Recreation.gov (camping reservations, all parks)	877-444-6777
California road conditions	800-427-7623
Police, Fire & Ambulance	911

Exchange Rates

Australia	A$1	$0.72
Canada	C$1	$0.78
Europe	€1	$1.16
Japan	¥100	$0.88
New Zealand	NZ$1	$0.66
UK	£1	$1.30

For current exchange rates, see www.xe.com.

Daily Costs

**Budget:
Less than $100**

➡ Park entrance fee: $20–35
➡ Campsite: $15–30
➡ Daily shower in park: $5
➡ Meal at inexpensive restaurant outside park or fast-food option inside park: $10
➡ Groceries from markets in or outside parks: $20

**Midrange:
$100–250**

➡ In-park lodging, midrange hotel or B&B: $80–200
➡ Non-fast-food meal at park restaurant: $20
➡ Yosemite bicycle or rafting rental: $31–35
➡ Sequoia Crystal Cave tour: $16

**Top end:
More than $250**

➡ Room in a top park hotel: $200–550
➡ Meal in a park-hotel restaurant: $40–60
➡ Yosemite rock-climbing instruction: $150

Opening Dates

Yosemite
Park open year-round, 24 hours a day. Tioga Rd closes approximately mid-October until early summer (average is last week in May). Glacier Point Rd beyond Badger Pass closes November through May.

Sequoia & Kings Canyon
Parks open year-round, 24 hours a day. Kings Canyon Scenic Byway closes mid-November through mid-April. Mineral King Rd closes late October through late May. Crystal Cave closes December through April.

Park Policies

➡ Wilderness permits, some by lottery, are required year-round for overnight backcountry trips. A permit is required to summit Half Dome.
➡ Yosemite campsites can be reserved up to five months in advance.
➡ Pets in national parks must be leashed and are restricted to certain areas.
➡ To protect wildlife, food and scented items must always be stored properly, usually in bear storage containers in camp areas.
➡ Anglers must possess a California fishing license.
➡ Wear bright-colored clothes if hiking in national forests during hunting season in October and November.

Getting There & Around

Fresno Yosemite Airport
YARTS buses run along Hwy 41 to Oakhurst and into Yosemite Valley ($16, nearly four hours); it's 57 miles on Hwy 180 to Kings Canyon, but you'll need a car.

Mammoth Yosemite Airport
Some lodgings provide free transfers and Mammoth Express buses (one way $3.50) ply the route to Mammoth Lakes. Mammoth Taxi does airport runs as well.

Los Angeles International Airport You'll need a rental car to reach Lone Pine on Hwy 395 or the southern entrance to Sequoia National Park.

San Francisco International Airport Gateway to northern Sierras, with northern Yosemite accessible by rental car.

For much more on **getting around**, see p248.

PLAN YOUR TRIP NEED TO KNOW

What's New

Mariposa Grove Restoration

Closed for nearly three years, the Mariposa Grove, one of Yosemite National Park's iconic attractions, reopened in the summer of 2018. Most of the parking has been torn out, new paths added, roads converted to hiking trails, and a new South Entrance hub, with a shuttle to the grove, has been established, all delivering a more 'natural' experience. (p110)

New Gold Rush

After years of prolonged drought, the winter of 2017 brought record precipitation and flooding to the Sierra Nevada and the runoff scoured stream beds and riverbanks, leaving previously concealed veins of rock exposed and hordes of hopeful prospectors dreaming of discovering gold in them hills.

Groveland Hotel

In the 19th century, the business of the small town of Groveland, on the northwestern edge of the Stanislaus National Forest and on the way to Yosemite, was ranching and mining. Those industries have faded, but some of the historic buildings remained. One, Main St's architectural crown jewel, was recently renovated and refurbished from top to bottom, reopening as a beautiful boutique hotel. (p139)

Ferguson Fire

Yosemite Valley was shut down to visitors for nearly three weeks in the summer of 2018 as a wildfire raged in the Merced River Canyon, the Sierra and Stanislaus National Forests and in Yosemite itself. Two firefighters were killed and 19 others wounded while battling the fire that scorched 97,000 acres. A large stretch of Hwy 41 from Wawona to Tunnel View was closed for a month.

Name Changes

When Aramark/Yosemite Hospitality took over the reins from Delaware North (DNC) of all Yosemite's lodgings, eateries and commercial tours and activities in 2016, DNC sued the federal government, claiming compensation for the intellectual property rights of various park property titles. In response, the names of several landmark buildings were changed, including the Majestic Yosemite Hotel (formerly the Ahwahnee Hotel), Half Dome Village (formerly Curry Village) and Big Trees Lodge (formerly Wawona Hotel). However, much of the park signage hasn't changed, which may cause some confusion.

For more recommendations and reviews, see lonelyplanet.com/usa

If You Like...

Hiking

The sights look lovely from the car, but hiking through the landscape allows you to stop, smell and touch.

High Sierra Trail Epic journey from Crescent Meadow to Lone Pine Creek. (p178)

Mt Hoffmann Share the sights with marmots at Yosemite's midpoint, a stark, high peak that's easy to summit. (p58)

Zumwalt Meadow Mosey around the wildflowers between river and canyon, listening for birds and looking for wildlife. (p191)

Mirror Lake An easy hike with a renowned reflection of Half Dome. (p49)

Little Lakes Valley Azure high-altitude lakes with vistas of enormous peaks. (p149)

Moro Rock Climb the steps to this iconic dome with views of peaks above and foothills below. (p188)

Backpacking

Break out that pack and put some distance between you and everyday life. With a wilderness permit, you're ready to roam.

Rae Lakes Loop Get acquainted with the Kings Canyon back-country on a jaunt along a chain of sparkling lakes. (p179)

High Sierra camps Feel a spring in your step while trekking without the weight of a tent or food. (p123)

Rancheria Falls Dodge bear scat along the Hetch Hetchy Reservoir during a spring hike past raging Wapama Falls. (p86)

Mt Whitney backdoor route Sneak up on Mt Whitney from Sequoia and forgo the permit lottery for this popular peak. (p164)

Ansel Adams Wilderness Area Some of the Sierra's most dramatic scenery, including spectacular high-altitude lakes, abuts Yosemite. (p148)

Hoover Wilderness Escape the summer crowds here, or use its trails to access Yosemite's northern backcountry. (p148)

Waterfalls

Mesmerized by springtime flow? Grab your rain jacket and let the never-ending spray work its magic.

Yosemite Falls The thundering cascades draw stares from across Yosemite Valley. (p102)

Mist Falls Kings Canyon has a trick or two up its sleeve, and this is one of its largest. (p176)

Bridalveil Fall After thundering in spring, its wispy summer trickle shows how it got its name. (p103)

Vernal Fall Hike here and to Nevada Fall to see the steps of the Great Staircase leap and plunge. (p55)

Rainbow Falls Be wowed by the prism that jets off its waters near the Devils Postpile National Monument. (p153)

Lundy Canyon A plethora of cascades surrounded by beavers' dams and shimmying aspen. (p145)

Tokopah Falls Sequoia's 1200ft beauty bounces off the canyon cliffs. (p37)

Views

Lift your eyes and adjust your road-weary pupils to stark mountains, ethereal lakes and vertiginous canyon cliffs. You could gaze for a lifetime – it never gets old.

Glacier Point A dizzying overlook onto Half Dome, with falls pouring from all sides. (p103)

Mono Lake Canoe through this beautiful blue bowl and discover why locals refused to let it die. (p146)

Alabama Hills Movie-set famous, its blazing orange hills give way to soaring snow-tipped peaks of granite. (p162)

Buck Rock Fire Lookout Summit this remote fire lookout atop a rocky mountain perch looking out over the Great Western Divide. (p189)

Mt Dana A grueling ascent pays off with an exquisite panorama of the High Sierra and Mono Lake. (p68)

Kings Canyon Scenic Byway This jaw-dropping scenic drive plunges into one of North America's deepest canyons. (p190)

Minaret Vista Eye-popping views of the Ritter Range, the serrated Minarets and the remote reaches of Yosemite. (p153)

Giant Sequoias

The biggest trees you'll ever see, thankfully preserved, and the original reason these parks were created. Sequoias are living lightning rods and habitats for incredible ecosystems.

Mariposa Grove More than 500 giants live on, including a walk-through tunnel tree. (p110)

Giant Forest Don't miss a gander at the hefty General Sherman Tree, by volume the largest living tree on earth. (p187)

General Grant Grove A virtual sequoia playground of hollow specimens and the site of the country's first ranger station. (p190)

Redwood Canyon In a land full of superlatives, this out-of-the-way spot earns another: the world's largest sequoia grove. (p190)

Tuolumne Grove Kids can tramp through a hollowed-out tunnel, and cross-country skiers make tracks here in winter. (p56)

Merced Grove Yosemite's smallest and most tranquil grove harbors 24 specimens. (p114)

KENRINGER/GETTY IMAGES ©

CAMPPHOTO/GETTY IMAGES ©

Top: Snow-dusted El Capitan (p103)

Bottom: Hot springs, Bridgeport (p147)

Winter Activities

Revel in the hushed pine forests, or scream down a powdery mountain chute. The bears may be slumbering, but you don't have to!

Mammoth Mountain Steel yourself for a gondola ride to 11,053ft and a season that practically lasts until summer. (p151)

Yosemite Ski & Snowboard Area Beginners will love the gentle hill at California's oldest ski resort. (p105)

Winter ski huts Strap on the skis or snowshoes and set out to rustic stone cabins. (p186)

Ice-skating Practice those rusty pirouettes alfresco under the gaze of Glacier Point. (p96)

Snow play Go tubing and sledding at dedicated areas in and outside the parks. (p148)

Extreme Adventures

Not one to seek out creature comforts or follow the pack? Up your adrenaline level with a few local favorites, but feel free to invent your own.

Rafting the Merced River Canyon Bounce over the spring runoff that ends up here as class III to VI rapids. (p92)

Hang gliding If you're certified, leap off a cliff at Glacier Point

and float down to Yosemite Valley. (p94)

El Capitan Summit the big wall of a lifetime. (p30)

Badwater Ultramarathon Push your mortal limits with a little jaunt between Death Valley and Mt Whitney. (p23)

Mammoth Mountain Bike Park Scream down the mountain on two wheels as you flirt with the perils of gravity. (p245)

History

Take a few steps back in time to see who and what has come before.

Bodie State Historic Park Journey down a back road to this beautifully preserved ghost town, among the best in California. (p146)

Manzanar National Historic Site A shameful chapter in the nation's history is memorialized at the remains of this Japanese internment camp. (p162)

Museum of Western Film History Densely packed exhibits tracing the Old West in film, especially movies shot in nearby Alabama Hills. (p162)

Eastern California Museum Highlights the work of Paiute and Shoshone basket makers, pioneer alpinists and Manzanar artists. (p161)

Laws Railroad Museum & Historic Site A slice of life from the late-1880s Eastern Sierra,

with old buildings and a historic railway station. (p158)

Yosemite Museum Rotating exhibits complement a re-created Native American village and excellent docent interpreters. (p99)

Swimming

Chock-full of deep lakes, careening rivers and veins of gentle streams, the region has endless water adventures to choose from. You can swan dive into pools, simmer in boiling liquid or plunge into an icy pond.

June Lake The rival to California coastal beaches, this sandy expanse is backed by towering mountains. (p39)

Merced River Suit up and wander down to Yosemite's best summer splashing, or sit on boulders and soak up some sun.

Hume Lake Sandy coves and beaches lure families to this pleasant lake and campground. (p191)

Eastern Sierra Hot Springs Find a solitary soaking spot with a mountain view and then strip down to your birthday suit. (p147)

Muir Rock Cannonball off John Muir's lecture site and do laps from shore to shore in the lazy summer sunshine. (p192)

Tenaya Lake Build sandcastles on the beach and coax those toes into the chilly water. (p113)

Month by Month

January

Short days and freezing temperatures mostly empty out the parks, but solitude has never looked so stunning. Skiing and other snow sports reign supreme.

☆ A Taste of Yosemite

At the Majestic Yosemite Hotel, meet top chefs from around the country as they lead cooking demonstrations and offer behind-the-scenes kitchen tours in January and February. It's all topped off by a sumptuous gala dinner.

February

Daytime temperatures gradually increase as the days get longer. The skiing season hits its stride and the long Presidents' Day weekend brings out the snow hounds.

◉ Horsetail Fall

For two weeks at the end of the month, this thin, seasonal cascade becomes Yosemite's most photographed attraction. When the sun sets on clear evenings, the flow lights up like a river of fire.

March

When it's sunny, Yosemite Valley can top out at almost 60°F (15°C), though ice forms in the evenings. There's a taste of spring at lower elevations.

☆ Yosemite Springfest

Yosemite Ski and Snowboard Area hosts this winter carnival on the last weekend of each ski season, usually in late March or early April. Events include slalom racing, costume contests, obstacle courses, a barbecue and snow sculpting. (p105)

April

Don't forsake the tire chains – there's still the possibility of snowstorms during winter's last gasp. But by the end of the month, the dogwoods start to bloom and the waterfalls begin awakening.

🏃 Fishing Season

Anglers froth at the mouth counting the days until the last Saturday of the month. Why? It's the kickoff date of the fishing season (www.wildlife.ca.gov), and the trout are just waiting to bite.

May

Things really start stirring on Memorial Day weekend, when flocks of vacationers flood the area and the spring snowmelt courses through park waterfalls. Chilly nights punctuate the occasional 70°F (21°C) day.

◉ Waterfall Season

For falls fanatics, the warmer weather means one thing: cascades gushing off the hook. Yosemite's most famous attractions demonstrate their vigor, and seasonal flows such as Hetch Hetchy's Tueeulala Falls, and Silver Strand Falls and Sentinel Falls in Yosemite Valley, briefly come to life. (p70)

June

The high country has begun to thaw and the summer visitor influx begins. It's the best time to explore trails below 8000ft, though you'll want snow gear to hike much higher.

🏃 Tioga Road Opens

Though it varies year to year, this trans-Sierra highway is usually plowed and open by now. The Eastern Sierra suddenly feels a little closer, and hikers get that itch to strike the trail.

⛺ Tuolumne Meadows Poetry Festival

Wildflowers and words take center stage during a weekend of workshops and readings in Tuolumne Meadows.

◉ Perseid Meteor Shower

Yosemite's Glacier Point, any primitive campground or a spot down a dirt road in the high Sierra are great places to take in the fiery cavalcade of shooting stars.

July

Snow has usually receded from higher elevations, though mosquitoes often wait to greet you there. On lower ground, summer heat may leave you wilting.

⛺ Badwater Ultramarathon

A race (www.badwater. com) between the highest and lowest points in the continental US? Why not? Over 60 hours, runners attempt a nonstop course from Death Valley (35 miles southeast of Lone Pine) to Whitney Portal.

August

Temperatures in Yosemite Valley and the lower areas of Sequoia and Kings Canyon keep rising, making an escape to the higher altitudes a refreshing relief.

September

The summer heat begins to fizzle as the month progresses, giving way to brisk days and frigid evenings. The crowds recede and waterfalls are at a trickle.

⛺ Dark Sky Festival

At Sequoia and Kings Canyon's early-September Dark Sky Festival there are astronaut talks, activities for kids, photography workshops and guided tours of the celestial firmament.

⛺ Yosemite Facelift

The year's biggest volunteer event – in Yosemite or any other national park – sees grateful souls arrive for a major cleanup (www.yosemiteclimbing.org) at the season's end.

October

The weather is hit and miss, with either Sierra Nevada sunshine or bucketfuls of chilling rain. Mountain businesses wind up their season and diehards take one last hike before the first snowflakes appear.

◉ Autumn Foliage

Fall colors light up the Sierra Nevada and leaf-peeping photographers joyride looking for the best shot. Black oaks blaze dramatically in the undulating foothills, but it's the stands of aspen that steal the show as they flame gold under the blue high-elevation sky.

November

Deep snow shuts Tioga Rd and, ta-da!, it's the unofficial start of winter. The Thanksgiving holiday reels in families, and backcountry campers tune up their cross-country skis.

December

Vacationers inundate the resorts during the week between Christmas and New Year's Day, though otherwise the parks remain frosted and solitary. Think snowshoe hikes and hot chocolate.

⛺ Bracebridge Dinner

Held at the Majestic Yosemite Hotel, this traditional Christmas pageant is part feast and part Renaissance fair. Guests indulge in a multicourse meal while being entertained by more than 100 actors in 17th-century costume.

Itineraries

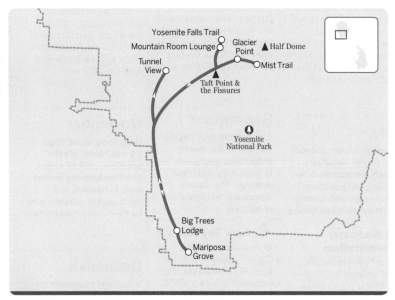

A Weekend in Yosemite

Feast on a multicourse banquet of Yosemite Valley attractions, scenic overlooks and giant sequoias.

Pack a lunch and head out to conquer the long climb of either the **Mist Trail** or the **Yosemite Falls Trail**, giving yourself lots of scenic breathers along the way. Quench your thirst post-hike with a celebratory drink at the Yosemite Valley Lodge's **Mountain Room Lounge**, and in the evening hear the rangers spin tales at a convivial campfire program.

On your second day, pack up and proceed to **Glacier Point**, stopping en route for a leisurely stroll to vertigo-inducing **Taft Point and the Fissures**. Save lunch for when you get to road's end, in full view of Half Dome and Vernal and Nevada Falls. Continue past Wawona to the South Entrance to take a gander at the giant sequoias of **Mariposa Grove**. Return to the historic **Big Trees Lodge** for dinner in its classy dining room. On your way home, stop at the magnificent **Tunnel View lookout**, taking in one last valley eyeful before you leave.

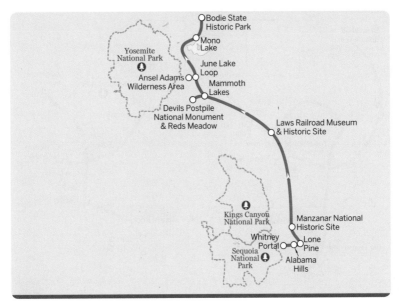

 ## Highway 395 (Eastern Sierra Scenic Byway)

Start in diminutive Lone Pine, exploring the fascinating paraphernalia from hundreds of movies in the **Museum of Western Film History**. Then head out to the nearby orange, round-earthen mounds of the otherworldly **Alabama Hills**, where many of the Old West Hollywood movies were shot. Day-trippers can make like they're on their way to climb the jagged peak of 14,505ft Mt Whitney by heading to **Whitney Portal** and Lone Pine Lake. Just up the road, near even tinier Independence, is the **Manzanar National Historic Site**, a museum dedicated to telling the story of a dark chapters in US history, located on the barren, windswept land of the former WWII-era internment camp.

You could then spend many days around Bishop, the second-largest town in the Eastern Sierra, hiking, cycling, fishing, bouldering... and hitting the **Laws Railroad Museum & Historic Site's** collection of antique railcars. Same goes for the year-round resort town of **Mammoth Lakes** (the mountain's ski season can run into June), with backcountry hikes galore, and a massive mountain-bike park. Don't miss **Reds Meadow**, just west of Mammoth Mountain, and the surreal 10,000-year-old **Devils Postpile National Monument**.

The drive around the **June Lake Loop**, under the shadow of Carson Peak, meanders through a horseshoe canyon, especially scenic in fall, and it's backed by the **Ansel Adams Wilderness Area** and its world-class high-country trails. In summer the swimming beach is a revelation of fun. For some geographic diversity, drive a little further north to **Mono Lake** to walk to its glassy surface and unearthly tufa towers. An appropriate coda to the trip is wandering among the frozen-in-time gold-rush-era buildings in the preserved ghost town of **Bodie State Historic Park**.

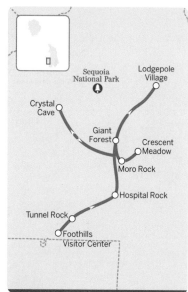

🏅8 DAYS Yosemite Complete

Pack in all of Yosemite's major sights on a tour of waterfalls, sequoias and high-country vistas. Spend your first day strolling the crowd-free **Yosemite Valley** loop trails. Next day, hike the drenched Mist Trail to **Vernal and Nevada Falls**. The following day float along the **Merced River** – the best rafting views you'll ever have. Reserve day four to huff and puff the Four Mile Trail to **Glacier Point** for vistas from the park's most famous viewpoint, or take a climbing class with the Yosemite Mountaineering School.

Drive out to Hetch Hetchy for a day trip and hike to **Tueeulala Falls** and **Wapama Falls**. Next morning, gobble down a filling breakfast at the historic **Big Trees Lodge**, park at Yosemite's South Entrance and humble yourself exploring the ancient **Mariposa Grove**. Pack a lunch and hike to thundering **Chilnualna Falls**, near Wawona. The following day, stop to marvel at **Olmsted Point** from the Tioga Rd viewpoint, and take in the dazzling views from the sandy shores of **Tenaya Lake**. Wind up your trip with a wander around the Sierra Nevada's biggest alpine meadow while camped at **Tuolumne Meadows**.

🏅1 DAY Sequoia National Park

Big trees, deep caves and high granite domes are all on the agenda for this day-long tour of Sequoia National Park.

Start your day at the **Foothills Visitor Center**, stopping long enough to get oriented. Head north on the Generals Hwy, hitting the brakes at **Tunnel Rock** – visualize squeezing through in a tin lizzie (small early-model car) – and to see Native American pictographs and grinding holes at **Hospital Rock**, near riverside swimming holes.

Arriving in **Giant Forest**, let yourself be dwarfed by the majestic General Sherman Tree, the world's largest tree. Learn more about giant sequoias at the kid-friendly Giant Forest Museum. Hop on the park shuttle for a wildflower walk around **Crescent Meadow** and to climb the puff-and-pant stairway up **Moro Rock** for bird's-eye canyon and peak views.

Picnic by the river at **Lodgepole Village**, then get back in your car and make your way to the chilly underground wonderland of **Crystal Cave**, where you can marvel at delicate marble formations while easing through eerie passageways.

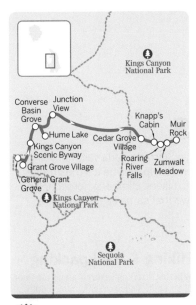

1 DAY Kings Canyon National Park

From giant sequoia crowns to the depths of the Kings River canyon, this twisting scenic drive is an eye-popping revelation.

Start in **Grant Grove Village** at the northern end of the Generals Hwy. Take a walk in **General Grant Grove**, encompassing the world's third-largest living tree and the gigantic Fallen Monarch.

Drive down the **Kings Canyon Scenic Byway** (Hwy 180), passing through the Giant Sequoia National Monument and stopping for a dip at **Hume Lake**. Back on the scenic byway, which starts descending precipitously, pull over to survey the canyon depths and distant peaks from lofty **Junction View**.

Cruise past **Cedar Grove Village**. Feel waves of spray from roadside **Roaring River Falls** and admire striking canyon views in verdant **Zumwalt Meadow**, a bird-watching spot with a boardwalk nature trail. At truthfully named Road's End, cool off at the beach by **Muir Rock** before turning around and driving back to catch a canyon sunset from historic **Knapp's Cabin**.

14 DAYS Sequoia to Alabama Hills

Kick off the trip with three to four days in **Sequoia and Kings Canyon National Parks**, touring their ancient trees, ethereal caves and showstopping river canyon. Heading north, camp at **Wawona** and budget a day for the southern reaches of Yosemite National Park. Spend at least three days exploring the miraculous falls and granite monoliths of **Yosemite Valley**, then hike the trails of Yosemite's high country while camped at **Tuolumne Meadows**.

East of the park, take a full day to explore the surreal countryside around **Saddlebag Lake** and then journey over to **Mono Lake**. Detour north to the ghost-town ruins of **Bodie State Historic Park** and then south for the mountain vistas buffering the **June Lake Loop**. From **Mammoth Lakes**, hike to the bizarre formation of the **Devils Postpile National Monument** before heading to the nearby **hot springs** at sunset. Next wind up the road to the **Ancient Bristlecone Pine Forest** to breathe the thin air and marvel at the gnarled, time-capsule trees. On your final day, tour the solemn remains of **Manzanar** and catch a film-worthy sunset at the Alabama Hills in **Lone Pine**.

Plan Your Trip
Activities

Every time you return home from a Sierra Nevada vacation, all you can think about for weeks is your next trip. Maybe it's the granite. Or the big, big trees. Whatever it is, hikers, climbers, horseback riders, river runners and skiers all have that same eager look here.

Best Time to Go

Backpacking June to September

Cycling May to October

Fall Foliage Viewing September to October

Hiking May to October

Horseback Riding June to August

Mountain Biking June to September

Rock Climbing April to October

Swimming July to August

White-water Rafting April to July

Winter Sports December to March

Top Outdoor Experiences

Backpacking John Muir Trail and summiting Mt Whitney

Cycling Yosemite Valley's paved trails

Hiking Half Dome high above Yosemite Valley

Mountain Biking Mammoth Mountain

Rock Climbing El Capitan in Yosemite Valley

Swimming, Tubing & Kayaking Merced River in Yosemite Valley

Skiing Downhill or Cross-country Around Mammoth Lakes

Snowshoeing Sequoia's Giant Forest

Stargazing Glacier Point

White-water Rafting Cherry Creek

Hiking & Backpacking

Whether strolling leisurely along the floor of Yosemite Valley or schlepping a 60lb pack over a high pass, hiking is the way most visitors experience the Sierra Nevada. And it's no wonder: more than 1600 miles of trails traverse a diverse and spectacular landscape, ranking the region's national parks among the world's most incredible hiking and backpacking destinations.

Some of the parks' most spectacular sights can be visited on short, easy trails, a few of which are wheelchair accessible. Many of the most famous hikes are day hikes, but they often involve steep ascents and descents. Avoid the crowds and blistering afternoon heat by starting early if you're tackling those trails in summer. Depending on last winter's snowpack, some trails may be closed until late spring or even midsummer, especially in the high country.

Permits are not required for day hikes into the backcountry, with the exception of Yosemite's Half Dome and Mt Whitney. All overnight backcountry trips in the parks require permits. If you're planning on hiking the most popular trails in summer, apply for permits many months in advance.

Maps, Books & Online Resources

Bulletin boards posted with trail maps and safety information are found at major trailheads. For short, well-established hikes, free maps handed out at park entrance stations and visitor centers are usually sufficient. Occasionally a more detailed topographic map may be necessary, depending on the length and difficulty of your hike. These are usually sold at park bookstores, visitor centers and wilderness-permit issuing stations.

The US Geological Survey (USGS; https://store.usgs.gov) offers topographic maps as free downloadable PDFs, or you can order print copies online. In-depth hiking and backpacking guides include Wilderness Press' excellent *A Complete Hiker's Guide* series, with titles for Yosemite, Sequoia and Kings Canyon. The Sequoia Parks Conservancy sells fold-out trail-map brochures with descriptions of several day hikes in each of the most-visited areas of Sequoia and Kings Canyon National Parks.

A couple of good online resources:

All Trails (www.alltrails.com) Hiking app with topographic and route detail.

Yosemite Hikes (www.yosemitehikes.com) Detailed descriptions of park hikes, as well as some in neighboring Sierra National Forest and some basic visitor information.

Group Hikes & Backpacking Trips

All national parks offer free ranger-guided walks and day hikes, most frequently in summer. Ask at visitor centers or check seasonal park newspapers for current programs and schedules. Paid guided hikes and outdoors classes are offered by the following:

Aramark/Yosemite Hospitality (☑888-413-8869; www.travelyosemite.com) Yosemite National Park concessionaire runs private and group guided hikes and overnight backpacking trips, including for beginners.

Road Scholar (☑800-454-5768; www.roadschol ar.org) Outdoors-oriented 'learning adventures' and hiking trips for those aged 50 and over.

Sequoia Parks Conservancy (Map p192; ☑559-565-4251; www.sequoiaparksconservancy.org; 47050 Generals Hwy; guided day hikes from $40; ☺day hikes begin at 9am (weather permitting), custom hike times vary) Private naturalist-guided hikes.

Sierra Club (☑415-977-5522; www.sierraclub. org) Day hikes, backpacking trips and volunteer vacations in the Sierra Nevada.

Southern Yosemite Mountain Guides (☑800-231-4575, 559-642-2817; www.symg.com) Long-established outfitter offering guided hiking, backpacking and packhorse-supported trips.

Yosemite Conservancy (☑209-379-3217; www. yosemiteconservancy.org) Guided natural-history, wildflower and photography hikes, plus overnight backpacking trips, including to Half Dome.

Long-distance Trails

Several long-distance trails pass through Yosemite, Sequoia and Kings Canyon National Parks, most famously the 211-mile John Muir Trail (JMT), which starts in Yosemite Valley and follows the Sierra Crest all the way to Mt Whitney (14,505ft). The daunting 2650-mile Pacific Crest National Scenic Trail (PCT) extends from Canada to Mexico, passing through the High Sierra. The province of experts, these trails can be a lifetime achievement for those who manage to through-hike the entire distance, but many people choose to hike them in smaller, more manageable sections. For more information on both trails, consult the Pacific Crest Trail Association (www.pcta.org); for trail conditions, call 888-728-7245.

Cycling & Mountain Biking

Bicycles are an excellent way to explore Yosemite Valley, where rentals are available. Twelve miles of mostly flat, paved trails pass nearly all of the valley's most famous sights. Wear a helmet and ride defensively – the path isn't always clearly marked and many visitors pay more attention to gawking than to steering.

For serious road cyclists, Yosemite's Glacier Point Rd ascends more than 1200ft over 16 miles. Tioga Rd/Hwy 120 is a more grueling route, climbing almost 6000ft from Yosemite Valley to lung-busting Tioga Pass, then dropping dramatically – make that *frighteningly* – down Lee Vining Canyon to finish at Hwy 395 near Mono Lake (a 45-mile total trip).

From Lee Vining, you can ride south on Hwy 395 and pick up Hwy 120 east again to knock out a spectacular Eastern Sierra loop by taking Benton Crossing Rd back west to Hwy 395. This is the route of the annual, early-September, open-registration **Mammoth Grand Fondo** (www.fallcen tury.org). The 16-mile June Lake Loop offers outstanding cycling, too, as does the road to Twin Lakes.

Sequoia and Kings Canyon don't have many places for cycling, although some paved roads in Sequoia's Giant Forest and from Cedar Grove to Road's End in Kings Canyon make for easy, mostly level rides – just watch for traffic. Hard-core cyclists could ride the Kings Canyon Scenic Byway, which drops almost 2000ft in 35 miles as it nerve-wrackingly winds its way down to the Kings River. Of course, you have to turn around and climb back up in order to get out – whew!

Note that all trails within the national parks are off-limits to mountain bikes. You'll need to head to Mammoth Mountain for mountain biking – it has more than 70 miles of singletrack, from downhill runs to free rides, plus shuttles, gondolas and chairlifts. Or you can head to Fish Camp south of Yosemite where there are dozens of miles of good trails, including to the Nelder Grove of giant sequoias and nearby Bass Lake.

For up-to-date advice and recommendations, check out MTBR (www.mtbr.com), an online forum with reviews of mountain-biking trails in California. The California Bicycle Coalition (www.calbike.org) has links to free online cycling maps, bike-sharing programs and community bike shops.

Rock Climbing & Bouldering

With 3000ft granite monoliths, sheer spires, near-vertical walls and a temperate climate, Yosemite is no less than the world's holy grail of rock. Camp 4, Yosemite Valley's cheap, no-reservations, walk-in campground, has for decades been the hangout for some of climbing's legendary stars. Yosemite's granite, mostly deemed impossible to climb until the 1940s, necessitated entirely new techniques, equipment and climbing styles. In 1947, using hand-forged steel pitons, Swiss climber John Salathé and Anton 'Ax' Nelson became the first to climb the Lost Arrow Chimney, regarded as the most difficult climb of its day. Next came a team of illustrious climbers who changed the sport forever, including Yvon Chouinard, founder of Patagonia, and Royal Robbins, a pioneer of clean-climbing techniques.

Attacking the world's greatest single slab of granite in stages between July 1957 and November 1958, big-wall pioneer Warren Harding took 45 days to climb El Capitan's now-world-famous Nose route. In 1994 Lynn Hill free-climbed the route in less than 24 hours, and in 2018 Alex Honnold and Tommy Caldwell speed climbed the Nose in just under two hours. Taking the Freerider route, Honnold completed the first free-solo climb (without ropes) in 2017; only a week before, he and a partner set the speed record with ropes on Freerider.

HOW HARD IS THAT TRAIL?

We've rated Sierra Nevada hikes by three levels of difficulty to help you choose the trail that's right for you.

➡ **Easy** Manageable for nearly all walkers, an easy hike is less than 4 miles, with fairly even terrain and no significant elevation gain or loss.

➡ **Moderate** Fine for fit hikers and active, older children, moderate hikes have a modest elevation gain in the range of 500ft to 1000ft and are usually less than 7 miles long.

➡ **Difficult** Hikes have elevation gains of more than 1000ft, are mostly steep, may have tricky footing and are often longer than 8 miles. Being physically fit is paramount.

All hikes, from day hikes to backcountry treks, follow marked, established trails and, unless otherwise noted, the distance listed in each hike description is for a round-trip journey. The actual time spent hiking will vary with your ability. When in doubt, assume trails will be harder and take longer than you think.

Today the climbing spirit soars as high as ever. During spring and fall, climbers flock to Yosemite Valley, and boulder-strewn Camp 4 remains ground zero. Need a climbing partner? Check the Camp 4 bulletin board. Looking for used climbing equipment? Camp 4. Want route information from fellow climbers? You guessed it.

Come summer, many climbers relocate to gentler, high-elevation Tioga Rd, especially around Tuolumne Meadows, where temperatures are cooler than in the valley and there's an abundance of glacially polished granite domes.

With so much glacial debris scattered about, Yosemite is also outstanding for bouldering, which involves climbing without a rope at short distances above the ground. The only bits of equipment required are shoes, a chalk bag and a bouldering mat, so it's a great way to enter the sport of climbing. Yosemite Valley and along Tioga Rd, including at Tuolumne Meadows, are the park's most popular bouldering spots.

Yosemite doesn't have a monopoly on rock climbing. Sequoia and Kings Canyon National Parks have some outstanding climbing with a fraction of the crowds, although some spots require a long back-country hike to access them. In the Eastern Sierra, Mammoth Lakes and the Owens River Valley and Buttermilks Country near Bishop are top climbing areas. There's also plenty of high-altitude climbing between Saddlebag Lake and Yosemite's Tioga Pass entrance. In winter Lee Vining Canyon is popular with ice climbers.

Mountain Project (www.mountainproject.com) Extremely detailed descriptions, practical information and reviews of climbing routes throughout the Sierras.

Sierra Rock Climbing School (www.sierrarockclimbingschool.com) Check with this Mammoth Lakes–based outfitter for climbing courses and guides in the Eastern Sierra.

Super Topo (www.supertopo.com) Active online forum for rock-climbing enthusiasts, with comprehensive threads on spots in the Sierra Nevada, especially Yosemite.

Yosemite Mountaineering School (p91) If you're new to climbing, or want to build on your techniques and knowledge, come to the Yosemite Mountain Shop between April and November. Ask about big-wall weekend climbing seminars and 'Girls on Granite' boot camps.

Horseback Riding

There's ample opportunity to saddle up within the parks. But don't imagine yourself galloping across a meadow with the wind at your back – stock animals must stick to trails. Keep in mind that, unless you're bringing your own horses, any 'horseback rides' offered within the parks are usually on tough, sure-footed mules.

From late spring through early fall, the Big Trees Lodge Stable (p92) offers two-hour and half-day trail rides in Yosemite; just outside the park's South Entrance, **Yosemite Trails Pack Station** (559-683-7611; www.yosemitetrails.com; 7910 Jackson/Big Sandy Rd, Fish Camp) offers four-hour Mariposa Grove rides ($195). In Kings Canyon, Grant Grove Stables (p183) and the Cedar Grove Pack Station (p183) offer short trail rides lasting one or two hours, as does the Horse Corral Pack Station (p183) in the Sequoia National Forest. If you want to get out into the wilderness, Cedar Grove Pack Station and Horse Corral Pack Station can arrange multiday backcountry trips, including for fishing.

The Eastern Sierra, with its mountain vistas, lakes and valleys, is ideal for horseback adventuring. Several outfitters run trips out of Mammoth Lakes and Bishop, putting riders within easy reach of the gorgeous Ansel Adams Wilderness and John Muir Wilderness. Pack trips also depart from Virginia Lakes, south of Bridgeport, and from June Lake, south of Lee Vining – at the latter, shorter trail rides last from one hour to all day.

Frontier Pack Train (summer 760-648-7701, winter 760-872-4038; www.frontierpacktrain.com; Silver Lake; 1hr/half-day/full-day rides $40/75/120; Jun-Sep) Area and backcountry horseback rides. Different trips go to various places, including Agnew or Gem Lake and Crest Creek. Longer treks have the option of fishing, swimming and picnicking in the wilderness.

Glacier Pack Train (760-938-2538; www.glacierpacktrain.com; Glacier Lodge Rd; day rides from $90; Jun-Sep) Journey into the mountains by horseback with this local outfit running camping, fishing and climbing trips during the summer months. Its trips are great for inexperienced hikers who want to get into high-altitude wilderness with all their gear.

McGee Creek Pack Station (☎760-935-4324, in winter 760 878 2207; www.mcgeecreek packstation.com; McGee Creek Rd; 1hr/half-day/full-day rides from $45/80/150; ☺vary; ⛺) Whether it's backcountry multiday packing trips or hour-long rides on nearby trails, the owners of this company offer decades of experience and knowledge. In summer, rides leave from McGee Creek Pack Station; in winter (when the road is closed) they're contactable at 8 Mile Ranch on Black Rock Springs Rd.

Rock Creek Pack Station (☎760-872-8331; www.rockcreekpackstation.com; 9006 Rock Creek Rd; half-/full-day rides from $65/120; ⛺) Old, experienced hands run this backcountry packing company high up in the Rock Creek wilderness. Many equine activities, as well as hiking and fishing trips, are on offer.

Virginia Lakes Pack Outfit (☎760-937-0326; www.virginialakes.com; Virginia Lakes Rd; 1½hr rides from $65, half-/full-day rides $90/150; ☺tour times vary, Jun-Sep only) Offers horseback riding trips with the possibility of a stop for lunch, hiking and fishing trips in the wilderness.

Swimming

Few sensations top the joy of jumping into a river or swimming in a mountain lake. However, you'd better be able to tolerate cold water here: rivers swollen with spring snowmelt don't become safe enough for swimming until midsummer, and alpine lakes stay chilly year-round.

In rivers, always swim near other people unless you're absolutely certain about the nature of the current. People drown every year in Sierra Nevada rivers. Watch out for slippery boulders, and never swim around,

LEAVE NO TRACE

Before you hit the trail, learn how to minimize your impact on the environment by talking with park rangers and visiting the Leave No Trace Center for Outdoor Ethics website (www.lnt.org).

Food

➡ Store food in a bear-resistant canister or locker.

➡ Never feed wildlife and avoid leaving any food scraps behind. Wild animals can become dependent on handouts, causing disease, starvation and aggressive behavior toward people.

Hiking & Camping

➡ Stay on the trail – making and taking shortcuts contributes to erosion.

➡ Camp at least 100ft from water and, if possible, the trail.

➡ Always yield to stock animals.

➡ Camp in existing sites or on durable surfaces. Keep campsites small.

Fires

➡ Don't start any campfires at altitudes above 9600ft, or above the tree line; additional restrictions may apply during the summer wildfire season.

➡ Below the tree line, collect only dead and downed wood. Use only sticks that can be broken by hand, not logs.

➡ If you make a campfire, keep it small and use existing fire rings only – don't build new ones.

Waste

➡ Discard all gray water at least 100ft from all water sources. Don't put any soap in the water (even biodegradable soap pollutes).

➡ Carry out all trash, including toilet paper. Toilet paper burns poorly and animals will dig up anything scented.

➡ Relieve yourself at least 200ft from any water source. For solid waste, dig a hole 6in deep (in snow, dig down to the soil).

above or below a waterfall, as you could drown if the current carries you over the top or if you're hit by rockfall.

Public swimming pools with lifeguards are open in summer at Half Dome Village and Yosemite Valley Lodge. The following are some good spots to swim:

➡ **Merced River** Yosemite's warmest waters are found along sandy beaches in the valley; more swimming holes are hidden around Wawona, too.

➡ **Tenaya Lake** This high-elevation lake is bordered by a half-moon sandy beach.

➡ **Eastern Sierra** Take your pick between Lundy Lake and June Lake, or visit local hot springs.

➡ **Kaweah River** Families picnic by the rocks and swim in the Foothills and Lodgepole areas of Sequoia National Park.

➡ **Kings River** Near Cedar Grove in Kings Canyon, Muir Rock and the Red Bridge are popular swimming holes.

➡ **Hume Lake** Off the Kings Canyon Scenic Byway, find family-friendly swimming beaches and water-sports equipment rental.

Rafting

During the summer months, floating along the Merced River in Yosemite Valley is a fun way to beat the heat (inflatable-raft rentals are available at Half Dome Village). All the white-water action happens in late spring, when snowmelt runoff creates lots of rapids along the Merced River.

The Yosemite region's white-water-rafting season usually kicks off in April. Typically the Tuolumne River runs into early September, while the Merced wraps up by mid-July, and both are well suited to beginner to intermediate rafters. For experts there's renowned Cherry Creek, a 9-mile stretch of the upper Tuolumne, offering nearly nonstop class IV to V+ rapids marked by narrow shoots, huge boulders, sheer drops, ledges and vertical holes.

In the Sierra National Forest, Kings River offers a scenic 10-mile stretch of exciting, mostly class III rapids that are good for beginners. With its headwaters in Sequoia National Park, the Kaweah River kicks out challenging class III to V rapids west of the park. Depending on snowmelt, the rafting season on these rivers runs from mid-April to mid-July, though in recent years drought has meant shorter seasons.

Guided River Trips

Several outfitters offer one-day, overnight and multiday white-water-rafting trips in the Sierra Nevada, with prices that vary by season and day of the week. All rafters should be strong swimmers and generally at least 12 years old.

All-Outdoors California Whitewater Rafting (☑925-932-8993; www.aorafting.com; 1250 Pine St, Walnut Creek; trips from $108) Veteran California outfitter runs Cherry Creek, as well as the Merced, Tuolumne and Kaweah Rivers.

ARTA River Trips (☑209-962-7873, 800-323-2782; www.arta.org; 24000 Casa Loma Rd; 1-/2-/3-day rafting $279/519/689; ⊗office hours vary, closed in winter) Nonprofit outfitter runs one-day and multiday Tuolumne River trips, as well as day trips on the Merced River.

Kings River Expeditions (☑800-846-3674, 559-233-4881; www.kingsriver.com; 1840 Shaw Ave, Clovis; 1-/2-day trips $145/289) Small, local operator for one- and two-day Kings River trips.

OARS (☑209-736-4677; www.oars.com) ✐ Worldwide rafting operator with a solid reputation and admirable environmental ethics. Offers trips on the Tuolumne and Merced Rivers.

Sierra Mac (☑209-591-8027; www.sierramac. com; 27890 Hwy 120; 1-/2-/3-day rafting $279/519/694; ⊗hours vary Apr-Oct) One of two outfitters running Cherry Creek; also offers Tuolumne and Merced River trips.

Whitewater Voyages (☑800-400-7238; www. whitewatervoyages.com) Runs trips on the Tuolumne, Merced, Kaweah, Kings and Kern Rivers.

Zephyr Whitewater Expeditions (☑209-532-6249, 800-431-3636; www.zrafting.com; 9988 Hwy 140, El Portal; half-/1-day trips per person from $112/158) Large, reputable outfitter offering trips on the Merced, Tuolumne and Kings Rivers.

Winter Activities

Downhill Skiing & Snowboarding

When it comes to downhill skiing and snowboarding, Mammoth Mountain in the Eastern Sierra reigns supreme. A top-rate mountain with excellent terrain for all levels of ability, Mammoth is known for its sunny skies, vertical chutes, airy snow and laid-back atmosphere. For a more local vibe, hit nearby June Mountain. Not for adrenaline junkies, Yosemite Ski and Snowboard Area is a historic spot: it's California's oldest ski resort. Gentle slopes, terrain parks, an excellent ski school and rental gear for the whole family make it an incredible spot for beginners. In the Sequoia National Forest, between Kings Canyon and Sequoia National Parks, novices can try out snowboarding at Montecito Sequoia Lodge.

Cross-Country Skiing

Outstanding cross-country skiing is found throughout the Sierra Nevada. Yosemite is an invigorating place for skiers of all skill levels, with options ranging from short scenic loops to challenging backcountry trails. Cross-country skiers can take their pick of almost 350 miles of well-marked trails and roads, with more than 25 miles of groomed trails accessed from the Yosemite Ski and Snowboard Area. Other popular

BUT WAIT, THERE'S MORE!

ACTIVITY	LOCATION	DESCRIPTION
Canoeing & kayaking	Yosemite Valley	Bring your own kayak or canoe to paddle the Merced River during early summer.
	Tenaya Lake	Bring your own motorless watercraft to this alpine lake in Yosemite's high country.
	Tioga & Saddlebag Lakes	Easy DIY put-ins at an alpine lake off Tioga Rd, east of Yosemite.
	Mono Lake	Paddle past bizarre-looking tufa formations; rentals & guided tours available in summer & early fall.
	June Lake	Lakeshore marinas rent canoes & kayaks in the Eastern Sierra.
	Mammoth Lakes	Eastern Sierra's best paddling is at Crowley Lake, Convict Lake & Lakes Basin; marinas rent canoes & kayaks.
	Hume Lake	Rent a canoe or kayak & paddle across this forested lake off the Kings Canyon Scenic Byway.
Caving	Crystal Cave	Explore Sequoia's most famous marble cave, carved by an underground river; tours run late spring through fall.
	Boyden Cavern	Go for a wet-and-wild guided walk deep in Kings Canyon; tours run late spring through early fall.
Fishing*	Yosemite Valley	Catch trout on the Merced River between Happy Isles & Foresta Bridge.
	Tuolumne Meadows	Trout swim the Lyell & Dana Forks of the Tuolumne River.
	Wawona	Some of Yosemite's best stream fishing for trout.
	Hetch Hetchy	Trout fishing in the reservoir & along the Tuolumne River.
	Eastern Sierra	Trout fishing in lakes, rivers & streams, especially Saddlebag Lake, June Lake & Mammoth Lakes.
	Kings Canyon	Cast for trout at Hume Lake & along the Kings River.
Golf	Wawona	Yosemite's historic nine-hole 'organic' golf course, open spring through fall.
Hang gliding	Yosemite	Advanced pilots with own equipment can soar from Glacier Point to Yosemite Valley.
Stargazing	Glacier Point	Join amateur astronomers & park rangers high above Yosemite Valley on summer weekends.
Tennis	Wawona	Tree-shaded outdoor court in southern Yosemite, open late spring through fall.

* California fishing license required for anyone over 16 years; state fishing laws apply (see www.wildlife.ca.gov/fishing). Ask about local fishing regulations at visitor centers and ranger stations.

park ski trails are found at Crane Flat and Mariposa Grove. With reservations, experienced skiers can overnight at the no-frills backcountry ski huts at Glacier Point, Ostrander Lake or Tuolumne Meadows.

In Sequoia and Kings Canyon, some 50 miles of marked but ungroomed trails crisscross the Giant Forest and General Grant Grove areas, with rental skis available at Wuksachi Lodge and Grant Grove Village. Backcountry skiers can try the challenging Lakes Trail from Lodgepole to the Pear Lake Ski Hut (p186; reservations required).

In the Eastern Sierra, Mammoth Lakes has some top-rated cross-country skiing, with more than 300 miles of ungroomed trails in town and in the Inyo National Forest. The Ansel Adams Wilderness, John Muir Wilderness and Saddlebag Lake area east of Yosemite's Tioga Pass offer endless exploring opportunities for experienced backcountry skiers.

Beginners might want to head to one of the following:

Montecito Sequoia Lodge (Map p192; ☑800-227-9900; www.mslodge.com; 63410 Generals Hwy; all-inclusive r from $189, ste from $269, cabins $169-379) Old-fashioned, family-oriented resort offers lessons, rents cross-country and skate skis, and maintains more than 30 miles of groomed trails for all skill levels in the Sequoia National Forest.

Tamarack Cross-Country Ski Center (p152) Hop on Mammoth Lakes' town shuttle to the Tamarack Lodge, where rentals and lessons are available. Almost 20 miles of meticulously groomed track runs through gorgeous scenery around Twin Lakes and the Lakes Basin.

Yosemite Cross-Country Ski School (☑209-372-8444; www.travelyosemite.com; 7082 Glacier Point Rd; ☺8:30am-4pm winter) Located in the Yosemite Ski and Snowboard Area, this school offers beginner-lesson-plus-rental packages, group and private lessons, ski-equipment rentals and guided tours. It also runs overnight trips to Glacier Point Ski Hut, a rustic stone-and-log cabin.

Snowshoeing

One of the easiest ways to explore the winter wilderness is to strap on a pair of snowshoes and head out on any of the hiking or cross-country-skiing trails. Just be sure not to tramp directly in ski tracks, which destroys them for any cross-country skiers who come after you.

You can rent snowshoes at the Yosemite Ski and Snowboard Area and explore on your own, or join a fun guided trip, ranging from two-hour moonlight walks to an all-day trek out to Dewey Point and back. If you bring your own snowshoes, Yosemite Valley, Mariposa Grove and Crane Flat are all scenic spots. Near Hetch Hetchy, Evergreen Lodge (p238) and, a little further afield, Rush Creek Lodge (p238) rent snowshoes and offer guided snowshoe hikes inside the park.

In Sequoia National Park, ranger-led snowshoe walks depart from Wuksachi Lodge (p197); reserve a spot by calling ahead or signing up in person in advance. Rental snowshoes are available at the Lodgepole Market Center (p201), Sequoia's Wuksachi Lodge (p197) and Kings Canyon's Grant Grove Village. For a backcountry adventure, score overnight reservations for Pear Lake Ski Hut (p186), accessible on snowshoes and cross-country skis.

Most cross-country-skiing centers rent snowshoes, as does Mammoth Mountain in the Eastern Sierra.

Skating, Sledding, Tubing & Snow Play

One of the most memorable winter activities for families in Yosemite is skating on Half Dome Village's outdoor rink (p96); rental skates are available. Or rent a snow tube and send yourself spinning downhill at the Yosemite Ski and Snowboard Area. At Montecito Sequoia Lodge (p35) in the Sequoia National Forest and at Mammoth Mountain and **Woolly's Tube Park and Snow Play** (☑760-934-7533; www.mammothmountain.com/winter/things-to-do/winter-activities/woollys-tube-park; 9000 Minaret Rd, Ste 200; adult/child from $39/34, snow play only $20; ☺10am-5pm, winter only; ⏺), you can rent a snow tube or a sled and go rocketing downhill. Sledding and tubing are also popular at designated snow-play areas throughout all three parks and in nearby national forests, but you'll have to bring your own gear. Just south of Yosemite, Tenaya Lodge (p140) has a small outdoor ice-skating rink (rentals available) and horse-drawn-sleigh rides.

Plan Your Trip

Travel with Children

Kids love the national parks, and bringing them along is a no-brainer. To find kid-oriented events, check the free seasonal park newspapers or consult the daily or weekly program calendars posted at visitor centers and some park lodgings and campgrounds. Spend days swimming, cycling and hiking. How about spying on the wildlife, marveling at waterfalls, peering over tall cliffs and exploring crazy-cool caves? For many kids, just sleeping in a tent for the first time is the biggest adventure.

Best Regions for Kids

Yosemite National Park

Drop by the Happy Isles Art & Nature Center (p100), be awestruck by Yosemite Valley's waterfalls, drink in views of Half Dome from Glacier Point and picnic by wildflower-strewn Tuolumne Meadows. When your kids get tired, simply hop on the bus and head back to your car, campsite or lodge.

Eastern Sierra

Ride a historic narrow-gauge railroad through pine forests, explore an Old West mining ghost town and ski the powder slopes of Mammoth Mountain or June Mountain.

Sequoia & Kings Canyon National Parks

In Sequoia learn all about giant sequoias in the Giant Forest, then scramble up Moro Rock and explore the creepy-crawly underground at Crystal Cave. In Kings Canyon duck inside the Fallen Monarch tree in General Grant Grove, cool off at Hume Lake and spot wildlife in Zumwalt Meadow.

Children's Highlights

Classes

Yosemite Conservancy (p248) Park partner offers outdoor classes and indoor programs that teach kids about ecology, history and more, as well as low-cost art classes taught at the Happy Isles Nature & Art Center in Yosemite Valley.

Ansel Adams Gallery (p98) Photography walks for budding shutterbugs explore Yosemite Valley.

Yosemite Mountaineering School (p91) Kids aged 10 and up can take a beginners' 'Go Climb a Rock' class in Yosemite Valley.

Cycling

Yosemite Valley (p87) Rent bikes or bring your own to pedal along paved, mostly level bike paths.

Mammoth Mountain (p151) Older kids and teens will go bananas over this giant mountain-bike park, open during summer.

Hiking

Yosemite

Yosemite Valley Loop (p48) Hike along primarily paved, flat trails, then hop on the shuttle bus back to where you started.

MY GOOD IMAGES/SHUTTERSTOCK ©

Giant sequoias in Sequoia National Park (p167)

Vernal Fall (p55) It's less than a mile to the footbridge below one of Yosemite Valley's most famous falls.

Mirror Lake (p49) Best in spring or early summer, when the lake's waters reflect iconic Half Dome.

Happy Isles Art & Nature Center (p100) Guided junior ranger walks start here during summer.

Sentinel Dome (p62) Yosemite's easiest granite-dome scramble, worth it for 360-degree views.

McGurk Meadow (p61) An easy-as-pie walk among wildflowers, just off Glacier Point Rd.

Mariposa Grove (p110) Ramble among majestic giant sequoias on newly restored nature trails.

Tuolumne Meadows (p64) Stroll by wildflowers and the Tuolumne River to Soda Springs, or climb nearby granite domes.

Sequoia & Kings Canyon

Big Trees Trail (p170) Marvel at giant sequoias along a short nature loop.

Moro Rock (p188) Climb with older kids up a granite dome for spectacular panoramas.

Crescent Meadow Loop (p170) Spy on black bears and peer inside the Chimney Tree.

Tokopah Falls (Map p192) Scenic riverside hike to a 1200ft-high cascade tumbling down cliffs.

General Grant Tree Trail (p174) Stare up at giant sequoias and step inside the Fallen Monarch.

Zumwalt Meadow (p191) A peaceful riverside ramble, with a good chance of spotting wildlife.

Eastern Sierra

Kaweah Oak Preserve (p206) Home to 324 acres of majestic oak trees; a gorgeous setting for easy hikes.

Devils Postpile National Monument (p153) Short trail to the top of Reds Meadow to see bizarre formations of molten lava.

History

Yosemite Valley Visitor Center (p242) Child-friendly, interactive natural and cultural history exhibits, plus afternoon junior-ranger talks and evening programs for little ones in the outdoor theater during summer.

Yosemite Museum (p99) Explore Yosemite's indigenous heritage, including at the recon-structed Indian Village of Ahwahnee. Don't miss the cross-section of a giant sequoia (count the rings!) out front.

Pioneer Yosemite History Center (p112) Wawona's atmospheric old buildings, stagecoaches and covered bridge are worth a look. In summer hop on a stagecoach for a short ride.

Yosemite Mountain Sugar Pine Railroad (p140) South of Yosemite, ride historic narrow-gauge trains into the forest.

Sequoia Parks Conservancy (p248) In summer this park partner puts on family-oriented living-history programs with a BBQ cookout at Wolverton Meadow and campfire storytelling at Wuksachi Lodge.

Hospital Rock (p188) Inspect ancient pictographs and Native American grinding holes in the Foothills area of Sequoia National Park.

Bodie State Historic Park (p146) Explore the ghostly ruins of a real 19th-century mining town in the Eastern Sierra that went from boom to bust.

Laws Railroad Museum & Historic Site (p158) A fun whistle-stop for train enthusiasts in the Eastern Sierra, with family-friendly special events.

Horseback Riding

Yosemite (p92) Hitch up in summer for a scenic two-hour trip to Mirror Lake in Yosemite Valley, or a two-hour ride along a pioneer-era wagon road in Wawona.

Yosemite Trails Pack Station (p31) Just south of the park, this outfit offers one- and two-hour creekside trail rides from April through early November, weather permitting.

Kings Canyon (p183) In summer, one- or two-hour horseback trips trek among giant sequoias in Grant Grove and along the Kings River from Cedar Grove.

Nature Centers

Happy Isles Art & Nature Center (p100) In this Yosemite Valley center you'll find great hands-on exhibits and dioramas depicting natural environments. Kids can learn about pine cones, rub their hands across granite, check out different animal tracks and even snicker at the display on animal scat.

Giant Forest Museum (p236) In Sequoia's Giant Forest, this family-friendly educational center has lots of stuff to touch, play with and explore, with

---

RAINY DAYS

Yosemite

Yosemite Conservation Heritage Center (p243) The cozy children's corner is full of ecofriendly books, games, puzzles, stuffed animals, fake bugs, crayons and an activity table.

Happy Isles Art & Nature Center (p100) Hands-on animal displays and identification activities (including on everyone's favorites – animal tracks and scat), plus drop-in family crafts and art classes.

Half Dome Village Lounge If you just need somewhere to sit out the storm, head to where the kids can do puzzles and play games by the fire (bring the cards!).

Sequoia & Kings Canyon

Kings Canyon Visitor Center (p236) Fun, nature-themed activity stations for kids are hidden at the back of the park's main visitor center in Grant Grove Village.

General Grant Grove (p190) and Giant Forest (p187) Pathways around these giant sequoias are generally shielded from all but the heaviest downpours by the massive trees themselves.

Eastern Sierra

Mammoth Rock 'n' Bowl (p152) Sleek complex of 12 lanes, plus Ping-Pong, Foosball and more.

Museum of Western Film History (p162) If too young to appreciate cinema history, the museum's own film about Westerns entertains.

KEEPING KIDS SAFE

Travel with kids always requires extra safety measures, but with a little preparation and common sense, your family can make the most of your park visit.

➡ Dress children (and yourself) in layers so they can peel clothing on or off as needed – mountain weather can change suddenly.

➡ Bring lots of high-energy snacks and drinks, even for short outings and easy hikes. Remember that kids dehydrate more quickly than adults.

➡ When hiking make sure your kids stay within earshot (if not sight). They may want to rush ahead, but it's easy to miss a trail junction or take a wrong turn.

➡ As an extra precaution while hiking, have each child wear brightly colored clothes and carry a flashlight and safety whistle.

➡ Make sure kids know what to do if they get lost on the trail (eg stay put, periodically blow the whistle) or anywhere else in the parks (eg ask a ranger for help).

➡ Be extra cautious with kids around waterfalls, near cliff edges and at viewpoints, not all of which have barrier railings; the same goes for any peaks or domes.

➡ At higher elevations kids may experience altitude sickness. Watch them for symptoms, especially while they're active outdoors. Descend to lower elevations immediately if any symptoms arise.

➡ Ensure your kids know what to do if they see a bear.

➡ Children are more vulnerable to spider and snake bites. Remind them not to pick up or provoke snakes (eg with sticks) and never to put their hands anywhere they can't see.

➡ Teach children to identify poison oak.

a walkway outside that dramatically shows the height of these giant trees.

Discovery Room At the back of the Kings Canyon Visitor Center (p236), kids can practice pine-cone identification and play a spot-the-species game with bilingual (Spanish/English) murals.

Swimming & Water Sports

June Lake (p149) In the Eastern Sierra hang out by the beach in summer or launch a canoe, kayak or paddleboat.

Merced River (p92) In summer go rafting or kayaking in Yosemite Valley or just splash around by the sandy shore.

Half Dome Village & Yosemite Valley Lodge (p93) Yosemite Valley's outdoor public swimming pools let families cool off.

Tenaya Lake (Tioga Rd) Build sandcastles on the beach of Yosemite's roadside high-altitude lake (warning: the water is chilly, even in summer!).

Hume Lake (p191) Along the Kings Canyon Scenic Byway, take a dip in this pretty forest lake with sandy beaches that's always crowded with families.

Kaweah River (p183) Families picnic, sunbathe on the rocks and splash around summertime swimming holes in Sequoia's Foothills and Lodgepole areas.

Muir Rock (p192) Late in summer this swimming spot along the Kings River near Road's End in Cedar Grove offers a small sandy beach.

Winter Sports

Yosemite Ski & Snowboard Area (p105) Gentle slopes and groomed cross-country tracks are excellent for beginners. The 'Badger Pups' kids' downhill program offers lessons for little skiers and boarders from four to six years old. Childcare is available for ages three to nine.

Half Dome Village (p96) Go ice-skating on an outdoor rink with superb scenery in Yosemite Valley. There's a smaller outdoor rink at Tenaya Lodge, just south of the park.

Wuksachi Lodge (p197) In Sequoia National Park, rent snowshoes and take the whole family for a hike around giant-sequoia groves, or join a ranger-guided snowshoe walk.

Mammoth Mountain (p151) In the Eastern Sierra near Mammoth Lakes, this superb skiing and snowboarding resort offers kids' lessons and childcare services. Families also love tamer and less crowded June Mountain (p149) ski resort nearby.

Montecito Sequoia Lodge (p35) In the Giant Sequoia National Monument, this family camp offers cross-country ski trails, snowboarding, snow tubing, sledding and daily children's activities.

Planning

Packing too much into your national-parks trip can cause frustration and spoil the adventure. Try to include the kids in the trip planning from the get-go. If they have a hand in choosing activities, they'll be much more interested and excited when you finally arrive.

For more advice and anecdotes, especially for families hitting the road together for the first time, read Lonely Planet's *Travel with Children*. Other helpful and encouraging reads for parents are *Babes in the Woods* by Jennifer Aist, *Outdoor Parents*, *Outdoor Kids* by Eugene Buchanan and the *Sierra Club Family Outdoors Guide* by Marlyn Doan.

Before You Go

Some great resources for getting kids psyched up about your trip:

➡ Yosemite's official website (www.nps.gov/yose/learn/kidsyouth) links to all kinds of junior-ranger and educational online activities, as does the 'Park Fun' page (www.nps.gov/yose/learn/kidsyouth/parkfun.htm).

➡ Sequoia and Kings Canyon's official website (www.nps.gov/seki/learn/kidsyouth/index.htm) lists free ranger-led programs and also includes a link to the *Sequoia Seeds* kids' newspaper.

➡ The National Park Service (NPS) WebRangers portal (www.nps.gov/kids) has dozens of fun, educational activities for aspiring junior rangers.

➡ Phil Frank's comic-strip books, *Fur and Loafing in Yosemite* and *Eat, Drink & Be Hairy*, are compilations of hilarious, bear-filled park adventures.

➡ Bishop Area Visitors Bureau (www.bishopvisitor.com/activities/kids) has recommendations and advice for families traveling in the Eastern Sierra.

➡ Ask questions and get advice from other travelers on Lonely Planet's Thorn Tree's 'Kids to Go' and 'USA' forums (www.lonelyplanet.com).

➡ Travel for Kids – High Sierra (www.travelforkids.com/Funtodo/California/highsierra.htm) has loads of tips for family activities, sightseeing, hiking and accommodations, plus recommended children's books.

Sleeping & Eating

The parks and nearby gateway towns all cater for families. Most lodgings allow kids under 12 years of age to sleep for free in the same room as their parents, though a rollaway cot may cost extra. A child-sized inflatable mattress or portable sleeping crib will fit into most motel or hotel rooms. Almost all restaurants in and around the parks have kids' menus with smaller portions and significantly lower prices. Dress codes are casual almost everywhere (except at the Majestic Yosemite Hotel's dining room).

Plan Your Trip

Travel with Pets

If you bring your pets, it's crucial that they stay comfortable and safe. Consider the availability of pet-friendly lodgings, potential interactions with other pets and wildlife, and local restrictions on recreational use, especially hiking. Be sure to check the different regulations governing each of the areas you plan to visit, too.

Policies & Regulations

Pets are allowed in the parks with some restrictions. Dogs aren't allowed on park shuttles, inside buildings or lodgings, on (almost any) hiking trails or in wilderness areas. Dogs are generally permitted in campgrounds and picnic areas but must be kept on a 6ft-long leash and accompanied at all times. Don't sneak dogs into backcountry or leave them tied up and unattended at campgrounds; it's illegal and you will be cited. And clean up your pooch's poop.

In the Sequoia National Forest, leashed dogs are permitted on trails and at campgrounds (maximum two pets per campsite), but they must sleep inside a tent or vehicle at night. Dogs aren't allowed at developed swimming areas.

For up-to-date policies:

Yosemite www.nps.gov/yose/planyourvisit/pets.htm

Sequoia & Kings Canyon www.nps.gov/seki/planyourvisit/pets.htm

Sequoia National Forest FAQ www.fs.usda.gov/sequoia

Service animals (eg guide dogs) may accompany visitors with documented disabilities on park shuttles, inside museums and visitor centers, and on hiking trails and into the backcountry. Ask about current regulations to see if any special permits are required or if any areas are off-limits. Ensure your service animal always wears its official vest and is kept on a 6ft-long leash.

Best Regions for Pets

Yosemite National Park

Dogs are allowed on most paved paths, including the scenic Yosemite Valley Loop, but *not* on hiking trails (with one or two exceptions). Almost all park campgrounds accept pets, and a few have facilities for horses as well.

Around Yosemite

Mammoth Lakes and the Eastern Sierra offer an abundance of dog-friendly trails and scenic backcountry stock trips, especially in the Inyo National Forest. National forests, including Sequoia National Forest, allow dogs on hiking trails and in campgrounds.

Sequoia & Kings Canyon National Parks

Dogs are prohibited on all park trails, but are allowed at park campgrounds. Backcountry stock trips are popular, with scenic trails starting from Mineral King and Cedar Grove.

Camping & Hiking

In Yosemite National Park, dogs are allowed on paved paths unless otherwise signposted – they're prohibited on paved trails leaving the Yosemite Valley floor, for instance. Dogs are not allowed on any unpaved roads or trails, except for the Wawona Meadow Loop and parts of Old Big Oak Flat Rd. You can bring pets into most developed campgrounds in Yosemite, except walk-in campgrounds (eg Camp 4 in Yosemite Valley).

In Sequoia and Kings Canyon National Parks, dogs are allowed in all developed campgrounds but not on any trails, paved or unpaved.

Bodie State Historic Park in the Eastern Sierra allows leashed dogs into the town site.

Dog-friendly Lodgings & Kennels

Except for service animals, dogs are not allowed inside any park lodgings. Some hotels and motels outside the parks accept pets, although a nightly surcharge, weight limits and breed restrictions may apply.

KEEPING PETS SAFE & HEALTHY

➡ Pets are extremely susceptible to overheating. Never leave your pet alone in a hot car, where they may experience brain and organ damage after only five minutes.

➡ Follow park regulations and keep your dog leashed at all times. Off leash there's more opportunity for your dog to roll in poison oak or get in a fight with another pet or a wild animal.

➡ Keep your dog healthy by periodically checking for ticks and being prepared for weather extremes. Bring plenty of water on hot days and blankets for chilly evenings.

➡ Remember that pet food is potentially bear food. Store your pet's food properly at all times (eg use bear lockers at campgrounds, trailheads and parking lots).

Not far from Yosemite's South Entrance, Tenaya Lodge (p140) offers dog-sitting and kennel services (surcharge applies) for hotel guests.

Yosemite Valley has a **dog kennel** (🖂209-372-8326; www.travelyosemite.com/discover/travel-tips/pets/; Yosemite Valley Stable; per dog per day $8.75; ☺late May–early Sep), though it's bare bones. Dogs are kept in outdoor cages (no food is allowed, due to wildlife concerns) and stay unattended. Boarding fees are per day (no overnight stays allowed). You must provide a written copy of immunization records. Reservations are strongly recommended.

Horse Trails & Facilities

On backcountry trails, stock users must follow strict guidelines on group size, grazing and dispersal of manure, as well as feed restrictions, to prevent the introduction of invasive plant species. Many trails are horse-friendly unless posted otherwise, but you'll need a special wilderness stockuse permit to use them.

Sequoia and Kings Canyon National Parks have several trails for stock trips, including those starting from the Mineral King and Cedar Grove areas. If you don't bring your own animals, talk to pack outfits in and around the parks about stock rentals and guided trips.

In Yosemite a handful of developed campgrounds have stock facilities, and Aramark/Yosemite Hospitality (p248), the park concessionaire, has some overnight boarding facilities available by reservation.

There's a primitive horse camp (p197) in the Sequoia National Forest, between Sequoia and Kings Canyon National Parks. There are more horse camps in the Eastern Sierra.

For up-to-date policies, permit regulations and camping and trails information, see the following:

Sequoia & Kings Canyon www.nps.gov/seki/planyourvisit/stockuse.htm

Sequoia National Forest www.fs.usda.gov/recmain/sequoia/recreation

Yosemite www.nps.gov/yose/planyourvisit/stock.htm

On the Road

Yosemite
National Park
p44

Around Yosemite
National Park
p134

Sequoia &
Kings Canyon
National Parks
p165

Yosemite National Park

Best Hikes

➡ Panorama Trail (p62)

➡ Cathedral Lakes (p65)

➡ May Lake & Mt Hoffmann (p58)

➡ Taft Point & the Fissures (p61)

➡ Lyell Canyon (p80)

Best Off the Beaten Trail

➡ Clouds Rest (p59)

➡ Alder Creek Falls (p70)

➡ Mono Pass (p67)

➡ Gaylor Lakes (p67)

Why Go?

The jaw-dropping head-turner of America's national parks, and a Unesco World Heritage site, Yosemite (yo-*sem*-it-ee) garners the devotion of all who enter. From the waterfall-striped granite walls buttressing emerald-green Yosemite Valley to the skyscraping giant sequoias catapulting into the air at Mariposa Grove, the place inspires a sense of awe and reverence – four million visitors wend their way to the country's third-oldest national park annually. But lift your eyes above the crowds and you'll feel your heart instantly moved by unrivaled splendors: the haughty profile of Half Dome, the hulking presence of El Capitan, the drenching mists of Yosemite Falls, the gemstone lakes of the high country's subalpine wilderness and Hetch Hetchy's pristine pathways.

Road Distances (Miles)

	Big Oak Flat Entrance	Arch Rock Entrance	Wawona	Yosemite Village
Arch Rock Entrance	20			
Wawona	40	30		
Yosemite Village	25	10	25	
Tuolumne Meadows	45	50	75	55

Entrances

There are five entrances to the park:

Arch Rock Entrance Hwy 140 runs through the Merced River Canyon before entering Yosemite Valley near this entrance on the western side of the park.

Big Oak Flat Entrance Hwy 120 W runs east from Groveland through the Stanislaus National Forest before entering the park at this entrance on the western side of Yosemite.

Hetch Hetchy Entrance Entrance to the least-visited part of the park in the northwest. Wilderness permits are issued here.

South Entrance The southern entrance to the park along Hwy 41 is just north of the town of Fish Camp and minutes to Mariposa Grove.

Tioga Pass Entrance Hwy 120 E traverses the park as Tioga Rd, connecting Yosemite Valley with the Eastern Sierra.

DON'T MISS

For two of the best views over Yosemite Valley, you don't even need to stroll far from your car. The best all-around photo op of the Valley can be had from **Tunnel View**, a large, busy parking lot and viewpoint at the east end of Wawona Tunnel, on Hwy 41. It's just a short drive from the Valley floor. The vista encompasses most of the Valley's greatest hits: El Capitan on the left, Bridalveil Fall on the right, the green Valley floor below, and glorious Half Dome front and center. This viewpoint is often mistakenly called Inspiration Point. That point was on an old park road and is now reachable via a steep hike from the Tunnel View parking lot.

The second view, known as **Valley View**, is a good one to hit on your way out. It offers a bottom-up (rather than top-down) view of the Valley and is a lovely spot to dip your toes in the Merced River and bid farewell to sights like Bridalveil Fall, Cathedral Rocks and El Capitan. Look carefully to spot the tip of Half Dome in the distance. As you head west out of the Valley on Northside Dr, look for the Valley View turnout (roadside marker V11), just over a mile past El Capitan Meadow.

When You Arrive

➡ The $35 vehicle entrance fee is valid for one week; keep your receipt to show when you exit the park.

➡ You'll receive a park map and the seasonal *Yosemite Guide* newspaper with information on activities, campgrounds, lodging, shuttles, visitor services and more.

➡ The park is open 24 hours daily. If you arrive at night and the gate is unattended, pay the entrance fee when you leave.

PLANNING TIPS

For 24-hour recorded information, including winter road conditions and summer road-construction updates, call 209-372-0200.

The park website (www.nps.gov/yose) offers free downloads of the park newspaper and helpful trip planning tips.

Fast Facts

➡ Total area: 1169 sq miles

➡ Designated wilderness area: 1101 sq miles (95% of park)

➡ Yosemite Valley elevation: 4000ft

Reservations

Recreation.gov handles reservations for all of Yosemite's reservable campgrounds and those in the surrounding national forests.

All noncamping reservations within the park are handled by Aramark/Yosemite Hospitality (p117) and can be made up to 366 days in advance; reservations are critical from May to early September.

Resources

Yosemite Conservancy (p248) Information, educational programs and activities such as art classes and backpacking trips by this nonprofit park-support organization.

Yosemite National Park

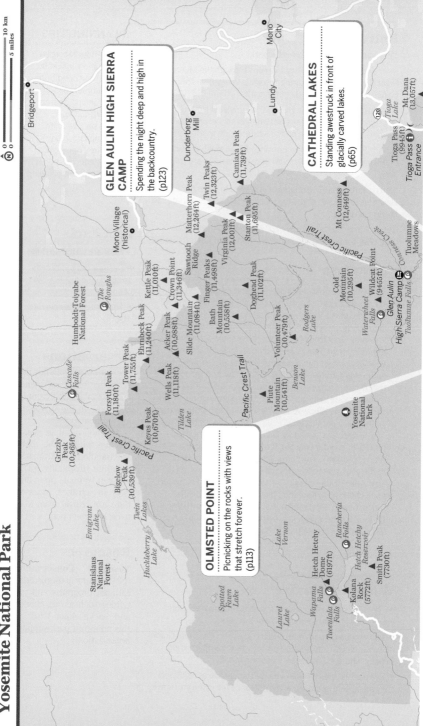

0 10 km
0 5 miles

Ⓝ

GLEN AULIN HIGH SIERRA CAMP

Spending the night deep and high in the backcountry. (p123)

CATHEDRAL LAKES

Standing awestruck in front of glacially carved lakes. (p65)

OLMSTED POINT

Picnicking on the rocks with views that stretch forever. (p113)

Bridgeport

Mono City

Mono Village (historical)

Lundy

Dunderberg Mill

The Roughs

Humboldt-Toiyabe National Forest

Mt Dana (13,057ft)

Tioga Lake

Tioga Pass (9945ft)

Tioga Pass Entrance

Mt Conness (12,649ft)

Conness Creek

Tuolumne Meadows

Camiaca Peak (11,739ft)

Twin Peaks (12,323ft)

Matterhorn Peak (12,264ft)

Kettle Peak (11,010ft)

Crown Point (11,346ft)

Ehrnbeck Peak (11,240ft)

Acker Peak (10,988ft)

Sawtooth Ridge

Virginia Peak (12,001ft)

Stanton Peak (11,695ft)

Cold Mountain (10,295ft)

Wildcat Point (9455ft)

Waterwheel Falls

Glen Aulin

High Sierra Camp

Tuolumne Falls

Pacific Crest Trail

Finger Peaks (11,498ft)

Slide Mountain (11,084ft)

Bath Mountain (10,558ft)

Doghead Peak (11,102ft)

Volunteer Peak (10,479ft)

Rodgers Lake

Benson Lake

Piute Mountain (10,541ft)

Pacific Crest Trail

Cascade Falls

Grizzly Peak (10,365ft)

Bigelow Peak (10,539ft)

Twin Lakes

Forsyth Peak (11,180ft)

Tower Peak (11,755ft)

Keyes Peak (10,670ft)

Wells Peak (11,118ft)

Tilden Lake

Emigrant Lake

Huckleberry Lake

Stanislaus National Forest

Spotted Fawn Lake

Laurel Lake

Lake Vernon

Rancheria Falls

Hetch Hetchy Reservoir

Hetch Hetchy Dome (6197ft)

Wapama Falls

Tueeulala Falls

Kolana Rock (5772ft)

Smith Peak (7730ft)

Yosemite National Park

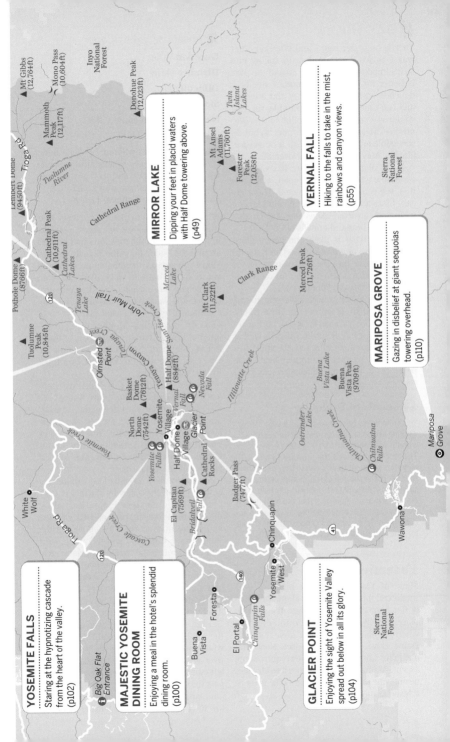

YOSEMITE FALLS

Staring at the hypnotizing cascade from the heart of the valley. (p102)

MAJESTIC YOSEMITE DINING ROOM

Enjoying a meal in the hotel's splendid dining room. (p100)

GLACIER POINT

Enjoying the sight of Yosemite Valley spread out below in all its glory. (p104)

MIRROR LAKE

Dipping your feet in placid waters with Half Dome towering above. (p49)

VERNAL FALL

Hiking to the falls to take in the mist, rainbows and canyon views. (p55)

MARIPOSA GROVE

Gazing in disbelief at giant sequoias towering overhead. (p110)

🚶 DAY HIKES

There's no better way – and often no other way – to see Yosemite than by hiking into it. It's impossible to say one area of the park is better for hiking than another. Really, it depends on the hiker's ability and interests and the time of year. For example, the vast wilderness surrounding Tuolumne (too-*ahl*-uh-*mee*) Meadows is a hikers' mecca, but it's accessible only when Tioga Rd is open (usually late May through early November).

Hikes along Tioga Rd are likewise only accessible when the road is open, and when it is, the walking is phenomenal. There are easy hikes and day hikes to splendid lakes – including Harden, Lukens and May Lakes – all sans the heat and crowds of the Valley.

Offering what is likely the park's finest view, Glacier Point is also a good jumping-off point for hikes into the backcountry to the south. The area is also popular for the Valley rim walks along the Pohono Trail.

Yosemite Valley is accessible year-round, but in the height of summer the heat can be brutal and the trails get crowded. Spring is a great time for hiking in the Valley as well as at Hetch Hetchy, another low-elevation area that experiences harsh summer heat. Temperatures in Wawona, which also sees fewer visitors, are similar.

ℹ️ Levels of Difficulty

Yosemite Valley offers hikes for all levels. Those seeking gentle strolls can visit Mirror Lake and wander the Valley Loop trails as far as they wish. The rest of the Valley's trails involve significant elevation gains. At the far end of the spectrum is the trek to the summit of Half Dome, perhaps the single most difficult (and popular) day hike in the entire park. Just remember that the altitude can make you short of breath before you become acclimatized. To assist you to choose the best hike for you, we rate the hikes from easy to difficult.

Yosemite Valley

Many of Yosemite's easiest hikes – some might call them strolls – are along the mostly flat floor of Yosemite Valley. It's a lovely place to wander, especially in the evenings when all the day-trippers are gone and Half Dome glows against the sunset. Nearly all day hikes from Yosemite Valley require some ascent. Assuming you can score a wilderness permit, the popular Half Dome hike is more relaxed as an overnighter.

🚶 Yosemite Valley Loop

Duration Varies
Distance Varies
Difficulty Easy
Start/Finish Varies
Nearest Town Yosemite Village
Transportation Shuttle
Summary Generally flat and paved, these trails are a great way to acquaint yourself with Yosemite Valley and its many historic sites. Plaques along the way explain the Valley's natural and human history.

Whether you want to plot a route from your campsite to the nearest hot shower, or take in the views from the meadows and bridges around the Valley floor, the vaguely defined loop trails are an undeniably great way to get to know Yosemite Valley. Parts are even wheelchair- and stroller-friendly, and they connect the Valley's most important historic and natural features. In some places the trail joins the road, while in other places it peters out only to reappear later. Generally, it follows alongside Northside and Southside Drs, with some sections tracing the routes of former wagon roads.

For the ambitious, a well-marked path leads up and down the entire Valley, but it's easily broken into segments, making the journey manageable for just about any level of hiker. Pick up a free Yosemite Valley hiking map at the Yosemite Valley Visitor Center for easy route-finding and labeled point-to-point distances.

You can walk a 2.6-mile loop around the eastern end of the Valley by starting at Half Dome Village. From here, head east along the edge of the day-use parking area, with the tent cabins on your right. When you hit the shuttle road, turn right and follow the road into and through the trailhead parking area. Southeast of the parking lot, two trails lead to Happy Isles: one skirts the shuttle road, and another leads into the trees and across a delicate meadow area known as the Fen. After visiting the Happy Isles Art & Nature Center, cross the Merced River and follow the trail alongside the road, veering left when you can to stay along the banks of the river. Just before you reach the stables, head left (southwest) on the road across the river, past the entrances to Lower and Upper Pines Campgrounds. Then look for the sign pointing to Half Dome Village. Further removed

Yosemite Valley – Day Hikes

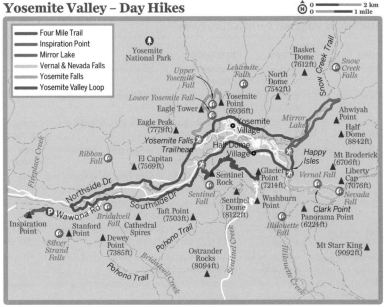

from the Valley's central commercial district and better for those seeking relative isolation, the 6.5-mile loop on the west end of the Valley passes good swimming spots on the Merced and offers fabulous views of El Capitan and Bridalveil Fall. The trail basically follows Northside and Southside Drives between the base of El Capitan and **Pohono Bridge**, the westernmost bridge over the Merced River.

🧍 Mirror Lake & Tenaya Canyon

Duration 1-2 hours

Distance 2–5 miles round-trip

Difficulty Easy–Moderate

Start/Finish Mirror Lake Trailhead

Nearest Town Half Dome Village

Transportation Shuttle stop 17

Summary Shallow Mirror Lake, reflecting Mt Watkins and Half Dome on its tranquil surface, is one of the Valley's most photographed sights. Further northeast, Tenaya Canyon offers one of the quietest corners of Yosemite Valley.

Formed when a rockfall dammed a section of Tenaya Creek, Mirror Lake has been slowly reverting to 'Mirror Meadow' ever since the park service stopped dredging it in 1971. Only

folks who visit in spring and early summer see the splendid sight for which Mirror Lake is named. By midsummer, it's just Tenaya Creek, and by fall, the creek has sometimes dried up altogether. Spring is also a marvelous time to visit for other reasons: the dogwoods are in full bloom and Tenaya Creek becomes a lively torrent as you venture further up the canyon. The Ahwahneechee called Mirror Lake Ahwiyah, meaning 'quiet water.'

From the Mirror Lake Trailhead, near shuttle stop 17, follow the Mirror Lake road to **Tenaya Creek Bridge**. Cross Tenaya Creek and follow the paved service road 1 mile to **Mirror Lake**, where interpretive signs explain the area's natural history. From here you can return back to the shuttle stop, or journey up Tenaya Canyon for a little solitude.

The trail continues along Tenaya Creek into **Tenaya Canyon**, in 1 mile passing the Snow Creek Trail junction and soon after crossing two tranquil footbridges. In 2009, a 115,000-ton rockfall cascaded almost 2000ft from Ahwiyah Point near Half Dome, burying a large section of the trail beyond here. A path now traverses the rockfall, and your heart may skip a beat when you hear the pinging sound of loose rocks in that area.

(Continued on page 54)

HIKING IN YOSEMITE NATIONAL PARK

NAME	REGION	DESCRIPTION	DIFFICULTY
Lukens Lake (p57)	Big Oak Flat Rd & Tioga Rd	Quick hike to small but attractive lake; lots of wildflowers	easy
Tenaya Lake (p57)	Big Oak Flat Rd & Tioga Rd	A level stroll around one of biggest lakes in the high country	easy
Tuolumne Grove (p56)	Big Oak Flat Rd & Tioga Rd	Descend along a portion of Old Big Oak Flat Rd to a small sequoia grove	easy-moderate
Merced Grove (p56)	Big Oak Flat Rd & Tioga Rd	The park's least-visited sequoia grove; downhill with a stiff ascent on the return	easy-moderate
Harden Lake (p58)	Big Oak Flat Rd & Tioga Rd	Follow the old Tioga Rd & the Tuolumne River for a rare warm lake swim	easy-moderate
North Dome (p60)	Big Oak Flat Rd & Tioga Rd	Astounding views of Yosemite Valley, Half Dome & Tenaya Canyon; includes 1000ft descent	moderate
May Lake & Mt Hoffmann (p58)	Big Oak Flat Rd & Tioga Rd	Short hike to May Lake High Sierra Camp, plus more challenging summit of nearby peak	moderate-difficult
Clouds Rest (p59)	Big Oak Flat Rd & Tioga Rd	Yosemite's largest expanse of granite; arguably its finest panoramic viewpoint	difficult
Tenaya Lake to Yosemite Valley (p77)	Big Oak Flat Rd & Tioga Rd	Includes 6321ft cumulative descent, with the option to summit Clouds Rest	difficult
Old Big Oak Flat Rd to Yosemite Falls (p76)	Big Oak Flat Rd & Tioga Rd	Inspiring hike from the heights of Yosemite Valley's north rim	difficult
McGurk Meadow (p61)	Glacier Point & Badger Pass	Short, flat walk to lush meadow; lots of wildflowers & old log cabin	easy
Taft Point & the Fissures (p61)	Glacier Point & Badger Pass	Major Valley viewpoint with interesting geological features	easy
Sentinel Dome (p62)	Glacier Point & Badger Pass	Easiest hike to top of a dome with amazing 360-degree views	easy-moderate
Panorama Trail (p62)	Glacier Point & Badger Pass	Descends from Glacier Point to Yosemite Valley floor, with postcard views the whole way down	moderate-difficult
Pohono Trail (p63)	Glacier Point & Badger Pass	Passes numerous Yosemite Valley viewpoints; requires car shuttle	moderate-difficult
Ostrander Lake (p79)	Glacier Point & Badger Pass	Out-and-back wildflower trail with distant views leads to a backcountry hut & amphitheater lake	moderate-difficult
Carlon Falls (p72)	Hetch Hetchy	Falls feed into two swimming spots on the western edge of the park	easy-moderate
Tueeulala & Wapama Falls (p70)	Hetch Hetchy	Undulating trail to base of Hetch Hetchy's roaring waterfalls; boasts views aplenty	easy-moderate
Poopenaut Valley (p72)	Hetch Hetchy	Steep descent to Tuolumne River and back up; break at the bottom for swim and solitude	difficult
Rancheria Falls (p86)	Hetch Hetchy	A popular introduction to Hetch Hetchy's lower altitude backcountry & waterfalls; best in spring	moderate-difficult
Dog Lake (p65)	Tuolumne Meadows	Picnicking & brisk swimming await at the end of this pine-forest trail	easy-moderate

 Drinking Water   Restrooms   Waterfall   Transportation to Trailhead   Swimming

DURATION	ROUND-TRIP DISTANCE	ELEVATION CHANGE	FEATURES	FACILITIES
1hr	1.6 miles	+200ft		
1-2hr	3 miles	+50ft		
1½hr	2 miles	+500ft		
1½-2hr	3 miles	+600ft		
2-3hr	5.8 miles	+400ft		
4½-5hr	8.5 miles	-1000/+422ft		
4-5hr	6 miles	+2004ft		
6-7hr	14.4 miles	+2205ft		
2 days (one way)	17.2 miles (one way)	+2205ft		
2 days (one way)	18.8 miles (one way)	+3080/-2700ft		
1hr	1.6 miles	+150ft		
1hr	2.2 miles	+250ft		
1hr	2.2 miles	+370ft		
5hr (one way)	8.5 miles (one way)	-3200/+760ft		
7-9hr (one way)	13.8 miles (one way)	-2800ft		
2 days	12.4 miles	+1550ft		
2hr	2.4 miles	+300ft		
2½-3hr	5.4 miles	+400ft		
3-4hr	2.8 miles	+1300ft		
7hr-2 days	13 miles	+786ft		
2hr	2.8 miles	+520ft		

 View   Wildlife Watching   Backcountry Campsite   Family Friendly   Picnic Tables   Ranger Station

NAME	REGION	DESCRIPTION	DIFFICULTY
Lyell Canyon (p80)	Tuolumne Meadows	Flat trail with superb views of Mt Lyell & its eponymous glacier	easy-moderate
Lembert Dome (p64)	Tuolumne Meadows	One of the best places to watch the sun set in Yosemite is atop this granite dome	moderate
Gaylor Lakes (p67)	Tuolumne Meadows	Short, steep hike with epic scenery of high country & lakes above Tioga Pass	moderate
Elizabeth Lake (p65)	Tuolumne Meadows	Great jaunt for acclimatizing in Tuolumne; superb views; lots to explore	moderate
Cathedral Lakes (p65)	Tuolumne Meadows	Easily one of Yosemite's most spectacular hikes	moderate
Glen Aulin (p66)	Tuolumne Meadows	Follow Tuolumne River past waterfalls to one of the High Sierra camps	moderate
Young Lakes (p81)	Tuolumne Meadows	Sweeping views of the Cathedral Range lead to a trio of lovely lakes	moderate
Mono Pass (p67)	Tuolumne Meadows	Outstanding day hike into high country above Tioga Pass	moderate-difficult
Vogelsang (p83)	Tuolumne Meadows	Multiday, high-country trip with astounding views of Cathedral Range	moderate-difficult
Mt Dana (p68)	Tuolumne Meadows	Lung-busting, thigh-burning hike to the park's second-highest peak	difficult
Waterwheel Falls (p85)	Tuolumne Meadows	Splendid series of waterfalls at head of Grand Canyon of the Tuolumne River	difficult
Wawona Meadow Loop (p68)	Wawona	Loop around meadow that's shaded & flat, but lots of horse manure	easy
Mariposa Grove to Wawona	Wawona	Woodsy, downhill alternative to shuttle bus	easy-moderate
Chilnualna Falls (p69)	Wawona	Uncrowded trail along cascading creek to top of waterfalls over Wawona Dome's shoulder	moderate-difficult
Alder Creek Falls (p70)	Wawona	Remote corner for quiet amid towering trees with splendid waterfall at end	moderate
Mirror Lake (p49)	Yosemite Valley	Best in spring, a relaxed stroll to the lovely sight of reflective Mirror Lake & beyond	easy
Yosemite Valley Loop (p48)	Yosemite Valley	Surprisingly uncrowded trails that pass all the major Valley sights	easy
Inspiration Point (p54)	Yosemite Valley	Some of the finest views of Yosemite Valley; easily extended to include other viewpoints	moderate-difficult
Vernal & Nevada Falls (p55)	Yosemite Valley	Justifiably popular hike to two of Yosemite's finest falls; mind-blowing scenery	moderate-difficult
Four Mile Trail (p54)	Yosemite Valley	One of the grandest viewpoints in the entire country; also accessible by car or shuttle	difficult
Yosemite Falls (p54)	Yosemite Valley	Sweat yourself silly & enjoy the views hiking to the top of Yosemite's highest falls	difficult
Half Dome (p74)	Yosemite Valley	The park's most difficult day hike is a strenuous push to the top of Yosemite's iconic dome	difficult

  Drinking Water   *Restrooms*   *Waterfall*   *Transportation to Trailhead*   *Swimming*

DURATION	ROUND-TRIP DISTANCE	ELEVATION CHANGE	FEATURES	FACILITIES
2 days	17.6 miles	+200ft		
2-3hr	2.4 miles	+850ft		
2-3hr	3 miles	+560ft		
2½-4hr	5.2 miles	+800ft		
4-7hr	8 miles	+1000ft		
6-8hr	11 miles	-600ft		
2 days	13 miles	+1400ft		
4hr	7.4 miles	+915ft		
3 days	27 miles	+3852ft		
6-7hr	5.8 miles	+3108ft		
2 days	18 miles	+2260ft		
1-1½hr	3.5 miles	+200ft		
2-3hr (one way)	6.5 miles (one way)	-2000ft		
4-5hr	8.6 miles	+2240ft		
4-5hr	8 miles	+1800ft		
1hr	2 miles	+100ft		
varies	varies	+330ft		
1½-2½hr	2.6 miles	+1000ft		
4-7hr	6.5 miles	+1900ft		
4-8hr	9.2 miles	+3200ft		
5-6hr	6.8 miles	+2400ft		
10-12hr	17 miles	+4800ft		

 View Wildlife Watching Backcountry Campsite Family Friendly Picnic Tables Ranger Station

(Continued from page 49)

From this opposite side of Tenaya Creek, the trail loops back through the canyon, passing Mirror Lake again.

🥾 Inspiration Point

Duration 1½–2½ hours

Distance 2.6-mile round-trip

Difficulty Moderate–Difficult

Start/Finish Tunnel View parking lot

Nearest Town Yosemite Village

Transportation Car

Summary Some of the best vistas in all Yosemite are granted to those who hike this steep trail to this classic viewpoint.

Sure, Tunnel View offers an amazing look into the Valley. But the view is even more impressive along the steep trail to Inspiration Point. Best of all, you'll leave the crowds behind.

Inspiration Point used to be a viewpoint along an old road into Yosemite Valley. The roadbed still exists, but this hike (actually the western end of the Pohono Trail) is now the only way to reach the point. You start by climbing a series of switchbacks from the upper Tunnel View parking lot (on Hwy 41 immediately east of the Wawona Tunnel). Almost immediately the view improves, with fewer trees and no bus tourists. Short spur trails lead to open viewpoints.

The climb is steep and steady but fairly short. The view from Inspiration Point itself – a large open area with views semi-obscured by trees – isn't as spectacular as on the way up, but it's a worthy destination nonetheless, quiet and perfect for a picnic. Better views can be had from cliffs just to the west. If you've got the energy, continue up the trail 2.5 miles to **Stanford Point** and even another half-mile on to **Crocker Point** (7090ft), and from there another half-mile on to **Dewey Point** (7385ft). All offer epic views. The Inspiration Point Trail is often doable in winter.

🥾 Yosemite Falls

Duration 6–8 hours

Distance 7.2-mile round-trip

Difficulty Difficult

Start/Finish Yosemite Falls Trailhead near Camp 4

Nearest Town Yosemite Village

Transportation Shuttle stop 7

Summary This classic hike along one of the park's oldest trails leads from the Valley floor to the top of the three-step falls. The stiff ascent (and equivalent descent) make it a real thigh-burning, knee-busting haul.

The heart-stopping views from atop Upper Yosemite Fall will make you quickly forget any pain endured on the hike up. If it seems a bit much, you can always hike just the first mile (and 1000 vertical feet) to **Columbia Rock** (5031ft), a justifiably classic viewpoint.

From the northeastern side of Camp 4, the Yosemite Falls Trail immediately starts in on the four dozen short switchbacks that zigzag up a talus slope through canyon live oaks. After 0.8 miles, the grade eases as the trail follows more switchbacks east to Columbia Rock.

In another 0.4 miles, the trail approaches the top of **Lower Yosemite Fall**, where breezes may shower you with a fine, cooling mist. After admiring the view of Upper Yosemite Fall, brace yourself for the numerous switchbacks that run steadily up a rocky cleft to the Valley rim. The falls once ran down this cleft.

The trail tops out 3.2 miles from the trailhead and bends east. At the junction, the trail going straight leads to **Eagle Peak** (7779ft). Turn right at this junction and follow the trail a short distance to the brink of Upper Yosemite Fall at the **Yosemite Falls Overlook** (6400ft). The view of the falls is impressive, but views of El Capitan and Half Dome are obscured. For a wider perspective, go the extra 1.6 miles (and nearly 600ft more in elevation) to **Yosemite Point** (6936ft), where you'll get incredible views of Half Dome, North Dome, Clouds Rest, Glacier Point, Cathedral Rocks and Lost Arrow.

Keep in mind that the falls are often dry by midsummer, so May and June (after the snow has cleared) are the best months to catch the scene in all its frothy glory. When you're done, retrace your steps to the trailhead.

🥾 Four Mile Trail

Duration 6–8 hours

Distance 9.6-mile round-trip

Difficulty Difficult

Start/Finish Four Mile Trailhead

Nearest Town Yosemite Village

Transportation El Capitan shuttle stop 5 (summer only), shuttle stop 7

Summary A fulfilling day hike from Yosemite Valley that ascends the Valley's southern wall to Glacier Point, the park's most famous viewpoint. The reward for the grunt is one of the finest vistas in the entire country.

Sure, you can easily get to Glacier Point by car or bus (an alternative preferred by many is to buy a one-way bus fare and hike down from the point), but there's something supremely rewarding about making the journey on foot. If the El Capitan shuttle isn't running yet, take the Valley shuttle to stop 7, and walk south along a paved footpath leading across Swinging Bridge to Southside Dr. From here walk parallel to the road a short distance west to the Four Mile Trailhead. (This adds about another half-mile each way.)

Today the Four Mile Trail actually spans closer to 4.6 miles, having been rerouted since it was first completed in 1872. It was originally intended as a toll pathway, at the time being the quickest way into the Valley.

The trail climbs steadily, passing 2000ft multi-tiered **Sentinel Fall** and **Sentinel Rock** (7038ft). At **Union Point**, 3 miles from the trailhead, you'll first catch a glimpse of Half Dome. Continue climbing until the trail levels out for the final leg to **Glacier Point**. Take in the views, fill up with more water and check out the snack bar.

When you're ready, return the way you came. Hardy hikers can turn this into an excellent loop trail (and avoid retracing their steps) by continuing on the Panorama Trail to Nevada Fall, then down to Happy Isles.

🏃 Vernal & Nevada Falls

Duration 4–6 hours

Distance 5.4-mile round-trip

Difficulty Moderate–Difficult

Start/Finish Vernal & Nevada Falls/John Muir Trailhead

Nearest Junction Happy Isles

Transportation Shuttle stop 16

Summary Affording views that are unmatched anywhere else in the park, this well-trodden partial loop ascends the so-called Giant Staircase: the route of the Merced River as it plunges over Nevada and Vernal Falls.

If you can only do a single day hike in Yosemite – *and it's springtime* – make this the one. Not only are Vernal and Nevada Falls two of Yosemite's most spectacular waterfalls, but Yosemite Falls and Illilouette Fall both make appearances in the distance from select spots on the trail. If you prefer a shorter excursion, and many do, stop at the top of Vernal Fall and return the same way you came.

There are two ways to hike this loop: up the **Mist Trail** and down the **John Muir Trail** (in a clockwise direction) or vice versa. It's easier on the knees to climb rather than descend the plethora of steep granite steps along the Mist Trail, so it's best to go for the clockwise route. Then you can lollygag along the John Muir Trail – which has astounding views of both falls – on the way down. The granite slabs atop Nevada Fall make for a superb lunch spot (as close to the edge as you want), with the granite dome of **Liberty Cap** (7076ft) towering above.

From the Happy Isles shuttle stop, cross the road bridge over the Merced River, turn right at the trailhead and follow the riverbank upstream. As the trail steepens, watch over your right shoulder for Illilouette Fall (often dry in summer), which peels over a 370ft cliff in the distance. From a lookout, you can gaze west and see Yosemite Falls. After 0.8 miles you arrive at the **Vernal Fall footbridge**, which offers the first view of 317ft Vernal Fall upstream.

Shortly beyond the Vernal Fall footbridge (just past the water fountain and restrooms), you'll reach the junction of the John Muir and Mist Trails. To do the trail clockwise, hang a left and shortly begin the steep 0.3-mile ascent to the top of **Vernal Fall** by way of the Mist Trail's granite steps. If it's springtime, prepare to get drenched in spray – wear some waterproof clothing! – and peer behind you as you near the top to see rainbows in the mist.

Above the falls, the Merced whizzes down a long ramp of granite known as the **Silver Apron** and into the deceptively serene Emerald Pool before plunging over the cliff. No matter how fun the apron looks on a hot day, *don't enter the water:* underwater currents in Emerald Pool have whipped many swimmers over the falls.

From above the apron, it's another 1.3 miles via granite steps and steep switchbacks to the top of the Mist Trail, which meets the John Muir Trail about 0.2 miles northeast of the falls. From this junction, it's

2.5 miles back to Happy Isles via the Mist Trail or 4 miles via the John Muir Trail.

Shortly after joining the John Muir Trail, you'll cross a footbridge (elevation 5907ft) over the Merced. Beneath it, the river whizzes through a chute before plummeting 594ft over the edge of Nevada Fall. Nevada Fall is the first of the series of steps in the Giant Staircase, a metaphor that becomes clear when viewed from afar at Glacier Point. Plant yourself on a slab of granite for lunch and views, and be prepared to fend off the ballsy Steller's jays and squirrels that will have your jerky in their jaws in no time, should you let down your guard.

Returning back from Nevada Fall along the John Muir Trail offers a fabulous glimpse of Yosemite Falls. The trail passes the Panorama Trail junction and traverses a cliff, offering awesome views of Nevada Fall as it winds down the canyon. Soon you'll reach Clark Point and a junction that leads down to the Mist Trail. From here it's just over 2 miles downhill, through Douglas firs and canyon live oaks to Happy Isles.

If you choose to do this hike in summertime, be sure to hit the trail early to avoid the crowds and afternoon heat.

Big Oak Flat Road & Tioga Road

Two of the area's main hikes lead to groves of giant sequoias. Though neither grove is as magnificent as Wawona's Mariposa Grove, the crowds are mercifully thinner.

Day hikes and backcountry excursions are plentiful in Yosemite's subalpine wilderness, which stretches north and south from either side of Tioga Rd. Like Tuolumne Meadows further east, this truly is a hikers' paradise. Several trails from the south side of the road lead to Yosemite Valley, and if you take the hikers' bus up from the Valley, they're more or less downhill all the way – an exquisite and rare treat.

🚶 Tuolumne Grove

Duration 1½ hours

Distance 2-mile round-trip

Difficulty Easy–Moderate

Start/Finish Tuolumne Grove Trailhead

Nearest Junction Crane Flat Gas Station

Transportation Car

Summary Descend into Yosemite's second-most-visited grove of giant sequoias (the walk back up is a bit of a haul). There's even a tree you can walk through.

You can reach this moderately sized grove of sequoias via a short, steep hike down a section of the Old Big Oak Flat Rd (closed to cars). Follow the road and a few switchbacks to the first trees, then meander through the grove and along an interpretive nature trail – from here you could continue another 4.2 miles to Hodgdon Meadow Campground (p122). The most popular attraction is the Tunnel Tree (or 'Dead Giant'), already a stump when a tunnel was cut into it in 1878. Another interesting specimen is the Leaning Towering Tree. It fell over in 1983, and now looks like a huge set of cracked vertebrae. At one end, its roots shoot out like flares, and the hollowed-out core makes a fun tunnel for kids to explore.

The only downside to this hike is the steady uphill climb back to the parking area (imagine the struggle of horses that once pulled stagecoaches up the slope). When it's hot, you'll be hurting – or panting at the very least. It's not awful though, and hikers of any age should be able to handle it given time and patience. Good for year-round visits.

🚶 Merced Grove

Duration 1½–2 hours

Distance 3-mile round-trip

Difficulty Easy–Moderate

Start/Finish Merced Grove Trailhead

Nearest Junction Crane Flat Gas Station

Transportation Car

Summary This hike leads down to a beautiful sequoia grove, with crowds rarely present to break the solitude. The walk follows a dirt road to a dense cluster of giant trees.

The smallest sequoia grove in the park, Merced is also the quietest, thanks in part to its distance from major park sights. If you seek solitude amid the sequoias, this is for you. You'll start from a small parking lot along Big Oak Flat Rd midway between Crane Flat and the Big Oak Flat gate. The trail follows a dirt road (closed to cars), which remains flat for the first half-mile before dipping downhill into the grove. A handful of the trees surround a small log cabin. Reserve your energy for the hike out.

Big Oak Flat Road & Tioga Road – Day Hikes

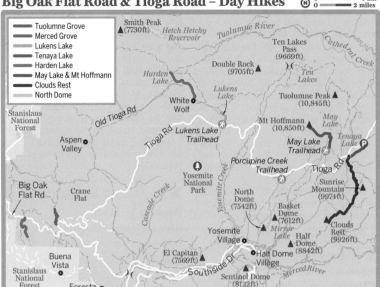

For even more quiet and solitude, head here in winter, either with cross-country skis, snowshoes or good boots.

🥾 Lukens Lake

Duration 1 hour

Distance 1.6-mile round-trip

Difficulty Easy

Start/Finish Lukens Lake Trailhead

Nearest Town White Wolf

Transportation Tuolumne Meadows hikers' bus or car

Summary A gentle, quick jaunt along a wildflower meadow and a peaceful lake edged by shaded forest. Even small children can do this walk with ease.

Hike up here early in the morning or late in the afternoon, especially on a weekday, and you just might have the quiet blue lake, green meadow and surrounding sea of colorful wildflowers all to yourself. (Weekends are a different story.) Corn lilies trace the path leading up to the lake, and thousands of orange and black butterflies cluster on the ground in summer. If you hold still and listen, you can hear the low hum of omnipresent bees. Purple and white flowers

erupt as you near the lakeshore, forming an exquisitely colored carpet. Revel in the idyllic setting and serenity in the 'golden hour' of early evening light. Even beginners can handle the short jaunt from Tioga Rd.

Start from the marked parking area a couple of miles east of the White Wolf turnoff. Cross the road and begin the trail in the soft woods. Climbing steadily, you'll reach a small ridge, then drop down to Lukens Lake. The trail follows the south shore to the west end, where you'll find plenty of shady spots to rest, picnic or simply sit in quiet contemplation.

An alternative 2.3-mile trail (one way) leads to the lake's west side from White Wolf Lodge, following the Middle Tuolumne River along the way.

🥾 Tenaya Lake

Duration 1-2 hours

Distance 3-mile round-trip

Difficulty Easy

Start/Finish East Tenaya Lake parking lot

Nearest Town Tuolumne Meadows

Transportation Tuolumne Meadows shuttle stop 9

Summary A back-and-forth stroll along

one of Yosemite's prettiest lakes, with no need to head high into the backcountry to reach it. A long sandy beach tempts you into trying the chilly blue water.

A pleasant stroll, this new loop trail skirts the shore of one of the park's biggest natural lakes. Begin from the upgraded parking area on the north shore. An accessible boardwalk on the east end leads to a popular sandy **beach**. Walk south along the beach, and look for the trail amid the trees just ahead. As the path traces the shore, small spurs lead down to the water. Though the shoreline is rocky, there are several nice spots for a picnic; summertime means masses of others have the same idea. There's now a boardwalk over wetlands on the western end (near the Sunrise Trailhead). For more privacy, head here first thing in the morning or late afternoon.

Harden Lake

Duration 2–3 hours

Distance 5.8-mile round-trip

Difficulty Easy–Moderate

Start/Finish White Wolf

Nearest Town White Wolf

Transportation Tuolumne Meadows hikers' bus or car

Summary Tracing a short section of the old Tioga Rd, this nicely forested out-and-back route is mostly level. Your reward is a tranquil and pretty lake basin that's good for a swim.

From the White Wolf Lodge parking area, start toward the direction of the White Wolf campground and follow the gravel road – a section of the old Tioga Rd – to the left of the campground entrance. The roadway passes a mixed forest of lodgepole pine and Jeffrey pine, running parallel to the Middle Fork of the Tuolumne River. A few areas of fire damage are visible just before a discreet sewage-treatment facility appears off to the left. Continue on, and at the 2-mile mark take a right off the (now dirt) road and onto a foot trail. Jittery leaves of quaking aspens flutter in the breeze, and the occasional pinedrops plant can be spotted by its unusual red stalks. The 2013 Rim Fire came perilously close to here, and the many blackened trees you see resulted from backfires set to contain it.

Follow the trail for almost a mile to the lake. On the path toward the small boulder-littered shore, a meadow erupts with bulbous yellow Bigelow sneezeweed and white sprays of yampa. If you continue on a bit further north to the far side of the lake, feast on tremendous views of the Grand Canyon of the Tuolumne River and the peaks in the park's northern wilderness.

Harden Lake is an unusually warm-water lake for these parts, primarily because it evaporates rapidly during summer. So bring a towel and splash around without feeling like a polar bear. Retrace your steps to the parking lot.

May Lake & Mt Hoffmann

Duration 4–5 hours

Distance 6-mile round-trip

Difficulty Moderate–Difficult

Start/Finish May Lake Trailhead

Nearest Town Tuolumne Meadows

Transportation Tuolumne Meadows hikers' bus or car

Summary May Lake is a relatively easy uphill jaunt to instant backcountry. A trail to Mt Hoffmann winds up its rocky slope, and the payoff is one of the best viewpoints of the park.

At the park's geographical center, **Mt Hoffmann** (10,850ft) commands outstanding views of Yosemite's entire high country. The broad summit plateau offers a superb perspective, a vista that drew the first California Geological Survey party in 1863. The peak is named after Charles F Hoffmann, the party's topographer and artist. The first peak climbed in Yosemite, Mt Hoffmann remains one of the park's most frequently visited summits.

Some hikers go no further than **May Lake** (9350ft), on the High Sierra Camps loop, a pristine mountain lake that cries out for a shoreline picnic. It alone is a satisfying destination, with great views of Half Dome, Cathedral Peak and Mt Clark along the way. The 1.2-mile stretch, a steady 500ft climb, takes only about 30 to 40 minutes, and if you have a wilderness permit you can overnight at the nice backpackers' campground next to the May Lake High Sierra Camp.

Start from the May Lake Trailhead (8846ft), 1.7 miles up a paved section of the old Tioga Rd. The turnoff from Tioga

Rd is 2.2 miles west of Olmsted Point and 3.2 miles east of the Porcupine Flat Campground. Be sure to use the bear boxes in the parking lot. (Note that the May Lake stop on the Tuolumne Meadows shuttle is a different trailhead east of Olmsted Point.)

At the lake the trail splits; the right fork leads to May Lake High Sierra Camp, the left traces the lakeshore and then ascends to Mt Hoffmann. The Hoffmann Trail winds through a talus field, where it follows a cairned path. Skirt the south edge of a meadow where the trail turns sharply toward Mt Hoffmann's east summit, and then aim for the higher west summit.

The last bit up involves some basic scrambling, so you'll want your hands free. Don't be surprised if some curious marmots pop their heads out of the rocks to check your progress. Be warned: the swarms of marmots living at the summit and in the rock piles are not shy – they'll come right up to you. If you sit down, keep an eye on your daypack!

Retrace your steps to the May Lake Trailhead.

🏃 Clouds Rest

Duration 7–10 hours, or 2-day trip

Distance 14.4-mile round-trip

Difficulty Difficult

Start/Finish Sunrise Lakes Trailhead

Nearest Town Tuolumne Meadows

Transportation Tuolumne Meadows shuttle stop 10 or car

Summary A fair amount of effort and distance is required for this classic hike, but you'll be amply rewarded with phenomenal 360-degree views from one of the park's best vantage points.

Yosemite's largest granite peak, Clouds Rest (9926ft) rises 4500ft above Tenaya Creek, with spectacular views from the summit and along the trail. More than 1000ft higher than nearby Half Dome, Clouds Rest may well be the park's best panoramic viewpoint. The hike involves a strenuous ascent and equally significant descent (make sure you have a cold drink waiting for you!), but getting here is definitely worth the effort. This hike forms part of the Tenaya Lake to Yosemite Valley hike.

Start from the Sunrise Lakes Trailhead at the west end of Tenaya Lake. Trailhead parking is limited, and the lot fills early. If you're staying in Tuolumne Meadows, it's easier to take the free shuttle bus to the trailhead.

Follow the trail along **Tenaya Creek** for your first glimpse of Clouds Rest and Tenaya Canyon's shining granite walls. As the trail climbs steadily up well-constructed switchbacks, the view expands to include prominent Mt Hoffmann (10,850ft) to the northwest and Tuolumne Peak (10,845ft) to the north. After a steady ascent, the grade eases atop soft earth amid large red firs. At 2.5 miles, continue straight past the Sunrise Lakes junction and descend southwest. As Yosemite Valley and Sentinel Dome come into view, the trail reaches the level floor west of Sunrise Mountain (9974ft). Paintbrushes, lupines and wandering daisies bloom here, alongside mats of pink heather and bushes of poisonous white-flowered Labrador tea. About 2 miles from the Sunrise Trail junction you'll reach a creek that's the last water source en route to the summit – so fill up here (and filter it).

At approximately 5 miles you'll reach the Forsyth Trail junction, although it's not labeled as such on the sign. Bear southwest and ascend the ridgeline that culminates in **Clouds Rest**. To the southeast are fabulous views of wedge-shaped Mt Clark (11,522ft), the Cascade Cliffs and Bunnell Point in Merced Canyon. The granite swell of Mt Starr King (9092ft) rises to the southwest. The trail soon passes over a low rise and through a slight but obvious saddle. At a large white pine about a mile beyond the saddle, a small unmarked trail forks left; this is recommended for those not willing or able to hike the more exposed summit path.

A sign reading 'Clouds Rest Foot Trail' directs you along the granite ridge, which narrows rather thrillingly in one place. Never less than 5ft wide, the narrowest section might look intimidating but takes only five to 10 seconds to cross. The summit itself offers breathtaking views of Half Dome and the Valley. The view stretches from the Sawtooth Ridge and Matterhorn Peak along the park's north border to Mt Ritter and Banner Peak, standing dark and prominent to the southeast. Mt Conness and Mt Dana on the Sierra Crest and the closer Cathedral Range are all outstanding. This is one of the Sierra Nevada's most inspiring viewpoints – savor the sights before retracing your steps to the trailhead.

You can extend your hike by continuing down to Yosemite Valley (as part of the Tenaya Lake to Yosemite Valley hike).

🏃 North Dome

Duration 4½–6 hours

Distance 11-mile round-trip

Difficulty Moderate

Start/Finish Porcupine Creek Trailhead

Nearest Town White Wolf

Transportation Tuolumne Meadows hikers' bus or car

Summary Perhaps the best vantage point along the Valley rim, this trail sees relatively few hikers. It's a downhill trek outbound, so you'll be doing the ascent on the return.

The trail descends 1000ft and rises 422ft on the way there, so be ready for a climb on the return trip. A side trip to the natural arch on Indian Ridge adds another 240ft climb. Note that North Dome is an exposed and hazardous place to be in a thunderstorm, and the final approach is not recommended in wet conditions.

From Tioga Rd, start at the Porcupine Creek Trailhead (8120ft), 1.2 miles east of Porcupine Flat Campground. To reach the trailhead from the campground, walk to the southern side of the highway from the camp entrance and follow the footpath that parallels the road.

An abandoned road leads beneath red firs until the pavement ends at 0.7 miles and the trail crosses Porcupine Creek via a log. After an easy ascent into the forest, you'll reach a few trail junctions in quick succession. Follow each in the signed direction of North Dome.

The trail climbs gently up Indian Ridge to an inviting view across the Valley to Sentinel Dome and Taft Point. The trail soon turns sharply and ascends steadily, leading to the marked Indian Rock trail junction at 3.6 miles from the trailhead.

A worthwhile but optional 0.6-mile (round-trip, included in hike mileage) side trip leads to Indian Rock (8360ft), Yosemite's only visible natural arch. Follow the short, steep spur trail to the arch. From the trail you can see the arch from all sorts of angles; the arch affords good views of Clouds Rest, the Clark Range, Mt Starr King and Sentinel Dome. Clamber onto the rock for a view of Half Dome framed by the arch.

At the Indian Rock Trail junction, the main trail continues south, leading to a spectacular viewpoint at the end of the ridge: front and center is Half Dome, and across the Valley is hard-to-see Illilouette Fall. North Dome lies directly below to the south, and Basket Dome's rounded peak (7612ft) lies to the southeast.

Hikers have created a number of indistinct use trails from here. The main trail curves around a large Jeffrey pine and drops southeast (left) off the ridgeline in the direction of Half Dome and then descends on switchbacks across open granite. Cairns lead to the marked North Dome Trail junction. Turn east for the final half-mile stretch. The rough trail descends steeply on a worn rock slab (that is dangerously slippery when wet) before a short final ascent to the summit.

West are the Sentinels, Cathedrals, El Capitan, the Three Brothers and Yosemite Point (Yosemite Falls lie hidden). To the northeast are Basket Dome, Mt Watkins and the distant peaks of the Cathedral Range. Horse Ridge rims the horizon to the south, while dominating the scene is the sheer north face of Half Dome – surely one of Yosemite's most impressive sights. Clouds Rest rises on the far side of granite-walled Tenaya Canyon.

Retrace your steps along Indian Ridge to return to the trailhead.

You can extend the hike by descending to the Valley on either the Snow Creek Trail (which heads down to Tenaya Canyon and Mirror Lake) or on the trail west to Yosemite Point and Yosemite Falls Overlook. From the latter, take the Yosemite Falls Trail down to Camp 4.

Use the hikers' bus from the Valley to reach the North Dome Trailhead in the morning. You can also start hiking from the Valley and visit North Dome on a very demanding round-trip of eight to 10 hours. For an especially vigorous day hike, traverse the Valley's north rim via North Dome by ascending the Snow Creek Trail's 100-plus switchbacks and returning via the Yosemite Falls Trail.

Glacier Point & Badger Pass

If you're looking for bird's-eye views of Yosemite Valley, then several Glacier Point Rd hikes will fit the bill perfectly. Dewey Point, Taft Point and the Sentinel Dome hikes all lead to spectacular overlooks of Yosemite

Valley. The Sentinel Dome hike offers perhaps the widest, finest view of all, and the trip to its summit takes a mere half-hour. Some of the hikes link up with other top-notch trails, such as the Four Mile Trail to Glacier Point and the trail from Wawona Tunnel to Inspiration Point (the westernmost leg of the Pohono Trail). Bask in views as you descend from Glacier Point and ogle some of Yosemite's best waterfalls.

🥾 McGurk Meadow

Duration 1 hour

Distance 1.6-mile round-trip

Difficulty Easy

Start/Finish McGurk Meadow Trailhead

Nearest Junction Bridalveil Creek Campground

Transportation Car

Summary An effortless and relaxing walk through grassy wildflower meadows, this is a nice choice for families or those who want an easier, less-crowded hike.

For a short stroll with solitude and tranquility, lush, open McGurk Meadow fits the bill. Park at a pullout along Glacier Point Rd just west of the Bridalveil Creek Campground

entrance; the posted trailhead is about 100yd west of the parking area.

Shaded by lodgepole pines, a level and sun-dappled path meanders through quiet forest. After about a mile, a historic one-room log cabin appears on the left. Kids will love playing in and around this former seasonal shelter for cattle ranchers; adults will need to double over to enter the low, half-scale doorway.

The meadow sits across a small footbridge just beyond the cabin, and its wildflowers peak in July, erupting in splashes of red, white and yellow. If you wish to continue on, another 3.2 miles takes you to Dewey Point (7385ft) and big, wide views down into the Valley.

🥾 Taft Point & the Fissures

Duration 1 hour

Distance 2.2-mile round-trip

Difficulty Easy

Start/Finish Sentinel Dome/Taft Point Trailhead

Nearest Junction Glacier Point

Transportation Car

Summary A hike over easy terrain leads to a spectacular overlook and drop-off at the

Glacier Point & Badger Pass – Day Hikes

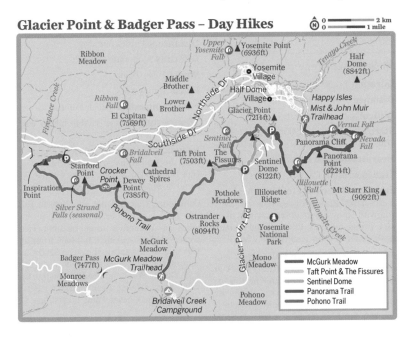

edge of a sheer 3000ft cliff. Sizable boulders fill a series of enormous granite cracks.

Park in the Sentinel Dome/Taft Point lot on the north side of Glacier Point Rd, about 13 miles from Chinquapin. Note that the main parking area is not that large and often fills up by midmorning; it is less packed in the afternoons.

Taft Point (7503ft) is a fantastic, hair-raising viewpoint at the edge of a sheer 3000ft cliff, with impressive views of El Capitan and Yosemite Valley. On the same promontory are the Fissures, a series of deep, narrow cracks in the granite, many with large boulders wedged inside. Choose your steps carefully, especially when accompanying small children.

After a gentle descent through pleasant forest, you'll emerge on an open, rocky slope dotted with hardy wind-shaped trees. On your right are the Fissures, which drop hundreds of feet along the edge of Profile Cliff. Across Yosemite Valley, you'll see the Three Brothers, with similar yet longer cracks in the rock.

Ahead is Taft Point, guarded only by a short metal railing. Unless you have a profound fear of heights, approach and peer over the edge – the sheer drop is mind-boggling. Look west through binoculars to spot climbers on the southeast face and nose of El Capitan. After soaking up the views, which include a close-up look at Cathedral Spires, return on a gentle uphill climb to the parking lot.

🏃 Sentinel Dome

Duration 1 hour

Distance 2.2-mile round-trip

Difficulty Easy–Moderate

Start/Finish Sentinel Dome/Taft Point Trailhead

Nearest Junction Glacier Point

Transportation Car

Summary The easiest trail up one of the park's fabled granite domes will reward you with sprawling panoramic vistas of high peaks and falls. Ravaged and surreal trees strain to grow against the wind.

For those unable to visit Half Dome's summit, Sentinel's summit (8122ft) offers an equally outstanding 360-degree perspective of Yosemite's wonders. A visit at sunrise, sunset or during a full moon is spectacular. You can also combine a trip up Senti-

nel Dome with a walk to Taft Point and the Fissures, an equidistant hike from the same trailhead, or combine the two to form a loop via the solitary Pohono Trail.

Park in the Sentinel Dome/Taft Point lot on the north side of Glacier Point Rd. From the parking lot, take the trail's gently rising right fork and head northwest across open granite slabs to the dome's base. Skirt the base to an old service road, which leads to the dome's northeast shoulder. From here, head up the gentle granite slope to the top (wear good hiking shoes).

The gnarled, bleached bones of a wind-beaten Jeffrey pine once crowned the top. The photogenic tree died in a drought in the late 1970s, but caused heartbreak for many when it finally fell in 2003.

From the top, the views take in almost the entire park. To the west are Cathedral Rocks and El Capitan, while to the north you'll spot Yosemite Falls and, in the distance, Mt Hoffmann. North Dome, Basket Dome and Mt Watkins line the Valley's northeast side, and Clouds Rest and Half Dome rise dramatically above Tenaya Canyon. In the distance, above Nevada Fall, you'll see the notable peaks of the Cathedral and Ritter Ranges. To the east lie Mt Starr King and the peaks of the Clark Range.

🏃 Panorama Trail

Duration 5 hours

Distance 8.5 miles one way

Difficulty Moderate–Difficult

Start Glacier Point

Finish Happy Isles

Nearest Junction Glacier Point

Transportation Glacier Point hikers' bus or car

Summary Picture-postcard views accompany this trail with eye-popping vistas of Half Dome. Visit Nevada Fall as you descend down, down, down to the Valley floor.

Connecting Glacier Point and Nevada Fall, this trail is gorgeous, comprising several miles of Yosemite's most picture-perfect scenery. Hikers seeking a full loop from the Valley must first tackle the steep 3200ft ascent on the Four Mile Trail. Those starting from Glacier Point and heading down to the Valley must arrange a car shuttle or reserve a seat on the Glacier Point hikers' bus. Or you can simply hike to Nevada Fall and return to Glacier Point the way you came.

At Glacier Point, look for the Panorama Trail signpost near the snack bar. Descend a fire-scarred hillside south toward Illilouette Fall. The route down is largely easy, with magnificent views to your left – including Half Dome, which from here looks like the tip of a giant thumb. If you're lucky, you'll also find blue grouse on the trail, hooting and cooing in gentle, haunting tones. Make sure you bring sunscreen and a hat, as most of the tree cover has burned away.

After about 1.2 miles you'll meet the trail from Mono Meadow. Turn left and take a short series of switchbacks down to Illilouette Creek. The best place to admire 370ft **Illilouette Fall** is a well-worn viewpoint above the creek on the left.

At the 2-mile mark, a footbridge crosses **Illilouette Creek**, whose shaded banks invite a picnic. The trail leaves the creek and climbs east to **Panorama Point**, then **Panorama Cliff**. This 760ft climb is the only significant elevation gain on the hike. Vantage points high above the Merced River afford amazing views of the Glacier Point apron, Half Dome, Mt Broderick (6706ft), Liberty Cap (7076ft) and Mt Starr King (9092ft).

The trail descends to a junction with the John Muir Trail. Turn right and follow the trail 0.2 miles to the top of **Nevada Fall**, 3.2 miles from Illilouette Creek.

To reach the Valley, descend the Mist Trail via Vernal Fall or take the slightly longer and gentler John Muir Trail. You'll emerge at Happy Isles on the Valley's east end (part of the Vernal and Nevada Falls hike).

🏃 Pohono Trail

Duration 7–9 hours

Distance 13.8 miles one way

Difficulty Moderate–Difficult

Start Glacier Point

Finish Tunnel View parking lot

Nearest Junction Glacier Point

Transportation Glacier Point hikers' bus or car

Summary A panoramic traverse of the southern Valley rim between Glacier Point and the Wawona Tunnel overlook, this hike descends along a scenic ridge above three waterfalls.

Romantically named Bridalveil Fall was called Pohono by the Ahwahneechee, who thought the fall bewitched. According to Native American legend, an evil spirit who breathed out a fatal wind lived at its base; to sleep near it meant certain death. Some claimed to hear the voices of those who had drowned, warning others to stay away.

As the trailheads are many miles apart, you'll need either two vehicles or to arrange for pickup following your hike. The Glacier Point hikers' bus can take you to Glacier Point from the Valley, but it doesn't stop at the Wawona Tunnel parking area.

It's best to go from east to west, starting at Glacier Point. (The trail descends more than 2800ft, so hiking the opposite direction would involve a strenuous climb.) Though it's generally downhill, the trail does make some noticeable climbs here and there. Highlights include Glacier Point (7214ft), Taft Point, Dewey Point, Crocker Point (7090ft), Stanford Point and Inspiration Point. The trail traverses an area high above three waterfalls – Sentinel, Bridalveil and Silver Strand.

Look for the well-marked trailhead near the snack bar at **Glacier Point**. After about a mile, you'll reach the trail junction for **Sentinel Dome**. You can either climb to the top or keep going, skirting just north of the dome along the Valley rim. After about 2 miles, you'll join the trail to **Taft Point**, which leads you across open rock, past the **Fissures** to the point itself. Peer over the railing before resuming your hike.

The trail continues west along the Valley rim, dipping to cross **Bridalveil Creek**. Past the creek, a trail veers left toward McGurk Meadow. Instead, bear right toward **Dewey Point** and another magnificent view (use extreme caution when peering over the edge). Across the Valley, you'll see 1612ft Ribbon Fall – when flowing, the highest single-tier waterfall in North America.

About a half-mile further west is **Crocker Point**, again worth a short detour for the view, which takes in Bridalveil Fall. Another short walk brings you to **Stanford Point**, the last cliff-edge viewpoint on this trail. Looking across the Valley from these western viewpoints, you can see the remains of the Old Big Oak Flat Rd, a white line traversing talus fields below on the north rim. Once you cross Meadow Brook and Artist Creek, you'll begin the steep, 2.5-mile descent to **Inspiration Point**, an overgrown viewpoint

Tuolumne Meadows – Day Hikes

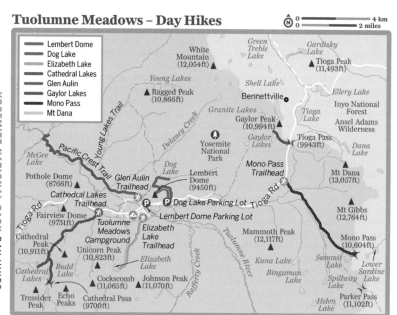

along an old roadbed. The final 1.3-mile leg ends at the Tunnel View parking lot.

Tuolumne Meadows

The many day hikes out of Tuolumne Meadows are some of the finest in all of Yosemite, especially in July, when colorful wildflowers – poking up wherever they can – bring the high country to life. If you don't need to return to the Valley the same day using public transportation, all of these hikes are reachable via the Tuolumne Meadows hikers' bus or the YARTS Hwy 120/395 bus.

Lembert Dome

Duration 2–3 hours

Distance 2.4-mile round-trip

Difficulty Moderate

Start/Finish Dog Lake parking lot

Nearest Town Tuolumne Meadows

Transportation Tuolumne Meadows shuttle stop 2

Summary The short hike (and scramble) to the top of Tuolumne's most iconic dome offers fun on granite and fantastic views in all directions, especially at sunset.

Lembert Dome (9450ft) rises from the meadows' east end, opposite the campground. Scrambling around the base of the dome's steep southwest face is a favorite Tuolumne pastime, but the real pleasure is hiking up the back side and standing atop the summit, where the views are staggering. Mt Dana, the Cathedral Range, Tuolumne Meadows, Pothole Dome, Fairview Dome and the Lyell Fork Tuolumne are all visible from the top. To the east, the Sierra Crest stretches from Mt Conness to the Kuna Crest. It's magical just before sunset.

This hike is doable for most walkers, but reaching the summit requires scrambling up the granite at the end – not recommended for the slippery-footed or faint at heart. Once you're on top, however, you can picnic upon a ledge or walk the ridge, scramble down some rock and cross a tree-filled saddle to the section of Lembert Dome that's so prominent from the road below.

Two similarly named trails lead to Lembert Dome. The one from the Lembert Dome parking lot, at the very base of the dome, is a steep, borderline unpleasant trail that's been damaged by storms. To reach the preferred Dog Lake Trail by car, drive east from the Tuolumne Meadows Campground and turn right onto the road leading to Tuolumne Meadows Lodge. Park in the Dog Lake parking lot, about a half-mile up this road. From the north side of the lot, follow the signed Dog Lake/Young Lakes trail up and across Tioga Rd.

This trail, almost entirely shaded in pine forest, is the quickest way up the back side of the dome. From the top, you can scramble up the granite to the dome's summit.

🚶 Dog Lake

Duration 2 hours

Distance 2.8-mile round-trip

Difficulty Easy–Moderate

Start/Finish Dog Lake or Lembert Dome parking lots

Nearest Town Tuolumne Meadows

Transportation Tuolumne Meadows hikers' bus; Tuolumne Meadows shuttle stop 2

Summary This short hike skirts the base of Lembert Dome and climbs gently through lodgepole pine forest to scenic Dog Lake, a great spot for an afternoon picnic and, if you can take it, a chilly dip.

Pine tree–ringed Dog Lake (9170ft) is accessible via the same trails that head to Lembert Dome. The better one leaves from the appropriately named Dog Lake parking lot, near Tuolumne Meadows Lodge. Follow this trail to the base of Lembert Dome. When you reach the turnoff for the summit, continue straight. A half-mile or so up the fairly flat trail is another junction; turn right toward Dog Lake (left is a steep downhill to the Lembert Dome parking lot). It's about another half-mile to the lake. Although most topo maps don't show it, a trail circles the lake, allowing you to hike around it before heading home.

Be prepared to share this subalpine gem with fellow hikers – on weekends it may resemble your local reservoir, as people lug abundant picnic supplies and even inflatable rafts up to the lake's forested shores.

🚶 Elizabeth Lake

Duration 2½–4 hours

Distance 5.2-mile round-trip

Difficulty Moderate

Start/Finish Elizabeth Lake Trailhead, Tuolumne Meadows Campground

Nearest Town Tuolumne Meadows

Transportation Tuolumne Meadows hikers' bus; Tuolumne Meadows shuttle stop 5

Summary At the foot of jagged Unicorn Peak, this easily reached alpine lake offers spectacular views and plenty of opportunity for exploration beyond the lake itself.

Any time is a good time for a hike to this beautiful lake, but it's a particularly good choice if you've just rolled into the Tuolumne Meadows area and need a short acclimatization hike before sunset. Because it's fairly short, the trail gets busy, but heading up in the late afternoon means you'll encounter fewer people. That said, you could easily stretch a day out of this hike by exploring the saddles and ridges around the lake or, if you're experienced, by attempting the summit of Unicorn Peak (10,823ft), a class 3–4 climb.

The trailhead lies in the upper 'B' section of Tuolumne Meadows Campground. When you pull in, ask the ranger on duty for a campground map, or follow the sign to Elizabeth Lake. Once you're on the trail, the climbing kicks in immediately, and most of the elevation gain is out of the way within the first mile or so. Most of this section is shaded by lodgepole pines. The first real treat is the trail's encounter with Unicorn Creek, which drains into Elizabeth Lake. After that, the trail widens and levels off, and finally meets a fork at the northeast end of the lake. Turn right, and you'll hit the water. Otherwise, you'll follow Unicorn Creek into a meadow (a reward in itself), where several side trails also lead to the lakeshore. Climbing the slopes on the south side of the lake affords views of Lembert Dome and, far beyond, 12,649ft Mt Conness. To return to the trailhead, retrace your steps.

If you choose to come earlier in the day, Elizabeth Lake makes a nice spot for a picnic lunch.

🚶 Cathedral Lakes

Duration 4–7 hours

Distance 8-mile round-trip (upper lake)

Difficulty Moderate

Start/Finish Cathedral Lakes Trailhead

Nearest Town Tuolumne Meadows

Transportation Tuolumne Meadows hikers' bus; Tuolumne Meadows shuttle stop 7

Summary Easily one of Yosemite's most spectacular hikes, this steady climb through mixed conifer forest ends with glorious views of Cathedral Peak from the shores of two shimmering alpine lakes.

If you can only manage one hike in Tuolumne, this should probably be it. Cathedral Lake (9588ft), the lower of the two lakes, sits within a mind-blowing glacial cirque, a perfect amphitheater of granite capped by the iconic spire of nearby **Cathedral Peak** (10,911ft). From the lake's southwest side, the granite drops steeply away, affording views as far as Tenaya Lake, whose blue waters shimmer in the distance. Although it's only about two hours to this lower lake, you could easily spend an entire day exploring the granite slopes, meadows and peaks surrounding it. Continuing to the **upper lake** (9585ft) adds less than an hour to the hike and puts the round-trip walk at 8 miles, including the stop at Cathedral Lake. Admittedly, the upper lake is less spectacular when measured against the lower lake, but by all other standards it's utterly sublime.

Parking for the Cathedral Lake Trailhead is along the shoulder of Tioga Rd, 0.5 miles west of Tuolumne Meadows Visitor Center. Due to the popularity of this hike, parking spaces fill up fast, so arrive early or take the free shuttle. Camping is allowed at the lower lake (despite what some maps show), but be absolutely certain you're 100ft from the water *and* the trail, and that you choose an already impacted site to prevent further damage. Better yet, camp somewhere near the upper lake or off the pass.

From the Cathedral Lake Trailhead on Tioga Rd, the hike heads southwest along the John Muir Trail. Almost immediately, it begins to climb through forest of lodgepole pine, mountain hemlock and the occasional whitebark pine. After ascending over 400ft, the trail levels out and a massive slab of granite – the northern flank of Cathedral Peak – slopes up from the left side of the trail. Soon you'll see Fairview Dome (9731ft) through the trees to your right.

Before long, the trail begins its second ascent, climbing nearly 600ft before leveling off and affording outstanding views of Cathedral Peak. Three miles from the trailhead, you'll hit the junction that leads 0.5 miles southwest to Cathedral Lake. This trail crosses a stunning **meadow** (turn around as you cross it for the head-on view of Cathedral Peak) before arriving at the granite shores of the lake. Be sure to follow the trail

around the lake and take in the views from the southwest side.

To visit the upper lake, backtrack to the main trail, turn right (southeast) and, after about 0.5 miles, you'll hit the lake. If you wish to stretch the hike out even further, you can continue past the upper lake to **Cathedral Pass** (9700ft), where you'll be rewarded with a stellar side view of Cathedral Peak and Eichorn Pinnacle (Cathedral's fin-like west peak). This side trip adds about 0.6 miles to the trip.

🏃 Glen Aulin

Duration 6–8 hours

Distance 11-mile round-trip

Difficulty Moderate

Start/Finish Glen Aulin Trailhead near Lembert Dome parking lot

Nearest Town Tuolumne Meadows

Transportation Tuolumne Meadows shuttle stop 4

Summary The first leg of the multiday hike through the Grand Canyon of the Tuolumne makes for a great day hike, offering stunning views of the Cathedral Range before reaching Glen Aulin High Sierra Camp.

Except for the dip in the final stretch, most of the elevation change along this hike is gradual. It's an uphill return, so save energy for the climb home. The hike follows a section of the Pacific Crest Trail (PCT), the same stretch that horse packers use to supply the High Sierra Camp. It's a beautiful walk, though it's well worn and there can be plenty of aromatic horse dung along the way.

The trailhead lies behind the Lembert Dome parking lot, which is immediately east of the Tuolumne Meadows Campground and bridge. Follow the dirt road northwest. When you reach the gate, swing west toward Soda Springs, watching for the Glen Aulin Trail signs to the right of Parsons Lodge.

The trail leads through open lodgepole pine forest, crosses shallow **Delaney Creek**, then continues to a signed junction with the Young Lakes Trail, 1.3 miles from Soda Springs. Take the left fork, heading northwest through lodgepole pines. You'll emerge on riverside meadows with outstanding views of Fairview Dome (9731ft), Cathedral Peak (10,911ft) and Unicorn Peak (10,823ft).

Continuing on, the level, cairn-dotted trail crosses a vast, glacially polished granite slab over which the **Tuolumne River** flows. The river's roar signals the end of Tuolumne Meadows and the start of a series of cascades that tumble toward the Grand Canyon of the Tuolumne.

The trail climbs briefly over a granite rib, affording distant views of Matterhorn Peak (12,264ft) and Virginia Peak (12,001ft) on Yosemite's north border and a first view of the huge, orange-tinged granite cliff above Glen Aulin. Descend through forest to a two-part wooden footbridge spanning the river, 2.3 miles from the Young Lakes Trail junction.

The trail descends steadily, alternating between forest and riverside before reaching **Tuolumne Falls**. Continue along the plunging river to a signed junction with the May Lake Trail and then a steel girder footbridge spanning the river. Cross it and you'll reach two trail junctions in close succession. To the right is the Glen Aulin High Sierra Camp. At the second junction, the PCT continues north (straight) to a backpackers' campground and on to Cold and Virginia Canyons.

You can hang out here, or turn west (toward Waterwheel Falls) and continue a short distance into Glen Aulin itself – a long, level forested valley where the river flows green and tranquil beneath a massive water-stained granite wall.

To extend this into an overnight excursion, consider taking the Waterwheel Falls hike.

🏃 Gaylor Lakes

Duration 2–3 hours

Distance 3-mile round-trip

Difficulty Moderate

Start/Finish Gaylor Lakes Trailhead & parking lot

Nearest Town Tuolumne Meadows

Transportation Tuolumne Meadows–Tioga Pass shuttle

Summary This spectacular and popular trail climbs gently up to Gaylor Lakes, set in pristine alpine territory just inside the park boundary near Tioga Pass.

The hike to Gaylor Lakes is a high-altitude hike, so prior acclimatization (such as a day in Tuolumne) is a good idea. There can be snow any time of the year. Sound good? It is.

The trail begins from the parking lot, immediately west of Tioga Pass Entrance, and wastes no time in starting its steep ascent. At the crest, **Lower Gaylor Lake** (10,334ft) lies in a basin below you, with great views everywhere you turn. The trail skirts the lower lake and then climbs to **Upper Gaylor Lake** (10,510ft).

For an extra bonus, head past the lake and climb again to the site of the old **Great Sierra Mine**, where the views are even more stunning. The alpine countryside here is knockout beautiful, so allow time for poking around.

🏃 Mono Pass

Duration 4 hours

Distance 7.4-mile round-trip

Difficulty Moderate–Difficult

Start/Finish Mono Pass Trailhead

Nearest Town Tuolumne Meadows

Transportation Tuolumne Meadows–Tioga Pass shuttle

Summary This outrageously scenic, high-altitude hike from Dana Meadows starts at 9689ft and follows an ancient Native American trail past meadows and through open forest to the vast, lake-crowned Mono Pass.

A saddle on the Sierra Crest between the rounded summits of Mt Gibbs (12,764ft) and Mt Lewis (12,296ft), Mono Pass was the highest point on an ancient Native American trade route that linked the Mono Lake area with Tuolumne and continued to Yosemite Valley via Cathedral Pass. Remnants of late-19th-century log buildings – relics of the mining years – remain along the trail among subalpine meadows and lakes. It's a fantastic walk through some of the highest of Tuolumne's readily accessible high country.

The Mono Pass Trailhead and parking lot is at road marker T37, 1.4 miles south of Tioga Pass. The trail leads southeast through open forest within the shadow of 13,057ft Mt Dana to the northeast. After an easy half-mile hike alongside **Dana Meadows**, the trail crosses the Dana Fork of the Tuolumne River, then crosses two small ridges before passing beneath lodgepole pines beside several small, buttercup-filled meadows. Emerging from the pines, the trail makes a gentle ascent along **Parker Pass Creek**, with the reddish bulk of Mt Gibbs above and to the east.

When you reach the signed Spillway Lake trail junction, follow the left fork toward Mono and Parker Passes. (You can also take the 1.4-mile trail to Spillway Lake for scenery and swimming. To return to the Mono Pass trail, there's a spur that leads east and back north from just north of the lake's shoreline.) The trail passes the remains of a log cabin and opens onto a large meadow beside a small creek, with impressive views of Kuna Crest and Mammoth Peak (12,117ft). Thirty minutes (1.4 miles) past the Spillway Lake junction, a small trail branches right toward Parker Pass. Keep going straight, however, past twisted whitebark pines and two small lakes to Mono Pass (10,604ft).

Tiny Summit Lake lies to the west, while east of the pass are Upper and Lower Sardine Lakes. Further down, Walker Lake lies in an area known as Bloody Canyon. Tree frogs chirp from the banks of Summit Lake in early summer. Flourishing in meadows along its north side are scrub willows, Sierra onions and yellow potentillas. At the south end of the pass sit three historic log cabins.

Retrace your steps to the trailhead. To make this an overnight trip, you must camp outside the park in the Ansel Adams Wilderness. Two worthy destinations are Upper Sardine Lake, only 0.3 miles east of Mono Pass, and a more strenuous 6 miles hike onward to Alger Lakes via Parker Pass and Koip Peak Pass.

🧍 Mt Dana

Duration 4–7 hours

Distance 5.8-mile round-trip

Difficulty Difficult

Start/Finish Unmarked trailhead immediately east of Tioga Pass Entrance

Nearest Town Tuolumne Meadows

Transportation Tuolumne Meadows–Tioga Pass shuttle or car

Summary Starting at 9945ft, this strenuous hike is a leg-working, lung-busting climb to the top of Yosemite's second-highest peak, which, at 13,057ft, offers stunning views in every direction.

Mt Dana, which takes its name from American geologist James Dwight Dana, offers unrivaled views of Mono Lake, the Grand Canyon of the Tuolumne and the rest of the Yosemite high country from its summit. Remember, though, that this is a steep, high-altitude hike which *starts* at nearly 10,000ft. Prior acclimatization will ease your struggle; bring clothing and gear for strong winds and sun.

The hiking season runs from July to mid-September, though snow may block the trail in early summer. Don't even start the hike if a storm threatens.

Parking is available at the Gaylor Lakes Trailhead just inside the Tioga Pass Entrance. From a small employee parking area beside the Tioga Pass Entrance kiosk, the trail heads east, passing between two broad, shallow pools before the ascent begins. At almost 1.5 miles, the trail passes through flower-filled meadows on a wide ridge, a natural place to pause and brace yourself for the final 1400ft ascent in the last mile.

There's no mapped trail to the top, but the many use trails here previously have been consolidated into one obvious path, with frequent cairns 2ft to 3ft tall leading the way up the rocky slope to the summit. The views from the summit of Mt Dana are outstanding enough to invite lingering, but no camping is permitted. From the summit, retrace your steps downhill to the trailhead or taken an alternative path back passing through the broad Dana Plateau.

Wawona

Mariposa Grove features quite a few lovely hiking trails, and you could easily spend a half-day or more crisscrossing its 250 acres. A trail connects the grove with Wawona, where an easy loop circles Wawona Meadow and a more difficult trail leads to Chilnualna Falls, one of the park's lesser-known waterfalls. From there, long-distance trails head to such remote areas as the Buena Vista Crest and the Clark Range.

🧍 Wawona Meadow Loop

Duration 1–1½ hours

Distance 3.5-mile round-trip

Difficulty Easy

Start/Finish Big Trees Lodge

Nearest Town Wawona

Transportation Car

Summary A relaxed loop on a former stagecoach road, this level hike surveys a pretty meadow, with wildflowers raging in late spring and early summer.

Though you won't huff and puff too much on this gentle, shaded loop around pretty Wawona Meadow, you will have to dodge copious amounts of smelly horse manure

Wawona – Day Hikes

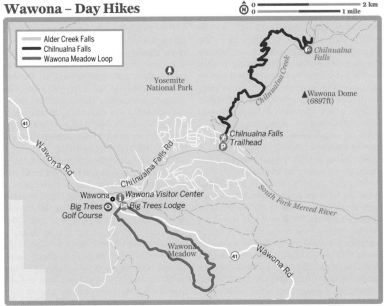

plopped and squashed along the entire trail. Horseback riders and stagecoaches use the loop, throwing up lots of dust – another unpleasant element, especially on an already hot summer day.

On the other hand, this short, easy trail is a nice way to spend an hour or two beneath the trees beside the meadow. It's especially lovely when native wildflowers are in bloom. If you're lucky, you might even be alone most of the way – aside from the horses and often loads of deer. Dogs are permitted here.

From the Big Trees Lodge, cross Hwy 41 on a small road through the golf course. The trail starts a short distance down on your left and follows an old dirt road around the meadow perimeter. On the return, you'll cross Hwy 41 again and wind up on the hotel's back lawn. Plunk down in an Adirondack chair and soak up the scene.

🏃 Chilnualna Falls

Duration 4–5 hours

Distance 8.2-mile round-trip

Difficulty Moderate–Difficult

Start/Finish Chilnualna Falls Trailhead

Nearest Town Wawona

Transportation Car

Summary Chilnualna Creek tumbles over the north shoulder of forested Wawona Dome in an almost continuous series of cascades. The largest and most impressive of these, Chilnualna Falls, thunders into a deep, narrow chasm.

Unlike its Valley counterparts, this fall is not free-leaping, but its soothing, white-water rush makes it an attractive day hike without lots of company. Carry plenty of water or a filter, as the route can be hot. The top is a nice picnic spot. Like all Yosemite waterfalls, Chilnualna Falls is best between April and June when streams are at their fullest. July and August are often too hot for an afternoon hike, and by September the fall is limited by low water.

The trailhead is at the eastern end of Chilnualna Falls Rd. Follow Hwy 41 (Wawona Rd) a quarter-mile north of the Big Trees Lodge and the Pioneer Gift & Grocery, and take a right just over the bridge on Chilnualna Falls Rd; follow it for 1.7 miles. The parking area is on the right, and the trailhead is marked.

The trail follows the northwest bank of Chilnualna Creek a short distance to the first series of tumbling cascades, which in spring shower the trail with a cool mist. Ascend several brief sets of granite steps beside the falls. Above, the stock trail joins the footpath along the Yosemite Wilderness boundary, a short but steep 0.2 miles and 600ft above the trailhead.

The trail rises gently yet continually through open, mixed-conifer forest, leveling out as it passes the rushing creek. It then moves away from the creek, taking you on long, sweeping switchbacks. The sheer granite curve of Wawona Dome fills the sky to the east as you rise above forested Wawona Valley. About halfway along the hike, you'll reach an unobstructed viewpoint from a granite **overlook** (5400ft); it offers the first good view of the fall. To the southwest are the forested Chowchilla Mountains.

The trail climbs several well-graded switchbacks, then a final dynamite-blasted switchback across a granite cliff to the top of **Chilnualna Falls** (6200ft). While you won't find any better view of the falls, it's worth continuing a quarter-mile further to a nice picnic spot along Chilnualna Creek. If you're on an overnight trip, head for the campsites further up both Chilnualna and Deer Creeks.

Retrace your steps 4.3 miles to the trailhead in two hours or so, past a sign that reads '5.6 miles to Wawona' (referring to the lodge and store, not the trailhead). At a junction 0.2 miles from the trailhead, avoid the tempting, broad horse trail (which comes out at a different trailhead) in favor of the footpath that bears left back down along the creek.

🚶 Alder Creek Falls

Duration 3–4 hours

Distance 8-mile round-trip

Difficulty Moderate–Difficult

Start/Finish Alder Creek Falls trailhead

Nearest Town Wawona

Transportation Car

Summary Far from the Valley crowds, or even those hiking nearby Chilnualna, this off-the-beaten-path trail offers refreshing solitude amid towering trees. The best time to make it all the way to the 100ft falls is early spring; it can get very hot in summer.

The small parking lot (basically a dirt turnout with a bear locker) for the trailhead is easy to find about a quarter-mile north of Hwy 41 along Chilnualna Falls Rd. Wawona Campground office (p110) is behind and below here and has a bathroom. The beginning of the trail, which begins on the opposite side of the

road alongside a park maintenance facility, is a little more difficult to locate.

It begins gradually uphill, soon picking up more elevation and passing sprinklings of wildflowers, like lupines, mariposa lilies and snow plants. There's a fork 3 miles in – the other trail leads to Hwy 41, another starting point for the hike – but the way forward is clearly signposted. Tree covering of black oaks, ponderosa pines, white firs and cedars grows denser as you reach a ridge. Several miles later, you cross several streams; the way may be muddy.

The trail gets wider and more exposed to the sun following an **old railroad bed** once used by the Yosemite Lumber Company – you can see some wire cables and wooden planks. Sections are also clearly still recovering from a 2007 fire. The gorge and Alder Creek Falls soon become visible below – depending on the time of year, you'll likely hear the falls before you see them. Spots around here are good for a picnic – it's not worth the trouble or consistent with Yosemite trail ethics to blaze your own way through dense foliage and unsteady boulders to the base of the falls.

You can continue on past the falls – the trail continues above them – but you've already seen the best scenery, so the falls make a logical turn-around spot for the downhill back to Wawona.

Hetch Hetchy

Hetch Hetchy offers some outstanding hiking, but day hikers are essentially limited to the Wapama Falls Trail, which traces the reservoir's scenic north shore, a fairly easy hike for just about anyone. You'll see some trees blackened by the 2013 Rim Fire.

🚶 Tueeulala & Wapama Falls

Duration 2½–3 hours

Distance 5.4-mile round-trip

Difficulty Easy–Moderate

Start/Finish Rancheria Falls Trailhead, O'Shaughnessy Dam

Nearest Junction Evergreen Lodge

Transportation Car

Summary This hike along the north shore of Hetch Hetchy Reservoir leads to the base of two neighboring falls: the free-leaping, seasonal Tueeulala Falls and

Hetch Hetchy – Day Hikes

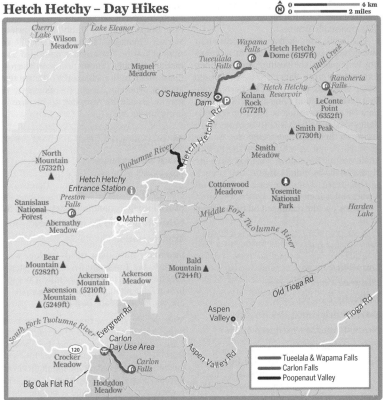

Tueeulala & Wapama Falls
Carlon Falls
Poopenaut Valley

the enormous triple cascades of year-round Wapama Falls.

Few – if any – trails in Yosemite bring you as close to the shower and roar of a giant waterfall as this one does to Wapama Falls. In springtime, after a good snowmelt, the falls can rage so mightily that the park occasionally has to close the trail itself as water rolls over the bridges. On your way, you'll pass the wispy Tueeulala Falls (*twee*-la-la), which spring spectacularly from the cliffs from more than 1000ft above the trail. All the while, **Hetch Hetchy Dome** (6197ft), on the north shore, and the mighty **Kolana Rock** (5772ft), on the south shore, loom over the entire scene. You can capture both falls and adjacent Hetch Hetchy Dome in a single striking photo. Kolana Rock's vertical north face provides nesting sites for peregrine falcons, once close to extinction but now present in healthier numbers. They are still a fully protected species, however, which

means Kolana Rock is off-limits to climbers during the springtime nesting season.

The gentle north shore trail is fairly flat, but does have a few ups and downs that will challenge unfit hikers in the summer heat. Plan the hike for mid- to late spring, when temperatures are cooler, butterflies are abundant, wildflowers are in bloom and the falls are full.

From the parking lot (3813ft), cross **O'Shaughnessy Dam** and pass through the tunnel on its far side. The broad, oak-shaded trail then heads northeast, above and parallel to the north shore of Hetch Hetchy Reservoir. In just over a mile, after rising gradually past several small seasonal streams, you'll reach a signed trail junction (4050ft).

Take the right (east) fork, following the sign to Wapama Falls. The trail descends gently, then bears left onto broad granite slabs before reaching Tueeulala Falls. Most of the falls end up flowing beneath the footbridge, but in spring a small section of the trail can fill with runoff. By June, the falls are usually dry.

The trail continues down a staircase that switchbacks gently to the base of thundering Wapama Falls (3900ft), where wooden footbridges span Falls Creek. In spring, water cascades over the trail beyond the first footbridge and almost covers the second. When the water is high, crossing is dangerous and ill-advised (two hikers were swept to their deaths in 2011 and another in 2017), but at other times the flow is ankle-deep. The frothy, gushing torrents create billowing clouds of mist that drench the entire area and make for a cool bath on a warm afternoon.

Return to the trailhead via the same route.

🥾 Carlon Falls

Duration 2 hours

Distance 4-mile round-trip

Difficulty Easy–Moderate

Start/Finish Carlon Day Use Area

Nearest Junction Evergreen Lodge

Transportation Car

Summary This short but sweet hike follows the South Fork Tuolumne River up to Carlon Falls, which cascade down granite slabs into perfect swimming holes.

Most people blow right by Carlon Falls on their way to Hetch Hetchy, but a quick stop for this short venture is well worthwhile. The hike is especially satisfying on a hot day, when the swimming holes beneath the falls are paradisaical. Folks who stay at Evergreen Lodge and Camp Mather frequent the falls, so arrive early to have the place to yourself. The only thing making this hike 'moderate' is a section of washed-out trail near the falls that requires surefootedness.

To get to the trailhead, drive northwest on Evergreen Rd, which departs Hwy 120 about 1 mile before the Big Oak Flat Entrance. About 1 mile after turning off, you'll see the Carlon Day Use Area at a bridge across the river. Park in the pullout on the far (north) side of the bridge and hike upstream from there. Although the trailhead is outside the Yosemite park boundary, you enter the park after about 0.1 miles.

Shaded by ponderosa pines, incense cedars and the occasional dogwood, the trail winds along the north bank of the river, through patches of fragrant kitkitdizze (an exceptionally pungent shrub also known as Sierran Mountain Misery) and finally arrives at Carlon Falls. Better described as a cascade, the falls tumble nearly 40ft across moss- and fern-draped granite into two separate swimming holes. There's plenty of granite around for sunning, so be sure to bring lunch.

🥾 Poopenaut Valley

Duration 3–4 hours

Distance 2.8 miles round-trip

Difficulty Difficult

Start/Finish Turnout on Hetch Hetchy Rd

Nearest Junction Evergreen Lodge

Transportation Car

Summary Burn those quads on your way down to the Tuolumne River via the steepest official hike in all of Yosemite. Cool off in several crystalline pools and keep an eye out for abundant bird life.

Most people visiting this area of the park cruise on down to the O'Shaughnessy Dam for panoramic views and the Wapama Falls hike. Locals, park staff and visitors who have already checked off the highlights head to this lesser known lung-busting trail. The reward is peace, quiet and a boulder-lined wilderness river after a steep 1300ft descent.

The blink-and-you-missed-it turnout with a few parking spots is on the right, a little under 3 miles after entering the park at the Hetch Hetchy entrance. Down, down, down you go, surrounded by white and Douglas firs, incense cedars, black oaks and sugar pines.

Watch out for poison oak; consider skipping this hike after major rains since the riverfront turns marshy, making it difficult to find a picnic spot.

🥾 OVERNIGHT HIKES

Backcountry hiking and sleeping beneath the stars is one of Yosemite's finest adventures. The vast majority of the almost four million people who visit Yosemite every year never leave the Valley floor, meaning the park's 1101 sq miles of wilderness is, relatively speaking, empty. There are a few painless bureaucratic hurdles to jump before head-

ℹ MANDATORY HALF DOME PERMITS

To stem lengthy lines (and increasingly dangerous conditions) on the vertiginous cables of Half Dome, the park now requires that all hikers obtain an advance permit to climb the cables. There are currently three ways to do this, though check www.nps.gov/yose/planyourvisit/hdpermits.htm for the latest information. Rangers check permits at the base of the cables.

Preseason permit lottery Lottery applications for 225 day hiking spots must be completed in March, with confirmation notification sent in mid-April; an additional $8 per person charge confirms the permit. Applications can include up to six people and seven alternate dates.

Daily lottery Approximately 50 additional day hiking permits are distributed by lottery two days before each hiking date. Apply online or by phone between midnight and 1pm Pacific Time; notification is available late that same evening. It's easier to score weekday permits.

Backpackers Those with Yosemite-issued wilderness permits that *reasonably include* Half Dome can request Half Dome permits ($8 per person) without going through the lottery process. Backpackers with wilderness permits from a national forest or another park can use that permit to climb the cables as long as their route also reasonably includes the area.

ing out, but a little planning will make your trek a triumph.

ℹ Wilderness Permits

Wilderness permits are required for all overnight backcountry trips (not for day hikes). To stem overuse of the backcountry, a quota system is in effect for each trailhead. You must spend your first night in the area noted on your permit – from there, you're free to roam.

Permits are available either in advance (between 26 weeks and two days ahead) or on a first-served basis from the nearest wilderness center. The park reserves 40% of its wilderness permits for walk-ups; these become available at 11am one day before the hike-in date. If you show up early the day before your hike, you should have no problem getting a permit. For popular hikes (such as Little Yosemite Valley, Cathedral Lakes or the High Sierra Camp routes), you should show up and get in line before the permit offices open the day before you hike. Always have a backup plan, as some spots fill very quickly.

Hikers who turn up at the wilderness center nearest the trailhead get priority over someone at another wilderness center. For example, if there is one permit left for Lyell Canyon, the Yosemite Valley Wilderness Center will call the Tuolumne Meadows Wilderness Center to make sure that no one breezing in to the Tuolumne office wants it before giving it to someone who has been waiting overnight in the Valley.

Reserving a wilderness permit is the best way to ensure you get one, and you can do so by fax (209-372-0739), phone (209-372-0740) or through the mail (PO Box 545, Yosemite, CA 95389). Faxes received between 5pm (the previous day) and 7:30am (the first morning you can reserve) get first priority. Reservations are not available from October to April, but you'll still need to get a permit.

In winter, wilderness permits are available at the Yosemite Valley Visitor Center (p130), the Hetch Hetchy Entrance Station (p115) and the seasonal ranger station at the Yosemite Ski & Snowboard A-frame building (p130). Self-registration permits are available 24 hours a day outside the Wawona and Big Oak Flat Information Stations and the Tuolumne Meadows Ranger Station. See www.nps.gov/yose/planyourvisit/permitstations.htm for more information.

Study your maps, read up and decide where you want to go before registering for a permit. Rangers can offer guidance about starting points and trail conditions, but they will not recommend one area over another because they don't know hikers' skills. See the National Park Service (NPS) website for updated trail conditions (www.nps.gov/yose/planyourvisit/wildcond.htm) or contact the wilderness centers.

ⓘ Backpackers Campgrounds

To accommodate backpackers heading into or out of the wilderness, the park offers walk-in backpackers' campgrounds in Yosemite Valley, Tuolumne Meadows, White Wolf and Hetch Hetchy. If you hold a valid wilderness permit, you may spend the night before and the night after your trip in one of these campgrounds. The cost is $6 per person per night, and reservations are unnecessary.

Long-distance cyclists may also use these campgrounds for one-night stays.

ⓘ Wilderness Regulations

For the sake of the bears more than your food, approved bear-resistant food canisters are required for all overnight hikes in the park. When you pick up your wilderness permit, you'll have to rent a bear canister or show that you have one. They're also sold at stores throughout the park. These canisters weigh just under 3lb each and, when carefully packed, can store three to five days' worth of food for one or two people. Keep the canisters closed when cooking.

Campfires are forbidden above 9600ft. Where available, use pre-existing campsites to reduce your impact, and camp at least 100ft from water sources and trails. Never put soap in the water, even 'biodegradable' types. Properly filter all drinking water or boil it for three to five minutes, and don't burn trash. Pack out everything you bring, including toilet paper.

Wilderness camping is prohibited within 4 trail-miles of Yosemite Valley, Tuolumne Meadows, Glacier Point, Hetch Hetchy and Wawona, and you must be at least 1 'air mile' from any road. No one is actually going to bust out the measuring tape – the idea is to keep people from simply wandering into the trees and camping when they can't find open campsites in the park. When you get a wilderness permit, you'll be asked to list the approximate location of your first campsite.

Yosemite Valley

Most hikes within and around Yosemite Valley proper are day hikes. Most overnight hikes from the Valley will take you out of its confines entirely. The hike to the top of Half Dome, Yosemite's most famous trek, is one major exception.

🚶 Half Dome

Duration 10–12 hours

Distance 14- to 16-mile round-trip

Difficulty Difficult

Start/Finish Vernal & Nevada Falls/John Muir Trailhead near Happy Isles

Nearest Junction Happy Isles

Transportation Shuttle stop 16

Summary Ideally done over two days, but doable as a grueling day hike, the demanding trek to the top of Yosemite's signature peak offers views (and crowds and sore muscles) like you wouldn't believe.

For many visitors, this is the ultimate Yosemite hike, an achievement to boast about to the grandkids some day. The stand-alone summit of this glacier-carved chunk of granite offers awesome 360-degree views, and peering down its sheer 2000ft north face offers a thrill you'll remember for the rest of your life. But, unless you get a crack-of-dawn start, you'll have people aplenty to deal with. Most importantly, advance permits are required for all hikers, making a Half Dome summit even harder to arrange.

Ideally, Half Dome is best tackled in two days, allowing you more time to rest up and enjoy the gorgeous surroundings. But since it's so popular, you'll have a hard time getting a wilderness permit to sleep overnight at the limited legal camping areas on the route (the most popular being Little Yosemite Valley). If you do attempt this hike in a single day (and many people do), and have a coveted permit, be ready for some serious exertion. Get an early start (like 6am – though the shuttle doesn't start until 7am), pack lots of water and bring a flashlight, because you may wind up hiking home in the dark.

Climbing gear is unnecessary. Instead, hikers haul themselves up the final 650ft to the summit between two steel cables. Climbing this stretch is only allowed when the cable route is open, usually late May to mid-October, depending on snow conditions. If planning an early-season or late-season trip, confirm ahead that the cables are in place.

Start at Happy Isles and ascend to the top of Nevada Fall on either the John Muir or Mist Trails. Continue over a low rise to level Little Yosemite Valley, which boasts views of Half Dome's south side. You'll also find so-

Half Dome and Vernal & Nevada Falls

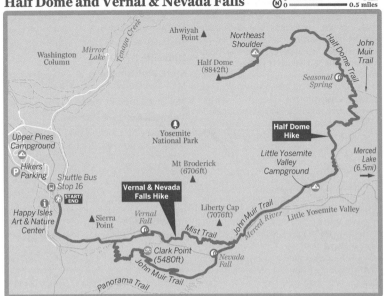

lar composting toilets, bear boxes and a seasonal ranger station, all welcome features at the well-used campground, which is one of the park's most heavily visited areas.

From the west end of Little Yosemite Valley, the Merced Lake Trail heads east along the river to the Merced Lake High Sierra Camp. Stay on the John Muir Trail, which turns north and climbs steeply through forest 1.3 miles to the Half Dome Trail junction, just 2 miles from the summit.

Take the left fork onto the Half Dome Trail. Just above the junction on the left is a hard-to-spot seasonal spring – the last source of water en route (filter or treat it). Continue on through forest and then up switchbacks to the northeast shoulder (7600ft), an alternative camping spot with spectacular views. Visit the summit at sunset and sunrise for exquisite solitude.

From here, a rocky trail snakes 650ft up two dozen switchbacks to reach a notch at the base of the **cables**. The twin steel cables are draped from posts bolted into the granite on the final 600ft ascent up an exposed 45-degree rock face. There are gloves available to protect your hands, and some intermittent wooden cross-boards provide footholds. A trip in light crowds takes only 15 minutes, but on crowded cables

(or if you're jittery), expect it to take much longer. 'Sharing the road' will be your biggest challenge.

A word of caution: do *not* ascend the cables if there's any chance of a storm. The exposed summit is no place to be when lightning strikes (should you have any doubts, read Bob Madgic's *Shattered Air;* 2005), nor do you want to get stuck halfway up with your hands wrapped around virtual lightning rods.

The **summit** is fairly flat and about 5 acres in size. From here, enjoy amazing views of Yosemite Valley, Mt Starr King, Clouds Rest, the Cathedral Range and the Sierra Crest. Camping on the summit is prohibited, and as tempting as it is to linger, watch the time carefully to avoid a hazardous descent in darkness.

If no wilderness permits are available from Happy Isles, other good starting points include Tenaya Lake and Glacier Point, the latter leading you along the gorgeous Panorama Trail.

Big Oak Flat & Tioga Road

Sometimes the best way to appreciate the beauty of Yosemite Valley is to sneak up on it from above. The Old Big Oak Flat Rd to

Old Big Oak Flat Road to Yosemite Falls

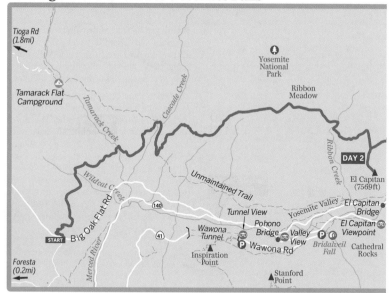

Yosemite Falls hike skirts the Valley's northern perimeter, while the Tenaya Lake to Yosemite Valley hike drops down from Tioga Rd.

🏃 Old Big Oak Flat Road to Yosemite Falls

Duration 2 days

Distance 18.8 miles one way

Difficulty Difficult

Start Old Big Oak Flat Trailhead

Finish Yosemite Falls Trailhead

Nearest Junction Crane Flat Gas Station

Transportation Tuolumne Meadows hikers' bus

Summary Climb up to bird's-eye views of Yosemite Valley, Half Dome and the Clark Range on a trail that never gets crowded. Spend the night on top of El Capitan before descending Yosemite Falls.

When planning this hike, note that some creeks along the way can be difficult to cross during peak spring runoff (Tamarack is the hardest), but run dry in summer. If you don't want to carry in *all* your water, this is best done as a late-spring trip. Ask at the Yosemite Valley or Big Oak Flat wilderness centers about water sources and creek levels en route.

DAY 1: OLD BIG OAK FLAT ROAD TRAILHEAD TO EL CAPITAN

7–8 HOURS / 10.1 MILES

From Yosemite Valley, ask the Tuolumne Meadows hikers' bus driver to drop you a quarter-mile west of Foresta turnoff on Big Oak Flat Rd, in the 'Old Big Oak Flat Rd' parking lot. The trailhead (across the street) begins with switchbacks, climbing through an area charred first by the 1990 Foresta fire and then retorched for good measure by the 2009 Big Meadow fire.

Over 4 miles, cross Wildcat Creek and then Tamarack Creek (a more challenging crossing with heavy runoff) before coming to a junction at a footbridge. To the left, it's just over 2 miles to Tamarack Flat Campground via the Old Big Oak Flat Rd. Instead continue right (southeast), crossing the footbridge over Cascade Creek. After half a mile, go left (northeast) at a junction and leave the spotty asphalt remains of the Old Big Oak Flat Rd, which continues fitfully down to the Valley through the Rockslides area, and is not maintained. The path is forested with red fir, Jeffrey pine and canyon live oak. Pass through Ribbon Meadow, with corn lilies and, in wet years, many mosquitoes. Cross Ribbon Creek and veer a quarter-mile south off the trail to camp on the sandy top of El Capitan (at just over 10 miles). Camp at an

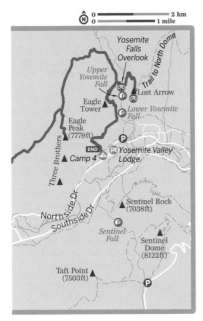

Transportation Tuolumne Meadows hikers' bus; Tuolumne Meadows shuttle stop 10; YARTS Hwy 120/395 bus

Summary Instead of driving between Tioga Rd and Yosemite Valley, why not hike it? The Tenaya Lake to Yosemite Valley hike is one of the classics, allowing you an up-close look at the major landscape changes.

The most spectacular trail from Tioga Rd to Yosemite Valley traverses the summit of Clouds Rest (9926ft), arguably Yosemite's finest panoramic viewpoint. An easier variation bypasses Clouds Rest completely and follows Sunrise Creek. Both hikes descend through Little Yosemite Valley and pass world-renowned Nevada and Vernal Falls to Happy Isles. Hearty hikers can also include a side trip to the top of Half Dome. On stormy days, steer clear of both Half Dome and Clouds Rest.

The trailheads are almost 50 miles apart by road. Unless you plan to shuttle two vehicles, use public transportation for the uphill leg.

DAY 1: TENAYA LAKE TO LITTLE YOSEMITE VALLEY
8–10 HOURS / 12.3 MILES

Start from the well-marked Sunrise Lakes Trailhead, at the west end of Tenaya Lake off Tioga Rd. Trailhead parking is limited, and the lot fills early. Those leaving from Tuolumne Meadows can instead use the free Tuolumne to Olmsted Point shuttle bus, which stops at the trailhead.

Follow the Clouds Rest hike for the trail to the summit. From there, head down steps off the south side to the ridge below. In 0.6 miles there's a signed junction with a bypass trail for horses. Continue straight, down through pines, chinquapins and manzanitas. Pass beneath granite domes and continue the descent on switchbacks. Near the bottom of the 2726ft descent, the trail enters shady forest.

At 3.8 miles from the summit of Clouds Rest, you'll reach the marked junction with the John Muir Trail (7200ft). Nearby Sunrise Creek offers several forested campsites and provides the first water since well before Clouds Rest. Turn west onto the John Muir Trail and descend a half-mile to the signed junction with the heavily traveled Half Dome Trail. Go south 1.3 miles to the established and busy campsites in Little Yosemite Valley (6100ft) along the Merced River. Beware: both Sunrise Creek and Little Yosemite Valley experience chronic problems with bears.

existing site to avoid trampling the undergrowth. At eye level, the surrounding peaks look like frothy waves, with the iconic Half Dome to the east. It's a stunning viewpoint from which to see the evening alpenglow.

DAY 2: EL CAPITAN TO YOSEMITE FALLS
6–7 HOURS / 8.7 MILES

Rejoin the trail and continue east for 1.7 miles to the Three Brothers. A half-mile jut takes you to Eagle Peak (7779ft), the upper of the trio, with more awesome and dizzying views of the Valley and the Clark Range. Continue northeast and, at the junction of the Yosemite Creek Trail, turn south to reach the top of Yosemite Falls in about a half-mile. It's 3.6 miles down more than a hundred switchbacks and 2700ft of knee-knocking descent to the Valley floor.

🥾 Tenaya Lake to Yosemite Valley

Duration 2 days

Distance 17.1 miles one way

Difficulty Difficult

Start Sunrise Lakes Trailhead

Finish Happy Isles

Nearest Town Tuolumne Meadows

Tenaya Lake to Yosemite Valley

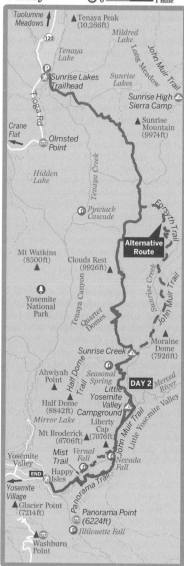

tually meets the trail from Clouds Rest and descends to Little Yosemite Valley.

To begin, follow the day one description for 4.7 miles to the signed junction (9100ft) with the Clouds Rest and Forsyth Trails. Bear southeast and follow the Forsyth Trail across a meadow into the pine and granite landscape. The trail leads down a slope of red firs, offering good views of the Clark Range, Merced Canyon and Mt Starr King. Follow Sunrise Creek until a slight ascent takes you to the marked junction (8000ft) with the John Muir Trail, also known here as the Sunrise Trail. Go southwest on the John Muir Trail 0.1 miles to another junction, where a trail to Merced Lake heads east. Stay on the John Muir Trail, heading west along Sunrise Creek, then descend switchbacks to the junction (7200ft) with the Clouds Rest Trail. Continue a half-mile to the busy Half Dome Trail, then turn south and descend the John Muir Trail to **Little Yosemite Valley**.

DAY 2: LITTLE YOSEMITE VALLEY TO HAPPY ISLES VIA THE JOHN MUIR TRAIL
2–3 HOURS / 4.8 MILES

Today you can follow either the Mist Trail or the John Muir Trail some 1065ft down to Happy Isles in Yosemite Valley. We recommend the John Muir Trail because the granite steps on the Mist Trail tend to pound your knees on the descent. If you do take the Mist Trail, it's 3.9 miles to Happy Isles.

From Little Yosemite Valley, follow the John Muir Trail for 0.5 miles, where it traces the Merced River and then contours to the south of Liberty Cap. At 1.1 miles, meet the Mist Trail (and follow it to the right, if you wish). Continue southwest along the John Muir Trail, fording the footbridge over the rushing Merced at **Nevada Fall**. Pass the junction with the Panorama Trail and, at approximately 4 miles, cross the river again. From here it's less than a mile to the trailhead, walking along the eastern riverbank.

Glacier Point & Badger Pass

Trails from the south and east side of Glacier Point Rd wind into some of Yosemite's largest wilderness tracts. Serious backpackers interested in longer hauls can explore such rugged areas as the Merced headwaters or the Clark Range, along the park's southeast border.

ALTERNATIVE ROUTE: TENAYA LAKE TO LITTLE YOSEMITE VALLEY VIA FORSYTH & JOHN MUIR TRAILS
7–9 HOURS / 10.9 MILES

Those not inclined to visit the Clouds Rest summit can follow an easier, forested alternative trail along Sunrise Creek, which even-

🏃 Ostrander Lake

Duration 2 days

Distance 12.4-mile round-trip

Difficulty Moderate–Difficult

Start/Finish Ostrander Lake Trailhead

Nearest Junction Bridalveil Creek Campground

Transportation Car

Summary A deservedly popular out-and-back trek to an atmospheric stone ski hut. A gorgeous granite-bowl lake cuts into the forest, with water perfect for a brisk dip.

Sure this trail is doable as a day hike, but what's the rush? Doing the trek over two days gives you the chance to check out regenerating forest, enjoy wildflowers and spy some wild strawberries.

Park at the Ostrander Lake Trailhead lot (just over 1 mile east of Bridalveil Creek Campground road) and use the bear boxes to stockpile any food that you're not packing in. You soon cross over a footbridge and the level trail starts through a swath of burned-through lodgepole forest. The trail, remaining level, fords through purple, yellow and white banks of waist-high wild-flowers, ecstatic bees and ground-hugging wild strawberries.

The hiking path that you're following was once a jeep road, but it is now also a winter route to the Ostrander Ski Hut, and yellow and orange cross-country ski markings are posted on trees the whole way there.

At almost 2 miles, bear left at a signed junction. Another junction comes within a mile, and once again bear left, following the trail sign to Ostrander Lake. The right-hand side trail goes to Wawona, among other places. A climb gears up slowly, and Horizon Ridge appears to your left (east) through the skeletons of burned-out trees and the dainty little puffs of young fir trees. The climb becomes steeper, but a clearing just past the ridge offers energizing views, just when you need the extra encouragement. The jagged Clark Range perches to the northeast, and you can spy on Basket Dome, North Dome and Half Dome as well. In approximately a half-mile, the pitched roof of the handcrafted stone **Ostrander Ski Hut** comes into view, framed by **Ostrander Lake** with a slope of rock boulders tumbling down its far shore from Horse Ridge.

You can trace the lake's western bank to find established campsites, and then cool off with a refreshing dip in the lake. When you're ready, you can return following the same trail.

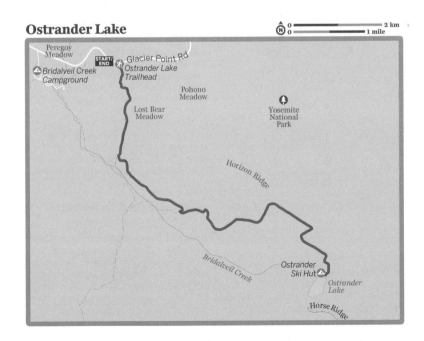

Ostrander Lake

Tuolumne Meadows

Several of the day hikes described earlier can also be extended into overnight excursions, including Cathedral Lakes and Glen Aulin.

🏃 Lyell Canyon

Duration 2 days

Distance 17.6-mile round-trip

Difficulty Easy–Moderate

Start/Finish Lyell Canyon Trailhead at Dog Lake parking lot

Nearest Town Tuolumne Meadows

Transportation Tuolumne Meadows hikers' bus; Tuolumne Meadows shuttle stop 1 or 3; YARTS Hwy 120/395 bus

Summary This flat section of the John Muir Trail meanders deep into Lyell Canyon to the base of Mt Lyell, the park's highest peak. Fishing, relaxing, views and side trips are all excellent.

If destinations like Cathedral Lake and Nevada Fall slap you in the face with their shockingly good looks, Lyell Canyon gently rolls its beauty over you like a blanket on a cool day. The Lyell Canyon Trail takes you through a special place, along a section of the John Muir Trail as it follows the Lyell Fork of the Tuolumne River through a gorgeous subalpine meadow hemmed in by tree-covered granite peaks. The final reward is the view of Lyell Peak and its eponymous glacier, towering over the meadow beyond Donohue Pass. This is also a great choice for those who loathe uphill climbs.

If you drove, the best place to park is the Dog Lake parking lot, off the road to Tuolumne Meadows Lodge. If that's full, park in the Tuolumne Meadows Wilderness Center parking lot, further west on the same road. From the latter, look for a trail sign reading

Lyell Canyon

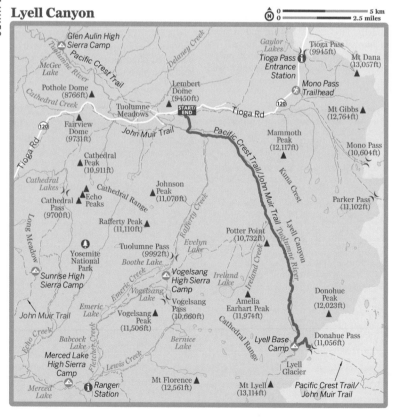

'John Muir Trail' and walk southeast, paralleling the road. After about 0.2 miles, you'll pass the trail that comes down from the Dog Lake parking lot. Soon, you'll cross the Dana Fork (Tuolumne River) by bearing right at a junction (continuing straight would take you to the lodge) and crossing the footbridge over the river. Soon you'll hit another junction; veer right toward Donohue Pass (hint: always head toward Donohue Pass). About 0.5 miles further, you'll cross the Lyell Fork over two footbridges and come to yet another junction. This time, bear left.

Another 0.5 miles on, the trail passes the Vogelsang/Yosemite Valley junction and crosses Rafferty Creek. Finally it turns southeast into Lyell Canyon, and you can start paying attention to the scenery rather than the trail junctions. After 4.2 miles you'll pass the turnoff to Ireland and Evelyn Lakes, cross Ireland Creek and pass beneath the inverted cone of Potter Point (10,732ft).

If you wish to camp in Lyell Canyon – a highlight of any Yosemite trip – you'll find several campsites alongside the river; just make sure you're at least 4 miles from the trailhead. Basically, anything south of Ireland Creek is fine. Some of the best campsites are about 0.5 miles before the head of the canyon, where you can see Mt Lyell (13,114ft) looming over the southeast end of the meadow. There are campsites on both sides of the river and above the trail. Once you start heading up the 'staircase' at the head of the canyon, campsites are few until you reach Lyell Base Camp, a busy climbers' camp below Donohue Pass.

You can take a day-long side trip to the summit of Mt Lyell, but only experienced climbers should attempt it. The ascent alone gains over 4000ft, and the difficult route traverses a glacier, involves steep and complex climbs, and requires safety ropes. Another option is setting up your own base camp in the canyon and continuing another few miles up the John Muir Trail to Donohue Pass (a 2000ft climb), admiring the impressive peaks and glaciers along the way.

On your second day, the task is simple: follow the John Muir Trail along the Lyell Fork back to the trailhead.

🚶 Young Lakes

Duration 2 days

Distance 13-mile round-trip

Difficulty Moderate

Start/Finish Dog Lake Trailhead near Lembert Dome parking lot

Nearest Town Tuolumne Meadows

Transportation Tuolumne Meadows hikers' bus; Tuolumne Meadows shuttle stop 4; YARTS Hwy 120/395 bus

Summary After climbing through forests of lodgepole pines, this trail opens up to offer sweeping views of the Cathedral Range before reaching shimmering Young Lakes, at the base of gnarly Ragged Peak.

DAY 1: TRAILHEAD TO YOUNG LAKES
3–4 HOURS / 6.2 MILES

Set at elevations between 9950ft and 10,050ft, the three Young Lakes make for a vigorous day hike but offer much more – particularly at sunrise and sunset – to those who make an overnight journey out of it. If the permit quota for Cathedral Lakes is full, this is a good alternative. Some walkers knock this off their favorite-hikes list because much of it is through pine forest, meaning fewer vistas. But the rewards at the lakes above make up for this tenfold.

Starting from the Lembert Dome parking lot, follow the Dog Lake trail into the trees, with Lembert Dome on your right. After 1.3 miles you'll pass the trail to Lembert Dome. After another 0.3 miles, you'll hit the junction to 9240ft Dog Lake, good for a quick detour and snack stop.

Back on the Young Lakes trail, you'll ascend gradually to about 9400ft before descending to Delaney Creek, which burbles along the edge of a lovely meadow. Cross Delaney Creek and follow the trail across the meadow and around the western side of a granite peak. Shortly thereafter, the trail meanders into a clearing and you'll see snarled Ragged Peak to the north. After entering a gently sloping meadow spotted with wildflowers and stunted whitebark pines, you're presented with a magnificent view to the south: the entire Cathedral Range and all its major peaks, including Cathedral Peak, Unicorn Peak and Echo Peaks (with Cockscomb just behind Unicorn). To the far left stands Mt Lyell (13,114ft), Yosemite's highest peak.

Cross Dingley Creek (a good spot to fill up the water bottles), and follow the trail over a small crest, with Ragged Peak on your right. The trail winds down through the pines and boulders to meet a junction (the return route). Keep to your right and continue around the northwest shoulder of Ragged Peak until, after 1.5 miles from

Young Lakes

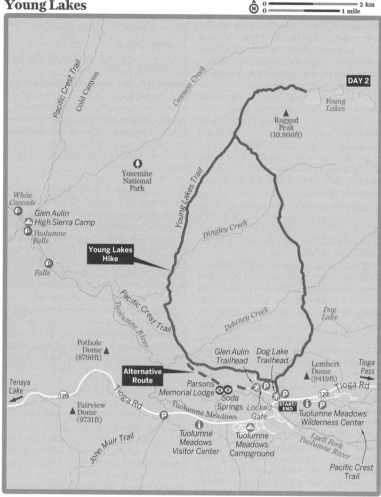

the junction, you arrive at the lowest of the **Young Lakes**. There are numerous places to camp along the northwest shore, and trees offer shade and shelter from any wind that might pick up. The lake itself sits within a sort of granite amphitheater formed by the northern flanks of Ragged Peak, which takes on a fiery golden glow at sunset, lighting up the lake with its reflection in the water.

From the northeast side of the lake, a trail leads up to **middle Young Lake**. From the middle lake's eastern shore, the trail climbs alongside a pretty waterfall – with one short section of easy scrambling alongside it – be-

fore reaching a meadow and gently sloping down to the third, **upper Young Lake**. It's a truly stunning alpine setting boasting marvelous views in every direction. There are a couple of campsites eked out above the northwestern shore.

DAY 2: YOUNG LAKES TO TRAILHEAD
3–4 HOURS / 6.8 MILES

To return from lower Young Lake, follow the same trail out until, after 1.5 miles from Young Lake, you reach the junction you passed on the way up. Stay to your right. The views are less impressive along the return trail, but it makes for variation. After 3.7 miles of mostly downhill walking you'll join the Pacific Crest Trail (PCT). After crossing Delaney Creek, the trail becomes extremely worn, sandy and mule-trodden. At a junction you can either stay to your left to reach the Lembert Dome parking lot, or head to your right to visit Soda Springs.

🏃 Vogelsang

Duration 3 days

Distance 27-mile round-trip

Difficulty Moderate–Difficult

Start/Finish Lyell Canyon Trailhead from Dog Lake parking lot

Nearest Town Tuolumne Meadows

Transportation Tuolumne Meadows hikers' bus; Tuolumne Meadows shuttle stop 1 or 3

Summary This exquisite but very popular semi-loop crosses Tuolumne and Vogelsang Passes through Yosemite's Cathedral Range, offering a remarkable circuit through John Muir's 'Range of Light.'

The sloping subalpine meadows and streams on either side of gentle Tuolumne Pass (9992ft) provide a scenic backdrop for some of the Sierra Nevada's most delightful hiking. The trail takes in multiple cascades and sweeping views of distant peaks in several mountain ranges, including the hard-to-see Clark Range. Camping at Vogelsang Lake and crossing the alpine Vogelsang Pass (10,660ft) rank among the highlights of this journey around Vogelsang Peak.

Vogelsang Peak, Lake and Pass, and High Sierra Camp, all take their name from the Vogelsang brothers, who headed the California Fish and Game Board from 1896 to 1910. The name itself translates aptly from German as 'a meadow where birds sing.'

DAY 1: LYELL CANYON TRAILHEAD TO VOGELSANG LAKE
4–6 HOURS / 7.2 MILES

On day one, follow the Lyell Canyon hike to the Pacific Crest/John Muir Trail. After 0.8 miles, at Rafferty Creek, turn south, leaving the John Muir Trail; the 2½-hour, 4.9-mile ascent along Rafferty Creek begins with a rugged uphill climb. Gouged out by the steel-shod hooves of packhorses and mules that supply the Vogelsang High Sierra Camp, the trail clambers over granite steps and cobblestones through forest for some

20 to 30 minutes before it eases and nears Rafferty Creek's left bank. To the north you'll see Mt Conness and White Mountain, while the Lyell Fork Meadows spread out some 500ft below to the east.

With the steepest part of the trail now behind you, you'll gradually ascend an attractive little valley, following the west bank of Rafferty Creek. The forested trail gently climbs, then enters a small open meadow. Passing beneath lodgepole pines and crossing several smaller streams, the well-worn trail finally emerges into a lovely meadow along Rafferty Creek. Finally, 6.1 miles from the trailhead, you'll arrive at gentle **Tuolumne Pass** (9992ft).

At the signed Tuolumne Pass junction, take the left fork and head southeast. The trail offers enticing views of Boothe Lake and the granite ridge above it as it travels 0.8 miles to Vogelsang High Sierra Camp (10,130ft). At a signed junction, a backpackers' campground lies to the left (east), while the trail to the right (west) descends to Merced Lake High Sierra Camp. Instead, continue straight (south) toward Vogelsang Pass. About 0.5 miles beyond the High Sierra Camp you'll reach large **Vogelsang Lake** (10,341ft), set in a picture-perfect cirque beneath Fletcher and Vogelsang Peaks. Above the northeast shore are campsites set among whitebark pines.

DAY 2: VOGELSANG LAKE TO EMERIC LAKE
5–7 HOURS / 10.2 MILES

The trail ascends above the southwest end of Vogelsang Lake, eventually crossing a large, cold stream just below its spring-fed source. The view of the lake below and Cathedral Range beyond is sublime. Five minutes' walk further you'll reach **Vogelsang Pass** (10,660ft), in the serrated granite ridge that descends from Vogelsang Peak (11,506ft).

From here the trail rises a bit and provides a long view of the upper Lewis Creek Basin. Lovely **Gallison Lake**, surrounded by meadow, issues forth a cascading stream. Large **Bernice Lake** spreads out at the base of a massive granite ridge beneath Mt Florence (12,561ft). Half a dozen more lakes lie hidden in a chain above Gallison Lake, fed by permanent snow from the slopes of Simmons Peak (12,503ft) at the valley's head. To the southwest is the more distant Clark Range, sweeping from the west to the southeast.

Descend the switchbacks that follow the course of a small stream. At the base, enter a forest along the level valley floor. Streams

Vogelsang

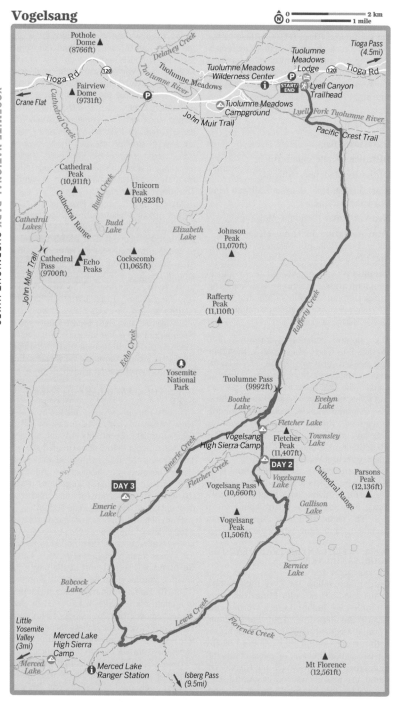

course across the meadow, involving a few crossings. Continue straight past the Bernice Lake junction, heading downstream along Lewis Creek as the descent grows steeper.

Three miles from Bernice Lake trail junction, you'll pass the Isberg Pass trail junction. Continue on 1 mile through a dramatic canyon for a view of distant Half Dome before passing the signed Merced Lake trail junction (8160ft). Turn north at the junction and follow the trail up Fletcher Creek. After crossing a footbridge, the trail climbs beside the creek, crosses several side streams and climbs high above the left bank of Fletcher Creek. The trail levels out about one hour past the footbridge, offering a fabulous vista over Merced Canyon and the Clark Range.

Leaving the views behind, head beneath lodgepole pines past the signed Babcock Lake trail junction. In 2 miles, the trail emerges in a lovely meadow and finally hits a four-way trail junction. Turn northwest and head 0.4 miles to the large Emeric Lake (9338ft). Cross its inlet to reach good campsites above the northwest shore.

DAY 3: EMERIC LAKE TO LYELL CANYON TRAILHEAD
4½–5 HOURS / 9.1 MILES
On Day 3, retrace your steps to the four-way junction. Turn north on the route to Boothe Lake (rather than the heavily used trail to Vogelsang High Sierra Camp). This lovely lake, which lies 2.7 miles from the junction, was the original site of the High Sierra Camp before the camp was moved and renamed Vogelsang. The trail stays well above the lake, where camping is prohibited. Arrive once again at Tuolumne Pass, 0.4 miles beyond Boothe Lake. From here, retrace your steps: 4.9 miles down Rafferty Creek to the John Muir Trail and 1.1 miles to the Lyell Canyon Trailhead.

🏃 Waterwheel Falls

Duration 2 days

Distance 18-mile round-trip

Difficulty Difficult

Start/Finish Glen Aulin Trailhead near Lembert Dome parking lot

Nearest Town Tuolumne Meadows

Transportation Tuolumne Meadows hikers' bus; Tuolumne Meadows shuttle stop 4; YARTS Hwy 120/395 bus

Summary Follow this hike along the Grand Canyon of the Tuolumne River to Waterwheel Falls. It's the last and most impressive of six cascades along the river,

Waterwheel Falls

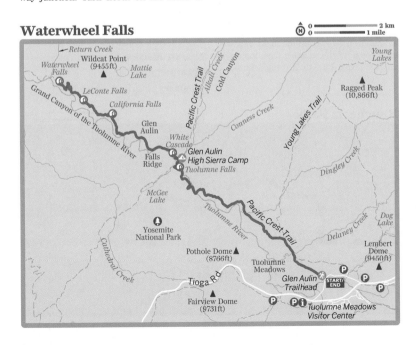

before it plunges into the canyon on its descent toward Hetch Hetchy Reservoir.

For the first several miles of the hike, follow the Pacific Crest Trail (PCT) to Glen Aulin. About 0.2 miles after Tuolumne Falls, head northwest along the trail to Waterwheel Falls, which is 3.3 miles downstream from where you leave the PCT. The trail meanders through ghost forest to the river's edge, inviting a dip in the placid waters, then crosses an area made marshy by a stream that descends from Cold Mountain to the north.

In just over a mile, you'll reach the far end of the peaceful glen, where the river flows briskly to the brink of the first in a series of near-continual cascades. The trail, too, plunges along the river, dropping over gorgeous orange-tinted granite. Ahead, the Grand Canyon of the Tuolumne stretches as far as the eye can see. The trail continues between the sheer, polished granite walls of Wildcat Point (9455ft) to the north and the 8000ft granite wall of Falls Ridge on the opposite bank. California Falls and LeConte Falls are the most prominent cascades in this section; most are unnamed. If you have to ask yourself, 'Is this Waterwheel Falls?' keep going – you'll know it when you see it.

About 2 miles beyond the glen, you'll reach a small unsigned junction where a spur trail branches southwest to a viewpoint of Waterwheel Falls. The obvious roar tells you this is the spot, although the falls remain hidden from view. From the main trail, walk to the edge of the massive falls, named for the distinctive 15ft- to 20ft-high plumes of water that curl into the air like a wheel midway down the more than 600ft-long falls.

After admiring the cascade, return to the main trail, turn west, and descend another 10 minutes. As you approach the scattered junipers beside an obvious dark granite rib perpendicular to the trail, turn south and head down a sandy slope through manzanita, following a trail that parallels the rocky rib. It leads to a large, forested campsite (6440ft) that's partly visible from the main trail above. Camp beneath big ponderosa pines and incense cedars, about 0.3 miles below Waterwheel Falls, with the green and tranquil Tuolumne River about 200ft away.

On day two, retrace your steps 9 miles to the trailhead.

Hetch Hetchy

Hetch Hetchy offers some excellent backpacking opportunities, as well as access to some of the park's most remote areas, north of the reservoir. Summers can be brutally hot, which is why the trails out here are busiest in spring and fall.

🏃 Rancheria Falls

Duration 7 hours–2 days
Distance 13-mile round-trip
Difficulty Moderate–Difficult
Start/Finish Rancheria Falls Trailhead
Nearest Junction Evergreen Lodge
Transportation Car
Summary This classic Hetch Hetchy

Rancheria Falls

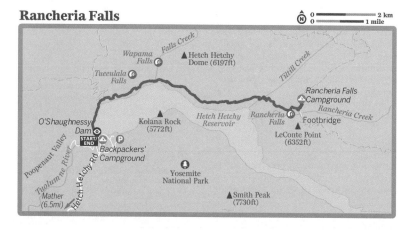

hike passes the spectacular Tueeulala and Wapama Falls, then takes you to the gentler Rancheria Falls, where swimming holes abound and the scenery is outrageous.

Rancheria Falls is doable as a day hike, but it's best enjoyed as an overnighter, allowing you to experience sunset over Rancheria Creek and Hetch Hetchy Reservoir. This part of Yosemite can be brutally hot in summer and, like the Tueeulala and Wapama Falls hike, is best in the spring. Still, it can be rewarding in July and even August, despite the heat, thanks to fewer people and the excellent swimming holes near the falls. Watch out for poison oak along the trail.

Follow the hike to **Wapama Falls**. After the falls, the trail climbs into the shade of black oaks and laurels, offering relief from the sun. It then ascends a series of switchbacks and skirts around the base of **Hetch Hetchy Dome** (6197ft), passing two epic viewpoints over the reservoir on the way. Alternately climbing and falling through shaded oak forest and hot, exposed stretches, the trail finally arrives at two footbridges over **Tiltill Creek**, which mark the end of the no-camping zone.

After climbing up from Tiltill Creek, you'll get your first glimpse of **Rancheria Falls** as they shoot down a granite apron into the reservoir below. Camping below the falls looks inviting but, because the area has become so impacted, it's best to continue 0.25 miles further to the established Rancheria Falls Campground.

After dropping your sack and pitching your tent, walk further up the trail, past the Tiltill Valley junction (stay to your right) to the footbridge over **Rancheria Creek**. During summer, when the water levels are low, there are two superb emerald-green swimming holes set in a chasm of granite, both with rock- and bridge-jumping opportunities for the adventurous. The views of Rancheria Creek and the reservoir from here are sublime.

To return on day two, retrace your steps.

🚗 DRIVING

Driving is hardly the proper way to see Yosemite Valley (unless you enjoy craning your neck in traffic to see the sights otherwise blocked by your roof), but it's an undeniably superb way to experience the high country – and beyond – via the spectacular Tioga Rd. This is the only road that bisects the park between its eastern and western borders. All park roads, however, are lined with beautiful scenery, so really you can't go wrong. If you're going to drive within Yosemite Valley, try to avoid doing it on weekends.

🚲 CYCLING

Mountain biking isn't permitted within the park, but cycling along the 12 miles of paved trails is a popular and environmentally friendly way of exploring the valley. It's also the fastest way to get around when valley traffic is at a standstill. Many families bring bicycles, and you'll often find kids doing laps through the campgrounds. Hardcore cyclists brave the skinny shoulders and serious altitude changes of the trans-Sierra Tioga Rd.

❶ Bicycle Rentals

If you can't bring your own bike, stands at Yosemite Valley Lodge (p130) and **Half Dome Village** (Map p124; per hr/day $12.50/30.50; ☺8am-6pm Mar-Oct) rent single-speed beach cruisers (per hour/day $12/33.50) or bikes with an attached child trailer (per hour/day $19.25/60). You're required to leave either a driver's license or credit card for collateral. Neither location accepts reservations, but you should be fine if you arrive before 11am or so.

Yosemite Valley Loops

Duration 1-3 hours
Distance Up to 12 miles round-trip

WATERFALL WARNING

On a blistering day, the park's waterways are a siren song for sweaty hikers with aching feet. But no matter how inviting, never enter rivers or creeks near a waterfall. Pay attention to posted warning signs (they're there because of prior fatalities), and use common sense if there aren't any. All it takes is one slip and within seconds you could be barreling toward a waterfall's precipice. Over a dozen visitors have died at Vernal Fall – please don't increase that statistic.

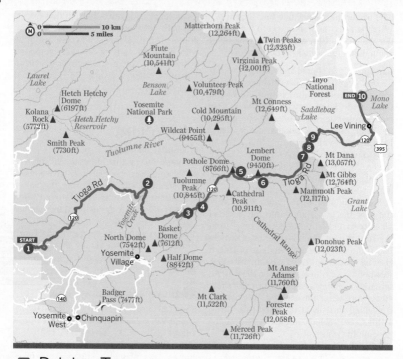

🚗 Driving Tour
Tioga Road to Mono Lake

START CRANE FLAT
END MONO LAKE
LENGTH 60 MILES; TWO TO FOUR HOURS

The highest elevation trans-Sierra highway and one of California's ultimate drives, Tioga Rd is open only during summer and fall, usually from late May to early November. Beginning at the ❶ **Crane Flat Gas Station** (p128), follow signs for Hwy 120 East. Gas up if you need to, as the next opportunity isn't until the very end of this drive.

In half a mile you'll see the trailhead lot for Tuolumne Grove, one of the park's giant sequoia groves. The road begins to climb through evergreen forest, gaining almost 2000ft over 14 miles to the White Wolf turnoff road, a section of the crooked old Tioga Rd, completed in 1883. Cross over a segment of ❷ **Yosemite Creek** and imagine the flow you see leaping off Yosemite Falls a few miles downstream.

Almost 10 miles on is the spacious must-do overlook of ❸ **Olmsted Point** (p113), with magnificent views of Half Dome and Tenaya

Canyon and interpretive displays about the geological masterpiece surrounding you. Granite domes buffer shimmering ❹ **Tenaya Lake** (p113), with climbers dangling like spiders.

Wildflowers carpet verdant ❺ **Tuolumne Meadows** (p106), and the spiky peaks of the Cathedral Range silhouette endless sky. Wedge-like Lembert Dome sits astride the ❻ **Tuolumne River**, whose waters make a lengthy journey to slake the thirst of San Francisco.

The road bears north in approximately 5 miles, skirting beautiful Dana Meadows at the approach to the road's dizzying apex, ❼ **Tioga Pass** (9945ft). The pinnacle of Mt Dana looms to the east as you exit the park, where you quickly pass the chilly waters of ❽ **Tioga Lake** and ❾ **Ellery Lake**, the highest lakes along the entire stretch of Hwy 120.

The road straightens and reorients to the east as it descends relentlessly along the abyss of Lee Vining Canyon. Downshift to preserve your brakes. As you reach road's end at Hwy 395, surreal ❿ **Mono Lake** (p88) comes into view.

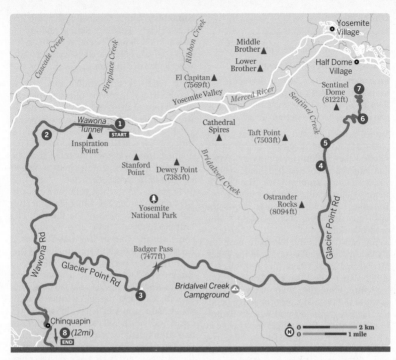

🚗 Driving Tour
Wawona Road & Glacier Point Road

START TUNNEL VIEW
END BIG TREES LODGE
LENGTH 52 MILES; TWO HOURS

Start your expedition from the east side of the Wawona Tunnel in the spectacular pull-off point of **❶ Tunnel View** (p45). No, you will not be staring at a dark traffic structure, but at the magnificent landscape to the east. Best in the spring when snowmelt has it gushing, 620ft Bridalveil Fall leaps off a plateau. When it thins out in summer, it sways like a string in the wind. The sheer wall of El Capitan rises to the north side of the Valley, and Half Dome pops out in the background.

Proceed west through Wawona Tunnel, the longest tunnel in the park at almost a mile. Two miles after your return to daylight, you approach **❷ Turtleback Dome**, a slab of exfoliating granite that looks like it's been sliced horizontally into pieces of crumbling bread.

In six more miles you'll come to the Chinquapin junction; turn left onto Glacier Point Rd to begin the forested 16-mile stretch to Glacier Point. In 2 miles is the wide western view of Merced Canyon, which descends 4500ft below you. The **❸ Yosemite Ski & Snowboard Area** (p105) appears in 3 more miles, though the lifts and lodge will be deserted in warm weather. In winter, the road is closed beyond here. Pass Bridalveil Creek Campground, with nearby views of the Clark Range to the east.

The road turns abruptly north near Mono Meadow, reaching **❹ Pothole Meadows**, where small bowls of water collect during wet months. A quarter-mile more lands you at the parking area for **❺ Sentinel Dome** (p62) (8122ft), one of the park's easiest-to-hike granite domes. Switchbacks descend through red fir forest to **❻ Washburn Point** (p105), which has views *almost* as good as those from Glacier Point. Winding through into **❼ Glacier Point** (p103), the peak of Half Dome parades before you.

Double back to the Chinquapin Junction, and turn left to continue south on the Wawona Rd (Hwy 41). The final 12-mile stretch crosses the South Fork of the Merced River before reaching the **❽ Big Trees Lodge** (p123).

Difficulty Easy

Start/Finish Yosemite Lodge

Nearest Town Yosemite Village

Transportation Shuttle stop 8

Summary Whether done in segments or in its entirety, this easy pedal around the floor of Yosemite Valley is as relaxing as it gets – and the views are amazing.

Twelve miles of paved, mostly flat bicycle paths run up and down the length of Yosemite Valley, making for some very relaxed and superbly enjoyable pedaling, whether you're solo or a family of five. The free Yosemite Valley hiking map provided at the Yosemite Valley Visitor Center shows the bike route in detail, and it's easy to whip out while riding.

You can pick up the bike path near just about anywhere you're staying in the Valley. Most people start where they rent bikes at either Half Dome Village or Yosemite Valley Lodge. From the latter, follow the path down to the riverside, past the lodge buildings, across a meadow and west to **Swinging Bridge** (which actually doesn't swing at all). Cross over the Merced River, veer east along Southside Dr, take in the magnificent view of Yosemite Falls, then Half Dome. Soon you'll pass Half Dome Village, the Royal Arches will appear on your left and you'll finally hit the road to Happy Isles. Pass the **Happy Isles Art & Nature Center** and continue along the road to loop around to North Pines Campground. Cross the Merced again, then cut north to Northside Dr, which you can follow back to Yosemite Valley Lodge.

If you only have time for one section, the route from Yosemite Village to the Mirror Lake road is especially serene after it splits from Northside Dr. Widening, it passes through thick woods and travels over the Merced, out of sight of any traffic and most people.

Carlon to Hetch Hetchy

Duration 3–4 hours

Distance 34-mile round-trip

Difficulty Moderate

Start/Finish Carlon Falls Day Use Area

Nearest Junction Evergreen Lodge

Transportation Car

Summary With a gentle ascent to the Hetch Hetchy Entrance Station and an adrenaline-spiking descent to the reservoir, this ride offers fabulous views and a spectacular destination.

With relatively little traffic, this ride to Hetch Hetchy Reservoir offers a splendid way to take in the scenery along the northwest boundary of the park. Fuel up with a good picnic lunch at the reservoir: the return climb is much more strenuous than the exciting drop on the way there. In summer, it can get extremely hot out here, so get an early start. In spring, it's divine.

To get to the starting point, drive northwest on Evergreen Rd, which departs Hwy 120 about 1 mile west of the Big Oak Flat Entrance. About 1 mile after turning off, you'll see the **Carlon Day Use Area** at a bridge across the South Fork Tuolumne River. Park in the parking lot and ride out to Evergreen Rd, cross the bridge and you're off. The first 9.5 miles rise and fall fairly gently with a modest overall elevation gain of about 550ft, and you'll pass by wildflower meadows, weathered wooden farmhouses and intermittent forest char remaining from the 2013 Rim Fire. About 1.5 miles after the park entrance (which lies about 7 miles from Carlon), you'll hit the crest of the ride (topping out around 5000ft) and begin the 1205ft descent to the reservoir. The views over the Poopenaut Valley are outstanding – be sure to stop for a breather at one of the viewpoints.

After you reach the reservoir, gobble down your energy bars, take a deep breath and slog your way back to the car.

OTHER ACTIVITIES

Rock Climbing & Bouldering

With its sheer spires, polished domes and soaring monoliths, Yosemite is rock-climbing nirvana. The main climbing season runs from April to October. Most climbers, including some legendary stars, stay at Camp 4 near El Capitan, especially in spring and fall. In summer, another base camp springs up at Tuolumne Meadows Campground. Climbers looking for partners post notices on bulletin boards at either campground.

The meadows across from El Capitan and the northeastern end of Tenaya Lake (off

Tioga Rd) are good for watching climbers dangle from granite (you need binoculars for a really good view). Look for the haul bags first – they're bigger, more colorful and move around more than the climbers, making them easier to spot. As part of the excellent **'Ask a Climber'** program, climbing rangers set up telescopes at El Capitan Bridge from 12:30pm to 4:30pm (mid-May through mid-October) and answer visitors' questions.

Climbers should pay attention to routes that are temporarily closed off to protect the nesting seasons of certain protected species like peregrine falcons and golden eagles. Closure notices are usually posted near trailheads to the sites.

Yosemite Valley

First, know this: all ropes lead to Camp 4. Most of the Valley's climbing activity revolves around this walk-in campground and historic hangout for climbing's most legendary figures. Camp 4 is where you go when you want to stop reading and start asking real people questions about where to climb, what to carry and what to expect. It's also where you'll find climbing partners, pick up used gear (among other things) and locate the car keys you left sitting at the base of the climb.

For many climbers, reaching the summit of El Capitan is a lifetime achievement, and hopefuls from around the world arrive to tackle its fabled routes.

As for bouldering, the possibilities are limitless. Popular areas include the west end of Camp 4, Sentinel Rock, the Four Mile Trail Trailhead, and the rocks near Housekeeping Camp and around Mirror Lake, to name only a few.

Big Oak Flat Road & Tioga Road

The big draw in these parts is Polly Dome, right next to Tenaya Lake. Stately Pleasure Dome, on the side of Polly adjacent to the lake, is the most popular spot, offering a good mix of easy and moderate routes. The granite rocks in this part of the park are well suited for slab and friction climbing, and both are well represented here.

For more difficult climbing, try the back side of Pywiack and Medlicott Domes, both just northeast of the lake toward Tuolumne Meadows. The beach at the east end of Tenaya Lake is an ideal spot for watching climbers.

For good bouldering, head to the Knobs, just over a mile north of Tenaya Lake on the west side of the road. Beginners will find excellent climbing on nearby Low-Profile Dome, particularly along the Golfer's Route.

Tuolumne Meadows

Come summertime, when temperatures in the Valley regularly top 90°F, climbers head to Tuolumne Meadows where the cool, high-country air is much more conducive to climbing. Thanks to the altitude,

---

YOSEMITE MOUNTAINEERING SCHOOL

Since 1969 **Yosemite Mountaineering School** (Map p124; ☎ 209-372-8344; www.travel yosemite.com; Half Dome Village; ⊙ Apr-Oct) has been teaching and guiding rock climbers, mountaineers and backcountry skiers of all levels. While you can learn everything from basic backpacking skills to building a snow cave, the school's specialty is teaching folks how to move their bodies up slabs of granite. Whether you're a 12-year-old who wants to learn the basics of climbing, belaying and rappelling or a sport climber who wants to learn the art of big walls, you'll find this school a gold mine of opportunity. Beginners over the age of 10 can sign up for the Welcome to the Rock seminar ($172 per person), which is pretty much guaranteed to inspire participants to go on for more. For parents, it's a great and constructive way to turn the kids loose for a day.

Other class offerings include anchoring, leading/multi-pitch climbing, self-rescue/aid and crack climbing, for which Yosemite is famous. You can even create your own custom climbing trip or hire guides to take you climbing.

The school is based out of the Yosemite Mountain Shop in Half Dome Village from April through November; it relocates to the Yosemite Ski & Snowboard Area in winter. The friendly and knowledgeable staff will offer suggestions based on your skill level and objectives.

the air is also thinner, so climbing here requires at least a day's acclimatization for most people.

Cathedral Peak and its fin-shaped west peak, the frightening Eichorn Pinnacle, are both epic and extremely popular climbs. It's fun watching climbers tackle these peaks from the Cathedral Lakes Trail. The Northwest Books route on Lembert Dome is one of the dome's most popular climbs. Mt Conness, on the park's eastern border, is a challenging all-day climb.

⚡Guided Trail Rides

The park's concessionaire runs guided trips to such scenic locales as Mirror Lake and Chilnualna Falls from Wawona's Big Trees Lodge Stable, as well as four- and six-day guided trips to the park's High Sierra camps. The season runs from May to October, although this varies slightly by location. No experience is needed, but reservations are advised, especially at Yosemite Valley Stable. The High Sierra camp trips operate by lottery. Some mounts are horses, but most likely you'll be riding a sure-footed mule.

Yosemite High Sierra
Camps Saddle Trips   HORSEBACK RIDING
(☑ freight 209-372-8348, lottery 888-413-8869; www.travelyosemite.com/lodging/high-sierra-camps; per person adult/child from $1040/806, freight per pound $5) These are far and away the most popular (though definitely not the cheapest) way to see the park from a saddle, with mules schlepping you and all the supplies. These four- to six-day trips include all meals and visit the spectacular High Sierra camps circuit. They fill up months in advance; check the park concessionaire's website for details.

You can also pay just to have mules carry your gear, or hire mules for custom trips to carry you and/or your gear to a destination of your choosing.

Big Trees Lodge Stable   HORSEBACK RIDING
(☑ 209-375-6502;   www.travelyosemite.com; ⊙ 7am-5pm mid-May–Sep) Located behind the Pioneer Yosemite History Center, this stable offers two-hour rides ($62 per person) around Wawona Meadow and to Chilnualna Falls. You need to arrive an hour prior to trip departure.

⚡Stock Camps

If you're bringing your own pack animal, you can use the stock camps at Tuolumne Meadows, Wawona and Bridalveil Creek campgrounds; you can reserve sites at www.recreation.gov. Stock are allowed on all Yosemite trails except those posted on the closure list, which also includes detailed information and restrictions (www.nps.gov/yose/planyourvisit/stock.htm).

⚡Rafting & Kayaking

From around late May to July, floating along the Merced River from Stoneman Meadow, near Half Dome Village, to Sentinel Bridge is a leisurely way to soak up Yosemite Valley views. Four-person **raft rentals** (Map p124; ☑ 209-372-4386; per person $30; ⊙ late May-late Jul) for the 3-mile trip are available from the concessionaire in Half Dome Village and include equipment and a shuttle ride back to the rental kiosk. Children must be over 50lb. Or bring your own raft and pay $5 to shuttle back. This activity is suitable for the mobility impaired.

Rafting is fun in Wawona on the South Fork of the Merced, between the campground and Swinging Bridge. On Tioga Rd, near Tuolumne Meadows, Tenaya Lake (p113) is a great place for a float and especially good for kayaking.

Serious paddlers are salivating over the new Merced River plan, which opens up the entire river to boaters with appropriate watercraft and personal flotation devices. River advocates swear that the best one-day river trip in California is between Clark's Bridge (near the stables) and the Pohono Bridge, especially in spring when the dogwoods are blooming overhead. A stretch of class IV white water from El Capitan Meadow and Pohono Bridge is certain to get your adrenaline pumping. For an overview of the policies, go to www.nps.gov/yose/learn/management/mrp.htm.

Whenever you disembark, be sure to do so only on sand or gravel bars – not vegetated riparian areas, which cannot handle the human impact.

Tuolumne River

River rats are also attracted to the fierce Tuolumne River, a classic class IV run that plunges and thunders through boulder gardens and cascades. Outfitters OARS (www.

oars.com) and Groveland-based Sierra Mac (www.sierramac.com) offer guided trips.

Swimming

On a hot summer day, nothing beats a dip in the gentle Merced River, though if chilly water doesn't float your boat, you can always pay to play in the scenic outdoor swimming pools at Half Dome Village (Map p124; adult/child $5/4; ⊘end May-Sep) and Yosemite Valley Lodge (p101); the price of admission includes towels and showers. With a sandy beach, Tenaya Lake is a frigid but interesting option. White Wolf's Harden Lake warms up to a balmy temperature by midsummer.

Yosemite Valley

Provided you don't trample the riparian life on your way, you can jump in the usually gentle Merced River just about anywhere, but there are several particularly good locations: at the beach just behind Housekeeping Camp; on the stretch behind Yosemite Valley Lodge; and at the Cathedral Beach and Devil's Elbow areas opposite the El Capitan Picnic Area. The beach immediately below Swinging Bridge is hugely popular and, thanks to calm waters, great for families. Tenaya Creek offers good swimming as well, especially near the bridge leading toward Mirror Lake.

Wawona

You'll find nice swimming holes near the campground and by Swinging Bridge. The latter is reached via a 2-mile drive east along Forest Dr, which parallels the south bank of the Merced River. Park in a lot beyond private Camp Wawona and walk the short distance to the river.

Big Oak Flat Road & Tioga Road

If you can handle cold water, Tenaya Lake offers some of the most enjoyable swimming in the park. It's hard to resist this glistening lake that beckons with sapphire waters. A sandy half-moon beach wraps around the east end. Sunbathers and picnickers are also drawn to the rocks that rim its north and west sides.

Want to work a little for that dip? May Lake is an easy hike and gorgeous, if a bit chilly. You can swim anywhere except a signed section of the western side where the

May Lake High Sierra Camp draws its drinking water. Further west, Harden Lake is unusually warm compared with other nearby lakes because much of its volume evaporates in summer. A late- or even mid-season swim is practically balmy.

Tuolumne Meadows

The Tuolumne River is an excellent choice for high-country swimming, with many easy-to-reach sandy-bottomed pools and slightly warmer temperatures than other High Sierra rivers. From the pullout at the west end of Tuolumne Meadows, follow the trail along Pothole Dome and the river for about a mile to a gorgeous waterfall and hidden swimming spot.

You'll also find a couple of small but good swimming holes at the twin bridges crossing the chipper Lyell Fork Tuolumne; to get there, head out on the trail to Lyell Canyon. If you don't mind hiking a bit further, the Lyell Fork also has some great (albeit shallow) swimming areas. Elizabeth Lake can be a bit bone-chilling, but on a hot summer day, plenty of people take the plunge and love it.

Fishing

Yosemite may not be the sort of place you go to catch whopping trophy trout, but the setting is fabulous, and wettin' a line, so to say, in the Merced or Tuolumne Rivers is pretty darn satisfying. Stream and river fishing is permitted only from the last Saturday in April until mid-November; lake fishing is OK year-round. In Wawona, the South Fork of the Merced offers some of the best stream fishing in the park. In and around the park you can fish the Merced River between Happy Isles and the Foresta Bridge in El Portal, although if you catch a rainbow trout, you'll have to throw it back. In Yosemite Valley, you're allowed only five brown trout per day, and bait is prohibited (artificial lures or barbless flies only).

You can pick up tackle and supplies at the stores in Tuolumne Meadows, Wawona and Crane Flat. Get in touch with Yosemite Sierra Flyfishing (☑831-345-8203; www.yosemitesierraflyfishing.com; half-/full day for 2 $335/435) and for more information on fishing in the park, see www.nps.gov/yose/planyourvisit/fishing.htm.

ℹ COFFEE WITH A RANGER

Rise and shine and schmooze with a perky park ranger at one of the morning Coffee with a Ranger sessions held at campgrounds throughout the park. This is a chance to get some quality time with the best sources of park information, and you can solicit suggestions for your day's adventures while enjoying a complimentary caffeine fix. Check the *Yosemite Guide* for locations and times, and don't forget to bring a mug!

🏃 Hang Gliding

You can actually hang glide from Glacier Point for a mere $5, provided you're an active member of the **US Hang Gliding & Paragliding Association** (USHPA; ☑800-616-6888, Colorado Springs 719-632-8300; www.ushpa.org; ☉8am-5pm), have level 4 (advanced standing) certification, and you preregister online with the **Yosemite Hang Gliders Association** (YHGA; Map p124; ☑650-773-6469; www.yosemitehg.org; ☉Jun-Sep). On weekend mornings from late May to early September, weather permitting, qualified hang gliders can launch from the overlook between 7am and 9pm, well before any thermal activity rolls in, and float down to Leidig Meadow, just west of Yosemite Valley Lodge. One of the best free shows in the park is watching the colorful gliders sprint off the edge and soar over the Valley like tiny paper airplanes.

🏃 Boating

Easy-to-access Tenaya Lake is hands down the best place for a motorless boat in the park. Lounging at the foot of John Muir's beloved Mt Hoffmann is tranquil May Lake, a lovely place to paddle an inflatable; that is, unless you want to hoof anything heavier for the 1.2 miles from the trailhead along Tioga Rd.

🏃 Golf

If you find the need to smack the ol' tiny white ball around, head to Yosemite's nine-hole, par-35 **Big Trees Golf Course** (☑20 9-375-6572; www.travelyosemite.com; green fees per 9/18 holes from $21.50/36; ☉8am-6pm mid-May–Sep), which was built in 1917. The course hails itself as one of the country's few 'or-ganic' golf courses, meaning no pesticides are used on the lawn and everything is irrigated with gray water. Cart and club rentals are available.

🏃 Campfire & Public Programs

There's something almost universally enjoyable about group campfire programs. Pull a bench around a roaring bonfire, with stars above, big trees behind you and lots of friendly folks all around, and it's as if you've left the world's troubles behind.

During the summertime, free campfire programs are held at the following Yosemite campgrounds: Tuolumne Meadows, Wawona, Bridalveil Creek, Crane Flat, White Wolf and Lower Pines. Check the *Yosemite Guide* for the week's programs and times. Rangers, naturalists and other park staff lead the programs, and topics include the history, ecology and geology of the local region, a few tips on dealing with bears, and maybe some stories and songs. They're geared toward families and people of all ages.

Similar evening programs are also held at amphitheaters behind Yosemite Valley Lodge and Half Dome Village – even in the absence of an actual campfire, the mood remains the same. These programs include general talks about the area, with occasional slide shows and films.

The Sierra Club's Yosemite Heritage Conservation Center also hosts programs on Fridays and Saturdays. More in-depth than the average campfire talk, these cover such topics as the founding of the John Muir Trail and the history of Hetch Hetchy.

Glacier Point rangers lead weekly programs at a lovely stone amphitheater near the snack bar, and sometimes offer sunset talks along the railing overlooking the Valley. Over at Tuolumne Meadows, talks take place at Parsons Memorial Lodge, reachable via an easy half-mile hike.

The busiest time is, of course, during the summer, usually June to September. Limited programs are offered in the low season, and they're held during cold weather at indoor locations such as Yosemite Valley Lodge and the Majestic Yosemite Hotel.

Monthly Yosemite Forum lectures focus on nature and science within the Sierra Nevada and take place in the auditorium of the Yosemite Valley Visitor Center.

🏃 WINTER ACTIVITIES

The white coat of winter opens up a different set of things to do, as the Valley becomes a quiet, frosty world of snow-draped evergreens, ice-coated lakes and vivid vistas of gleaming white mountains sparkling against blue skies. Winter tends to arrive in full force by mid-November and peter out in early April.

A free shuttle bus connects the Valley and the Yosemite Ski & Snowboard Area. Roads in the valley are plowed, and Hwys 41, 120 and 140 are usually kept open, conditions permitting. Tioga Rd (Hwy 120 E), however, closes with the first snowfall. Be sure to bring snow chains with you, as prices for them double once you hit the foothills.

🏃 Cross-Country Skiing

Cross-country skiers can explore 350 miles of skiable trails and roads, including 90 miles of marked trails and 25 miles of machine-groomed track near the Yosemite Ski & Snowboard Area. The scenic but grueling trail to Glacier Point (21 miles round-trip) also starts from here. More trails are at Crane Flat and Mariposa Grove. The ungroomed trails can also be explored with snowshoes.

Glacier Point Road & Around

Twenty-five miles of groomed track and 90 miles of marked trails fan out from the Yosemite Ski & Snowboard Area (p105). From here, you can schuss out to the Clark Range Vista and Glacier Point, an invigorating 21-mile round-trip. Pick up a trail map or download one from the Yosemite National Park (www.nps.gov/yose/planyourvisit/upload/badger-winter.pdf) website.

The Yosemite Cross-Country Ski School (p35) offers learn-to-ski packages ($46), guided tours (from $102 per person), telemark instruction ($49), private lessons (starting at $37) and equipment rental ($25 for skis, boots and poles). It also leads very popular overnight trips to the Glacier Point Ski Hut.

WAWONA

Mariposa Grove contains a series of well-marked cross-country skiing trails, including an 8-mile loop trail from the South Entrance. Trail maps can be purchased at the park or printed from the park website at www.fs.usda.gov/activity/sierra/recreation/wintersports. The trails also connect to marked **Sierra National Forest** trails just south of the park in Goat Meadow and along Beasore Rd.

Big Oak Flat Road & Tioga Road

You'll find good, marked cross-country skiing and snowshoeing trails in the Crane Flat area, including Old Big Oak Flat Rd, which leads to Tuolumne Grove (p56) and Hodgdon Meadow. Snowcapped Clark Range is visible from the **Crane Flat Lookout**, a 3-plus mile round-trip from the eponymously named parking lot on Big Oak Flat Rd – expect peaceful solitude and clear views. Trail maps are available at the park and at www.nps.gov/yose/planyourvisit/brochures.htm. When Tioga Rd is closed in winter, it becomes a popular, though ungroomed, ski route.

🏃 Downhill Skiing & Snowboarding

California's oldest ski slope, Yosemite Ski & Snowboard Area sits at 7300ft on Glacier Point Rd, about 22 miles from the Valley. Known as a family-friendly mountain geared toward beginners and intermediates, it features an 800ft vertical drop, nine runs, two terrain parks, five lifts, a full-service lodge and equipment rental ($37 for a full set of gear). For great money-saving deals, check out the stay-and-ski packages at the Big Trees Lodge, Yosemite Valley Lodge and Majestic Yosemite Hotel, and note that lift-ticket prices drop considerably midweek. It also rents tubes for snow tubing.

The excellent on-site **Yosemite Ski & Snowboard Area School** (www.travelyose mite.com; group/private lessons from $80/89.50) is highly regarded for its top-notch instruction, particularly for beginners. Group lessons start at $80 and private lessons start at $89.50 per hour for one. Badger's gentle slopes are well suited for first-time snowboarders.

In winter, a free daily shuttle runs from the Valley to the Yosemite Ski & Snowboard Area in the morning, returning to the Valley in the afternoon.

🏃 Snowshoeing

It wouldn't be difficult to argue that Yosemite Valley is at its very best just after a fresh snowfall. Snowshoeing around the Valley,

WORTH A TRIP

WINTER SKI HUTS

When Yosemite National Park is hushed and white, three classic ski huts are open for overnight guests who make the trek on snowshoes or cross-country skis. The journeys aren't easy, but certainly worth the work. Make sure to self-register for a wilderness permit before you head out.

In winter, the concession stand at Glacier Point fills with bunk beds and becomes the Glacier Point Ski Hut (Map p124; ☏209-372-8444; ☉Dec-Mar). It's operated by the park concessionaire and reached by a 10.5-mile trip on an intermediate trail. Guided trips are led by the Yosemite Cross-Country Ski School (p35); one-night trips cost $350 per person, two nights $550. These tariffs include meals, wine, accommodations and guides. Or you can get there without a guide (reservation required) and pay $146 per day for meals and lodging.

The handcrafted stone Ostrander Lake Ski Hut (☏209-379-5161; www.yosemiteconservancy.org; bunks weekday/weekend $35/55), operated by the Yosemite Conservancy (p248), can accommodate up to 15 skiers in a gorgeous lakeside spot beneath Horse Ridge. Cooking facilities are provided, but you must ski in with all of your supplies. The 10-mile trip requires experience and a high fitness level. Staffed throughout winter, the hut is open to backcountry skiers and snowshoers; a draw is held for reservations in November.

Are you up to a 16-mile trek from the eastern side of the park, summiting Tioga Pass? In winter, the Tuolumne Meadows Campground reservation office (☏209-372-4025; Tioga Rd; ☉8am-5pm Jul-Sep) reinvents itself as the free Tuolumne Meadows Ski Hut. It has a wood-burning stove, sleeps 10, and is first come, first served. Tuolumne winter rangers post helpful conditions updates at www.nps.gov/yose/blogs/tmconditions.htm. If you're hesitant to try this on your own, the Cross-Country Ski Center runs infrequent six-day tours for $876 per person. The center is in a stone building facing Tioga Rd, just west of the bridge across the Tuolumne River, right at the entrance to the campground.

past icy monoliths, frozen waterfalls and meadows blanketed in snow, is a truly magical activity. The John Muir Trail, which begins at Happy Isles, is a popular destination.

You can rent snowshoes ($23/18 per half-/full day) at the Yosemite Ski & Snowboard Area, and sometimes at the Half Dome Village Ice Skating Rink (p96), where rangers lead two-hour naturalist treks that are informative, fun and cheap ($5). Check the *Yosemite Guide* for schedules. Rentals are also available at the Crane Flat gas station (p128). From January to March, rangers offer two-hour 'Full Moon Snowshoe Walks' (with equipment rental $35) on nights of, and leading up to, a full moon. Sign up at the Yosemite Valley Lodge Tour Desk (☏209-372-1240; www.travelyosemite.com/things-to-do; 9006 Yosemite Lodge Dr, Yosemite Valley; ☉7:30am-7pm) or call 209-372-1240.

🏃 Ice-Skating

A delightful way to spend a winter's afternoon is twirling about on the large outdoor Half Dome Village Ice Skating Rink (Map p124; 2hr session adult/child $10/9.50, skate rental $4; ☉1:30-7pm Mon-Fri, noon-9pm Sat & Sun Nov-Mar; ⛸). Daily sessions begin at 3:30pm and 7pm, with additional sessions at 8:30am and noon on weekends and holidays.

🏃 Snow Camping

There are no quotas or reservations for winter camping, but you still need to get a wilderness permit.

Destinations accessed from Glacier Point Rd are some of the most popular places to enjoy snow camping. There are restrictions on staying at overlooks, and you must camp at least 1.5 miles from the Yosemite Ski & Snowboard Area. See www.nps.gov/yose/planyourvisit/wildwinter.htm for more information as well as a winter trail map.

Off-limits in summer, Wawona's peaceful and protected Mariposa Grove is open for camping from December to mid-April when snow closes the road. You must set up your tent uphill from Clothespin Tree. The Wawona Campground also stays open for winter camping on a first-come, first-served basis.

The Yosemite Cross-Country Ski School (p35) offers an overnight trip from the Yosemite Ski & Snowboard Area ($292 per person, including meals), with instruction in snow camping fundamentals and survival.

🏃 Sledding & Tubing

If tubing down a hill is more your fancy, there's a snow-play area located in Crane Flat. The Yosemite Ski & Snowboard Area (p105) also has a tubing area for younger kids, with two-hour sessions ($17) starting at 11:30am and 2pm, tubes included. In the Sierra National Forest a mile south of the South Entrance, the free Goat Meadow Snow Play Area is another good location if you have gear.

⊙ SIGHTS

Everywhere you look in Yosemite, there are sights: lofty granite domes, sheer cliffs, turbulent rivers, glassy lakes, hypnotizing waterfalls and serene meadows; not to mention spectacular viewpoints to take in all of these and more in a panoramic vision. No section of the park is lacking. However, the time you have and your mode of transportation – whether private vehicle, shuttle bus, bike or foot – will determine your best plan of attack.

Visitor activity is concentrated in Yosemite Valley, especially in Yosemite Village, which has the main visitor center, a museum, eateries and other services. Half Dome Village is another hub. Some of the park's most recognizable natural features such as Half Dome, El Capitan and Yosemite Falls are here, as well as trailheads for popular hikes.

Notably less busy, Tuolumne Meadows, toward the eastern end of Tioga Rd and only open in summer, draws hikers, backpackers and climbers to its pristine backcountry for trails and routes that run the gamut from meadow strolls to strenuous scrambles and long-distance overnights.

Glacier Point, another section of the park with no road access outside summer (except for the ski area), offers spectacular views. Wawona, the park's southern focal point, also has good infrastructure, if a much reduced trail network. The Big Oak Flat Rd area and western Tioga Rd, have several giant sequioa groves. In the northwestern corner, Hetch Hetchy, which has no services at all, but notably impressive waterfalls and several recommended hikes, receives the smallest number of visitors, but shouldn't be overlooked.

⊙ Yosemite Valley

The park's crown jewel, spectacular meadow-carpeted Yosemite Valley is bisected by the rippling Merced River and hemmed in by some of the most majestic chunks of granite anywhere on earth. Ribbons of water, including some of the highest waterfalls in the US, fall dramatically before crashing in thunderous displays. The counterpoint to the sublime natural scene is bustling Yosemite Village.

ℹ Orientation

Meadow-carpeted Yosemite Valley is 7 miles long and 1 mile wide (at its widest point). The Merced River meanders down its middle, within sight of Half Dome on the east end, westward past El Capitan, and out of the park into the Merced River Canyon.

Northside and Southside Drives parallel the valley on either side of the river, each one way for most of its route (the former heads west, the latter heads east). Four bridges span the river, including Sentinel Bridge, which leads to Yosemite Village, the Valley's commercial center.

The Majestic Yosemite Hotel sits about a half-mile east of the village, while Yosemite Valley Lodge is near the base of Yosemite Falls, less than a mile west of the village. Half Dome Village and the three Pines campgrounds lie south of the river, about a mile east of Sentinel Bridge.

Three highways diverge at the west end of the Valley. Big Oak Flat Rd leads north to Crane Flat (where it meets Hwy 120), Hetch Hetchy and Tuolumne Meadows; Hwy 140 heads west out of the park to El Portal and Mariposa; and Hwy 41 runs south to Glacier Point Rd, Wawona and Mariposa.

Yosemite Village & Around

Regardless of your feelings toward commercial development in one of the world's natural wonders, you'll probably wind up here at one point or another, as the village offers just about every amenity – from pizzas and ice cream, to firewood and wilderness permits and, yes, even a Starbucks.

Commercial development began in the Valley almost as soon as the public became aware of the park. Quite a few hotels opened around the turn of the 20th century, and by the 1920s a collection of businesses – including hotels, photo studios, a dance pavilion

Yosemite Valley Region

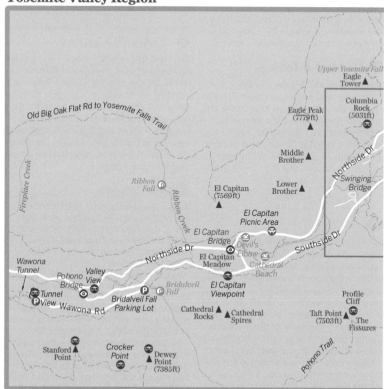

and even a cinema – had risen just south of the river near Sentinel Bridge. This was the original Yosemite Village. By the 1950s, however, it was downgraded to the 'Old Village,' as businesses moved north of the river. The site of the Old Village has since reverted to meadow (look for road marker V20), though the chapel remains, albeit in a slightly different spot. A few buildings were moved to the Pioneer Yosemite History Center in Wawona, and Best's Studio was moved to the present-day village and eventually renamed the Ansel Adams Gallery.

Rarely do visitors spend much time in the Valley without a stop at the park's main visitor center (p130). If you've never been to Yosemite, it's an excellent place to load up on information.

At the main desk, rangers answer tourists' questions (remaining amazingly friendly amid the barrage) and can pretty much settle any query you might have. An excel-

lent free Valley hiking map is available, and weather reports, campground availability, and trail and road conditions are posted behind the desk.

To the right of the help desk is the **exhibit hall**, which offers an interactive walk through Yosemite's history from the dinosaurs to the present.

Ansel Adams Gallery   GALLERY
(Map p124; ☑ 209-372-4413; www.anseladams. com; 9031 Village Dr; ☺ 9am-5pm) Few know about it, but *original* Ansel Adams photographic prints are shown at Yosemite Valley's Ansel Adams Gallery. A number of walks and classes are also offered, including the fascinating 'In the Footsteps of Ansel Adams' offered every Tuesday and Saturday afternoon ($95); call in advance to reserve a spot. For budding photographers, free guided camera walks are offered Tuesday, Thursday and Saturday mornings in summer;

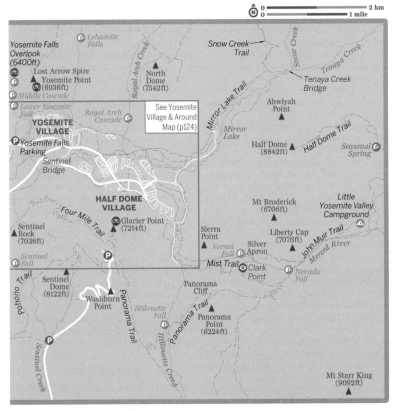

space is limited to 15 people and three days' advance reservation is requested.

The gallery is also a recommended **gift shop**, with fine art reproductions of Yosemite landscape photos and a **bookstore**, with an excellent selection of nonfiction and novels about the West.

Yosemite Museum MUSEUM

(Map p124; www.nps.gov/yose; 9037 Village Dr, Yosemite Village; ⊙ 9am-5pm summer, 10am-4pm rest of year, often closed noon-1pm) 🅿 **FREE** The Yosemite Museum has Miwok and Paiute artifacts, including woven baskets, beaded buckskin dresses and dance capes made from feathers. Native American cultural demonstrators engage visitors with traditional basket weaving, toolmaking and crafts. There's also an **art gallery** with paintings and photographs from the museum's permanent collection. Behind the museum, a self-guided **interpretive trail** winds past the reconstructed 1870s **Indian Village** of Ahwahnee, with pounding stones, an acorn granary, a ceremonial roundhouse and a conical bark house.

Yosemite Conservancy has a small gift shop here, with mostly a selection of jewelry.

Yosemite Community Church CHURCH

(The Chapel; Map p124; ☑ 209-372-4831; www.yo semitevalleychapel.org; ⊙ services 9:15am, 11am & 6:30pm Sun, 7pm Thu summer, 9:15am & 6:30pm Sun winter) Built in 1879, this chapel is Yosemite's oldest structure that still remains in use, including for weddings. In 1885, President Ulysses Grant's memorial service was held at the church's original location near the base of the Four Mile Trail; in 1901, the chapel was moved about a mile to its present site. Sunday-morning services are nondenominational.

Half Dome Village & Around

Lying directly below Glacier Point, Half Dome Village is home to Yosemite Valley's second-biggest collection of restaurants, stores and overnight accommodations. Originally called Camp Curry, it was founded in 1899 by David and Jennie Curry as a place where everyday visitors could find 'a good bed and a clean napkin at every meal.' Starting with just a handful of tents, the camp quickly grew, thanks in large part to David Curry's entrepreneurial drive and booming personality. One of his biggest promotional schemes was the Firefall (p106), a nightly event and significant tourist draw.

More than 100 years later, the Camp Curry sign still hangs over the entrance (a temporary sign on top reads 'Half Dome Village'), but this sprawling complex retains few traces of its turn-of-the-20th-century roots. From the parking lot, a sea of tent cabins fans out toward the base of Glacier Point, radiating from a central cluster of stores and snack bars – not exactly a vision of rustic glory. Still, it's pleasant to settle in for pizza and beer on the patio that faces the amphitheater out back. There's even a small cocktail bar. Or you can head to the charming deck of the old **Camp Curry Lounge** for a catnap in one of the rocking chairs.

Yosemite Mountain Shop (Map p124; ☑ 209-372-8396; Half Dome Village; ☺ 8am-8pm summer, shorter hours rest of year) offers the Valley's best selection of camping, mountaineering and backpacking supplies and is the home of the Yosemite Mountaineering School (p91). It's also world-renowned for its selection of big-wall climbing gear.

Happy Isles   AREA
(Map p124; ☐ shuttle stop 16) Where the Merced River courses around two small islands lies Happy Isles, a popular area for picnics, swimming and strolls on marked paths and a small boardwalk over a marshy area. It also marks the start of the **John Muir Trail** and **Mist Trail** to several waterfalls and Half Dome. The **Happy Isles Art & Nature Center** (Map p124; ☑ 209-372-4207; artcenter@ yosemiteconservancy.org; classes $10-20) operates out of here as well.

**Yosemite Conservation
Heritage Center**   HISTORIC BUILDING
(Map p124; ☑ 209-372-4542; www.sierraclub.org/ education/leconte; ☺ 10am-4pm Wed-Sun & evenings Fri & Sat May-Sep; ☞; ☐ shuttle stop 12) Built by the Sierra Club in 1903, this small, rustic, granite-and-wood lodge offers a glimpse of a relatively unknown chapter of California architecture. Designed by Berke-

ley architect John White, the building sits firmly within a style known as the First Bay Tradition, a movement that was intimately linked with the 20th-century Arts and Crafts movement. The First Bay Tradition placed great importance on reflecting the natural world and insisted that each work of architecture be specific to its surroundings.

The Sierra Club built the lodge in honor of Joseph LeConte (1823–1901), a University of California Berkeley geologist and a cofounder of the Sierra Club. The building was initially erected in Camp Curry and then moved here in 1919. Formerly called LeConte Lodge, it's one of three National Historic Landmarks in Yosemite, along with the former Ahwahnee Hotel (now the Majestic Yosemite Hotel) and the Rangers' Club (a valley building currently used as employee housing).

Sierra Club members staff the lodge, which houses exhibits and information on LeConte, Sierra Club cofounder John Muir and photographer Ansel Adams, along with an excellent library of park-related ecology, geology and other nature books for browsing. There's also a fun children's corner. Evening activities take place most Fridays and Saturdays and are posted out front and in the *Yosemite Guide*.

Majestic Yosemite Hotel

Almost as iconic as Half Dome itself, the elegant Majestic Yosemite Hotel has drawn well-heeled tourists through its towering doors since 1927. Of course, you needn't be wealthy in the least to partake of its many charms. In fact, a visit to Yosemite Valley is hardly complete without a stroll through the **Great Lounge** (aka the lobby), which is handsomely decorated with leaded glass, sculpted tiles, Native American rugs and Turkish kilims. You can relax on the plush but aging couches and stare out the 10 floor-to-ceiling windows, wander into the Solarium, or send the kids into the walk-in fireplace (no longer in use) for a photo. You can even sneak up the back stairs for a peek into the private **Tudor Room**, which has excellent views over the Great Lounge.

Take a wander around the outside, too. The hotel was built entirely from local granite, pine and cedar – against the backdrop of the Royal Arches it's truly a sight to see. There's no mistaking the reasoning behind its National Historic Landmark designation. Dropping in for a meal at the **restaurant** or a drink and a snack at the **bar** are great

YOSEMITE'S ARTISTS

From its very beginnings as a park, Yosemite has inspired a body of art nearly as impressive as the landscape itself. The artists who came to Yosemite with the first generation of tourists revealed a world of extraordinary beauty, even as miners, ranchers and lumbermen were tearing it apart in their lust for profit. From the illustrations of Thomas Ayres to the photographs of Carleton Watkins, art played a key role in the bid to establish Yosemite as a national park.

In the mid-19th century, the Hudson River School and related movements in American art strived to capture the face of God in the wild magnificence of nature. A parallel trend in literature expressed a distinctly American spiritualism tied to the wilderness; writers who explored such transcendental themes included Ralph Waldo Emerson, Walt Whitman, Emily Dickinson and Henry David Thoreau. Into this intellectual moment, which flourished on the East Coast, came the first paintings of Yosemite by a recognized artist, Albert Bierstadt, in 1863.

At that time, San Francisco was becoming the epicenter for a distinctly Californian school of art. Inspired by the vistas that Bierstadt and the photographers were capturing in Yosemite, many other artists embraced the Sierra as a subject matter. Mountain landscapes by Charles Nahl, Thomas Hill and William Keith soon adorned Victorian mansions in San Francisco and Sacramento, and painters became a regular fixture in the haunts of John Muir, who occasionally led groups of them on sketching expeditions into remote locations. Hill set up a studio at Wawona in 1884, beginning the tradition of resident artists and galleries in the park.

While the painters were often content to set up their easels in the meadows, photographers became known for seeking out more inaccessible regions. Sierra Club photographer-mountaineers such as Joseph LeConte and Norman Clyde captured extremely remote areas of the park. Yosemite's best-known photographer, of course, was Ansel Adams, who developed a level of craft not seen in the work of his predecessors. An early proponent of the idea that photography could adhere to the same aesthetic principles used by fine artists, he also became a strong advocate for the preservation of the wilderness, working on the frontlines of the growing conservation movement.

In 1929 Adams married Virginia Best, whose father's gallery in Yosemite Valley was the precursor to the Ansel Adams Gallery (p98), found today in Yosemite Village. In 1940 Adams held a photography workshop at the gallery with fellow photographer Edward Weston, beginning a tradition of photography education that continues to this day.

Three of Adams' assistants – John Sexton, Alan Ross and Ted Orland – are lesser known but equally important to the greater body of Yosemite photography, and photographer-mountaineer Galen Rowell, who Adams himself highly regarded, took some of the most extreme photos of the park, continuing to expose those faraway places to the public eye.

ways to experience this historic hotel without coughing up three car payments' worth of cash in order to spend the night.

Originally named the Ahwahnee, the hotel was built on the site of a former Ahwahneechee–Miwok village. To promote the relatively young national park, National Park Service (NPS) director Stephen Mather dreamed up the idea of a majestic hotel to attract wealthy guests. The site was chosen for its exposure to the sun and its views of Half Dome, Yosemite Falls and Glacier Point. The hotel was designed by American architect Gilbert Stanley Underwood, who also designed Zion Lodge, Bryce Canyon Lodge

and Grand Canyon North Rim Lodge. If the hotel's lobby looks familiar, perhaps it's because it inspired the lobby of the Overlook Hotel, the ill-fated inn from Stanley Kubrick's *The Shining*.

Yosemite Valley Lodge

Near the base of Yosemite Falls, the collection of buildings known as Yosemite Valley Lodge includes modern, motel-like accommodations, restaurants, including the recently upgraded Base Camp eatery and Starbucks, shops, a bar, a bicycle-rental stand, a **pool** (Map p124; adult/child $5/4; 🚻),

LEGEND OF HALF DOME

According to Native American legend, one of Yosemite's early inhabitants came down from the mountains to Mono Lake, where he married a Paiute named Tesaiyac. The journey back to the Valley was difficult, and by the time they reached what was to become Mirror Lake, Tesaiyac decided she wanted to return to her people at Mono Lake. Her husband refused to live on such barren, arid land with no oak trees where he could get acorns. With a heart full of despair, Tesaiyac fled toward Mono Lake, her husband in pursuit. When the spirits heard the couple quarreling, they grew angry and turned the two into stone: he became North Dome and she became Half Dome. The tears she cried made marks as they ran down her face, forming Mirror Lake.

a tour desk (p96) and other amenities. The amphitheater hosts regular evening programs, and the pool is open to the public.

Unlike the Majestic Yosemite Hotel, it's not a very striking development. Despite efforts to blend it into the natural surroundings, the place feels strangely like a suburban condo development. Though it doesn't appear very old, the lodge dates back to 1915. It underwent extensive redesign and remodeling in 1956, 1998 and 2014, retaining little to suggest its history.

The Yosemite Valley shuttle bus stops right out front, as do **Yosemite Area Regional Transport System** (YARTS; ☑877-989-2787; www.yarts.com) buses. All guided tram tours, ski shuttles and hiker buses also leave from here; tickets are available from the tour desk in the lobby.

Yosemite Falls

One of the world's most dramatic natural spectacles, Yosemite Falls is a marvel to behold. Naturalist John Muir devoted entire pages to its changing personality, its myriad sounds, its movement with the wind and its transformations between the seasons. No matter where you are when you see it (and it regularly pops into view from all over the Valley), the falls will stop you in your tracks.

In spring, when snowmelt gets Yosemite Creek really pumping, the sight is astounding. Another sign of springtime is 'frazil ice,' the strange slurry – not exactly ice or snow – that moves like lava from the bottom of the falls under Yosemite Creek bridges. On nights when the falls are full and the moon is bright, especially in May and June, you might spot a 'moonbow' (aka lunar rainbow or spraybow). In winter, as the spray freezes midair, an ice or snow cone, depending on its density, forms at the base of the falls and can top out at several hundred feet.

Dropping 2425ft, Yosemite Falls is considered the tallest in North America and the fifth highest in the world (Angel Falls in Venezuela occupies the top spot). Some question that claim, however, as Yosemite Falls comprises three distinct tiers: towering 1430ft Upper Yosemite Fall, tumbling 675ft Middle Cascade and the final 320ft drop of Lower Yosemite Fall. It's also possible to make the grueling hike to the top. The easternmost route of the loop trail is wheelchair accessible.

To get to the base of Lower Yosemite Fall, get off at shuttle stop 6 (or park in the lot just north of Yosemite Valley Lodge) and join the legions of visitors for the easy quarter-mile stroll. Note that in midsummer, when the snowmelt has dissipated, both the upper and lower falls usually dry up – sometimes to a trickle, at other times stopping altogether.

Half Dome

Rising 8842ft above sea level, and nearly a mile above the Valley floor, Half Dome serves as the park's spiritual centerpiece and stands as one of the most glorious and monumental (not to mention best-known) domes on earth.

Its namesake shape is, in fact, an illusion. While from the Valley the dome appears to have been neatly sliced in half, from Glacier or Washburn Points you'll see that it's actually a thin ridge with a back slope nearly as steep as its fabled facade. As you travel through the park, witness Half Dome's many faces. For example, from Mirror Lake it presents a powerful form, while from the Panorama Trail it looks somewhat like a big toe poking out above the rocks and trees.

Half Dome towers above Tenaya Canyon, a classic, glacially carved gorge. Across this canyon rise North Dome and Basket Dome, examples of fully intact domes. In contrast, Half Dome's north face shattered along cracks as a small glacier undercut the dome's base. The resulting cliff boasts a 93% vertical grade (the sheerest in North America), attracting climbers from around the world. Hikers with a permit (p73) can reach its summit from the Valley via a long series of trails (never do it with rain in the forecast). The final 45-degree stretch to the top was first made accessible by George Anderson, a local blacksmith who drilled holes in the granite in 1875 and installed a rope system (later replaced by the steel cables in use today).

Bridalveil Fall

In the southwest end of Yosemite Valley, Bridalveil Fall tumbles 620ft. The Ahwahneechee people call it Pohono (Spirit of the Puffing Wind), as gusts often blow the fall from side to side, even lifting water back up into the air. This waterfall usually runs year-round, though it's reduced to a whisper by midsummer. Bring rain gear or expect to get wet when the fall is heavy.

Take the seasonal El Capitan shuttle or park at the large lot where Wawona Rd (Hwy 41) meets Southside Dr. From the lot, it's a quarter-mile walk to the base of the fall. The path is paved, but probably too rough for wheelchairs, and there's a bit of an uphill at the very end. Avoid climbing on the slippery rocks at its base – no one likes a broken bone. The Yosemite Conservancy is planning to remodel the usually overflowing parking lot and trail access to make it more visitor friendly.

If you'd rather walk from the Valley, a trail (part of the Loop Trails) follows Southside Dr, beginning near the Yosemite Heritage Conservation Center and running about 3.8 miles west to the falls.

El Capitan

At nearly 3600ft from base to summit, El Capitan ranks as one of the world's largest granite monoliths. Its sheer face makes it a world-class destination for experienced climbers, and one that wasn't 'conquered' until 1958. Since then, it's been inundated. Look closely and you'll probably spot climbers reckoning with El Cap's series of cracks and ledges, including the famous 'Nose.' At night, park along the road and dim your headlights; once your eyes adjust, you'll easily make out the pinpricks of headlamps dotting the rock face. Listen, too, for voices.

The meadow across from El Capitan is good for watching climbers dangle from granite (you need binoculars for a really good

DON'T MISS

HORSETAIL FALL

For two weeks in late February, if the sky's clear and the water flow right, visitors can behold a fiery spectacle at Horsetail Fall. A seasonal ribbon of water dropping off the eastern edge of El Capitan blazes like a stream of molten lava when the fall catches the sunset. Many compare it to witnessing the Glacier Point Firefall, and photographers flock to the El Capitan Picnic Area for views. The National Park Service (www.nps.gov) put in place rules to reduce the severe congestion.

YOSEMITE NATIONAL PARK SIGHTS

view). Look for the haul bags first – they're bigger, more colorful and move around more than the climbers, making them easier to spot. As part of the excellent 'Ask a Climber' program, climbing rangers set up telescopes at El Capitan Bridge from 12:30pm to 4:30pm (mid-May through mid-October) and answer visitors' questions. See the *Yosemite Guide* listing for a schedule.

◉ Glacier Point & Badger Pass Region

Constructed to replace an 1882 wagon road, the modern 16-mile stretch of Glacier Point Rd leads to what many people consider the finest viewpoint in Yosemite. A lofty 3200ft above the valley floor, 7214ft Glacier Point presents one of the park's most eye-popping vistas and practically puts you at eye level with Half Dome.

❶ Orientation

From Yosemite Valley, it's 30 miles (about an hour's drive) to Glacier Point. Glacier Point Rd runs east from the Chinquapin junction on Hwy 41, dead ending at Glacier Point itself. The road rises from about 6000ft at Chinquapin to 7700ft at the Sentinel Dome parking lot, then down again to 7214ft at Glacier Point. From the Chinquapin turnoff, Yosemite Ski & Snowboard Area lies about 5 miles to the east; in winter, Glacier Point Rd is closed east of the ski area.

Glacier Point lies at the far eastern end of winding Glacier Point Rd. Along the road, hiking trails lead to more spectacular viewpoints such as Dewey Point and Sentinel Dome. The road also passes Bridalveil Creek Campground, adjacent to Bridalveil Creek, which runs north and drops into Yosemite Valley as Bridalveil Fall.

The only services in the area are at Glacier Point, where there's a small snack bar and gift shop.

Rangers are stationed at viewpoint areas but the closest visitor center is in Yosemite Valley. No wilderness permits are available in the vicinity (except at Yosemite Ski & Snowboard Area in winter); you must backtrack to either Yosemite Valley or Wawona if you develop warm-weather backcountry urges.

A Valley–Glacier Point bus service operates in summer, and a Valley–Yosemite Ski & Snowboard Area service in winter.

Glacier Point

If you drove, the views from 7214ft Glacier Point might make you feel like you cheated – superstar sights present themselves to you without your having made barely any physical effort. A quick mosey up from the parking lot and you'll find the entire eastern Yosemite Valley spread out before you, from Yosemite Falls to Half Dome, as well as the distant peaks that ring Tuolumne Meadows. Half Dome looms practically at eye level, and if you look closely you can spot hikers on its summit.

To the left of Half Dome lies U-shaped, glacially carved Tenaya Canyon, while below you'll see Vernal and Nevada Falls. On the Valley floor, the Merced River snakes through green meadows and groves of trees. Sidle up to the railing, hold on tight and peer 3200ft straight down at Half Dome Village. The aqua rectangle of its swimming pool is clearly visible, as is the Majestic Yosemite Hotel just to the north. Basket Dome and North Dome also rise to the north of the Valley, and Liberty Cap and the Clark Range can be seen to the right of Half Dome.

At the tip of the point is Overhanging Rock, a huge granite slab protruding from the cliff edge like an outstretched tongue, defying gravity and once providing a scenic stage for daredevil extroverts. Through the

Glacier Point & Badger Pass Region

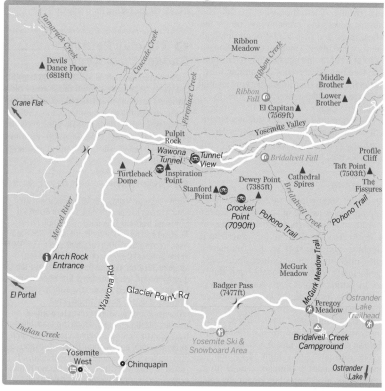

years, many famous photos have been taken of folks performing handstands, high kicks and other wacky stunts on the rock. You'll have to stick to the pictures now though, as the precipice is off-limits.

Almost from the park's inception, Glacier Point has been a popular destination. It used to be that getting up here was a major undertaking. That changed once the Four Mile Trail opened in 1872. While not exactly an easy climb – neither then nor today – the trail did offer a more direct route to the point. James McCauley, an early Yosemite pioneer, financed the formation of the trail, for which he charged a toll; he later took over the reins of the Mountain House hotel, built in 1873 atop Glacier Point. In the 1870s he also conceived the famous Firefall, though the former Curry Village later picked up and heavily promoted the event.

A wagon road to the point was completed in 1882, and the current Glacier Point Rd was built in 1936. As far back as 1929 (and

again in the 1970s), there was talk of building an aerial tramway to ferry tourists from Yosemite Valley to Glacier Point. But since the cables would be an eyesore and the system would disturb fragile ecosystems, plans thankfully were abandoned. The spectacularly situated Glacier Point Hotel stood on the point from 1917 until 1969, when it burned down along with the adjacent McCauley Mountain House.

Washburn Point

Named for the brothers who built the Big Trees Lodge, this viewpoint along Glacier Point Rd is magnificent, though not quite as expansive as Glacier Point. The point faces east towards the Clark Range and lacks sweeping views of Yosemite Valley. Still, a stop here serves as a great warm-up to Glacier Point, less than a mile down the road.

Yosemite Ski & Snowboard Area

The California ski industry essentially got its start in Yosemite Valley, and Badger Pass, now called the **Yosemite Ski & Snowboard Area** (209-372-8430; www.travelyosemite. com; lift ticket adult/child $55/32; 9am-4pm mid-Dec–Mar), was California's first alpine ski resort. After Yosemite's All-Year Hwy (now Hwy 140) was completed in 1926 and the Ahwahnee Hotel (now the Majestic Yosemite Hotel) opened its doors the following year, Yosemite Valley quickly became a popular winter destination.

As the 1929 Winter Olympics approached, the newly formed Curry Company and the Yosemite Winter Club submitted an impassioned bid to host the games. They lost, and instead the events were held at Lake Placid, New York – where, in a freakish irony, no snow fell that winter. (The 2017–18 winter was a bleak one for Yosemite snowfall, at least early in the season, and the ski area never opened.) Bales of hay were used in lieu of snow, while the Sierra saw record snowfalls.

When Wawona Tunnel opened in 1933, skiers began congregating at Badger Pass. In 1935, a new lodge opened on Glacier Point Rd, and a newfangled device called 'the upski' was installed at the pass. The crude lift consisted of nothing more than two counterbalanced sleds, but it worked, and this place became California's first alpine ski resort.

Map: Yosemite area showing Yosemite Falls Overlook (6400ft), Yosemite Point (6936ft), North Dome (7542ft), Upper Yosemite Fall, Yosemite Village, Mirror Lake, Half Dome (8842ft), Four Mile Trail, Half Dome Village, Tenaya Creek, Union Point, Glacier Point (7214ft), Vernal Fall, Nevada Fall, Sentinel Fall, Snack Bar & Gift Shop, Sentinel Dome (8122ft), Washburn Point, Panorama Point (6224ft), Sentinel Dome & Taft Point Trailhead, Illilouette Fall, Panorama Trail, Pothole Meadows, Illilouette Creek, Ostrander Rocks (8094ft), Mono Meadow. Scale: 4 km / 2 miles.

THE FIREFALL

Imagine the ruckus that would ensue today if someone built a bonfire and sent it toppling over Glacier Point. Rangers and fire crews would swarm the scene, and rangers would no doubt press arson charges. So it's hard to believe that this was a Yosemite evening tradition for 88 years, inciting public rapture and no official park condemnation. It sounds horrific to those schooled in the 'leave no trace' wilderness ethic, but countless Valley campers still testify to the beauty and excitement of the Firefall, regarded as a sublime summer moment in the enchantment of a summer's evening. Even the echoing signal call to Glacier Point from the Camp Curry campfire, 'Let the fire fall!' became a spine-tingling element of the tradition.

The Firefall originated around 1872, when a hotel was being built at the top of James McCauley's new 4-mile toll trail to Glacier Point. Perhaps as an advertisement for his enterprise, McCauley pushed his campfire off the cliff, creating a glowing waterfall of sparks that was so appealing that tourists in Yosemite Valley called on McCauley to repeat it. His sons transformed the Firefall into a family business, collecting $1.50 from each person who wanted to see it happen. When they found enough takers, a fire builder went up the trail to build a large fire of fir bark and pushed it off the cliff just after nightfall.

The McCauleys left Yosemite in 1897, but two years later David Curry reintroduced the Firefall as a way to draw business to his newly created Camp Curry. Apart from two brief hiatuses, one in 1913 and the other during WWII, the Firefall continued to hold a place in Yosemite evening activities until the National Park Service (NPS) ended it in 1968, finally declaring the tradition to be incompatible with natural land management.

To read a compilation of Firefall memories, visit http://firefall.info.

In winter, a free shuttle bus runs between the Valley and the Yosemite Ski & Snowboard Area. Also in winter, wilderness permits are available by self-registration at the A-frame building (p130), where the first-aid station and ski patrol are also situated. Rangers usually staff the office from 8am to 5pm.

◉ Tuolumne Meadows

Arriving at Tuolumne Meadows after the drive up from Yosemite Valley is like stepping into another world, even though the two areas are only about 55 miles apart. Instead of being surrounded by waterfalls and sheer granite walls, you emerge in a subalpine wonderland marked by jagged peaks, smooth granite domes, brilliant blue lakes and the meadows' lush grasses and wildflowers. The flowers, which peak in July, are truly a highlight of any visit to Yosemite.

Flowing from the Sierra Crest, the Lyell and Dana Forks of the Tuolumne River – not to mention creeks such as Budd, Unicorn and Delaney – all converge at Tuolumne Meadows (8600ft elevation). At 2.5 miles long, the main flat cradles the Sierra's largest subalpine meadow. The surrounding peaks and domes make Tuolumne a paradise for climbers and hikers, with trails stretching in all directions.

Lying deep in the high country of the Sierra, the Tuolumne Meadows region enjoys a brief but glorious summer and, depending on weather conditions, is only accessible roughly between June and November. Despite the short season, Tuolumne is far quieter than the Valley, although the area around the store, campground and visitor center can get crowded, especially on midsummer weekends. Many hiking trails, such as Dog Lake, are also well traveled, but with a little effort you'll quickly find solitude.

At the Tuolumne Meadows Visitor Center, about a mile west of the campground, rangers answer questions, sell books and hiking maps, and have helpful handouts describing local trails. There are a few good displays that explain common glacial features. Especially handy is the wildflower display, which will help you identify what you see on your hikes.

The Tuolumne Meadows Wilderness Center is the place to go for wilderness permits and trail information. Since Tuolumne's mountains, lakes and trails are such a draw for backpackers, it's often a busy spot. It stocks a small selection of books and maps, and has information on current trail conditions. The center sits on the south side of Tioga Rd just east of Lembert Dome, on the spur road leading to Tuolumne Meadows Lodge.

The Tuolumne Meadows Store stocks groceries and supplies and has a post office.

❶ Orientation

Tuolumne Meadows sits along Tioga Rd (Hwy 120) west of the park's Tioga Pass Entrance.

Temperatures in Tuolumne Meadows and the surrounding high country are 15°F to 20°F cooler than in Yosemite Valley, a benefit for hikers and anyone else who struggles in the heat. At the same time, nights are much chillier up here, so pack warm clothes. And remember, snow can fall here in any month of the year, though typically no later than June and no earlier than September.

Main Meadow

Stretching nearly 3 miles from Pothole Dome in the west to Lembert Dome in the east, Tuolumne's main meadow is a beautiful sight to behold, especially during sunset, when golden light ripples across the green grass and lashes up the sides of distant peaks into the still blue sky. Grab a fishing pole and dip into the gently rolling **Tuolumne River** as the sunlight drifts away, or just find a quiet spot to sit and stare at the landscape as the mood shifts and the colors shimmer.

While the meadow is perfect for quiet contemplation, there's actually a lot of activity going on here. Blanketed in snow for most of the year, it explodes to life in summer, when the wildflowers, taking full advantage of the short growing season, fill the grassy expanse with color. For an explanation of what's happening beneath the meadow's deceptively still surface, check out the interpretive signs that line the dirt road between the Lembert Dome parking lot and Soda Springs.

Soda Springs SPRING

Above the north shore of the Tuolumne River, carbonated mineral water burbles silently out of Soda Springs, a small natural spring that turns its surroundings into a cluster of mineral-crusted, rust-red puddles. People (and animals) used to drink the stuff, though the park service now discourages the practice due to possible surface contamination – no big deal, as it's not exactly an appealing method for quenching your thirst anyway.

The springs are a short, pleasant walk across the flat middle of the meadow. There are two approaches, both about 0.75 miles long. The first starts opposite the Tuolumne Meadows Visitor Center on Tioga Rd. The other begins in the Lembert Dome parking area.

Parsons Memorial Lodge HISTORIC BUILDING

This simple but beautifully rugged cabin was built in 1915 from local granite. It initially served as a Sierra Club meeting room and was named for Edward Taylor Parsons (1861–1914), an adventurer and active Sierra Club member who helped found the club's outings program. Today it opens as a shelter during thunderstorms (there's a huge fireplace inside), as well as for special events, ranger talks and other programs. See the *Yosemite Guide* for the current schedule.

Walk from the Tuolumne Meadows Visitor Center or Lembert Dome parking areas.

Pothole Dome

Pothole Dome marks the west end of Tuolumne Meadows. It's small by Yosemite standards, but the short, 200ft climb to the top offers great views of the meadows and

---

DON'T MISS

SUMMER STARGAZING

On many Friday and Saturday nights in summer, the Glacier Point amphitheater hosts various astronomy clubs, which set up telescopes and let the public take a closer-than-usual look at what's deep in the night sky – from the moon's mottled surface to fuzzy, faraway star clusters and even the Andromeda galaxy. These programs are accompanied by 'Stars Over Yosemite' discussions, during which rangers point out constellations in the sky above Glacier Point. Bring the kids.

On most summer nights, there are also four-hour **stargazing tours** (☏ 209-372-1240, 209-372-4386; www.travelyosemite.com; adult/child 5-12yr $45/30; ⊗ departure 7pm; 🚌) from the Valley to Glacier Point that include an hour-long astronomy program.

Throughout the summer, astronomy walks are also regularly hosted by amateur astronomers in Tuolumne Meadows, Yosemite Valley and Wawona. In Tuolumne you can walk out into the meadow, lie on granite still warm from the afternoon sun and gaze up at the star-blazoned sky.

Check the *Yosemite Guide* for schedules.

Tuolumne Meadows Region

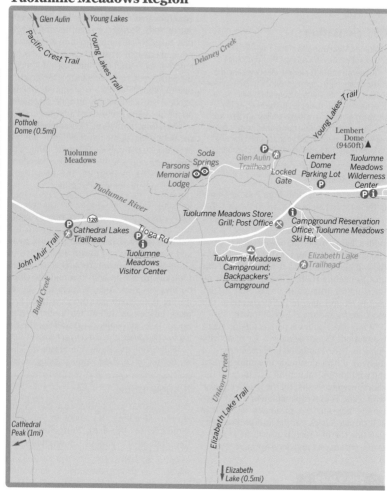

surrounding peaks – especially, of course, at sunset. Park along Tioga Rd, then follow the trail around the dome's west side and up to its modest summit. It's a fairly quick trip and well worth the effort.

Lembert Dome

Prominently marking the eastern end of the main meadow, Lembert Dome towers about 800ft above the Tuolumne River. Its summit, which chalks in at 9450ft above sea level, is easily one of the finest places to watch the sunset in Yosemite. Its steep western face is

a de facto granite playground for everyone from kids (who stick around the gently sloping bottom) to climbers (who rope up and head to the top). Nonclimbers can reach the summit by hiking up the back side. The dome was named for 19th-century shepherd Jean-Baptiste Lembert, who homesteaded in Tuolumne Meadows.

Cathedral Range

Dominating the views to the south of Tuolumne Meadows, the jagged Cathedral Range runs roughly northwest from the Sier-

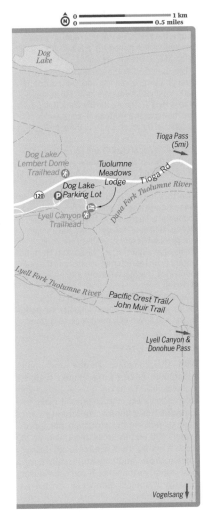

the range, as does the trail up to Young Lakes (p81). The Cathedral Lakes (Tuolumne Meadows) hike is the classic must-do hike into the range itself.

Tioga Pass

Tioga Rd (Hwy 120) climbs steadily toward Tioga Pass, which at 9945ft is the highest auto-route over the Sierra. The short ride by car or free shuttle bus from Tuolumne Meadows takes you across dramatic, wide open spaces – a stretch of stark, windswept countryside near the timberline. You'll notice a temperature drop, and possibly, widespread patches of snow.

Tioga Rd parallels the Dana Fork of the Tuolumne River, then turns north, where it borders the beautiful Dana Meadows all the way to Tioga Pass. To the east you'll see great views of Mt Gibbs (12,764ft) and 13,057ft Mt Dana, the park's second-highest peak after Mt Lyell (13,114ft).

On most maps of California, you'll find a parenthetical remark – 'closed in winter' – printed next to the pass. While true, this statement is also misleading. Tioga Rd is usually closed from the first heavy snowfall in October until May, June or even July! If you're planning a trip through Tioga Pass in spring, you're likely to be out of luck. According to official park policy, the earliest date the road will be plowed is April 15, yet the pass has been open in April only once since 1980 (the average opening date is May 26). It's a complex and hazardous endeavor because of avalanche zones, rockfalls, fallen trees, snow pack depth and even heavy snow during the clearing process. Other mountain roads further north, such as Hwy 108, Hwy 4 and Hwy 88/89, may also be closed due to heavy snow, albeit only temporarily. Call 800-427-7623 for road and weather conditions.

ra Crest, marking the divide between the Tuolumne and Merced Rivers. Its granite pinnacles are immediately striking, in particular Cathedral Peak (10,911ft), visible from numerous spots in the region, including along Tioga Rd. At certain angles, its summit appears to be a near-perfect pinpoint, though in reality it's a craggy, double-pronged affair. Other mountains in the range include Tresidder Peak, Echo Peaks, the Matthes Crest and Unicorn Peak (10,823ft), another standout with a horn-shaped protuberance, just east of Cathedral Peak. Soda Springs offers a particularly good vantage point for viewing

◉ Wawona

Wawona, about 27 miles south of Yosemite Valley, is the park's historical center, home to its first headquarters (supervised by Captain AE Wood on the site of the Wawona Campground) and its first tourist facilities. The newly restored Mariposa Grove of giant sequoias lies just inside the park's South Entrance.

The park's first headquarters was a simple wayside station run by Galen Clark, who homesteaded in Wawona in 1856. A decade later, Clark was appointed state guardian of the Yosemite Grant, which protected Yosemite Valley and the Mariposa Grove. In 1875 he sold his lodge to the Washburn brothers, who built what's known today as the Big Trees Lodge (formerly the Wawona Hotel). The Washburns also renamed the area Wawona – thought to be the local Native American word for 'big trees.'

Completed in 1875, the original Wawona Rd opened the floodgates for tourists curious to see the big trees – as well as wondrous Yosemite Valley to the north. The road was modernized in 1933, following construction of the Wawona Tunnel.

From 1891 to 1906, the current Wawona Campground site was home base for the US cavalry, who were appointed as the first official protectors of the newly formed national park. The cavalry moved its headquarters to Yosemite Valley in 1906. Curiously, considering its significant role in the park's history, Wawona remained private property for decades and wasn't incorporated into the boundaries of Yosemite National Park until 1932. Some parts of the area are still in private hands, including the houses that line Chilnualna Falls Rd.

A blend of Victorian elegance and utilitarian New England charm, the Big Trees Lodge is the commercial hub of the area. The unassuming white wooden building sits behind a large, manicured green lawn and a fountain inhabited by very vocal frogs.

The Wawona Visitor Center (p130) doubles as the area's visitor center and wilderness center. It issues wilderness permits and bear canisters, answers general park questions and sells some maps and books. The station is located inside Hill's Studio, a historic 1886 building (it was the studio of landscape painter Thomas Hill) adjacent to the Big Trees Lodge. Small exhibits in the studio include reproductions of his work. When the office is open for the season, it issues wilderness permits for all areas of the park. During the months it's closed, backcountry-bound visitors can self-register for wilderness permits at the Wawona campground office (☑209-375-9535; Wawona District Circle) for Chilnualna Falls and Alder Creek Falls only. Bear canisters can be rented at the general store when the office is closed.

❶ Orientation

Wawona lies on Hwy 41 (Wawona Rd), 4 miles north of the park's South Entrance, which is about 63 miles north of Fresno. Yosemite Valley is a 27-mile drive north. From the Big Trees Lodge, the YARTS Hwy 41 bus route services Yosemite Valley (round-trip adult/child under 13 years $13/9) a few times daily.

The South Fork of the Merced River passes through Wawona, running northwest out of the park. Most visitor services lie just to its south. Across Hwy 41, there's the Big Trees Golf Course and the expansive Wawona Meadow, which doubled as the local airport in the early 20th century.

At the corner of Hwy 41 and Forest Dr, just north of the hotel, are a general store, post office, ATM and gas station (24 hours with credit card).

North of the river is Chilnualna Falls Rd, which runs east into a development of private homes and rental properties. The horse stables, the Pioneer Yosemite History Center and a small Campground Reservation Office are along Chilnualna Falls Rd, as are the Bassett Memorial Library (with free internet access) and the year-round Pine Tree Market, about a mile northeast of Hwy 41.

Some 6 miles southeast of Wawona stands the Mariposa Grove of giant sequoias, the park's largest and deservedly popular sequoia grove.

Mariposa Grove

With their massive stature and multi-millennium maturity, the chunky high-rise sequoias of Mariposa Grove (⊘8am-8pm summer, hours vary other times) will make you feel rather insignificant. The largest grove of giant sequoias in the park, there are approximately 500 mature trees towering over 250 acres. Walking trails wind through this very popular grove, and you can usually have a more solitary experience if you come during the early evening in summer or anytime outside of summer.

A major restoration project completed in June 2018 added a new trail that follows along the old Washburn stagecoach road of the late 19th century, including accessible boardwalks. The removal of most of the parking lot and grove roads should translate to less traffic congestion and a more natural visitor experience. Exhibits on sequoia ecology from the Mariposa Grove Museum are due to be permanently relocated to the South Entrance hub.

On your right as you enter the lower grove, you may recognize the Fallen Monarch from an iconic 1899 photo of the US 6th Cavalry – and their horses – posed on the tree's length. Its exposed root system

Wawona

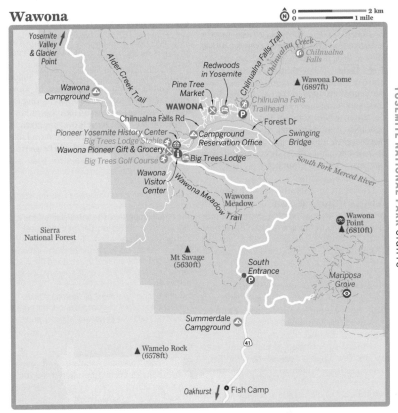

illustrates the sequoias' shallow but diffuse life-support system.

Walk a half-mile up to the 1800-year-old Grizzly Giant, a bloated beast of a tree with branches that are bigger in circumference than most of the pine trees in this forest. The walk-through California Tunnel Tree is close by, and the favored spot for 'I visited the tall forest' photos. Incredibly, this tree continues to survive, even though its heart was hacked out back in 1895.

In the upper grove, the more famous Fallen Wawona Tunnel Tree, however, fell over in a heap in 1969 – its 10ft-high hole gouged from a fire scar in 1881. Other notable specimens include the Telescope Tree and the Clothespin Tree. Three miles from the parking lot, the wide-open overlook at Wawona Point (6810ft) takes in the entire area. It's about a mile round-trip from the Fallen Wawona Tunnel Tree.

Depending on your energy level, you could spend half an hour or a few hours exploring the forest. Between the new shuttle stop and the Wawona Tunnel Tree in the upper grove, the elevation gain is about 1000ft, but the trail is gentle.

In summer, on weekends and during holidays, parking at the grove is limited to visitors with accessible placards; others must take the free shuttle bus from the South Entrance, unless they arrive outside of the to-be-determined shuttle hours. It takes at least an hour to drive from Yosemite Valley to the grove shuttle at the South Entrance. Snowfall closes the Mariposa Grove Rd to cars from about November to April, but you can always hike, ski or snowshoe in (2 miles, 500ft of elevation gain) and experience it in its quiet hibernation.

Pioneer Yosemite History Center HISTORIC BUILDING
(☎ 209-372-0200; www.nps.gov/yose/planyour visit/upload/pyhc.pdf; Wawona; rides adult/child $5/4; ⏱ 24hr, rides 10am-2pm Wed-Sun Jun-Sep; P ♿) FREE Off Wawona Rd, about 6 miles north of Mariposa Grove, you can take in the manicured grounds of the elegant Big Trees Lodge and cross a covered bridge to this rustic center, where some of the park's oldest buildings were relocated. It also features stagecoaches that brought early tourists to Yosemite, and offers short horse-drawn stagecoach rides in summer.

⊙ Along Tioga Road

The only road that bisects the park is Tioga Rd, a 56-mile scenic highway that runs between Crane Flat in the west (starting from Crane Flat junction) and Hwy 395 at Lee Vining, about 12 miles east of Tioga Pass, the park's easternmost gate. Along the way it traverses a superb High Sierra landscape. Be prepared to pull over regularly to gawk at sights such as glorious Tenaya Lake, mighty Clouds Rest and Half Dome from Olmsted Point.

Along Tioga Road

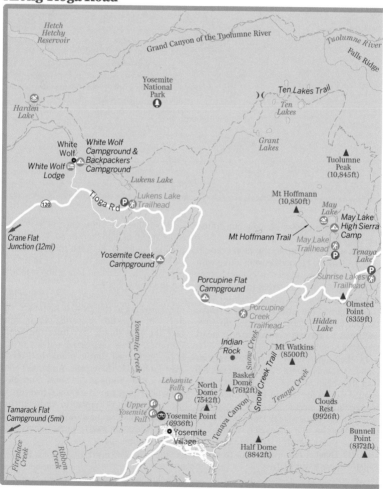

Initially called the Great Sierra Wagon Rd, the road was built by the Great Sierra Consolidated Silver Company in 1882–83 to supply a mine at Bennettville near Tioga Pass. Ironically, no significant silver was ever found, and the mine closed soon after the road was completed. Tioga Rd was realigned and modernized in 1961. Only a few sections of the original roadbed remain, including the rough, 4.5-mile stretch that leads to Yosemite Creek Campground. Head down this narrow, tortuous road for a glimpse of how much more treacherous park roads used to be – and not even that long ago. You'll re-turn to Tioga Rd with new-found respect for this engineering marvel.

As Tioga Rd heads east toward Tuolumne Meadows, it passes four campgrounds. Some 15 miles northeast of Crane Flat is White Wolf (p122), with a small lodge with tent cabins and a store that sells mostly snacks and drinks. White Wolf sits on a short spur road a mile north of Tioga Rd.

During summer, a Yosemite Valley–Tuolumne Meadows bus run by the park concessionaire is an excellent transportation option for one-way hikes that depart from Tioga Rd.

Olmsted Point   VIEWPOINT

This 'honey, hit the brakes!' viewpoint, mid-way between the May Lake turnoff and Tenaya Lake, is a lunar landscape of glaciated granite with a stunning view down Tenaya Canyon to the back side of Half Dome. Looming over the canyon's eastern side is 9926ft Clouds Rest, a massive mountain comprising the largest exposed chunk of granite in Yosemite. (As its name implies, clouds often settle atop the peak.) Rising 4500ft above Tenaya Creek, it makes for a strenuous, but rewarding day hike: it's a 14-mile out-and-back with 1775ft of elevation gain.

Not surprisingly, the viewpoint and its parking lot are swamped with visitors. You'll have to clamber down some rocks to grab a tiny bit of solitude. To experience an even better view, and without the company of other awestruck visitors, stroll a quarter-mile down to the overlook, where you can get past the tree cover and see even deeper into the canyon. Because of extreme avalanche hazards, Olmsted Point is the last area of Hwy 120 to be plowed before the road opens.

The point was named for Frederick Law Olmsted (1822–1903), who was appointed chairman of the first Board of Commissioners to manage the newly established Yosemite Grant in 1864. Olmsted also helped design Central Park in New York City and did some landscaping for the University of California and Stanford University.

Tenaya Lake   LAKE

Just east of Olmsted Point, the shiny blue surface of Tenaya Lake (8150ft) looks absolutely stunning framed by thick stands of pine and a series of smooth granite cliffs and domes. Dominating its north side is Polly Dome (9806ft). The face nearest the lake is known as Stately Pleasure Dome, a popular spot with climbers – you may see them working

Waterwheel Falls
Wildcat Point (9455ft)
LeConte Falls
California Falls
Pacific Crest Trail
Conness Creek
Glen Aulin High Sierra Camp
Young Lakes Trail
Tuolumne Falls
McGee Lake
Pacific Crest Trail
Cathedral Lakes Trailhead
Fairview Dome (9731ft)
John Muir Trail
Tioga Pass; Lee Vining (Hwy 395)
Polly Dome (9806ft)
120
Cathedral Peak (10,911ft)
Unicorn Peak (10,823ft)
Cathedral Lakes
Budd Lake
Tenaya Peak (10,266ft)
Tenaya Lake Beach
Tressider Peak (10,600ft)
Echo Peaks
Rafferty Peak (11,096ft)
Mildred Lake
Matthes Lake
Sunrise Lakes
Sunrise Mountain (9974ft)
Sunrise High Sierra Camp
John Muir Trail
Vogelsang Trail
Echo Valley
Merced Lake

0   5 km
0   2.5 miles

their way up from the road. Sloping up from the lake's south shore are Tenaya Peak (10,266ft) and Tresidder Peak (10,600ft).

The lake takes its name from Chief Tenaya, the Ahwahneechee chief who aided white soldiers, only to be driven from the land by white militias in the early 1850s. Tenaya allegedly protested the use of his name, pointing out that the lake already had a name – Pywiack ('Lake of Shining Rocks'), for the polished granite that surrounds it.

◎ Big Oak Flat Road

If arriving on Hwy 120 and entering the park at the Big Oak Flat entrance, many just pass through this section, but the campgrounds at Hodgdon Meadow and Crane Flat keep the area humming with people.

Big Oak Flat Rd was the second route into the park, completed in 1874, just a month after Coulterville Rd. Both were toll roads. Today, Big Oak Flat Rd follows a modified route into the Valley, though a portion of the old road remains open to cyclists and hikers headed for Tuolumne Grove. In winter the road is popular with cross-country skiers.

Going east on Big Oak Flat Rd (Hwy 120) past the Big Oak Flat Entrance, you'll find the Big Oak Flat Information Station (p130). It serves as a mini visitor center with a good variety of books, maps and postcards for sale. The staff can answer questions and there is a courtesy phone inside to check available concessionaire-run lodging inside the park. In the same office is the wilderness permit desk, which issues permits and doles out bear boxes ($5 per week).

At Crane Flat junction, Crane Flat Gas Station & More (p128) sells firewood, ice, beer, and a smattering of groceries and last-minute camping supplies. Perhaps most importantly, it also has decent fresh coffee. The gas station operates 24 hours year-round with a credit card, and there's a payphone outside.

At Crane Flat, throngs of sandhill cranes once rested here as they crisscrossed the Sierra Nevada, and the birds gave the meadow (and surrounding area) its name. About 4 miles east of the entrance is the road to the Merced Grove, a seldom-visited giant sequoia grove. At 6000ft, a springtime Valley rainstorm often translates to snow flurries here. In winter, the area is a hub for cross-country skiing and snow play. Beautiful views, and giant sequoias in Tuolumne and Merced Groves, await after many a bend in the road. Heavy snowfall keeps it closed from about November until May.

Big Oak Flat Road & Crane Flat

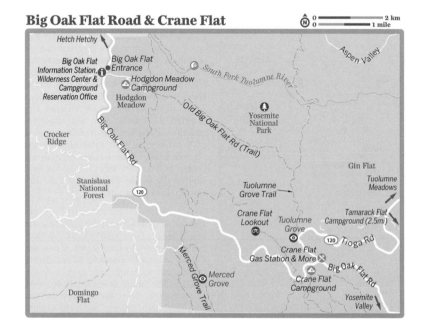

◉ Hetch Hetchy

In the park's northwestern corner, Hetch Hetchy, which is Miwok for 'place of tall grass,' gets the least amount of traffic yet sports waterfalls (Tueeulala and Wapama are easily accessible; the latter flows year-round) and granite cliffs that rival its famous counterparts in Yosemite Valley. The main difference is that Hetch Hetchy Valley is now filled with water.

The 8-mile-long reservoir, its placid surface reflecting clouds and cliffs, stretches behind O'Shaughnessy Dam, site of a parking lot and trailheads. It's a lovely, quiet spot and well worth the 40-mile drive from Yosemite Valley, especially if you're tired of the avalanche of humanity rolling through the area. The 2013 Rim Fire charred a huge section of the forest in this region, and while its impact is immediately apparent, the area's beauty has not been significantly diminished.

From the park's Big Oak Flat Entrance, drive a mile or two west on Hwy 120 and look for the signed turnoff to Hetch Hetchy along Evergreen Rd; turn right (north), drive 8 miles to Mather and turn right (east) onto Hetch Hetchy Rd. The **Hetch Hetchy Entrance Station** (☑209-379-1922; ⊙7am-9pm summer, 8am-7pm winter) is just a mile beyond the junction; from here it's about a 9-mile twisty descent to the parking lot beside O'Shaughnessy Dam.

There are bathrooms but no other visitor services at Hetch Hetchy. Its low elevation makes Hetch Hetchy an especially suitable hiking destination in spring and fall. In summer, it can be very hot and dry.

The road is open only during daylight hours. The gate is locked at night, and the road may close in winter due to heavy snows (carry chains). Vehicles over 25ft are not permitted on the narrow, winding road.

Exercise caution when crossing the falls, especially on the potentially dangerous

Hetch Hetchy Region

boardwalk over Wapama. Keep an eye out for rattlesnakes and the occasional bear, especially in summer.

Hetch Hetchy Valley was filled with water only after a long political and environmental battle that lasted a dozen years during the early 20th century. Despite the best efforts of John Muir, who led the fight against it, the US Congress approved the 1913 Raker Act, which allowed the city of San Francisco to construct O'Shaughnessy Dam in the Hetch Hetchy Valley. This blocked the Tuolumne River and created Hetch Hetchy Reservoir. Muir's spirit was crushed, and he died a year later, supposedly of a broken heart.

Today the reservoir and dam supply water and hydroelectric power to much of the Bay Area, including Silicon Valley. When you turn on a tap in San Francisco, out pours Tuolumne River water from the Hetch Hetchy Reservoir. Some politicians and environmentalists (particularly the Sierra Club) still argue for pulling the cork and draining the valley. And who knows? Stranger things have happened in California.

There's one good thing you can say about the dam: by filling in the valley, it has prevented the overdevelopment that plagues Yosemite Valley. Hetch Hetchy remains a lovely, quiet spot – good for a quick day trip or as a jumping-off point for a serious backcountry experience.

🛏 SLEEPING

One of the biggest questions facing Yosemite visitors is where to spend the night. More than four million people visit Yosemite each year, many as day visitors but many also vying for one of the approximately 1500 campsites or 1300 rooms and tent cabins available in the park. During the height of summer, visitors fill open reservations faster than blue jays descend on a picnic. Newcomers with visions of sleeping soundly under the stars often find that campsites and rooms are full, having been reserved months in advance.

Most lodges and campgrounds both inside and outside the park open and close at slightly different times each year, depending on weather. Always check before you go. If you're stuck without a place to sleep inside the park, look outside its borders.

Those hoping to get in touch with nature may find they're more in touch with their neighbors, who are often clanging pans, slurping beer by the fire or snoring in their tents just 10ft or 20ft away. It gets especially crowded in Yosemite Valley. Overnighters looking for a quieter, more rugged experience are better off in spots like Bridalveil Creek, Yosemite Creek and Porcupine Flat.

Campgrounds in Yosemite range from primitive tent-only sites to developed ones that can accommodate large RVs. Most have flush toilets and potable water. The exceptions are the park's three primitive sites (Tamarack Flat, Yosemite Creek and Porcupine Flat) and the Yosemite Valley backpackers' campground, which have vault (pit) toilets and require you to bring your own water or a means of purifying water from nearby streams. None of the campgrounds have showers.

Campground elevations are important to consider. The campgrounds along Tioga Rd and in Tuolumne Meadows, some of which sit above 8000ft, may boast warm weather during the day, but come nightfall you'll be wishing you'd packed that wool sweater.

Yosemite has four campgrounds open all year: Upper Pines, Camp 4, Wawona and Hodgdon Meadow. The rest are open seasonally.

🛏 Yosemite Valley

Camping

While Yosemite Valley campgrounds are convenient to many of the park's major sights and activities, they're also very crowded, often noisy and definitely lacking in privacy. Don't camp here expecting to get away from it all – for solitude, you're better off in less visited areas of the park.

Yosemite Valley's three Pines campgrounds (North Pines, Upper Pines and Lower Pines) are all located east of Yosemite Village at the far end of the Valley and are open to both RVs and tent campers.

Backpackers' Campground   CAMPGROUND **$**
(Map p124; tent sites per person $6; ☺ Apr–late Oct) The 20 quiet, wooded sites at Yosemite Valley's campground are open only to backpackers holding valid wilderness permits (and only for a night before and after a wilderness trip). It's a walk-in, self-registration campground, reached via a bridge over Tenaya Creek from the western end of North

Pines Campground. It has vault toilets but no potable water.

Camp 4
CAMPGROUND $

(Map p124; www.nps.gov/yose; shared tent sites per person $6; ☺year-round) Walk-in campground at 4000ft, entwined in climbing history and popular with climbers who tend to be long-term occupants; sites are shared.

Lower Pines Campground
CAMPGROUND $

(Map p124; www.nps.gov/yose; tent & RV sites $26; ☺Apr-Oct; ⚋) Jam-packed and noisy, with 60 sites at 4000ft, some along the Merced River; reservations required.

Upper Pines Campground
CAMPGROUND $

(Map p124; www.nps.gov/yose; tent & RV sites $26; ☺year-round; ⚋) Busy, busy, busy – and big (238 sites, 4000ft); reservations required mid-March through November. Sites are fairly small and close to one another. However you can find relative privacy the further back you go; that is, towards the Happy Isles Art & Nature Center.

North Pines Campground
CAMPGROUND $

(Map p124; tent & RV sites $26; ☺Apr-Oct; ⚋) Within walking distance of some of the valley's most popular trailheads, North Pines (4000ft) has 81 sites near Mirror Lake, with some spots along the Merced River; reservations required. Can feel crowded and cramped with RVs.

Lodging

Yosemite Valley offers a fair range of accommodations, from simple tent cabins to comfortable motel units to luxurious lodg-

ings. Tent cabins at Half Dome Village and Housekeeping Camp are great for families who wish to avoid both exorbitant hotel costs and the labor of setting up camp.

Housekeeping Camp
CABIN $$

(Map p124; www.travelyosemite.com; Southside Dr; q $119; ☺Apr-Oct) This cluster of 266 cabins, each walled by concrete on three sides and lidded by a canvas roof, is crammed and noisy, but the setting along the Merced River has its merits. Each unit sleeps six and has electricity, light, a table and chairs, and a covered patio with picnic tables. Laundry (8am to 10pm) and shower facilities are open to guests and nonguests.

Bring your own sleeping bag, or linens can be rented; for the latter, be sure to have extra layers of clothes for chilly nights.

Half Dome Village
CABIN $$

(Map p124; ☐front desk 209-372-8333, reservations 888-413-8869; www.travelyosemite.com; tent cabins from $143, r from $260, cabins with/without bath from $225/170; ☺daily mid-Mar–late Nov, Sat & Sun early Jan–mid-Mar; Ⓟ☻☎⚋) Founded in 1899 as summertime Camp Curry, Half Dome Village has hundreds of units squished together beneath towering evergreens. The canvas cabins (heated or unheated) are basically glorified tents, so for more comfort, quiet and privacy, get one of the cozy wood cabins, which have vintage posters. There are 18 motel-style rooms in Stoneman House, including a loft suite that sleeps six.

Cabin 819, with its fireplace, sofa bed and king-sized bed, is probably the most luxurious of the bunch. The village is off Southside Dr.

LODGING RESERVATIONS IN YOSEMITE

All noncamping reservations within the park are handled by **Aramark/Yosemite Hospitality** (☐888-413-8869; www.travelyosemite.com) and can be made up to 366 days in advance; reservations are critical from May to early September. Rates – and demand – drop from October to April. If you're flexible, there's often some space available on short notice, especially midweek. That said, it's important to remember that rooms rarely become available midsummer. You can go on the website and easily view everything that's available.

The only accommodations outside of that system are the Ostrander Ski Hut and the homes and cabins in Foresta (a private vacation settlement south of Big Oak Flat Rd), Yosemite West and the Redwoods in Yosemite.

If you roll into the park without a reservation, the Yosemite Valley Visitor Center and all the lodging front desks have courtesy phones so you can inquire about room availability throughout the park.

Other park visitors overnight in nearby gateway towns like Fish Camp, Midpines, El Portal, Mariposa and Groveland; however, commute times into the park can be long.

★ **Majestic Yosemite Hotel** HISTORIC HOTEL $$$

(Map p124; ☑ reservations 888-413-8869; www.travel
yosemite.com; 1 Ahwahnee Dr; r/ste from $480/600;
🅿 ⊜ @ 🛜 🌊) The crème de la crème of Yo-
semite's lodging, this sumptuous historic
property (formerly called the Ahwahnee)
dazzles with soaring ceilings and atmospheric
lounges featuring mammoth stone fireplaces.
Classic rooms have inspiring views of Glacier
Point and partial vistas of Half Dome. Cottag-
es are scattered on the immaculately trimmed
lawn next to the hotel. For high season and
holidays, book a year in advance.

Ask for one of the over 90 rooms reno-
vated in 2017–18 with new carpets, curtains
and bathroom fixtures; keep in mind some
rooms have more natural light than others.
Suite 332 has a fireplace, a chandelier and
incredible panoramic views.

The Majestic is the gold standard for up-
scale lodges, but even if you're not staying
here, you can still soak up the ambience
during afternoon tea, a drink in the bar or
a gourmet meal.

Worth noting is that the hotel is a dead
zone as far as cell-phone reception goes.

Yosemite Valley Lodge MOTEL $$$

(Map p124; ☑ reservations 888-413-8869; www.
travelyosemite.com; 9006 Yosemite Lodge Dr; r
from $260; 🅿 ⊜ @ 🛜 🌊) 🏊 A short walk from
Yosemite Falls, this low-slung complex contains a wide range of eateries (some newly
renovated), a lively bar, a big pool and other
amenities. The rooms, spread out over 15
buildings, feels like a cross between a motel
and a lodge, with rustic wooden furniture
and nature photography. Rooms have cable
TV, fridge and coffeemaker, and small patios
or balcony panoramas.

🛏 Glacier Point & Badger Pass

Camping

Bridalveil Creek Campground CAMPGROUND $
(www.nps.gov/yose; tent & RV sites $18;
⊙ Jul–early Sep; 🐾) Quieter than the Yosemite Valley campgrounds, with 110 sites at
7200ft.

Lodging

Scenic Wonders ACCOMMODATION SERVICES $$$
(☑ 888-967-3648; www.scenicwonders.com; con-
dos/cabins from $210/265) This management
company rents out dozens of houses, cabins
and studios spread around Yosemite West,
Wawona and the Oakhurst area. There's
some wi-fi availability, but in this woodsy
location it's not guaranteed.

Yosemite West High Sierra B&B B&B $$$
(☑ 209-372-4808; www.yosemitehighsierra.com;
7460 Henness Ridge Rd; r $280-340, apt $360-
520; 🛜) Conveniently located in the park
but away from the Yosemite Valley crowds,
this five-room B&B also has an apartment
that sleeps up to five. The owners have
been exploring Yosemite for over 35 years,
so they have a wealth of knowledge to
share, and guests swoon over the sunsets
from the deck. Minimum stay of two to
three nights.

B&B rooms sleep up to three. Rates are
based on double occupancy.

SHOWERING IN & AROUND YOSEMITE

Yosemite campers have one thing in common: they all need a wash. No campgrounds in
the park have showers. Should you feel the need to remove that four-day layer of grime
or wash your hair, head to the public showers at Half Dome Village (p117), it's located
between the dining and dining pavilion towards the back of the development's main building, or Housekeeping Camp (p117). Both places have hot showers and charge $5 for
nonguests (open 24 hours, but closed for cleaning from 10am to 11am and 10:30pm to
midnight). Showers at the Tuolumne Meadows Lodge are only open to guests. No public
shower facilities exist at Wawona.

Other handy pay showers outside the park:

Mono Vista RV Park (p143) The closest pay showers for Tuolumne Meadows campers;
located in Lee Vining.

Indian Flat RV Park (☑ 209-379-2339; www.indianflatrvpark.com; 9988 Hwy 140)

HOW TO SCORE A CAMPSITE

Competition for sites at one of the park's 13 campgrounds is fierce from May to September, when arriving without a reservation (seven take reservations) and hoping for the best is tantamount to getting someone to lug your Barcalounger up Half Dome. Even first-come, first-served campgrounds tend to fill by noon, especially on weekends and around holidays.

All campgrounds have flush toilets, except for Tamarack Flat, Yosemite Creek and Porcupine Flat, which have vault toilets and no potable water. Those at higher elevations get chilly at night, even in summer, so pack accordingly. The Yosemite Mountaineering School (p91) rents camping gear.

If you hold a wilderness permit, you may spend the nights before and after your trip in the backpacker campgrounds at Tuolumne Meadows, Hetch Hetchy, White Wolf and behind North Pines in Yosemite Valley. The cost is $5 per person, per night, and reservations aren't necessary.

Opening dates for seasonal campgrounds vary according to the weather.

Reservations

Reservations for the seven campgrounds (this includes all car campgrounds) within the park that aren't first-come, first-served are handled by Recreation.gov (877-444-6777). Campsites can be reserved up to five months in advance. Reservations become available from 7am on the 15th of every month in one-month blocks, and often sell out within minutes.

If you still have questions regarding the whole process or simply wish to speak with a human being in Yosemite, call the Yosemite Valley Campground Reservation Office and leave a message (209-372-8502); they'll return your call. Also, check the website of Yosemite National Park (www.nps.gov/yose/planyourvisit/camping.htm).

If you already have a reservation, proceed directly to the campground gate to check in. If you're going to be more than 24 hours late, call the campground office; otherwise you may lose your reservation. At check-in, the person listed on the reservation is required to be present and show identification (at least by the following day if they arrive late), and it is no longer possible to change the name on a camping reservation without canceling it.

First Come First Served

Without a booking, your only chance is to hightail it to an open first-come, first-served campground or proceed to one of four campground reservation offices in Yosemite Valley, Wawona, Big Oak Flat and Tuolumne Meadows (the latter three are only open seasonally). Try to get there before they open at 8am (the Yosemite Valley office may open at 7:30am in summer), put your name on a waiting list and then hope for a cancellation or early departure. Return when the ranger tells you to (usually 3pm) and if you hear your name, consider yourself very lucky indeed.

If you want to stay in Yosemite Valley, you have two options, though in summer you'll need to be there before opening time for either. Option one is the first-come, first-served, walk-in campground at Camp 4. A lawn chair line starts forming by 6:30am for summer weekends, and the benefit of getting a site here is that you can stay for up to seven nights.

Option two is the Yosemite Valley Campground Reservation Office in the day-use parking lot near Camp Curry. It rarely has multiple-night cancellations, but it has more potential sites available than Camp 4.

Outside the Valley, the first-come, first-served campgrounds are Bridalveil Creek, Tamarack Flat, White Wolf, Yosemite Creek, Porcupine Flat and half the sites at Tuolumne Meadows. Or you can stop by one of the other reservation offices:

Wawona (☏ 209-375-9535; ☺ 8am-5pm late May–early Oct) On Chilnualna Falls Rd.

Big Oak Flat (p121) Next to the Big Oak Information Station; no waiting list so be here when it opens to scoop up cancellations.

Tuolumne Meadows (p96) Near the campground entrance.

YOSEMITE NATIONAL PARK CAMPGROUNDS

CAMPGROUND	LOCATION	DESCRIPTION	NO OF SITES	ELEVATION
Hodgdon Meadow (p122)	Big Oak Flat Rd	Close to park entrance; utilitarian, can be crowded & noisy; easy drive to Yosemite Valley	105	4872ft
Crane Flat (p121)	Crane Flat	Large family campground across five loops; varied sites; easy drive to Yosemite Valley	166	6192ft
Bridalveil Creek (p118)	Glacier Point Rd	Near Glacier Point; some attractive sites; removed from Valley crowds	110	7200ft
Porcupine Flat (p122)	Tioga Rd	Primitive, close to road but relatively quiet; RV access front half only	52	8100ft
Tamarack Flat (p122)	Tioga Rd	Quiet, secluded, primitive; accessed via rough 3-mile road; tent only	52	6315ft
White Wolf (p122)	Tioga Rd	Only nonprimitive campground in area; walking distance to store & restaurant	74	8000ft
Yosemite Creek (p122)	Tioga Rd	Park's most secluded, quiet, primitive campground; accessed via rough 4.5-mile road; tent only	75	7659ft
Tuolumne Meadows (p123)	Tuolumne Meadows	Park's biggest campground, many sites well dispersed over large, forested area	304	8600ft
Wawona (p123)	Wawona	Located along river; nicer sites in back section (open summer only); short drive to store	93	4000ft
Camp 4 (p117)	Yosemite Valley	Walk-in campground, popular with climbers; fee is per person; campers share sites; tent only	35	4000ft
Lower Pines (p117)	Yosemite Valley	Smaller Valley campground; minimum privacy	60	4000ft
North Pines (p117)	Yosemite Valley	Smaller Valley campground; pleasant sites, slightly removed from development; adjacent to stables	81	4000ft
Upper Pines (p117)	Yosemite Valley	Largest Valley campground, expect little privacy, especially in summer; close to Happy Isles	238	4000ft

Drinking Water	Flush Toilets	Ranger Station Nearby	Wheelchair Accessible	Dogs Allowed (On Leash)

All of the above campgrounds have bear-proof boxes, parking, picnic tables, fire pits and trash cans.

🛏 Big Oak Flat Road & Tioga Road

Camping

If you're in the mood for some solitude and crisper evening air, you'll find a number of options along Tioga Rd (Hwy 120) as it heads east from Crane Flat to Tuolumne Meadows. When it's been a light snow season, early birds may get the place all to themselves. The four campgrounds along Tioga Rd operate on a first-come, first-served basis, and two of them are the most rugged, quiet and beautiful in the park. White Wolf offers flush toilets and running water, while the other three are primitive, with only vault

OPEN	RESERVATION REQUIRED?	DAY FEE	FACILITIES
year-round	mid-Apr–mid-Oct	$18-26	
Jun–mid-Oct	yes	$26	
Jul-early Sep	no	$14	
Jul-Sep	no	$12	
late Jun-Sep	no	$12	
Jul-early Sep	no	$18	
Jul-early Sep	no	$12	
Jul-Sep	half reserved	$26	
year-round	Apr-Sep	$18-26	
year-round	no	$6 per person	
Apr-Oct	yes	$26	
Apr-Sep	yes	$26	
year-round	mid-Mar–Nov	$26	

 Grocery Store Nearby   Restaurant Nearby   Payphone RV Dump Station

toilets and no water tap, so be sure to bring your own water or be prepared to purify it from adjacent streams.

Next door to the Big Oak Flat Information Station, the staff at the small Campground Reservation Office (209-379-2123; 8am-5pm mid-Apr–mid-Oct) offer advice on camping options and post information on site availability at the first-come, first-served campgrounds at Tamarack, Yosemite Creek, Porcupine Flat and White Wolf, though they don't assign sites. Come in at 8am to see if there are any cancellations at Hodgdon Meadow or Crane Flat campgrounds.

Crane Flat Campground CAMPGROUND $
(www.nps.gov/yose; Big Oak Flat Rd; tent & RV sites $26; Jul-mid-Oct;) Large family campground at 6192ft, with 166 sites; reservations

required. The Clark Range overlook hike, 4 miles out and back, begins from here.

Yosemite Creek Campground
CAMPGROUND $

(www.nps.gov/yose; tent sites $12; ☺ Jul-early Sep; ✷) The most secluded and quiet campground (7700ft) in the park is reached via a rough 4.5-mile road. There are 75 first-come, first-served primitive sites (no potable water).

Tamarack Flat Campground
CAMPGROUND $

(Old Big Oak Flat Rd; tent sites $12; ☺ late Jun-Sep; ✷) Quiet and primitive (pit toilets only) at 6315ft; the 52 tent sites are a rough 3-mile drive off Tioga Rd. Despite its relatively secluded location, you'll need to show up early to snag a spot, especially on weekends. Bring plenty of water.

White Wolf Campground
CAMPGROUND $

(www.nps.gov/yose; tent & RV sites $18; ☺ Jul-early Sep; ✷) Attractive setting at 8000ft, but the 74 sites are fairly boxed in. Trailheads for Harden and Lukens Lake hikes are nearby.

Porcupine Flat Campground
CAMPGROUND $

(www.nps.gov/yose; tent & RV sites $12; ☺ Jul-mid-Oct; ✷) Primitive 52-site area at 8100ft; some sites near the road.

CAMPFIRES
....

Everyone loves a campfire, but take note of a few rules. Fires in Yosemite campgrounds are allowed only within established fire rings or barbecue pits. Wood and kindling gathering is illegal in the Valley, so you'll have to buy firewood. To improve air quality, from May through September campfires in the Valley are allowed only between 5pm and 10pm. Those staying in campgrounds outside the Valley are allowed to gather wood, but it must be downed (on the ground) and dead. It's often easier (and always more environmentally sound) to simply buy a bundle, preferably from within a 50-mile radius to thwart invasive pests.

After having a campfire, make sure it's completely out. Stir the fire and coals with water a half-hour before going to bed or leaving the site, then hold your hand close to check for any lingering hot spots.

Hodgdon Meadow Campground
CAMPGROUND $

(Tuolumne Grove Rd; tent & RV sites $18-26; ☺ year-round; ✷) Utilitarian and crowded 105-site campground at 4900ft; reservations required mid-April to mid-October.

Lodging

★ Rush Creek Lodge
LODGE $$$

(☏ 209-379-2373; www.rushcreeklodge.com; 34001 Hwy 120; r & 2-bedroom villas $345-545; ✳ @ ☇ ✷) ✎ Luxurious country chic sums up this fabulous family-friendly resort surrounded by the Stanislaus National Forest and situated a half-mile from Yosemite's Big Oak Flat Entrance. Most rooms have a deck with mountain views. Villas and lodge rooms feature colorful sliding barn doors, industrial-style luggage racks and internet-connected radios. The large pool and giant hot tubs are the property's social hub.

Groups of six can get good value from the hillside villas with two king beds (or one king and two singles) and a sofa sleeper (especially good deals at off-peak times). Most of the buildings are made from recycled blue pine from the 2013 Rim Fire. Maples and aspens are being planted in a many-years-long effort to replenish the tree cover and a nature trail is being built in partnership with the forest service.

A recreation concierge is on hand to help visitors sort through what to see and do. There are free daily family-friendly activities, including s'mores, afternoon talks and scheduled hikes with guides, plus an elaborately designed indoor playground, bocce court, bike paths, mini-ziplines and a giant slide for kids. The large restaurant, an updated version of the classic summer-camp dining hall, offers an airy space, hearty breakfasts, and dishes like king salmon and New York strip steak for dinner. The tavern bar and lounge serves creative Californian cuisine and there are regular poolside barbecues in summer. For a small resort, the grocery–snack bar–gift shop is well curated and stocked and good for a meal on the go. In-room massage services are offered.

Nearby in Yosemite are the Tuolumne and Merced groves of giant sequoias, as well as Hetch Hetchy Reservoir.

White Wolf Lodge
CABIN $$

(www.travelyosemite.com/lodging/white-wolf-lodge; White Wolf Rd; tent cabins without bath $140, cabins $170; ☺ Jun-early Sep) This complex enjoys its own little world a mile up a spur road, away from the hubbub and traffic of Hwy 120 and Yosemite Valley. There are 24 spartan four-bedded tent cabins without electricity and four very-in-demand hard-walled cabins that feel like rustic motel rooms. The generator cuts out at 11pm, so you'll need a flashlight until early morning.

There's also a dining room with somewhat pricey fare and a tiny counter service store.

🛏 Tuolumne Meadows

Camping

Tuolumne Meadows Campground   CAMPGROUND $
(www.nps.gov/yose; Tioga Rd; tent & RV sites $26; ☺ Jul-Sep; 🐾) Biggest campground in the park (8600ft), with 304 fairly well-spaced sites; half of these can be reserved.

Lodging

Tuolumne Meadows Lodge   CABIN $$
(☑ reservations 888-413-8869; www.travelyosem ite.com; tent cabins $145; ☺ mid-Jun–mid-Sep) Set amid the magnificent high country, about 60 miles from Yosemite Valley off Tioga Rd, this option attracts hikers to its 69 canvas tent cabins with two or four beds each, a wood-burning stove and candles (no electricity); showers available. Breakfast and dinner are offered (surcharge applies; dinner reservations required). A fork of the Tuolumne River runs through the property.

🛏 Wawona

Camping

Wawona Campground   CAMPGROUND $
(www.nps.gov/yose; Wawona; tent & RV sites $26; ☺ year-round; 🐾) Idyllic riverside setting at 4000ft with 93 well-spaced sites; reservations required May to September.

Lodging

Big Trees Lodge   HISTORIC HOTEL $$
(☑ reservations 888-413-8869; www.travelyosem ite.com; 8308 Wawona Rd; r with/without bath from $220/150; ☺ mid-Mar–late Nov & mid-Dec–early Jan; 🅿 ♿ 🛜 🏊) This National Historic Landmark, dating from 1879, is a collection of six graceful, whitewashed New England-style buildings flanked by wide porches. The 104 rooms – with no phone or TV – have Victorian-style furniture and other period items, and about half the rooms share bathrooms, with nice robes provided for the walk there. Wi-fi is available in the annex building only.

The grounds are lovely and fairly idyllic on sunny spring days, with a spacious lawn dotted with Adirondack chairs.

Redwoods in Yosemite   ACCOMMODATION SERVICES $$$
(☑ 209-375-6666, 877-753-8566; www.redwoods inyosemite.com; 8038 Chilnualna Falls Rd; per night $243-1480; 🛜 🏊) This private enterprise rents more than 130 fully furnished accommodations of various sizes and levels of comfort, from rustic log cabins to spacious six-bedroom vacation homes (hot tub, anyone?). The office (with free coffee and tantalizing fresh popcorn) is 2 miles east of Hwy 41 on Chilnualna Falls Rd; look for the junction just north of the Pioneer Gift & Grocery.

There's a three-night minimum stay in summer and during holidays; two nights otherwise.

🛏 Hetch Hetchy

Camping

The only place to stay in this area is the **backpackers' campground** (tent sites per person $6; ☺ year-round), which is one of the

---

WORTH A TRIP

HIGH SIERRA CAMPS

In the backcountry near Tuolumne Meadows, the exceptionally popular High Sierra camps provide shelter and sustenance to hikers who'd rather not carry food or a tent. The camps – called Vogelsang, Merced Lake, Sunrise, May Lake and Glen Aulin – are set 6 miles to 10 miles apart along a loop trail. They consist of dormitory-style canvas tent cabins, plus showers (at May Lake, Sunrise and Merced Lake – subject to water availability) and a central dining tent. Rates include breakfast and dinner. Organized hiking/saddle trips led by ranger naturalists also available (from $670/1040).

Yosemite Village & Around

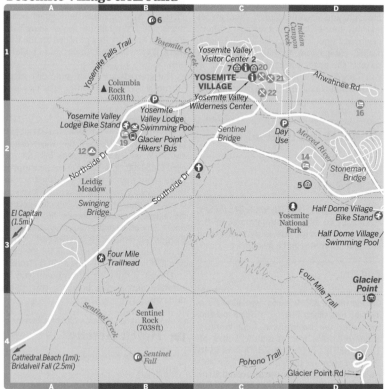

park's nicest. But it's brutally hot in summer and available only to holders of valid wilderness permits for Hetch Hetchy.

Once you leave the park, the nearest official campground is the pleasant **Dimond O Campground** (☎877-444-6777; www.recreation. gov; Evergreen Rd; tent & RV sites $24; ☉May–Sep), which lies 6 miles north of Hwy 120 on Evergreen Rd, in the Stanislaus National Forest. Some sites can be reserved; others are first-come, first-served.

Lodging

★**Evergreen Lodge**   CABIN **$$$**
(☎209-379-2606; www.evergreenlodge.com; 33160 Evergreen Rd, Groveland; tents $110-145, cabins $230-495; ☉usually closed Jan–mid-Feb; P☺❄@☎☒) ✿ Outside Yosemite National Park near the entrance to Hetch Hetchy, this classic, nearly century-old resort con-

sists of lovingly decorated and comfy cabins (each with its own cache of board games) spread among the trees. Accommodations run from rustic to deluxe, and all cabins have private porches without distracting phone or TV. Roughing-it guests can cheat with comfy, prefurnished tents.

The place has just about everything you could ask for, including a tavern (complete with pool table), a general store, a fantastic restaurant serving all meals, live music, horseshoe pits, Ping-Pong, bocce ball, a giant outdoor chess set, a kids' zipline, s'mores every night, and all sorts of guided hikes and outdoor activities – many of them family oriented. Seasonal equipment rentals are also available. Evergreen uses hydroelectric power and has an electrical-car charging station. Off-peak rates are especially good value.

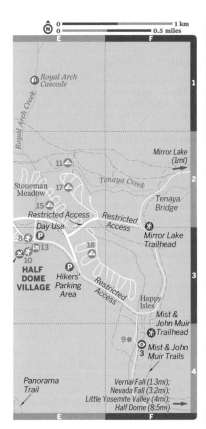

Yosemite Village & Around

✗ EATING & DRINKING

You can find food options for all budgets and palates within the park, from greasy slabs of fast food to swanky cuts of top-notch steak. All places carry good vegetarian options. The Village Store has the best selection (including health-food items and some organic produce), while stores at Half Dome Village, Wawona, Tuolumne Meadows and the Yosemite Valley Lodge are more limited.

✗ Yosemite Valley

Yosemite Village

Village Store SUPERMARKET **$**
(Map p124; ☉ 8am-8pm, to 10pm summer) The biggest and best grocery store in the park is located smack in the center of Yosemite Village. Whether you're after last-minute items or full-fledged dinners, there's no denying the place comes in handy. The store carries decent produce, fresh meat and fish,

FOOD STORAGE

Bringing in or buying your own food saves money, but remember that you must remove it – along with any other scented items such as soap and shampoo – from your car (or backpack or bicycle) and store it overnight in a bear-resistant box (locker) or canister. Boxes are located at nearly every major trailhead and some park facilities, including Half Dome Village and Housekeeping Camp. For backcountry campers, canisters – no hanging using the counterbalance or pulley system – may be rented for $5 per week (with a $95 deposit) at the wilderness and visitors centers. For locations and details, check www.nps.gov/yose/planyourvisit/bearcanrentals.htm.

and even some surprising items like tofu hot dogs, hummus, udon noodles and polenta.

You'll also find a small section of camping supplies, along with plenty of souvenirs.

Degnan's Kitchen   AMERICAN $
(Map p124; www.travelyosemite.com; 90015 Village Dr; mains $6-15; ⊘7am-9pm) Occupying the space of the former Degnan's Deli, off Village Dr, this thoroughly updated version mixes contemporary decor with deli-style sandwiches, a wide variety of salads, pizza, espresso drinks, fresh doughnuts and other baked goodies, and an emphasis on locally sourced produce and meats. Bottles of beer are shockingly cheap ($1 to $1.60); check the fridge for half-off sandwiches, salads and fruit bowls.

The open space ordering area and 'system' is a bit disorganised and on busy days can feel stressful, like trying to board a subway at rush hour.

Loft at Degnan's   PIZZA $
(Map p124; www.travelyosemite.com; mains $8-11; ⊘noon-9pm) Above Degnan's Kitchen, off Village Dr, the Loft has received a top-to-bottom remodeling. Kick back and enjoy tacos, burritos, artisan pizzas and appetizing Asian-style chicken, beef and vege bowls, as well as beer, wine and sake. The space has high-beamed ceilings and a many-sided fireplace.

Village Grill   FAST FOOD $
(Map p124; Yosemite Village; mains $6-13; ⊘11am-6pm mid-Mar–Oct; ⊠) Fight the chipmunks for burgers, hot sandwiches, wraps, chili,

salads and fries alfresco. Expect crowds and lines.

Half Dome Village

Half Dome Village Pizza Deck   PIZZA $
(Map p124; pizzas from $9; ⊘11am-10pm, shorter hours winter) Enjoy tasty pizza at this buzzing eatery that becomes a chatty après-hike hangout in the late afternoon. Specialty pizzas like the Hog Heaven (pepperoni, Canadian bacon, sausage and more bacon) runs $26 for a large.

**Half Dome Village
Gift & Grocery**   MARKET $
(Map p124; ⊘8am-10pm summer, shorter hours winter) The Half Dome Village store is undoubtedly handy if you're in the neighborhood and need food, snacks, camping supplies, sodas, gifts or beer.

Meadow Grill   FAST FOOD $
(Map p124; mains $7.25; ⊘11am-8pm mid-Apr–Sep) Hot dogs, burgers and a few salads are available on a deck near the parking area. Even when lines are long, the food's served up fairly quickly.

Half Dome Village Pavilion   CAFETERIA $$
(Map p124; adult/child breakfast $9/5.75, dinner $13.50/7; ⊘7-10am & 5:30-8:30pm late Mar-Oct; ⊠⛹) The cafeteria-style setup here has all the charm of a train-station waiting room. The quality of the food has improved a tad since the restaurant transitioned from a buffet format, though it's still pretty unexciting. Portions, however, are large and the high-ceilinged, airy dining room makes a good spot for the little ones to run wild.

The dinner prices refer to main, plus two sides and bread. The entire pavilion, including the Peets coffee area, are scheduled for a renovation to be completed by spring 2019.

Half Dome Village Bar   BAR
(Map p124; ⊘11am-10pm) Directly beside the Half Dome Village Pizza Deck window, this tiny and charming bar, literally a hole-in-the-wall, pulls a couple of decent microbrews ($7) and pours a full range of cocktails ($11).

Majestic Yosemite Hotel

**Majestic Yosemite
Dining Room**   CALIFORNIAN $$$
(Map p124; ☎209-372-1489; 1 Ahwahnee Dr, Yosemite Valley; breakfast mains $11-19, lunch mains $15-22, dinner mains $27-48; ⊘7-10am & 11:30am-

3pm Mon-Sat, 5:30-9pm daily; 🍴) 🗲 The formal ambience (mind your manners!) may not be for everybody, but few would not be awed by the sumptuous decor, soaring beamed ceiling and palatial chandeliers here. The menu is constantly in flux, but most dishes have perfect pitch and are beautifully presented. There's a dress code at dinner, but otherwise shorts and sneakers are OK.

Sunday brunch (adult/child $55/22; 7am to 2pm) is amazing. Reservations highly recommended for brunch and dinner.

Majestic Hotel Bar BAR
(Map p124; www.travelyosemite.com; 1 Ahwahnee Dr, Yosemite Valley; ⊙11:30am-11pm) The perfect way to experience the Majestic Yosemite Hotel without dipping too deep into your pockets; settle in for a drink at this cozy bar completely remodeled in 2016. Appetizers and light meals ($11 to $21) provide sustenance.

Yosemite Valley Lodge

Base Camp Eatery CAFETERIA $
(Map p124; 9006 Yosemite Lodge Dr, Yosemite Valley; mains $8-17; ⊙6:30am-10pm, to 8pm winter; 🖾) Formerly a dated and stodgy food court, this large space has been completely redesigned and modernized. Several self-service stations serve a variety of cuisines, including Asian-style noodle dishes, artisan pizzas, healthy salads and the usual burgers and chicken tenders. And whatever your view on things (park staff are generally enthused), it's a bit startling to find a Starbucks attached.

★**Mountain Room**
Restaurant AMERICAN $$$
(Map p124; 🕿 209-372-1281; www.travelyosemite.com; 9006 Yosemite Lodge Dr, Yosemite Valley; mains $21-39; ⊙9am-1pm & 5-10pm; 🍴🖾) 🗲 With a killer view of Yosemite Falls, the window tables at this casual yet elegant contemporary restaurant are a hot commodity. Plates of NY strip steak, grilled pork mole and locally caught mountain trout woo diners, who are seated beside gallery-quality nature photographs. Reservations accepted only for groups larger than eight.

Mountain Room Lounge BAR
(Map p124; www.travelyosemite.com; 9006 Yosemite Lodge Dr, Yosemite Valley; ⊙4:30-11pm Mon-Fri, noon-11pm Sat & Sun) Catch up on the latest sports news while knocking back draft brews at this large bar that buzzes in wintertime. The small food menu (mains

$8 to $16) features nachos, sandwiches and chili. Order a s'mores kit (graham crackers, chocolate squares and marshmallows) to roast in the open-pit fireplace. Kids welcome until 10pm.

✖ Glacier Point Road & Badger Pass

When the road is open, the unexciting snack bar (Map p124; hot dogs $5; ⊙9am-7pm) at Glacier Point is your only food option.

In the wintertime (until 4pm), the Yosemite Ski & Snowboard Area runs a fast food grill (Yosemite Ski & Snowboard Area; mains $7-12) serving pizza, burgers, nachos and chicken strips. Upstairs, the walls of the Snowflake Room (Yosemite Ski & Snowboard Area; mains under $10; ⊙8am-4pm winter) are covered with cool old ski photos and pieces of vintage ski equipment. On weekends and holidays, the cozy wood-beamed room offers sandwiches and salads, a bar and a view of the lifts.

✖ Wawona

**Wawona Pioneer Gift &
Grocery** SUPERMARKET $
(🕿209-375-6574; Rte 41; sandwiches $7; ⊙8am-5pm) Well-stocked market with good camping supplies, sandwich counter, coffee and large gift shop in the back.

Pine Tree Market MARKET $
(🕿209-375-6343; 7995 Chilnualna Falls Rd; ⊙9am-6:30pm Mon-Thu & Sun, to 7pm Fri & Sat) This tiny and super-friendly market sells groceries and bags of divine locally roasted coffee (take a deep breath in the aisles), and in summer it sells crates of seasonal fruit grown by regional farmers. It's located a mile east of Hwy 41 amid the redwoods in Yosemite; turn east off Chilnualna Falls Rd, which is just north of the Pioneer Yosemite History Center.

You pass the market on the way to the Chilnualna Falls Trailhead.

Big Trees Lodge Dining Room AMERICAN $$$
(www.travelyosemite.com; Big Trees Lodge, 8308 Wawona Rd; breakfast & lunch mains $14-17, dinner mains $22-32; ⊙7-10am, 11am-2pm & 5:30-9pm Easter-Dec; 🍴🖾) 🗲 Beautiful sequoia-painted lamps light this old-fashioned white-tablecloth dining room, and the Victorian detail makes it an enchanting place to have an upscale – though somewhat

overpriced – meal. ('Tasteful, casual attire' is the rule for dinner dress.) There's a barbecue on the lawn from 5pm to 7pm every Saturday during summer.

The hotel's wide white porch makes a snazzy destination for evening cocktails. Listen for veteran pianist Tom Bopp in the lobby.

✖ Big Oak Flat Road & Tioga Road

A mile north of Tioga Rd, the White Wolf Lodge (p122) area has a miniscule store that sells snacks, ice-cream bars and coffee. At lunchtime, it has prepared sandwiches available, and there's always a vegetarian option.

Crane Flat Gas Station & More SUPERMARKET $
(Big Oak Flat Rd; ⊘8am-7pm Mar-Oct) Gas-station store stocking snacks, camping supplies, souvenirs, beer, wine and a wide selection of food items. Gas pumps open 24 hours with card. Also has an ATM.

★ Rush Creek Lodge Tavern CALIFORNIAN $$
(Rush Creek Lodge, 34001 Hwy 120; mains $10-19; ⊘noon-3pm & 5:30-10pm; 🖰) Warm and welcoming, with high ceilings and sports on the large-screen TV and occasional music in summer, Rush Creek's tavern is ideal for a taste of low-key comfort after a day on the trails. And the quality and creativity of the menu far exceeds expectations: vegetarian flatbreads, cheese boards and so-called small plates (portions are big), like wild boar bolognese and bison meatballs.

The bar does great cocktails and serves area craft beers. Children are well served with their own menu and coloring kits.

White Wolf Lodge Dining Room AMERICAN $$
(☑209-372-8416; White Wolf Lodge, White Wolf Rd; breakfast buffet $12, dinner mains adult/child $35/10; ⊘7:30-9:30am & 6-8pm; 🖋) The small, rustic dining room of the White Wolf Lodge is open for a buffet breakfast and in the evening for family-style dinners inside or on the front porch. Reservations are strongly advised for dinner, with four seating times available. It seems pricey for the lackluster quality of the fare.

✖ Tuolumne Meadows

As with everything else along Tioga Rd, the eating establishments in Tuolumne Meadows are open roughly late June to mid-September only. Exact dates depend on snowfall.

Tuolumne Meadows Grill FAST FOOD $
(Tioga Rd; mains $5-11; ⊘8am-5pm mid-Jun–mid-Sep) You can hardly say you've visited Tuolumne without scoffing down a chili dog or burger in the parking lot in front of the Tuolumne Meadows Grill. The soft-serve ice-cream cones and hearty breakfasts – not to mention the people-watching at the picnic tables – are equally mandatory.

Tuolumne Meadows Store MARKET $
(Tioga Rd; ⊘8am-8pm end May-end Sep) Browse the busy aisles of the Tuolumne Meadows Store, which stocks just about every necessity you could possibly have forgotten: wine, beer, chips, dehydrated backpacking food, a smattering of produce, tofu dogs, dorky hats, camp cups, firewood, candy bars, fishing tackle and camping supplies, all at marked-up prices.

Tuolumne Meadows Lodge AMERICAN $$
(☑209-372-8413; mains breakfast $6-11, dinner $10-25; ⊘7-9am & 5:45-8pm mid-Jun–Oct; 🖰) For a classic Yosemite experience, make a dinner reservation (for breakfast, just show up) at the Tuolumne Meadows Lodge. The place is as basic looking as they come, but the breakfasts are hearty; the dinners, in terms of both choice and quality, are OK. But good company is pretty much guaranteed: tables are shared.

Craft beer from the Mammoth Brewing Company and California wines available.

✖ Hetch Hetchy

There are no eating establishments or stores in Hetch Hetchy, just one excellent place a mile outside the park border.

★ Evergreen Lodge AMERICAN $$
(☑209-379-2606; www.evergreenlodge.com; 33160 Evergreen Rd; breakfast & lunch mains $12-15, dinner mains $15-32; ⊘7-10:30am, noon-3pm & 5-10pm; 🖋🖰) Creative and satisfying, the Evergreen's restaurant serves some of the best meals around, with big and delicious breakfasts, three types of burger (Black Angus beef, buffalo and veggie) and dinner choices including rib-eye steak, lobster risotto and vegetarian chickpea curry.

The homey wooden tavern is a perennial favorite for evening cocktails, beers on tap over a game of pool and live music on select weekends. A general store fills the gaps with to-go sandwiches, snacks and dreamy gelato.

ℹ Information

BOOKSTORES

Almost every park store, from the gift shop at Yosemite Valley Lodge to the convenience stores at Wawona and Crane Flat, offers a variety of books and park maps. For the best selection of information about the park and Sierra Nevada region, visit the Yosemite Conservancy Bookstore (www.yosemiteconservancystore.com), adjacent to the Yosemite Valley Visitor Center. The store is operated by the nonprofit Yosemite Conservancy, and proceeds benefit the park.

Hiking maps and guides can be found in all the park's shops, visitor centers and wilderness centers.

The Ansel Adams Gallery (p98) in Yosemite Village also carries a great selection of books, including fine-art and photography volumes.

DANGERS & ANNOYANCES

Hiking in the wilderness is no joke. And most of Yosemite is wilderness. However, even the front country can be dangerous. There's a reason the exploits of Yosemite's search and rescue teams have been documented in a film and a book, *Off the Wall: Death in Yosemite,* about all of the fatalities that have occurred in the park (there were 16 in 2016, down from 20 in 2015). Two experienced climbers tragically fell to their deaths from El Capitan and another was killed by rockfall in 2018.

Landslides frequently close trails and steep paths get slippery after rains and flooding. Sometimes the valley itself can flood, and the park closes and visitors are told to leave with little warning.

Wild animals can transmit diseases, namely lyme, rabies, plague and hantavirus cardio-pulmonary syndrome (HCPS), a serious and sometimes fatal respiratory disease. Avoid direct contact with and exposure to animal droppings, especially rodents, even those charming-looking squirrels, chipmunks and marmots. And never touch a dead one! This means avoiding sleeping on the ground; always use a cot, hammock, sleeping bag or other surface.

Yosemite is prime black bear habitat. However, according to the National Park Service, there has never been a bear attack resulting in a fatality or serious injury in Yosemite. Incidents do happen. However, these are down dramatically, from 165 in 2014 to only 38 in 2016. Follow park rules on proper food storage and utilize bear-proof food lockers when parked overnight.

Mountain lion sightings are uncommon, but are a possibility. If you see one, do not run; rather, attempt to scare it away by shouting and waving your arms. The same warning applies for coyotes, which are more frequently seen. Report sightings to park dispatch (☏ 209-372-0476).

Mosquitoes can be pesky in summer, especially at high elevations in August, so bug spray's not a bad idea. And please don't feed those squirrels. They may look cute but they've got a nasty bite.

INTERNET ACCESS

Yosemite Valley Lodge, Majestic Yosemite Hotel, Half Dome Village and Big Trees Lodge offer free wi-fi to guests.

Mariposa County Public Library (☏ 209-372-4552; 58 Cedar Ct, Girls Club Bldg, Yosemite Valley; ◷ 9am-noon Mon & Tue, to 1pm Wed & Thu; 🛜) Free internet terminals and wi-fi.

LEGAL MATTERS

➡ Carrying concealed firearms, with proper permitting, is allowed (oddly, slingshots are explicitly prohibited). However, no firearms allowed inside federal and some park facilities.

➡ Pepper spray and bear spray are illegal.

➡ No hunting.

➡ No BASE jumping, punishable with jail and/or fine; hang gliding within park restrictions is legal.

➡ Possession and use of marijuana, even medical, is illegal.

➡ No drones.

➡ No feeding wildlife.

➡ No collecting plants, reptiles and butterflies.

➡ No metal detectors.

➡ No picking up archaeological items.

➡ No driving in meadows.

➡ No biking off paved roads.

MEDIA

For newspapers in Yosemite Valley (*San Francisco Chronicle, Fresno Bee, Modesto Bee* and *Merced Sun-Star),* hit the coin-operated boxes outside Degnan's Kitchen, in front of the stores at Half Dome Village and at Housekeeping Camp. In Tuolumne Meadows, they're sold in front of the store and at the Tuolumne Meadows Lodge.

MEDICAL SERVICES

Yosemite Medical Clinic (☏ 209-372-4637; 9000 Ahwahnee Dr, Yosemite Village; ◷ 9am-7pm daily late May-late Sep, to 5pm Mon-Fri late Sep-late May) A 24-hour emergency service is available.

MONEY

Stores in Yosemite Village, Half Dome Village and Wawona all have ATMs, as do the Yosemite Valley Lodge (p118) and the Majestic Yosemite Hotel (p118).

POST

The main **post office** (9017 Village Dr; ⊗8:30am-5pm Mon-Fri, 10am-noon Sat) is in Yosemite Village, but **Wawona** (☑209-375-6574; 1 Forest Dr; ⊗9am-5pm Mon-Fri, to noon Sat) and the **Yosemite Valley Lodge** (Yosemite Valley Lodge, 9006 Yosemite Lodge Dr; ⊗12:30-2:45pm Mon-Fri) also have year-round services. A seasonal branch operates in **Tuolumne Meadows** (☑209-372-8236; ⊗9am-5pm Mon-Fri, to noon Sat, closed mid-Sep–mid-Jun).

TELEPONE

There are payphones at every developed location throughout the park. Cell-phone reception is sketchy, depending on your location; AT&T and Verizon have the only coverage and both are generally good in the Yosemite Village area.

USEFUL WEBSITES

Discussion forums with good local advice can be found at www.yosemite.ca.us/forum and www.yosemitenews.info.

Yosemite Conservancy (www.yosemiteconservancy.org) Information and educational programs offered by the nonprofit park-support organization.

Yosemite National Park (www.nps.gov/yose) Official Yosemite National Park Service site with the most comprehensive and current information. News and road closures/openings are often posted first on its Facebook page (www.facebook.com/YosemiteNPS).

VISITOR CENTERS

Yosemite's entrance fee is $30 per vehicle, $25 per motorcycle or $15 for those on a bicycle or on foot and is valid for seven consecutive days. Passes are sold (you can use cash, checks, traveler's checks or credit/debit cards) at the various entrance stations, as well as at visitor centers in Oakhurst, Groveland, Mariposa and Lee Vining. Upon entering the park, you'll receive a National Park Service (NPS) map and a copy of the seasonal *Yosemite Guide* newspaper, which includes an activity schedule and current opening hours of all facilities. The official NPS website (www.nps.gov/yose) has the most comprehensive and current information.

For recorded park information, campground availability, and road and weather conditions, call 209-372-0200.

The park has a bare-bones dog kennel (p42), at which dogs are kept in outdoor cages (no food is allowed, due to wildlife concerns) and stay unattended. No overnight stays are allowed. You must provide a written copy of vet immunization records. Reservations are strongly recommended.

A-frame Building (☑209-372-0409; Yosemite Ski & Snowboard Area; ⊗9am-4pm winter) In winter, wilderness permits are available by self-registration at the A-frame Building, where the first-aid station and ski patrol are also situated. Rangers usually staff the office from 8am to 5pm.

Big Oak Flat Information Station

(☑209-372-0200; ⊗8am-5pm late May-Oct) Has a wilderness permit desk.

Tuolumne Meadows Visitor Center

(☑209-372-0263; ⊗9am-6pm Jun-Sep) Information desk, bookstore and small exhibits on the area's wildlife and history.

Tuolumne Meadows Wilderness Center

(☑209-372-0309; ⊗8am-5pm late May–mid-Oct) Issues wilderness permits.

Wawona Visitor Center (☑209-375-9531;

Wawona; ⊗8:30am-5pm May-Oct) Located off Wawona Rd in the historic studio of artist Thomas Hill; has information and issues wilderness permits.

Yosemite Valley Visitor Center (Map p124;

☑209-372-0200; 9035 Village Dr, Yosemite Village; ⊗9am-5pm; 🖢) Park's busiest information desk. Shares space with bookstore run by Yosemite Conservancy and part of the museum complex in the center of Yosemite Village.

Yosemite Valley Wilderness Center (Map

p124; ☑209-372-0745; Yosemite Village; ⊗8am-5pm May-Oct) Wilderness permits, maps and backcountry advice.

WILDERNESS CENTERS

Yosemite's two main wilderness centers are in Yosemite Valley and Tuolumne Meadows. At both, hikers can buy maps and guidebooks, check current weather and trail conditions, get helpful tips on planning and packing, and – most importantly – obtain wilderness permits. You can also rent bear-proof food canisters ($5 per week, with $95 deposit). Wawona, Big Oak Flat and Hetch Hetchy visitor centers also rent canisters in summer; the latter, together with the Yosemite Valley Visitor Center, are the only ones to rent year-round.

Advance reservations for wilderness permits cannot be made through the wilderness centers themselves. Note also that reservations are not necessary for winter camping, but you still need to get a wilderness permit during wintertime.

The Wawona Visitor Center also issues wilderness permits.

ⓘ Getting Around

BICYCLE

Cycling is an ideal way to take in Yosemite Valley. You can rent a wide-handled cruiser (per hour/day $12/33.50) or a bike with an attached child trailer (per hour/day $19.26/60) at the **Yosemite Valley Lodge** (Map p124; per hr/day $12/33.50; ⊗8am-7pm) or Half Dome Village (p87). Strollers and wheelchairs are also rented here.

CAR & MOTORCYCLE

Roadside signs with red bears mark the many spots where bears have been hit by motorists (many hundreds have been injured, including 27 alone in 2016 and more than 100 killed since 1995), so think before you hit the accelerator, and follow the pokey posted speed limits – they are strictly enforced. Valley visitors are advised to park and take advantage of the Yosemite Valley Shuttle Bus. Even so, traffic in the valley can feel like rush hour in LA.

Glacier Point and Tioga Rds are closed in winter. Even if driving a rental vehicle, sometimes tire chains are required and it's recommended to always have them on hand from November to March.

Nonguests can generally park in the lots for Half Dome Village, Valley Lodge and Majestic during the day – dashboard parking permits for guests only are checked after 5pm.

The closest gas station to the Valley is in El Portal, which you have to leave the park to access, 15 miles away. Next best, and in the park, is at Crane Flat a little over 17 miles away. **Wawona Chevron** (Hwy 41; ⊙8am-6pm) has high-priced gas, but is the only option between Oakhurst and Yosemite Valley. Electric vehicle charging stations are located in the parking lot of the Village Store and the Majestic Yosemite Hotel.

Village Garage (☑209-372-8320; Tecoya Rd; ⊙8am-noon & 1-5pm, towing 24hr) provides emergency repairs and even gasoline when you're in an absolute fix.

If you're driving a hard-top and looking for a rental with more pizzazz and open to the elements, try **Sierra Nevada Motorsports** (☑833-533-7494; www.sierranevadamotorsports.com; 42515 Hwy 41, Oakhurst; ⊙summer 8am-6pm, other months 9am-4pm; 4/8hr rental Slingshot $199/299, Jeep $99/149) in Oakhurst; it rents Slingshots (manual transmission, like a miniature race car) and Jeeps.

For the latest on road conditions, call the 24-hour National Park Service line at 209-372-0200.

RV

Consider the following if you're visiting Yosemite National Park in a RV:

➡ There are no electrical hookups.

➡ Generators can be used in campgrounds only during certain hours.

➡ In Yosemite Valley, the maximum length for RVs is 40ft, for trailers 35ft.

➡ No vehicles over 25ft on Mariposa Grove Rd; trailers aren't permitted. No vehicles over 25ft on Hetch Hetchy Rd; maximum width 8ft mirror to mirror.

➡ No trailers or vehicles over 30ft on Glacier Point Rd past the Sentinel Dome/Taft Point Trailheads.

➡ RVs over 24ft are not recommended for Yosemite Creek and Tamarack Flat campgrounds or for Porcupine Flat or White Wolf.

➡ Yosemite's only year-round dump station is in Yosemite Valley near the Upper Pines Campground. Wawona and Tuolumne Meadows stations open in summer.

➡ For more information see www.nps.gov/yose/planyourvisit/rv.htm.

SHUTTLE & BUS

The free, air-conditioned **Yosemite Valley Shuttle Bus** (www.nps.gov/yose/planyourvisit/upload/valleyshuttle.pdf) is a comfortable and efficient way of traveling around the park. Buses operate year-round from 7am to 10pm at 20- to 30-minute intervals and stop at 20 numbered locations, including parking lots, campgrounds, trailheads and lodges. These get very crowded in late spring and summer. For a route map, see the *Yosemite Guide* or check www.nps.gov/yose/planyourvisit/upload/valleyshuttle.pdf.

Free buses also operate between Yosemite Valley and the Yosemite Ski & Snowboard Area (winter only). The **Tuolumne Meadows Shuttle** (one-way adult/child 5-12yr $9/4.50; ⊙7am-7pm Jun–mid-Sep) runs between Tuolumne Lodge and Olmsted Point in Tuolumne Meadows (usually mid-June to early September), and the **El Capitan Shuttle** runs a summertime valley loop from Yosemite Village to El Capitan.

Two fee-based hikers' buses also travel from Yosemite Valley. For trailheads along Tioga Rd, catch the **Tuolumne Meadows Hikers' Bus** (☑209-372-1240; www.travelyosemite.com), which runs once daily in each direction. Fares depend on distance traveled; the trip to Tuolumne Meadows costs $14.50/23 one way/return. The **Glacier Point Hikers' Bus** (Map p124; ☑888-413-8869; one-way/return $27/54; ⊙mid-May–Oct) is good for hikers as well as for people reluctant to drive up the long, windy road themselves. Reservations are required.

1. El Capitan (p103)
One of the world's largest granite monoliths makes a challenging climb.

2. Bridalveil Creek (p63)
A number of hikes cross this creek near a quiet campground.

3. Vernal Fall (p55)
Misty trails lead to this 317ft fall.

4. Yosemite Valley (97)
This meadow-carpeted valley is the crown jewel of Yosemite National Park.

Around Yosemite National Park

Best Places to Eat

➡ Skadi (p155)

➡ Erna's Elderberry House (p142)

➡ Erick Schat's Bakery (p159)

➡ Convict Lake Resort Restaurant (p157)

➡ Ohanas 395 (p150)

Best Places to Stay

➡ Hotel Charlotte (p139)

➡ Mammoth Mountain Inn (p153)

➡ Yosemite Bug Rustic Mountain Resort (p136)

➡ Tenaya Lodge (p140)

➡ Inn at Benton Hot Springs (p152)

Why Go?

Though many consider Yosemite the crème de la crème of the Sierras, you may just find you prefer the flavor of other regions around it. You'll find many who'd argue the unbeatable merits of the Eastern Sierra, which is home to sights such as Mono Lake, Mammoth Lakes, hidden hot springs, shimmering alpine lakes and some of the state's most dramatic mountain scenery.

Heading to Yosemite by car or bus, you'll travel along one of four primary approaches. To the west, Hwys 120 and 140 provide the main access routes, with wonderful little goldrush-era towns and groovy old-time saloons. To the south, Hwy 41 passes by pastoral fishing lakes and mountain roads, and the eastern route over Tioga Pass is the highest auto pass in California.

Road Distances (Miles)

	Mariposa	Yosemite Valley	Mammoth Lakes	Tioga Pass
Yosemite Valley	45			
Mammoth Lakes	135	105		
Tioga Pass	95	65	40	
Oakhurst	25	45	145	105

Around Yosemite National Park ⊙ ━━━━ 50 km / ━━━━ 25 miles

MONO LAKE

A unique and fragile ecosystem that nurtures vast populations of migratory birds, its mirrored surface reflects stark Sierra peaks. Paddle around the eerie tufa formations or hike the shores of this massive alkaline lake. (p146)

BODIE STATE HISTORIC PARK

The Wild West lives on in this sprawling high-altitude ghost town, where hundreds of decaying wooden buildings bring to life a lawless 19th-century mining boomtown. (p146)

MAMMOTH LAKES

A four-season recreation hot spot, this town is catnip for the outdoorsy set. Shred fresh powder at the Mammoth Mountain resort, soak in natural hot springs and ramble along its phenomenal hiking trails. (p151)

BISHOP

In-the-know climbers and hikers flock to this unassuming Owens Valley town, a gateway to High Sierra trails and passes, renowned Buttermilk Country bouldering and hidden troves of ancient petroglyphs in the Volcanic Tablelands. (p157)

MERCED RIVER

Bounce and splash through white-water rapids in the spectacular Merced River Canyon. When the Sierra snowmelt courses from the mountains, springtime rafting reaches its frothy apex. (p136)

ALABAMA HILLS

There are dozens of weird and wonderful shapes to look out for while exploring these otherworldly rock formations. (p162)

MT WHITNEY

West of Lone Pine, the jagged incisors of the Sierra surge skyward in all their raw and fierce glory, topping off at the highest summit in the contiguous US. (p164)

Map labels

NEVADA / CALIFORNIA

Humboldt-Toiyabe National Forest

Fales Hot Springs (395) (182)

Closed in Winter (108)

Pinecrest Lake
Pinecrest

Bridgeport
Potato Peak (9957ft)

Bodie State Historic Park

Hoover Wilderness

Conway Summit (8143ft) (270) (167)

Stanislaus National Forest

Emigrant Wilderness

Dunderberg Peak (12,374ft)

Black Mountain (11,797ft)

Mono Lake

Hetch Hetchy Reservoir

Saddlebag Lake

Lee Vining

Hetch Hetchy Entrance Station

Yosemite National Park

Tioga Pass (9943ft)

Groveland

Buck Meadows (120)

Big Oak Flat Entrance

Yosemite Village

Half Dome (8842ft)

Tioga Pass Entrance (120) (158)

Inyo National Forest

Benton

June Lake

Benton Hot Springs (6)

El Portal
Arch Rock Entrance

Closed in Winter

June Mountain (10,090ft)

Briceburg (140) (41)

Ansel Adams Wilderness

Mammoth Lakes

Lake Crowley

Midpines

South Entrance

Mammoth Mountain (11,053ft)

(395)

Tom's Place

Mariposa

Bootjack (49)

Fish Camp

Merced (14mi) (140)

Ancient Bristlecone Pine Forest

Oakhurst

Bishop (168)

Aspendell (395)

Inyo National Forest

Big Pine

Merced (35mi)

Pine Flat Lake

Sierra National Forest

Kings Canyon National Park

Clovis (99) (41)

Independence

Fresno (180)

Squaw Valley

Hume

Kanawyers

(180)

Wilsonia

Cedar Grove Village

Alabama Hills (395)

Pinehurst

Mt Whitney (14,505ft)

Lone Pine

Hanford

Visalia

Sequoia National Park

Death Valley (105mi)

(198) (99)

Los Angeles (210mi)

Tulare

YOSEMITE GATEWAYS

Gateway towns to Yosemite National Park are spread over a large and disparate region. While they're not unappealing in their own right, the towns are overshadowed by the parks nearby. Oakhurst is the least charming of the gateway towns, but it's a logical choice if you're combining a visit to Yosemite with a trip to Kings Canyon and Sequoia National Parks. Fish Camp is only 3 miles from Yosemite's southern entrance, but its sleeping and eating options are comparably scarce. Groveland, the most northern gateway, offers access to lesser-visited sections of Yosemite. However, drives can be long if you plan to visit Yosemite Valley in summer. It's the same with Mariposa, which has a busy Main St and several Old West museums. Scenic Merced River Canyon is the closest to the valley, but most of its lodgings are of debatable value.

Highway 140

The approach to Yosemite via Hwy 140 is one of the most scenic routes to the park, especially the section that meanders through Merced River Canyon. Unless you're up at the crack of dawn, it can get crowded at the height of summer. Right outside the Arch Rock entrance, and primarily inhabited by park employees, El Portal is a convenient Yosemite base.

YARTS ([✔]209-388-9589, 877-989-2787; www.yarts.com) buses from Mariposa stop at Midpines ($1 one way) and El Portal ($3 one way) on their way to Yosemite Valley ($6 one way). YARTS journeys to Yosemite National Park include free entry: one child under 12 goes free with a paying adult. Several buses depart per day between 6am and 8pm.

Midpines & Merced River Canyon

There's not much to see or do in Midpines, a rural community about 25 miles west of Yosemite's Arch Rock Entrance. From Midpines, Hwy 140 drops down into the beautiful Merced River Canyon. The springtime runoff makes this a spectacular spot for **river rafting** with many miles of class III and IV rapids (age minimums vary with water levels). Worldwide rafting operators with solid reputations run trips; Zephyr Whitewater Expeditions (p33) has a seasonal office a few miles west of El Portal. Right outside the Arch Rock entrance, and primarily

inhabited by park employees, El Portal is a convenient Yosemite base.

🛏 Sleeping

Several USFS campgrounds lie on the northern side of the Merced River (no potable water) and there are three primitive **Bureau of Land Management** (BLM; www.blm.gov/visit/merced-river; Briceburg; tent & RV sites $10; ♿) campgrounds with to-die-for campsites right on the river just off Hwy 140 near the Briceburg visitor center.

★ Yosemite Bug
Rustic Mountain Resort   HOSTEL, CABIN $
([✔]209-966-6666; www.yosemitebug.com; 6979 Hwy 140, Midpines; dm from $29, tent cabins from $60, r with/without bath from $135/95; P ⊖ @ 🛜) 🏊 This friendly, folksy place feels like a secret oasis tucked away on a forested hillside about 25 miles from Yosemite. A wide range of accommodations lines its narrow ridges (cabins, dorms, private rooms and permanent tents). The June Bug Cafe is highly recommended and worth the trip alone, as are the massages and spa with hot tub ($12 per day).

Yoga lessons are also available and dorm dwellers have access to a communal kitchen. The basic tent cabins can get chilly at night: you'll probably need to sleep in thermals even with the blankets provided, and nighttime bathroom trips aren't convenient.

The YARTS bus stops a quarter mile up the driveway.

Yosemite View Lodge   MOTEL $$
([✔]209-379-2681; www.stayyosemiteviewlodge.com; 11136 Hwy 140, El Portal; r $189-269, ste $329-559; P ❄ @ 🛜 ♨ ♿) Two miles from the park entrance, this big, modern complex has hot tubs, an on-site restaurant and swimming pools. Decor is dated, but the 338 rooms feature kitchenettes, and some have gas fireplaces and Merced River or mountain views. Ground-floor rooms have big patios. No cell reception; wi-fi is patchy ($10 per day).

Cedar Lodge   MOTEL $$
([✔]209-379-2612; www.stayyosemitecedarlodge.com; 9966 Hwy 140, El Portal; r $169-189, ste $439-560; ❄ 🛜 ♿) Approximately 9 miles west of Yosemite's Arch Rock entrance, Cedar Lodge is a sprawling establishment with more than 200 adequate rooms, an indoor pool, a seasonal outdoor pool and a couple of restaurants. The balcony rooms are the best of the bunch. No cell service; the sluggish wi-fi costs $10 per day.

Eating

★ June Bug Cafe
CALIFORNIAN $$

(🕿 206-966-6666; www.yosemitebug.com/cafe; Yosemite Bug Rustic Mountain Resort, 6979 Hwy 140, Midpines; mains $8-22; ⏰ 7-10am, 11am-2pm & 6-9pm; 🅿 🛜 🖉 🚼) 🍴 Guests of all ages and backgrounds convene at this friendly eatery, decorated with adventure equipment. While sharing hiking stories, folks eat delicious, freshly prepared meals (or drink beer and wine in the evenings). More than a half-dozen inexpensive healthy and hearty (and almost gourmet!) dishes are on the menu and are served cafeteria-style, so clear and stack your own plate.

Cedar House Restaurant & Bar & Grill
AMERICAN $$

(🕿 209-379-2316; Yosemite Cedar Lodge, 9966 Hwy 140, El Portal; dinner mains $18-29; ⏰ 7-9am & 5:30-8:30pm) Don't expect much at this restaurant catering to the captive guests of the Yosemite Cedar Lodge and people entering/exiting the park. The basic burger- and diner-style fare on the menu at the attached grill is somewhat better value, but expect long waits and slow service at both. The restaurant has more variety (from seared ahi to chicken marsala).

Mariposa

🕿 209 / POP 2170 / ELEV 1949FT

About halfway between Merced and Yosemite Valley, Mariposa (Spanish for 'butterfly') is the largest and most interesting town near Yosemite National Park. Established as a mining and railroad town during the gold rush, it has the oldest courthouse in continuous use (since 1854) west of the Mississippi, loads of Old West pioneer character and a couple of good museums dedicated to the area's heritage, plus annual festivals celebrating the history of the place.

⊙ Sights

Mariposa Museum & History Center
MUSEUM

(🕿 209-966-2924; www.mariposamuseum.com; 5119 Jessie St; adult/child $5/free; ⏰ 10am-4pm; 🚼) Mariposa's past comes alive, well, as much as possible considering the fairly fusty objects displayed in this museum. Menus, logbooks, train tickets, photos and so on are organized in small diorama-style rooms to tell the stories of specific historical epochs or people. Some gems, like actual gold-miners' letters, can be found if you have the time.

California State Mining & Mineral Museum
MUSEUM

(🕿 209-742-7625; www.parks.ca.gov/?page_id=588; 5005 Fairgrounds Rd; adult/under 13yr $4/free; ⏰ 10am-5pm Thu-Sun May-Sep, to 4pm Oct-Apr) Rock hounds should drive to the Mariposa County Fairgrounds, 2 miles south of town on Hwy 49, to see the 13lb 'Fricot Nugget' (the largest crystallized gold specimen from the California gold-rush era, dating back to 1864) and other gems and machinery at the California State Mining & Mineral Museum. There is also a very cool exhibit on glow-in-the-dark minerals.

🛏 Sleeping

Mariposa Hotel Inn
HISTORIC HOTEL $$

(🕿 209-966-7500; www.mariposahotelinn.com; 5029 Hwy 140; r $149-169; ❄ 🛜) This atmospheric, creaky 1901 building is filled with things from the past. Old photos, mirrors, newspaper clippings and an antique phone with a vintage earpiece hang on the corridor's walls, while vintage chairs, beds and dressers decorate the six king or queen rooms. Room 6 has a claw-foot tub. Hummingbirds love the flowery back patio where breakfast is served.

River Rock Inn
MOTEL $$

(🕿 209-966-5793; 4993 7th St; r $135-189; 🅿 ❄ 🛜 🐾) Updated kitchenette rooms are done up in artsy earth tones at this inn that claims to be the oldest motel in town. It features a courtyard deck and a small cafe serving breakfast (included) to guests. It's a block removed from Hwy 140 on a quiet side street.

Mariposa Lodge
MOTEL $$

(🕿 800-966-8819, 209-966-3607; www.mariposalodge.com; 5052 Hwy 140; r $139-169; ❄ 🛜 🏊 🐾) More of a generic motel, the simple, well-kept Mariposa sports clean, quiet rooms with triple-sheeted beds and friendly staff. It earns extra marks for the good-sized kitchenette rooms and for the blooming flowers that border the grounds.

✕ Eating

★ Happy Burger
DINER $

(🕿 209-966-2719; www.happyburgerdiner.com; cnr 5120 Hwy 140 & 12th St; mains $8-14; ⏰ 6am-9pm; 🛜 🖉 🚼 🐾) Burgers, fries and shakes served with a heavy dose of nostalgic Americana. Happy Burger, decorated with old album covers, boasts the largest menu in the Sierra. It's also one of the cheaper meals in town. Besides burgers, there's sandwiches,

Mexican food, salads and a ton of sinful ice-cream desserts. Patio games and a 'doggy dining area' can be found outdoors.

Sugar Pine Cafe

AMERICAN $

(☑209-742-7793; www.sugarpinecafe.com; 5038 Hwy 140; mains breakfast $7-15, lunch $9-15; ☺7am-3pm) Gussied up with chrome soda-counter stools and red circular booths, this 1940s-era diner serves yummy breakfast items like omelets, buttermilk pancakes or granola with fruit and Greek yogurt. For lunch, choose hot or cold sandwiches, and black Angus beef burgers served on an English muffin (or a regular bun).

Sal's Taco Truck

FOOD TRUCK $

(☑209-742-3177; Jessie St; tacos from $1.50, burritos from $2; ☺11am-7pm, longer hours in summer) Located in the parking lot opposite the Mariposa Museum & History Center, this Mexican food truck is a local favorite and has the cheapest menu in town. It serves up grilled tilapia tacos, cheese quesadillas and chile verde supreme. Our favorite is Sal's burrito bowl.

Savoury's

AMERICAN $$

(☑209-966-7677; 5034 Hwy 140; mains $17-41; ☺5-9:30pm; ☑) Upscale yet casual Savoury's is the best restaurant in town. Black lacquered tables and contemporary art create tranquil window dressing for dishes like caramelized pork chop prepared with Sierra cider, pan-seared scallops with ginger and orange zest, Cajun-spiced New York steak with pan-seared onions, and crab cakes with cilantro-lime aioli.

Charles Street Dinner House

STEAK $$$

(☑209-966-2366; www.charlesstreetdinnerhouse.net; cnr Hwy 140 & 7th St; mains $19-38; ☺11am-2pm & 5-10pm Tue-Sat, 9am-2pm Sun) As old school as it gets: expect wooden booths, wagon wheels for decor and hearty steaks on the menu. It's classic fare done well. Order hand-cut steaks, lobster tail or barbecue ribs. The portions are large enough to satisfy the heartiest appetite.

🍷 Drinking & Nightlife

★Alley

BAR

(☑209-742-4848; www.thealleylounge.com; 5027 Hwy 140; ☺4-10pm Mon-Thu, to midnight Fri & Sat) Small batch, Californian boutique wines and 16 craft beers are served up in a sophisticated, contemporary space. But it's the lovely backyard beer garden, open in warm months, that puts the Alley at the top. Nibble on artisan appetizer plates while enjoying the laid-back atmosphere. There's live music some nights.

Casto Oaks

WINE BAR

(☑209-742-2000; www.castooakswine.com; 5022 Hwy 140; ☺11am-5pm Wed-Sat, until 4pm Sun) 🍷 Stop by this tasting room to try the local tipple. Casto Oaks manages 6 acres of vineyards in Mariposa, and some of their batches have won national awards. The Casto family produces Zinfandel, Cabernet, Cabernet Franc and Merlot.

1850 Brewing Company

BREWERY

(☑209-966-2229; www.1850restaurant.com; 5114 Hwy 140; ☺11:30am-8:30pm Tue-Thu, 11am-9pm Fri & Sat) Brewing their own local beer on site, this new space is modern, earthy and serves around nine rotating beers. Choose from pale ales, pilsners, strong reds, browns, dark wheats and coffee stouts. Sampling flights are $14 for four 1850 brews. A full menu (mains $8 to $23) includes steaks, burgers and small plates (nachos, sausage platters, salmon cakes etc).

Highway 120 (West)

Most folks visiting from the San Francisco Bay area take Hwy 120 into the park, entering Yosemite at the Big Oak Flat Entrance. This is also the main route to Hetch Hetchy. A few quality hotels are in Groveland proper and there's a variety of accommodations to the east along Hwy 120 in the Stanislaus National Forest. Staying at one of the latter, while not far away as the crow flies, feels worlds away from Groveland's conveniences.

The two approaches to Groveland from the west both involve steep mountain climbs with switchbacks. YARTS runs at least one morning trip daily between Sonora and Yosemite Valley via the Big Oak Flat entrance, with a stop in Groveland ($9 one way, 1¾ hours). YART journeys to Yosemite National Park include free entry to the park.

Buck Meadows & Around

A former stagecoach stop en route to Yosemite, tiny Buck Meadows is only 20 minutes' drive from the park entrance, and a good alternative to staying inside the park. The **Rainbow Pool** (www.fs.usda.gov/stanislaus; P♿) **FREE**, in the Stanislaus National Forest, is a popular swimming hole with a small cascade; it's signed on the south side of Hwy 120.

There are three convenient campgrounds in the Stanislaus National Forest between Groveland and Buck Meadows. On a rural road right off Hwy 120, **Blackberry Inn Bed & Breakfast** (☑209-962-4663; www.blackberry-inn.com; 7567 Hamilton Station Loop; r $210-305; ⊗mid-Mar–Oct; ❋@🤶) is a stunningly converted yellow-and-white house with sumptuous rooms with wraparound porches, stained-glass scenes of Yosemite, soaking tubs and electric fireplaces that give off real heat and a cozy ambience. The big breakfasts can be delivered to your room or patio so you can spy on the hummingbirds. **Yosemite Westgate Lodge** (☑800-253-9673, 209-962-5281; www.yosemitewestgate.com; 7633 Hwy 120; r $229-329; ❋⚟), only 12 miles from the entrance to Yosemite, has remodeled hotel-style rooms and a pool.

Groveland

☑209 / POP 600 / ELEV 3136FT

From the Big Oak Flat entrance to Yosemite, it's 22 miles to Groveland, an adorable town with restored gold-rush-era buildings and lots of visitor services.

🛏 Sleeping

★**Hotel Charlotte**   BOUTIQUE HOTEL $$
(☑209-962-6455; www.hotelcharlotte.com; 18736 Main St; r $129-259; ❋@🤶🐾) Casually sophisticated and designed with a mix of contemporary touches and vintage chintz, the Charlotte is the nicest spot in central Groveland. Some of the rooms have beautifully restored, claw-foot bathtubs, and the owners, a husband-and-wife team, work diligently to help guests enjoy their Yosemite stay.

Groveland Hotel   HOTEL $$
(☑209-962-4000; www.groveland.com; 18767 Main St; r $149-200, ste $225-295; ❋@🤶🐾) The historic and tastefully decorated Groveland dates from 1850. It houses a small bar and 18 bright, recently renovated rooms with wooden platform beds and white linen; some give subtle nods to the Old West, including cow hides and carved headboards. Rooms also have wraparound verandas and coffee machines. Suites come with Murphy beds and sleep up to four people.

🍴 Eating

Provisions   AMERICAN $
(Groveland Hotel, 18767 Main St; mains $8-16; ⊗7am-9pm) Groveland Hotel's newly opened Provisions stocks yogurt parfaits, artisan salads, fresh-made hummus, a wide selection of local wines and craft beers. A changing dinner menu of homemade specialties includes dishes like chili honey-glazed pork shank and fettuccine with lamb meatballs. There are a few indoor seats, some on the patio, or order to go.

Kevin N Randi's Old Fashioned Meat Market   DELI $
(☑209-962-5500; www.facebook.com/kevinandrandismeatdeli/; 18687 Main St Ste B1; salads from $3, sandwiches from $7; ⊗10am-5pm Tue-Sat, kitchen closes at 4pm; 🅿) If you need a packed lunch, this is the place to get a loaded, made-to-order sandwich or healthy salad (the edamame and bean salad is delicious!). You can also pick up grass-fed beef, organic poultry, deli meats, cheeses and homemade cookies and cakes.

Cocina Michoacana   MEXICAN $
(☑209-962-6651; 18730 Main St; mains $10-16, a la carte tacos from $4.40; ⊗10am-10pm) Quick and friendly service and large servings of tasty Mexican fare make this a popular restaurant with locals. There's a large menu, with familiar dishes such as carne asada, steak ranchero, burritos and fajitas. The chicken mole is especially recommended and there's a good selection of Mexican beer. Decor is simple: wooden tables and traditional Mexican artifacts on the walls.

Priest Station Cafe   AMERICAN $$
(☑209-962-1888; www.prieststation.com; 16756 Old Priest Grade; mains $11-25; ⊗11am-3pm Mon-Thu, 8am-8pm Fri-Sun) Pleasant mountain views from the deck of this roadside restaurant around 5 miles west of Groveland are worth stopping for. Good biscuits and gravy for breakfast and classic sandwiches and burgers are bonuses. It's also the oldest family-run business in the area: six generations of Ankers have owned the property since 1853, when it was a miner's supply store.

🍺 Drinking & Nightlife

★**Iron Door Grill & Saloon**   BAR
(☑209-962-6244; www.iron-door-saloon.com; 18761 Main St; ⊗restaurant 7am-10pm, bar 11am-1am, shorter hours winter) Claiming to be the oldest bar in the state (est. 1852 when it served liquor to thirsty miners), the Iron Door is a dusty, atmospheric place, with swinging doors, a giant bar, high ceilings, mounted animal heads and hundreds of dollar bills tacked to the ceiling. It has live

music on summer weekends and also hosts open-mic and karaoke nights.

Mountain Sage CAFE
(18653 Main St; drinks $2-6, snacks $4-8; ⏲7am-5pm during summer, 7am-3pm Thu-Mon during winter, later during ad hoc events; 🅿) 🍴 This popular cafe is also an art gallery, nursery and live-music venue all rolled into one, with fair-trade coffee, tasty baked treats and an excellent summer concert series (www.mountainsagemusic.org). It's also the site of a Saturday farmers market in summertime. Smoothies, homemade quiche, cookies, breakfast burritos, oatmeal and other goodies are also available.

🔒 Shopping

Yosemite Adventure Supplies SPORTS & OUTDOORS
(📞209-962-0923; www.facebook.com/Yosemite AdventureSupplies; 18911 Ferretti Rd, Bldg A; ⏲9am-5pm) Forgotten your hiking poles or missing something from your camping gear? Fear not. This local store has you covered before you enter the park, with all the supplies you could need for an adventure. They also do mountain bike rentals ($20 for half a day), plus fishing gear and snow chain rentals.

SOUTH OF YOSEMITE (HIGHWAY 41)

If you're heading up from Los Angeles or another Southern California point, this is the highway you'll likely wind up driving. Plus, Fresno Yosemite International Airport is only 64 miles south of Oakhurst and is the closest airport to the park. Hwy 41 runs north out of Oakhurst, slowly gains elevation and turns into a twisty mountain road just south of Fish Camp before continuing into Yosemite.

YARTS has five daily buses (two are extremely early in the morning) between Fresno (both the airport and the train station) and Yosemite Valley, with stops along Hwy 41, including in Oakhurst ($8 one way from Fresno, $10 one way on to Yosemite Valley). YARTS journeys to Yosemite National Park include free entry. For every adult ticket purchased, one child (12 and under) can ride for free.

Fish Camp

📍559 / POP 60 / ELEV 5062FT
Fish Camp, just south of Yosemite on Hwy 41, is more of a bend in the road than a destination, but it does have some good lodging options as well as the ever-popular Sugar Pine Railroad, a historic steam train that chugs through the woods on a 4-mile loop.

🛏 Sleeping & Eating

Summerdale Campground CAMPGROUND $
(www.fs.usda.gov; Hwy 41; tent & RV sites $32-34; ⏲May-Sep; 🐾) The closest campground to Yosemite (only 1.5 miles away off Hwy 41), Summerdale is a pleasant spot along Big Creek, with 28 well-dispersed sites in a grassy meadow with trees for shade. Each campsite has a picnic table, grill and campfire ring. Vault toilets and potable water are available. It can be booked online.

⭐**Narrow Gauge Inn** INN $$
(📞559-683-7720; www.narrowgaugeinn.com; 48571 Hwy 41; r Nov-Mar/Apr-Oct from $79/175, ste from $248; ❄@🛜🐾) Next door to the Sugar Pine Railroad (📞559-683-7273; www.ymsprr.com; 56001 Hwy 41; rides adult/child $24/12; ⏲mid-Mar–Oct; 🐾), this friendly and comfortable 26-room inn has a seasonal hot tub and pool, a small bar and the finest **restaurant** (mains $15-25; ⏲5-9pm late Apr-Oct; 🅿🛜🐾) in the area. Each tastefully appointed room features unique decor and a pleasant deck facing the trees and mountains, and all have flat-screen TVs. The breakfast buffet, included in room rates, is excellent.

White Chief Mountain Lodge MOTEL $$
(📞559-683-5444, 559-683-2615; www.whitechief mountainlodge.com; 7776 White Chief Mountain Rd; r $159-179; ⏲Apr-Oct; 🅿🛜) The cheapest and most basic option in Fish Camp, this 1950s-era motel has 26 simple kitchenette rooms with dated furnishings. Rooms include coffee machines, refrigerators and cable TV. It's located a few hundred yards east of Hwy 41; watch for the sign and go up the wooded country road.

Tenaya Lodge HOTEL $$$
(📞800-722-8584, 559-683-6555; www.tenaya lodge.com; 1122 Hwy 41; r $169-500; 🅿❄@🛜🐾) A sprawling complex just 2 miles from Yosemite's south entrance, this large resort, conference center and upscale spa is ideal for families looking for a rustic luxury feel. Activities range from mountain biking

and flashlight hikes to wine-and-watercolor nights. It has three pools, a games room kids won't want to leave, five restaurants and a general store.

There are also five sleek and contemporary, adults-only suites (no pets either) with a sort of Scandinavia-meets-Miami-meets-mountain aesthetic and top-of-the-line boutique touches and small patios. Across the road, surrounded by towering pine and cedar trees, is a village of family-style cottages with outdoor decks, all renovated in 2017. An additional 54 contemporary, stand-alone cabins will open in March 2019, part of a 30-acre expansion.

The breakfast buffet is massive and the Sierra Restaurant, especially recommended, has lured a talented chef from San Francisco who's especially good with innovative and tasty small dishes. S'mores, snowshoeing and ice skating are on offer in the winter.

Tenaya now offers all-day tours ($145/80 per adult/child) of Yosemite in Mercedes buses with retractable roofs that offer better views than windows would allow.

Two dozen baby giant sequoias have been planted around the property. One day maybe they'll grow to rival the specimens in nearby Mariposa Grove.

Big Creek Inn B&B　　　　B&B $$$
(☏559-641-2828; www.bigcreekinn.com; 1221 Hwy 41; r $259-309; 🛜) Each of the three white-palette rooms has peaceful creek views and a private balcony; two have gas fireplaces. From the comfortable rooms or the back patio you can often spot deer and beavers, or hummingbirds lining up at the patio feeder. Amenities include in-room DVD/Blu-ray players and a large movie library, a kitchenette and big soaking tubs with bath salts.

Oakhurst

☏559 / POP 2900 / ELEV 2274FT

Although only about 16 miles south of Yosemite's southern entrance (and the Mariposa Grove), at the junction of Hwys 41 and 49, Oakhurst feels worlds away from the park's natural majesty. It's the most quotidian of Yosemite's gateway towns: think strip malls and fast-food joints. For park-goers it functions primarily as a convenient service town and is your last chance to stock up on reasonably priced groceries, gasoline and camping supplies.

🏃 Activities

Yosemite Bicycle & Sport　　MOUNTAIN BIKING
(☏559-641-2453; www.yosemitebicycle.com; 40680 Hwy 41; rentals per day from $50; ⊙11am-6pm Mon-Fri (summer), 11am-6pm Tue-Fri Feb-Nov, 10am-5pm Sat) There are plenty of biking options around Oakhurst, from off-road single tracks to fire roads, making for a great way to see the vistas and countryside. This local outfit rents out a good selection of bikes (basic, mountain bikes and full suspension bikes), plus bike racks for cars. They'll also offer advice on the best rides in the area.

🛏 Sleeping

High Sierra RV Park　　CAMPGROUND $
(☏559-683-7662; www.highsierrarv.com; 40389 Hwy 41; camping per site up to 5 people $13-30; ⊙office open 8-11:30am & 1-6pm year-round; 🅿🛜🐾) Tent campsites include water, electric hookups and free showers. There's a snack-and-supplies shop, laundry and pay phone on site. Reservations are available online. RVs are also welcome. Nonguests can use the showers for $7.

★**Sierra Sky Ranch**　　LODGE $$
(☏559-683-8040; www.sierraskyranch.com; 50552 Road 632; r $99-304; ❄🛜🏊🐾) This 1875 former ranch encompasses 14 attractive acres. The homespun rooms are phone-free and pet friendly, with double doors that open onto shady verandas. The rambling and beautiful old lodge has vintage Western furniture and loads of comfortable lounging areas. The owners were renovating the restaurant during our last visit.

Hounds Tooth Inn　　B&B $$
(☏559-642-6600; www.houndstoothinn.com; 42071 Hwy 41; r $140-260; ❄🛜) A few miles north of Oakhurst, this gorgeous garden B&B is swimming in rosebushes and Victorianesque charm. Its 12 individually designed airy rooms and two cottages, some with spas and fireplaces, have a slight English-manor-house feel. Complimentary wine, hot drinks and snacks are available in the afternoon, like a kind of 'club status' if you will.

Château du Sureau　　BOUTIQUE HOTEL $$$
(☏559-683-6860; www.chateausureau.com; 48688 Victoria Lane; r $420-645, 2-bedroom villas $2950; ❄@🛜🏊🐾) Never in a billion years would you expect to find a place like this in Oakhurst. This luxe Relais & Chateaux property has discreet service and lavish European style throughout, plus a world-class

AROUND YOSEMITE NATIONAL PARK OAKHURST

spa. Inside, the Austrian owner honors the Provençale aesthetics of France with period furnishings, balconies, shuttered windows and enormous frescos, plus chandeliers and four-poster beds.

Eating

Love Cafe
VEGAN $

(☑ 559-642-5683; www.facebook.com/lovecafe oakhurst/; 39993 Hwy 41; mains $11-14; ⊙ 7am-3pm Tue-Sat; 🅿 🗷) 🍴 You can't miss the giant vintage-style, red-headed woman in park ranger gear on the side of this recently opened cafe – the first vegan cafe in the county. From the menu, you may be forgiven for thinking you're in a carnivore's cafe – it has chicken curry salads, Bridge burgers and meatball marinara subs. However, all dishes are entirely meat free.

Pete's Place
DINER $

(☑ 559-683-0772; 40093 Hwy 41; burgers from $3.95, specials from $10, meal deals from $8.50; ⊙ 7am-3pm Sun-Tue, 7am-8pm Wed Sat; 🗷) Fill up on a hearty meal at this basic place before entering the park. The menu is extensive, with most kinds of classic American fare, plus some Greek dishes. Breakfast specials include veggie scramble, chicken fried steak and biscuits and gravy. For lunch, you can't go wrong with the enormous Greek salad or a burger – patties are fat and flavorsome.

South Gate Brewing Company
PUB FOOD $$

(☑ 559-692-2739; www.southgatebrewco.com; 40233 Enterprise Dr; mains $12-29; ⊙ 11am-9pm; 🛜 🗷) About a quarter mile west of the junction of Hwys 41 and 49, this popular microbrewery pub serves primo burgers (made with grass-fed beef), brick-oven pizzas, sandwiches and salads. Try a Glacier Point pale ale with a bacon Deadwood Porter BBQ burger or the blonde-ale-beer-battered fish and chips. Steaks, meatloaf and pasta are served too.

★ Erna's Elderberry House
CALIFORNIAN, FRENCH $$$

(☑ 559-683-6860; www.chateausureau.com/ernas-elderberry-house-restaurant; Château du Sureau, 48688 Victoria Lane; prix-fixe dinner $75-112, Sun brunch mains $18-24, tasting menu $68; ⊙ brunch 11am-1pm Sun, dinner 5.30-8pm daily; 🗷) With wall tapestries, oil paintings and ornate chandeliers, the Californian-French restaurant at Château du Sureau could be a castle. But you don't have to be royalty to eat at this haute cuisine restaurant, which boasts excellent service. Dishes change frequently and range from caramelized onion velouté and foie gras parfait to truffle gnocchi and dark chocolate raspberry torte.

Tioga Pass to Lee Vining

Tioga Pass

The stretch of Hwy 120 between Tioga Pass and Lee Vining is the most epic route into or out of Yosemite National Park – and one of the most stunning anywhere in California (it's closed from sometime in November to June, depending on the snow conditions). The roadbed is scratched into the side of steep, dramatic Lee Vining Canyon, with sheer drop-offs, rugged rock walls and sweeping views. It's incredible to witness how quickly and significantly the scenery changes from one side of Tioga Pass to the other. Once you cross the pass heading east and start downhill, you'll leave behind the lush grasses and tall pines of Tuolumne and Dana Meadows for the dry, sagebrush-coated landscape of the Great Basin Desert. At the end of Hwy 120 lies Mono Lake, a massive expanse of saltwater at the edge of the Great Basin Desert.

Reflecting its bleak, high-alpine surroundings at an elevation of 10,087ft, **Saddlebag Lake** (actually a reservoir) lies at the end of a 2.5-mile dirt road that branches north from Hwy 120, about 2 miles east of Yosemite's Tioga Pass Entrance. With countless lakes and stunning views of North Peak (12,242ft) and Mt Conness (12,590ft) on the Yosemite border, and pointy Tioga Peak (11,526ft) to the southeast, the area is utterly spectacular. Saddlebag Lake is California's highest car-accessible lake and a favorite haunt for anglers.

🛏 Sleeping & Eating

Saddlebag Lake
CAMPGROUND $

(www.fs.usda.gov; 10087 Saddlebag Lake Rd; tent & small RV sites $22) Perched atop a hill at 10,000ft and overlooking the reservoir, this is a favorite with anglers. All 20 sites are small and well kept and some have splendid views over the lake. No reservations. Has drinking water and vault toilets.

★ Sawmill Walk-in
CAMPGROUND $

(www.fs.usda.gov; Saddlebag Lake Rd; tent sites $17) One of the most scenic established campgrounds in the entire Sierra Nevada, Sawmill offers 12 sites on the edge of the beautiful Monroe Hall Research Area (day hiking only). It's about a quarter-mile walk to the campground. Vault toilets; no water source other than a nearby creek. No reservations.

Tioga Lake Campground
CAMPGROUND $
(www.fs.usda.gov; Hwy 120; tent & small RV sites $22; ☉closed during winter, open when snow has cleared; ☂) The campground closest to Tioga Pass is at Tioga Lake, and has a handful of sunny, exposed sites right on the lake but visible from the road. No reservations. It has potable water, bear lockers and vault toilets. It's situated at the northwest shore of the lake.

Junction Campground
CAMPGROUND $
(www.fs.usda.gov; cnr Hwy 120 & Saddlebag Lake Rd; tent & RV sites $17; ☉closed winter) Named for its location at the intersection of Hwy 120 and Saddlebag Lake Rd, this 13-site campground offers a sunny location near Lee Vining Creek. It has vault toilets and bear lockers. No reservations.

★Tioga Pass Resort
CABIN $$
(www.tiogapassresort.com; Hwy 120; d $145, cabins $180-280; ☉Jun-Sep) Situated at a whopping 9550ft and only 2 miles east of Tioga Pass, this is as close to a Yosemite experience as you can get without staying in the park. Founded in 1914, this high-country resort attracts a fiercely loyal clientele to its quiet, comfortable, woodsy cabins (most with full kitchen) beside Lee Vining Creek. Walk-ins can sometimes snag a cancellation.

The thimble-sized cafe serves excellent fare all day at a few tables and a broken horseshoe counter, with a house pastry chef concocting dozens of freshly made desserts. At the time of update the resort was closed due to damage caused by a record snowfall; it's predicted that it will reopen in the summer of 2019.

Lee Vining
📍442, 760 / POP 220 / ELEV 6780FT
Highway 395 skirts the western bank of Mono Lake, rolling into the gateway town of Lee Vining, where you can eat, sleep, gas up (for a pretty penny) and catch Hwy 120 to Yosemite National Park when the road's open. A superb base for exploring Mono Lake, Lee Vining is only 12 miles (about a 30-minute drive) from Yosemite's Tioga Pass entrance. **Lee Vining Canyon** is also a popular location for **ice climbing**.

🛏 Sleeping

Mono Vista RV Park
CAMPGROUND $
(☎760-647-6401; www.monovistarvpark.net; 57 Beavers Lane; tent/RV sites $27/35; ☉mid-Apr–Oct) Located behind a Chevron gas station, it can get crowded at this campground just a block from the highway. On offer are grassy sites for tents, and the closest showers ($3) east of Tuolumne Meadows.

El Mono Motel
MOTEL $
(☎760-647-6310; www.elmonomotel.com; cnr Hwy 395 & 3rd St; r $76-103; ☉mid-May–Oct; ☂) Grab a board game or soak up some mountain sunshine in this friendly place attached to an excellent cafe (p144). In operation since 1927, it's often booked solid, and each of its 11 simple rooms (a few share bathrooms) is unique, decorated with vibrant and colorful art and fabrics.

Lake View Lodge
LODGE $$
(☎760-647-6543; www.lakeviewlodgeyosemite.com; 51285 Hwy 395; r & cabins from $79-294; ☉year-round; ☂☂) A large complex anchoring the southern end of town with a variety of room types, from standard motel accommodation to postage-stamp-sized cabins with full kitchens and even a 'glamping trailer.' The largest cabins sleep up to eight. Many are furnished with red and blue focus walls. Only a few have views.

Murphey's Motel
MOTEL $$
(☎760-647-6316; www.murpheysyosemite.com; 51493 Hwy 395; r $88-290; ☉year round; ☂☂☂) At the northern end of town, this large, two-story, log-cabin-style place offers comfy, but dated, rooms. It's one of the few hotels in Lee Vining open year-round. Rooms have refrigerators and coffee makers, the largest is cosy, but sleeps six on three queen beds.

Yosemite Gateway Motel
MOTEL $$
(☎760-647-6467; www.yosemitegatewaymotel.com; 51340 Hwy 395; r from $107-299; ☂☂) Think vistas. This is the only motel on the eastern side of the highway, and the views of Mono Lake and surroundings from some of the rooms are phenomenal. The somewhat-tired rooms have comfortable beds with thick duvets and big bathrooms. Family units and suites sleep up to six.

🍴 Eating

★Mono Cone
BURGERS $
(☎760-647-6606; 51508 Hwy 395; burgers $7; ☉11am-6pm mid-Apr–Oct; ☎) Looking to

AROUND YOSEMITE NATIONAL PARK TIOGA PASS TO LEE VINING

satisfy your nostalgia for summertime vacations of yore or want to introduce your kids to a classic roadside joint? Mono Cone will not disappoint. Chow down on juicy burgers, fries and thick shakes at one of the outdoor picnic tables. Waits can be long at the height of summer lunch hour.

Latte Da Coffee Cafe CAFE $
(☑760-647-6310; cnr Hwy 395 & 3rd St; sandwiches from $6; ☺7am-8pm May-Oct; ☜) Located at the El Mono Motel (p143), this cafe is a charming spot for sandwiches, scones and good organic espresso drinks. There's a cozy wood-floored interior, front porch and tiny backyard garden.

Nicely's DINER $
(☑760-647-6477; Hwy 395 & 4th St; mains $6-12; ☺7am-9pm) This diner is so old school it has Kraft macaroni and cheese on its menu. Burgers, eggs Benedict and old-fashioned buttermilk pancakes are more appealing choices.

Mono Market MARKET $
(www.leeviningmarket.com; 51303 Hwy 395; sandwiches $8; ☺7:30am-8pm, shorter hours winter; ☑) Stock up on quality groceries at the local market, whose diverse selection seems more like that of a big-city grocery store, even with British and Aussie favorites such as Marmite and Vegemite. On our visit there was a batch of fresh organic locally grown tomatoes. The deli serves delicious breakfast burritos, pastries and coffee, all to go.

★**Whoa Nellie Deli** AMERICAN $$
(☑760-647-1088; www.whoanelliedeli.com; Tioga Gas Mart, 22 Vista Point Rd; mains $7.50-19; ☺6:30am-9pm late-Apr–Oct; ☟) Years after its famed chef moved on to Toomey's (☑760-924-4408; www.toomeyscatering.com; 6085 Minaret Rd; breakfast items $5.50, mains from $16-36; ☺7am-9pm; ☟) at Mammoth Lakes, this Mobil-gas-station restaurant off Hwy 120 is still, surprisingly, a darn good place to eat. Stop in for delicious burgers, fish tacos, wild-buffalo meatloaf and other tasty morsels. There are live bands some nights.

★**Mono Inn** AMERICAN $$$
(☑760-647-6581; www.themonoinn.com; 55620 Hwy 395; small plates $16-18, mains $32-38; ☺5-9pm Tue-Sat, to 8pm Sun Apr–mid-Nov) A restored 1922 lodge owned by the family of photographer Ansel Adams, this elegant yet casual lakefront restaurant makes everything from scratch and has correspondingly delectable

lake views inside and on the terrace. Stop in for the occasional live band on the creekside terrace. It's located about 5 miles north of Lee Vining. Call ahead for reservations as opening hours are subject to change.

🛍 Shopping

Beaver's Sporting Goods SPORTS & OUTDOORS
(☑760-647-6406; 51328 Hwy 395; ☺9am-6pm) One-stop shop for everything fishers need. Plus camping supplies. Business hours are subject to change, particularly in winter.

ℹ Information

Mono Lake Committee Information Center
(☑760-647-6595; www.monolake.org; cnr Hwy 395 & 3rd St; ☺9am-5pm, later hours in summer) Internet access ($2 for 15 minutes), maps, books, info about Mono Lake and passionate, preservation-minded staff. Public restroom too. Plus local handmade gifts such as candles, pottery and balms.

ℹ Getting There & Away

Eastern Sierra Transit Authority (☑760-872-1901; www.estransit.com) Buses stop in Lee Vining on their way between Lone Pine ($19, 2½ hours) and Reno, NV ($37, three hours); buses depart once a day in either direction between Monday and Friday.

EASTERN SIERRA

Cloud-dappled hills and sun-streaked mountaintops dabbed with snow typify the landscape of the Eastern Sierra, where slashing peaks – many over 14,000ft – rush abruptly upward from the arid expanses of the Great Basin and Mojave Deserts. It's a dramatic juxtaposition that makes for a potent cocktail of scenery. Pine forests, lush meadows, ice-blue lakes, simmering hot springs and glacier-gouged canyons are only some of the beautiful sights you'll find in this region.

The Eastern Sierra Scenic Byway, officially known as Hwy 395, runs the entire length of the range. Turnoffs dead-ending at the foot of the mountains deliver you to pristine wilderness and countless trails, including the famous Pacific Crest Trail, John Muir Trail and main Mt Whitney Trail.

ℹ Getting There & Away

Mammoth Yosemite Airport (MMH; www.visitmammoth.com/fly-mammoth-lakes; 1300

Airport Rd) the most convenient airport, but flights are limited to a few West Coast cities.

Airports in Los Angeles and Las Vegas, both over 200 miles away from Lone Pine, make logical starting points for a south-to-north exploration of the Eastern Sierra. Otherwise, it makes sense to fly into Reno, NV, and travel south. Either way, if you want to avoid backtracking, try to fly into one airport and out of another.

ℹ Getting Around

The Eastern Sierra is easiest to explore under your own steam. Keep in mind that some mountain roads close in winter, as do most of the passes that take you over the Sierras from east to west, including Tioga Rd (Hwy 120) to Yosemite.

Eastern Sierra Transit Authority buses make a round trip between Lone Pine and Reno ($59, six hours) on Monday, Tuesday, Thursday and Friday, stopping at all Hwy 395 towns in between. Fares depend on distance, and reservations are recommended. There's also an express bus between Mammoth and Bishop ($7, one hour, around three times daily) that operates Monday to Friday.

In summer, connect to Yosemite via YARTS bus in Mammoth Lakes or Lee Vining. Mammoth to Lee Vining costs $6 one-way, while Mammoth to Yosemite Valley is $18 (including free park entry, plus one free under-12s ticket per adult ticket purchased), with one to two early morning departures per day.

North of Mono Lake

The spine of the Mono Lake region, Hwy 395, has turnoffs into the mountains to the west or the high desert to the east. No matter which direction you choose, Mono Lake's unique and almost meditative profile beckons. For a time warp back to the gold-rush era, swing by Bodie, one of the West's most authentic and best-preserved ghost towns. Virginia Lakes and Lundy Lake provide quick access to backcountry wilderness trails. Even the drives here are magnificent, passing through deep canyons with steep mountain slopes rising ahead.

Lundy Lake

After Conway Summit, Hwy 395 twists down steeply into the Mono Basin. Before reaching Mono Lake, Lundy Lake Rd meanders west of the highway for about 5 miles to Lundy Lake. This is a gorgeous spot, especially in spring, when wildflowers carpet the canyon along Mill Creek, or in fall when the landscape is brightened by colorful foliage.

Before reaching the lake, the road skirts first-come, first-served **Lundy Canyon Campground** (www.monocounty.ca.gov/facilities/page/lundy-lake-campground; Lundy Lake Rd, near Hwy 395; tent & RV sites $16; ⊘ late Apr-Oct; 🐾). At the end of the lake, there's a ramshackle resort on the site of an 1880s mining town, plus a small store and boat rentals.

Past the resort, a dirt road leads into Lundy Canyon; after 2 miles, it dead-ends at the trailhead for the Hoover Wilderness Area (p148). A fantastic 1.5-mile hike follows Mill Creek to the 200ft-high **Lundy Falls**. Industrious beavers define the landscape along the trail, with gnawed aspens scattered on the ground and a number of huge dams barricading the creek. Ambitious types can continue on via Lundy Pass to Saddlebag Lake and the **Twenty Lakes Basin**, though the final climb out of the canyon uses a rocky and very steep talus chute.

Note: Lundy Lake Rd can be snow-covered in winter and impossible to pass.

Virginia Lakes

South of Bridgeport, Hwy 395 gradually arrives at its highest point, Conway Summit (8143ft), where you'll be whipping out your camera to capture the awe-inspiring panorama of Mono Lake, backed by the Mono Craters, and June and Mammoth Mountains.

Also at the top is the turnout for **Virginia Lakes Road** (closed in winter), which parallels Virginia Creek for about 6 miles to a cluster of lakes flanked by Dunderberg Peak (12,380ft) and Black Mountain (11,797ft). A trailhead at the end of the road gives access to the Hoover Wilderness Area and the **Pacific Crest Trail**. The trail continues down Cold Canyon through to Yosemite National Park. With a car shuttle, the excellent 10.5-mile hike to **Green Creek** visits a bevy of perfect lakes; an extra mile (each way) takes you to windswept – check out the mammoth tree blowdown! – **Summit Lake** at the Yosemite border. Check with the folks at the **Virginia Lakes Resort** (📱 760-647-6484; www.virginialakesresort.com; Virginia Lakes Rd; cabins from $117; ⊘ mid-May–mid-Oct; 🐾), opened in 1923, for maps and tips about specific trails (open seasonally between May and October). Nearby, Virginia Lakes Pack Outfit offers horseback-riding trips.

DON'T MISS

MONO LAKE

North America's second-oldest lake (www.monolake.org; off Hwy 395) is 70 sq miles, and a quiet and mysterious expanse of deep blue water. The glassy surface reflects jagged Sierra peaks, young volcanic cones and the unearthly tufa (too-fah) towers that make the lake so distinctive. Jutting from the water like drip sand castles, tufas form when calcium bubbles up from subterranean springs and combines with the lake's carbonate waters. The biggest grove (Test Station Rd, near Hwy 120; adult/child $3/free; P 🚻) is on the southern rim, with a mile-long interpretive trail.

Rising above the southern shore of the lake, Panum Crater (Mono Crater Rd, Near Mono Lake Basin Rd & Hwy 120) is the youngest (about 640 years old), smallest and most accessible of the craters that string south toward Mammoth Mountain. A panoramic trail circles the crater rim (about 30 to 45 minutes), and a short but steep 'plug trail' puts you at the crater's core.

On the north shore of Mono Lake are the Black Point Fissures, narrow crags that opened when a lava mass cooled and contracted about 13,000 years ago. Access is from three places: east of Mono Lake County Park; from the western shore off Hwy 395; or south off Hwy 167.

The best place for swimming is at Navy Beach (Navy Beach Rd, off Hwy 120). It's also the best place to put in canoes or kayaks. Contact the Mono Lake Committee or Caldera Kayaks (☑760-934-1691; www.calderakayak.com; tours from $75 for 3 or more people; ☺mid-May–early Oct) for canoe and kayak tours.

In *Roughing It*, Mark Twain described Mono Lake as California's 'dead sea.' Hardly. The brackish water teems with buzzing alkali flies and brine shrimp, both considered delicacies by dozens of migratory bird species that return here year after year. So do about 85% of the state's nesting population of California gulls, which take over the lake's volcanic islands in spring and summer. The Mono Lake Wilderness Trail is a good place to spot them.

A short drive north of Lee Vining, the Mono Basin Scenic Area Visitor Center (☑760-647-3044; www.fs.usda.gov/inyo; 1 Visitor Center Dr; ☺8am-5pm mid-Apr–Nov; 🚻) offers advice and maps.

To get to the reserve, head south from Lee Vining on Hwy 395 for 6 miles, then east on Hwy 120 for 5 miles to the dirt road leading to a parking lot. Pay via the honesty box.

Bodie State Historic Park

At Bodie State Historic Park (☑760-647-6445; www.parks.ca.gov/bodie; Hwy 270; adult/child $8/5; ☺9am-6pm Apr-Oct, to 4pm Nov-Mar; road often closed in winter; P 🚻), a gold-rush ghost town is preserved in a state of 'arrested decay.' Weathered buildings sit frozen in time on a dusty, windswept plain. To get there, head east for 13 miles (the last 3 miles are unpaved) on Hwy 270, about 7 miles south of Bridgeport. The access road is often closed by snow in winter.

Gold was first discovered here in 1859, and within 20 years the place grew from a rough mining camp to an even rougher boomtown with a population of 10,000 and a reputation for unbridled lawlessness. Fights and murders took place almost daily, the violence no doubt fueled by liquor dispensed in the town's 65 saloons, some of which did double duty as brothels, gambling halls or opium dens. The hills disgorged some $35 million worth of gold and silver in the 1870s and '80s, but when production plummeted, so did the population, and eventually the town was abandoned to the elements.

Peering through the windows of the 200 weather-beaten buildings, you'll see stocked stores, furnished homes, a schoolhouse with desks and books, and workshops filled with tools. The jail is still there, as are the fire station, churches, a bank vault and many other buildings.

The former Miners' Union Hall now houses a museum and visitor center. Rangers conduct free general tours. In summer, they also offer tours of the landscape and the cemetery; call for details. The second Saturday of August is Friends of Bodie Day (www.bodiefoundation.org), with stagecoach rides, history presentations and lots of devotees in period costumes.

Bridgeport

☑ 442,760 / POP 575 / ELEV 6465FT

Barely three blocks long, set amid an open high valley and in view of the peaks of Sawtooth Ridge, Bridgeport flaunts classic Western flair with charming old storefronts and a homey ambience. Almost everything shuts down or cuts back its hours for the brutal winters, but the rest of the year the town is a magnet for anglers, hikers, climbers and hot-spring devotees.

🏃 Activities

★ Travertine Hot Spring — HOT SPRINGS

FREE A bit southeast of town, head here to watch a panoramic Sierra sunset from three small but entirely natural hot pools set amid impressive rock formations. To get here, turn east on Jack Sawyer Rd just before the ranger station, then follow the dirt road uphill for about 1 mile. The pools are located over the mound behind the toilet block, and are free to bathe in.

🛏 Sleeping

Bridgeport Inn — HISTORIC HOTEL $

(☑ 760-932-7380; www.thebridgeportinn.com; 205 Main St; r with shared bathroom $59-89, historic rooms from $139) Step back in time at this vintage country-style hotel, dating back to 1877. The walls are decorated with Victorian wallpaper, the stairs have original bannisters, there's an original wood-burning stove in the lounge and the ceilings have ornate chandeliers. There's a good restaurant and bar on site too.

Virginia Creek Settlement — MOTEL $

(☑ 760-932-7780; www.virginiacreeksettlement.com; Hwy 395; converted wagons from $36, tent cabins from $40, d from $87; 🐾) Easily found on the highway 6 miles south of Bridgeport (look for the old-fashioned windmill by the roadside), Virginia Creek has a number of accommodation types, all designed with a retro Old West theme. Ever wanted to bed down in a covered wagon like a pioneer? Tent cabins and woodsy motel rooms are also available – the latter can be a little musty. The on-site restaurant (mains $12-33; ⊙ 7am-9pm) is one of the best in the area, serving hearty Italian fare.

Bodie Victorian Hotel — HISTORIC HOTEL $

(☑ 760-616-1977; www.bodievictorianhotel.com; 85 Main St; r from $78; ⊙ May-Oct; ❋🐾) To experience an 1800s boarding house in all its rickety glory, try a room in this building transplanted from the abandoned mining town of Bodie. It can feel rundown despite the great-great-grandmother-style antiques, bold Victorian wallpaper and striking bordello accoutrements. If no one's here, poke your head into the Sportsmens Bar & Grill next door to rustle up an employee.

Silver Maple Inn & Cain House — MOTEL $$

(☑ 760-932-7383; www.silvermapleinn.com; 340 Main St; r $130-200; ❋🐾) A good choice, whether you stay in one of the standard rooms in the whitewashed classic roadside motel, or one of the more contemporary and luxurious rooms in the next-door Cain House. The two share an immaculately maintained lawn with chairs laid out for enjoying sunny days.

🍴 Eating & Drinking

High Sierra Bakery — BAKERY $

(☑ 760-914-4002; www.highsierrabakery.com; 172 Main St; donuts from $3; ⊙ 6am-4:30pm late May–early Sep) With a wooden facade that could be straight out of a Wild West town, this family-owned bakery prepares handmade donuts, croissants, scones and breads daily. Plus they serve espresso drinks, salads and sandwiches.

Bridgeport Inn Restaurant — AMERICAN $$

(www.thebridgeportinn.com; 205 Main St; mains $9-35; ⊙ 7am-9pm mid-Mar–Oct; 🐾) Stop in at the country-kitchen dining room of this whitewashed 1877 building for burgers, pot roast, steaks and seafood, and a dip into its modest wine list. Watch the world stream by from a classic soda-fountain stool on the long front porch. The cozy bar in front is open evenings much of the year. Breakfast is classic American fare.

Rhino's Bar & Grille — GRILL $$

(☑ 760-932-7345; 226 Main St; mains $10-23; ⊙ 8am-9:30pm Thu-Sun) All-American bar with flags, patches, license plates and beer pumps decorating the walls and ceilings. Typical bar food includes breakfasts, sandwiches and burgers (the Rhino Burger comes with bacon, cheese and nitro wing sauce). Pool tables in the back.

❶ Getting There & Away

Eastern Sierra Transit Authority buses stop here on their way between Lone Pine ($22, three hours) and Reno, NV ($32, 2½ hours);

ℹ WILDERNESS AREAS

The backside of Yosemite, Sequoia and Kings Canyon is easily the rival of the national parks in terms of ethereal landscapes with endless opportunities for backcountry hiking. The following is a list of the major areas, a puzzle of interlocking county, state and national forests and federally protected lands.

Ansel Adams Wilderness Area (www.fs.usda.gov)The spectacular Ansel Adams Wilderness Area abuts Yosemite National Park, Mammoth Lakes, June Lake and Inyo National Forest. It contains some of the most dramatic alpine scenery in the Sierra Nevada, including beautiful lakes, high peaks, gorges and a few small glaciers.

Hoover Wilderness (www.fs.usda.gov) Constituting 128,000 acres of backcountry paradise, Hoover includes the Virginia Lakes, Lundy Lake and high peaks to the west bordering Yosemite National Park.

Humboldt-Toiyabe National Forest (www.fs.usda.gov) At 6.3 million acres, this is the largest national forest in the lower 48 states. Most of it is in Nevada, with a small portion around Bridgeport in California.

Inyo National Forest (www.fs.usda.gov/inyo) An enormous area of nearly 2 million acres of dense forests, high peaks and lakes, as well as nine wilderness areas, Inyo covers a good chunk of California's Eastern Sierra and White Mountains. It encompasses a vast network of trails and campgrounds, with ranger stations in Lone Pine, Bishop, Mammoth Lakes and Mono Basin.

John Muir Wilderness Area (www.fs.usda.gov) Named for the naturalist who devoted much of his life to protecting the Sierra Nevada and Yosemite regions, this wilderness area (around 600,000 acres) abuts Kings Canyon and Sequoia national parks and several other wilderness areas subsumed under the Inyo National Forest.

Wilderness Permits

➡ Free wilderness permits for overnight camping are required year round in the Ansel Adams, John Muir, Golden Trout and Hoover Wilderness areas.

➡ For the first three areas, trailhead quotas are in effect from May to October; about 60% of the quota may be reserved online at www.recreation.gov for a $5 fee (per person), or $15 (per person) if entering the Mt Whitney Zone.

➡ From November to April, you can pick up permits at most ranger stations; permits are bookable around six months in advance. If you find a station closed, look for self-issue permits outside the office.

➡ Wilderness permits for the Inyo National Forest can be picked up in Lone Pine, Bishop, Mammoth Lakes or its Mono Basin ranger stations.

➡ For information, call the **Inyo National Forest Wilderness Permit Office** (p160) in Bishop.

➡ Yosemite's Tuolumne Meadows Wilderness Center can also issue permits for trips from Saddlebag Lake and has a self-registration permit station.

➡ Permits for the Hoover Wilderness that depart from the Humboldt-Toiyabe National Forest (seasonal quotas on some trails) are issued at the **Bridgeport Ranger Station & Visitor Center** (☎ 760-932-7070; www.fs.usda.gov/htnf; Hwy 395; ⊙ 8am-4:30pm).

➡ The forums on High Sierra Topix (www.highsierratopix.com) are an excellent resource for planning trips.

one bus leaves daily in either direction Monday to Friday. Highway 182 heads northeast from Bridgeport into Nevada. Most people carry on north to Carson City or Reno, NV.

Mammoth Lakes Region

Mammoth Lakes may be famous for its world-class skiing mountain, but the surrounding region is just as appealing, especially in summer. Explore the area around the main town for geothermal sites, waterfalls, surreal volcanic formations, glorious mountaintops and lush canyon meadows popping with scores of clear blue lakes.

South off Hwy 395 (roughly equidistant between Mammoth Lakes and Bishop), Rock Creek Rd travels 11 miles to reach hiking access with some of the dreamiest landscapes in the Sierra. **Little Lakes Valley Trail**, part of the John Muir Wilderness area, offers a rewarding trek through some 10,300ft of elevation and glacier-carved canyon views peppered with multicolored flora in spring. In wintertime there's a Sno-Park 7 miles along Rock Creek Rd, and during summer there are horseback-riding trail rides from its location just before the trailhead.

June Lake Loop

Under the shadow of massive Carson Peak (10,909ft), the stunning 16-mile June Lake Loop (Hwy 158) meanders through a picture-perfect horseshoe canyon, past the relaxed resort town of **June Lake** and four sparkling, fish-rich lakes: Grant, Silver, Gull and June. It's especially scenic in fall, when the basin is ablaze with golden aspens.

On the northern edge of June Lake is one of the high Sierra's most idyllic swimming spots, an expansive sandy beach cradled by the spectacular shimmering lake and awe-inspiring mountains.

June Lake is 2 miles west of Hwy 395 (a few miles south of Lee Vining) on Rte 158. The loop around Silver Lake is usually closed in winter.

Activities

Hiking

June Lake is backed by the Ansel Adams Wilderness Area, which runs into Yosemite National Park. Hiking and horseback-riding trips into the backcountry are as impressive as any in the Sierra Nevada. The **Rush Creek Trailhead** (near June Lake Loop Rd) offers access to awesome backcounty at Agnew, Gem and Waugh Lakes; eventually the path meets up with the Pacific Crest Trail. The route is a moderate-to-hard 8.4-mile round-trip to Agnew Lake and 10-mile round-trip to Gem Lake.

Other Activities

Cyclists can zip around the entire loop, a moderate 22-mile circle including a section

of Hwy 395. Boat and tackle rentals, as well as fishing licenses, are available at five marinas. In June Lake village, **Ernie's Tackle & Ski Shop** (📞 760-648-7756; 2604 Hwy 158; ⊙7am-6pm in winter, 6am-7pm rest of year) can get you geared up.

In wintertime, ice climbers flock to the area's frozen waterfalls. The **June Mountain Ski Area** (📞 888-586-3686, 24hr snow info 760-934-2224; www.junemountain.com; Hwy 158; lift tickets adult/13-22yr & senior/under 13yr $119/98/free; ⊙8:30am-4pm winter only; 🚡), much smaller and less crowded than nearby Mammoth Mountain is good for beginners. Mammoth lift passes can be used here.

🛏 Sleeping

There are a handful of highly recommended campgrounds surrounding June and other lakes in the area. **Oh! Ridge Campground** (📞 800-444-7275; www.recreation.gov; off Pine Cliff Rd; tent & RV sites $25-28; ⊙late-Apr–Oct; 🐾) is especially popular with families because of its access to a swimming beach on June Lake.

June Lake Villager Motel   MOTEL **$**
(📞 760-648-7712; www.junelakevillager.com/en-us; 2640 Hwy 158; r from $95-145, cabins $145-295; 🅿🛜) Located in town, June Lake Villager Motel has simple, light and airy rooms, some with kitchenettes and ski memorabilia. Larger suites and cabins have fireplaces, patios and barbecues and sleep five to seven people.

Fern Creek Lodge   CABIN **$**
(📞 760-648-7722; www.ferncreeklodge.com; 4628 Boulder Dr; cabins from $125; 🛜) Around since the late 1920s, this place is a good choice if you don't mind slightly bland furnishings in exchange for some homey privacy. Each cabin has a fully stocked kitchen and a deck or front porch to take in the stupendous mountain views. The on-site general store (7am to 7pm) has all the basics you'll need for a cookout at the central barbecue.

Silver Lake Resort   CABIN **$$**
(📞 760-648-7525; www.silverlakeresort.net; 6957 Hwy 158; cabins from $144-304; ⊙May–mid-Oct) Across the road from Silver Lake and astride Alger Creek, this sweet cabin compound dating from 1916 has a duck pond and boat rentals in addition to 17 rustic cabins with full kitchens. Its tiny old-time **cafe** (mains $8-11; ⊙7am-2pm May-Oct; 🅿) displays the requisite

WORTH A TRIP

TWIN LAKES

Eager anglers line the shoreline of Twin Lakes, a gorgeous duo of basins cradled by the fittingly named Sawtooth Ridge. The area's famous for its fishing – especially since some lucky guy bagged the state's largest ever brown trout here in 1987 (it weighed in at a hefty 26lb). Stop by **Ken's Sporting Goods** (☑760-932-7707; www.kenssport.com; 258 Main St; ⊙7am-7pm Mon-Thu, to 8pm Fri & Sat mid-Apr–Oct, 9am-4pm Tue-Fri rest of year) in Bridgeport for gear and information. Lower Twin is quieter, while Upper Twin allows boating and waterskiing. Other activities include mountain biking and, of course, hiking in the Hoover Wilderness Area and on into the eastern, lake-riddled reaches of Yosemite National Park.

Also check out **Buckeye Hot Spring** (www.monocounty.org/places-to-go/hot-springs/buckeye-hot-springs/; off Buckeye Rd, near Hwy 395; ⊙road access may be closed during winter; P) FREE, where piping hot water emerges from atop a steep hillside and cools as it trickles down into several rock pools right by the side of lively Buckeye Creek. Clothing is optional. To get there, turn right at Doc & Al's Resort (7 miles from Hwy 395), driving 3 miles on a graded dirt road. Cross the bridge at Buckeye Creek (2.5 miles on), and bear right at the Y-junction, following signs to the hot spring. Go uphill a half-mile until you see a flattish parking area on your right. Follow the hillside trail down to the pools.

Accommodations in the area include several forest service campgrounds **Kearsarge Pass Trailhead** (Onion Valley Rd) and **Annett's Mono Village** (☑760-932-7071; www.monovillage.com; 13425 Twin Lakes Rd; tent/RV sites $25/35, r $85, cabins $95-215; ⊙late Apr-Oct; @ 🛜), a huge and rather chaotic tumbledown resort on Upper Twin Lake; pay showers available.

antique winter-sports equipment and serves diner fare.

Double Eagle Resort & Spa   RESORT $$$
(☑760-648-7004; www.doubleeagle.com; 5587 Hwy 158; r/cabins from $249/349; 🛜❄🐾) A swanky spot for these parts, Double Eagle has sleek two-bedroom log cabins and comfortable balconied hotel rooms. Worries disappear at the elegant spa, and there's a heated indoor pool and a fully equipped gym. The restaurant exudes rustic elegance, with cozy booths, a high ceiling and a huge fireplace.

🍴 Eating

★ **Ohanas 395**   FOOD TRUCK $
(www.ohanas395.com; 131 S Crawford Ave; mains $7-17; ⊙noon-6pm) This very good food truck, in the parking lot near June Lake Brewing (p151), serves wait-worthy 'Hawaiian soul food' with a dash of Mexican fusion. It's pretty much the only food like this on offer in the area, and you can order up dishes such as Honolulu fried noodles, slow-cooked kalua pig tacos, a classic plate lunch or an *ahi poke* (raw-fish salad) bowl.

Eagle's Landing Restaurant   CALIFORNIAN $$
(☑760-648-7004; www.doubleeagle.com/eagles-landing-restaurant; 5587 Hwy 158, Double Eagle Resort & Spa; mains $11-36; ⊙7:30am-9pm; P🐾) The restaurant at the Double Eagle Resort (p150) exudes rustic elegance, with cozy booths, a high ceiling and a huge fireplace. Breakfast is especially hearty and dinner mains include salmon, pasta, rotisserie chicken and several cuts of steak.

Tiger Bar   AMERICAN $$
(☑760-648-7551; www.tigerbarcafe.com; 2620 Hwy 158; mains $9-22; ⊙8am-9pm, bar open until 1am) After a day on the slopes or trails, people gather at the long bar or around the pool table of this no-nonsense, no-attitude place, which has been around in some form or another since 1932. The kitchen feeds all appetites, with burgers, salads, tacos and other tasty grub, including homemade fries; there are fresh-baked pies for dessert.

Carson Peak Inn   AMERICAN $$$
(☑760-648-7575; www.carsonpeakinn.com; Hwy 158; meals $24-40; ⊙5-10pm) Inside a cozy house with a fireplace, this restaurant is much beloved for its tasty old-time indulgences, such as fried chicken, pan-fried trout and chopped sirloin steak. Portion sizes can be ordered for regular or 'hearty' appetites. Its opening hours are shorter during winter.

🍺 Drinking & Nightlife

★ **June Lake Brewing** MICROBREWERY
(☏858-668-6340; www.junelakebrewing.com; 131 S Crawford Ave; ☺noon-8pm Mon, Wed, Thu, Sun, to 9pm Fri & Sat; 🐾) A top regional draw, June Lake Brewing's open tasting room serves around 10 drafts, including a 'SmoKin' Porter, Deer Beer Brown Ale and some awesome IPAs. Brewers swear the June Lake water makes all the difference. Flights are around $6.

ℹ Getting There & Away

Eastern Sierra Transit offers a June Lake Loop stop on its Reno, NV, to Lone Pine route, but it requires 24-hour advance notice (call 760-872-1901 to book). There are two trips daily in either direction between Mammoth Lakes and June Mountain Ski Area ($6.50 one way, 30 minutes), and to Lone Pine ($18, 2½ hours) and Reno ($40, 3½ hours).

YARTS connects two stops in June Lake (the ski area and Rush Creek trailhead) with Mammoth Lakes, Lee Vining, Tuolumne Meadows ($4 to $6 depending on the stop, one way) and Yosemite Valley ($15 one way) in summer. Reservations required.

Mammoth Lakes

🔗 442,760 / POP 8100 / ELEV 7880FT
Mammoth Lakes is a famous mountain-resort town endowed with larger-than-life scenery – active outdoorsy folks worship at the base of its dizzying 11,053ft Mammoth Mountain. Long-lasting powder clings to these slopes, and when the snow finally fades, the area's an outdoor wonderland of mountain-bike trails, excellent fishing, endless alpine hiking and blissful hidden spots for hot-spring soaking. Eastern Sierra's commercial hub and a four-season resort, Mammoth is backed by a ridge line of jutting peaks, ringed by clusters of crystalline alpine lakes and enshrouded by the dense Inyo National Forest.

⦿ Sights

★ **Earthquake Fault** NATURAL FEATURE
(Minaret Rd) **FREE** On Minaret Rd, about 1 mile west of the Mammoth Scenic Loop, detour to gape at Earthquake Fault, a sinuous fissure half a mile long gouging a crevice up to 20ft deep into the earth. Ice and snow often linger at the bottom until late summer, and Native Americans and early settlers used it to store perishable food. Accessibility is difficult during winter.

🏃 Activities

Mammoth Mountain SNOW SPORTS
(☏760-934-2571, 760-934-2571, 24hr snow report 888-766-9778; www.mammothmountain.com; access via Minaret Rd; adult/13-18yr/5-12yr/under 5yr $159/130/64/free; 🅿) A skiers' and snowboarders' dream resort, where sunny skies, a reliably long season (usually November to June) and more than 3500 acres of fantastic tree-line and open-bowl skiing are a potent cocktail. At the top you'll be dealing with some gnarly, nearly vertical chutes. The longest run is 3 miles.

The other stats are just as impressive: 3100 vertical feet, 150 trails and 28 lifts (including nine high-speed quads). Boarders, meanwhile, will find world-class challenges in 11 terrain parks with three intense half-pipes (12ft to 22ft), 95 jumps and 126 rails, boxes and jibs.

There are five hubs at the base of the mountain: Main Lodge, Canyon Lodge, Eagle Lodge, the Mill Cafe and the Village, each with ticket offices and parking lots. Free ski shuttles pick up throughout town. Alternatively, hop on the Village Gondola (free to all), which whisks you up to Canyon Lodge – the base of several chairlifts – in six minutes.

Mammoth Mountain Bike Park MOUNTAIN BIKING
(☏800-626-6684; www.mammothmountain.com; day pass adult/7-12yr $45/24; ☺9am-6pm Jun-Sep) Come summer, Mammoth Mountain morphs into the massive Mammoth Mountain Bike Park, with more than 80 miles of well-kept single-track trails. Several other trails traverse the surrounding forest. In general, Mammoth-style riding translates into plenty of hills and soft, sandy shoulders, which are best navigated with big, knobby tires.

But you don't need wheels (or a medic) to ride the vertiginous **gondola** (☏800-626-6684; www.mammothmountain.com; Minaret Rd; adult/13-18yr/5-12yr $34/29/12; ☺hours vary; 🅿🐾) to the apex of the mountain, where there's a cafe and an interpretive center with scopes pointing toward the nearby peaks. And for kids 12 years and under, a $40 Adventure Pass buys unlimited day access to a zipline, climbing wall, bungee trampoline and child's bike-park area.

When the park's open, it runs a free mountain-bike **shuttle** (9am to 5:30pm) from the Village area to the Main Lodge. Shuttles depart every 30 minutes, and mountain bikers

INN AT BENTON HOT SPRINGS

Soak in your own hot-springs tub and snooze beneath the moonlight at **Benton Hot Springs** (☑ 866-466-2824, 760-933-2287; www.historicbentonhotsprings.com; Hwy 120, Benton; tent & RV sites for 2 people $50-60, B&B r from $119; P ❄ 🛜 🐾), a small, historic resort in a 150-year-old former silver-mining town nestled in the White Mountains. Choose from 11 well-spaced campsites with private tubs or a room in the themed, antique-filled B&B, with semiprivate tubs. Daytime dips are available, subject to availability. Reservations essential.

The inn is reachable from Mono Lake via Hwy 120 (in summer), Mammoth Lakes by way of Benton Crossing Rd or Bishop via Hwy 6; the first two options are undulating drives with sweeping red-rock vistas that glow at sunset, and all take approximately one hour. An Eastern Sierra Transit Authority bus connects Bishop and Benton ($6, one hour) on Tuesday and Friday, stopping right at the resort.

If you have time, ask for directions to the Volcanic Tablelands petroglyphs off Hwy 6, where ancient drawings decorate scenic rock walls.

with paid mountain passes get priority over pedestrians.

Tamarack Cross-Country Ski Center   SKIING
(☑ 760-934-2442; www.tamaracklodge.com/xc-ski-center; 163 Twin Lakes Rd; all-day trail pass adult/senior/child $29/23/5; rental packages adult/senior/child $29/29/24; ⊙ 8:30am-5pm) Tamarack Lodge has almost 20 miles of meticulously groomed tracks (for cross-country skiing) amid magnificent scenery around Twin Lakes and the Lakes Basin. Rentals and lessons available. The rental center is in a large tent at the back of the parking lot.

The terrain is also great for snowshoeing. The orange-line town shuttle runs from the Village to Tamarack Lodge.

Agnew Meadows Trailhead   HIKING
(Agnew Meadows Rd, off Postpile Rd; ⊙ Postpile Rd closed during winter.) Has access to the famous John Muir Trail and Pacific Crest Trail, the latter immortalized by Cheryl Strayed's novel *Wild* and the movie of the same name starring Reese Witherspoon, among other hikes. Shadow Lake is also a stunning 7-mile day hike from Agnew Meadows.

Mammoth Rock 'n' Bowl   BOWLING
(☑ 760-934-4200; www.mammothrocknbowl.com; 3029 Chateau Rd; per game adult $5-8, under 13yr $3-5, shoe rental adult/child $4/2; ⊙ 4pm-midnight Mon-Fri, noon-midnight Sat & Sun; 🐾) A psychedelic mural of the Devils Postpile crowns this stylish and modern 12-lane complex. The ground floor has foosball, ping-pong and darts, plus TVs for watching sports, and a bar. Upstairs has an upscale French-style eatery (p155), and some high-def golf simulators

(per hour $30 to $40) that let you whack real golf balls across virtual courses.

Lakes Basin Path   CYCLING
(Lake Mary & Minaret Rd) One of Mammoth's fantastic multi-use paths, the 5.3-mile Lakes Basin Path begins at the southwestern corner of Lake Mary and Minaret Rds and heads uphill (1000ft, at a 5% to 10% gradient) to Horseshoe Lake, skirting lovely lakes and accessing open views of the Sherwin Range. For a one-way ride, use the free Lakes Basin Trolley, which tows a bicycle trailer.

Volcom Brothers Skate Park   ADVENTURE SPORTS
(☑ 760-934-8989; 1390 Meridian Blvd; ⊙ sunrise to sunset; 🐾) **FREE** Whether you are a skateboarding fan or not, the 40,000 sq ft Volcom Brothers Skateboard Park is something to behold. Skaters come from around the US to ride here. Spectators can stand on the sidelines and watch the skateboarders perfecting their tricks and attempting the 90-degree bowl. Skaters must wear helmets and pads. Has seasonal restrooms.

🛏 Sleeping

Mammoth B&Bs and inns rarely sell out midweek, when rates tend to be lower. During ski season, reservations are recommended at weekends and essential during holidays. Many properties offer ski-and-stay packages. Condo rentals often work out cheaper for groups.

Moderne Hostel   HOSTEL $
(☑ 760-934-2414; https://holidayhausmoteland hostel.com; 3905 Main St; dm from $34-55, d from $72-104; P ❄ 🛜) One of Mammoth's few

REDS MEADOW & DEVIL'S POSTPILE

One of the most beautiful and varied landscapes near Mammoth Lakes is the Reds Meadow Valley, west of Mammoth Mountain. Drive on Hwy 203 as far as **Minaret Vista** (off Minaret Rd; ⊘ road closed during winter) for eye-popping views (best at sunset) of the Ritter Range, the serrated Minarets and the remote reaches of Yosemite National Park.

The most fascinating attraction in Reds Meadow is the surreal volcanic formation of **Devils Postpile National Monument** (☏ 760-934-2289; www.nps.gov/depo; access off Minaret Summit Rd/Reds Meadow Rd; shuttle day pass adult/child $7/4; ⊘ Jun-Oct, weather depending). The 60ft curtains of near-vertical, six-sided basalt columns formed when rivers of molten lava slowed, cooled and cracked with perplexing symmetry. This honeycomb design is best appreciated from atop the columns, reached by a short trail. The columns are an easy half-mile hike from the Devils Postpile Ranger Station.

From the monument, a 2.5-mile hike passing through fire-scarred forest leads to the spectacular **Rainbow Falls** (⊘ road closed during winter), where the San Joaquin River gushes over a 101ft basalt cliff. Chances of actually seeing a rainbow forming in the billowing mist are greatest at midday. The falls can also be reached via an easy 1.5-mile walk from the Reds Meadow area, which has a cafe, a store, the Reds Meadow campground and a pack station.

The valley road provides access to six campgrounds along the San Joaquin River. Tranquil, willow-shaded **Minaret Falls Campground** (www.fs.usda.gov; off Minaret Rd; tent & RV sites $23; ⊘ road closed during winter season; 🐾) is a popular fishing spot where the best riverside sites have views of the namesake cascade.

The road to Reds Meadow is only accessible from about June until September, weather permitting. To minimize impact when it's open, the road is closed to private vehicles beyond Minaret Vista unless you are camping, have lodge reservations or are mobile impaired, in which case you must pay a $10 fee per car at the Minaret Vista entrance station. Otherwise you must use a mandatory shuttle bus ($7/4 adult/child one-way; children under two years go free). The bus leaves from a lot in front of the Adventure Center (next to the mammoth statue/gondola) approximately every 30 minutes between 7am and 7pm, and you must buy tickets inside the Adventure Center before joining the line. There are also three direct departures from the Village (on Canyon Blvd, under the gondola) before 9am, plus the option of using the free mountain-bike shuttle between the Village and the Adventure Center. The bus stops at trailheads, viewpoints and campgrounds before completing the one-way trip to Reds Meadow (45 minutes to an hour).

hostels offers well-kept, contemporary-style dorm rooms with personal lockers and reading lights, plus an equipped kitchen. Rooms have communal bathroom facilities. There's also board and ski storage, and a lounge area with TV. It shares an office and driveway with the Holiday Haus.

Davison Street Guest House   HOSTEL $
(☏ 760-924-2188;   www.mammoth-guest.com; 19 Davison St; dm $49-52, d $106-140; 🛜) This charming and interesting five-room A-frame chalet hostel on a quiet residential street has a stocked kitchen, plus mountain views from the living room (with fireplace) or sundeck. There's a nifty electronic self-registration system when the manager isn't around. Fills with long-distance backpackers in June and July.

★**Mammoth Mountain Inn**   INN $$
(☏ 760-934-2581; www.themammothmountaininn. com; 10400 Minaret Rd; r from $129-239, condos from $259-1199; 🅿 @ 🛜 ♨) Warm and cozy, oozing traditional ski-lodge appeal, and only steps from the base of the Panorama Gondola, this is the best address for skiers and snowboarders. Though prices come down out of ski season, at 9000ft it's a spectacular location no matter the time of year. It's a low-slung complex with a pool and hot tubs to soothe aching limbs.

Tamarack Lodge   LODGE, CABIN $$
(☏ 760-626-6684,   760-934-2442;   www.tamaracklodge.com; 163 Twin Lakes Rd; r with shared/private bath from $99/127, cabins from $255-425; 🅿 🐾 @ 🛜 ♨) 🍃 In business since 1924, this charming year-round resort on Lower Twin Lake has a cozy fireplace lodge, a bar and

excellent restaurant, 11 rustic-style rooms and 35 cabins. The cabins range from very simple to simply deluxe, and come with full kitchen, private bathroom, porch and wood-burning stove. Some can sleep up to 10 people. Daily resort fee is $20.

Austria Hof Lodge   LODGE $$
(🖉 866-662-6668, 760-934-2764; www.austriahof. com; 924 Canyon Blvd; r incl breakfast $89-275; 🛜) Close to Canyon Lodge, rooms here have modern knotty-pine furniture, thick down duvets and DVD players. Ski lockers, fireplaces, flat screen TVs and a sundeck hot tub make winter stays here even sweeter. Continental breakfast included with stays. In the evening, the lodge restaurant serves meaty gourmet German fare (such as bratwurst sampler plates and wiener schnitzel) in a cellar dining room.

Mammoth Creek Inn   INN $$
(🖉 760-934-6162; www.mammothcreekinn.com; 663 Old Mammoth Rd; r from $149-240, lofts from $389-675; @🛜🏊) It's amenities galore at this pretty inn at the end of a commercial strip, with down comforters and fluffy terry robes, a sauna, hot tub and a fun pool-table room. Lofts overlook the majestic Sherwin Mountains, have full kitchens and can sleep up to six. Ski and board storage available, plus pet-friendly rooms. Resort fee $22.

Alpenhof Lodge   HOTEL $$
(🖉 760-934-6330; www.alpenhof-lodge.com; 6080 Minaret Rd; r $99-229; P@🛜🏊) A snowball's toss from the Village, this Euro-flavored inn has updated lodge rooms with tasteful accent walls and ski racks; larger rooms and cottages have gas fireplaces or kitchens. The basement houses the Clocktower Cellar.

Juniper Springs Lodge   LODGE $$
(🖉 760-924-1102; www.juniperspringsmammoth. com; 4000 Meridian Blvd; studios from $129; P🛜🏊) You can't beat the location of this ski-in and -out five-floor resort next to Eagle Lodge, with 180 suites and townhouses. Rooms have classic furnishings and kitchens. Communal facilities include a fitness center, games room and coffee shop, plus a laundry. There's two heated swimming pools and six outdoor hot tubs. Bike rentals available in summer. Free airport pickup.

Cinnamon Bear Inn   B&B $$
(🖉 800-845-2873, 760-934-2873; www.cinnamon-bearinn.com; 133 Center St; r $99-195; @🛜) At this down-to-earth inn you'll sleep like a log in chunky wooden beds, and most rooms have cozy gas fireplaces. Swap stories about the day's adventures with other guests over wine, cheese and crackers in the evening, or soak away soreness in the small outdoor Jacuzzi. Home-cooked breakfasts are available in the mornings.

Campgrounds

About 15 USFS campgrounds are scattered in and around Mammoth Lakes, and all are petfriendly, with flush toilets but no showers. Many sites are available on a first-come, first-served basis, and some are reservable. Note that nights get chilly at these elevations, even in July. All close in winter and charge about $23. Stop by the Mammoth Lakes Welcome Center or check its website for a full list of campgrounds and public shower locations.

Some of the nicest campgrounds are in the lakes basin around Twin Lakes, Lake Mary and Lake George, with well-spaced sites in a pine forest and along crackling creeks. Less picturesque but close to town, New Shady Rest and Old Shady Rest are two sprawling options right behind the Mammoth Lakes Welcome Center.

 Eating

Dessert'D   DESSERTS $
(🖉 760-924-0877; www.dessertd.com; 588 Old Mammoth Rd; cupcakes from $3.75; ⊗11am-7pm Mon-Sat, 11am-5pm Sun; 🍴) Sweet treats such as cookies, marshmallows, jams, cakes, sweet cream pie and brownies are made on site at this ridiculously good dessert shop. Everything is made using organic ingredients and natural flavorings and there are lots of vegan and gluten-free options. Hot drinks include old-fashioned hot cocoa (in original, almond, banana, cherry, coconut or salted caramel flavor), with whipped cream.

Ramenya   JAPANESE $
(🖉 760-965-0520; 4 Alpine Circle; sushi rolls from $6, ramen from $14; ⊗5-9pm Sun-Mon, to 9:30pm Wed-Thu, to 10pm Fri & Sat; P🍴) Lit by fairy lights, this sleek white and wood dressed tent-shaped restaurant serves big hot bowls of flavorsome noodle soup. Choose from *shoyu ramen* (with roasted pork), *ajo ramen* (with salt butter and garlic soup and chicken) or *midori ramen* (veggie or chicken broth with broccoli, spinach, onions and carrot). Dumplings, sushi and kimchi also available.

Giovanni's Pizzeria ITALIAN **$**
(☑760-934-7563; www.giovannismammoth.com;
437 Old Mammoth Rd; small pizzas from $8, pasta
from $14; ☺11:30am-9pm) This low-key Italian restaurant has been open for 30 years
and is a local favorite. It serves good-sized
plates of classic pasta, with two sides, while
pizzas are hand-tossed and served with
thick crusts. Service is occasionally slow.
No reservations.

Old New York Deli & Bagel Co DELI **$**
(☑760-934-3354; www.oldnewyork.com; 6201
Minaret Rd; bagels from $2, mains $4-11; ☺6am-
4pm) While the bagels here may not rival
those actually made in the city, New Yorkers won't be disappointed by the selection
of healthy, large salads and pastrami and
roast-beef sandwiches. Just a few flights of
stairs from the base of the Village Gondola.

Nik-n-Willie's PIZZA **$**
(☑760-934-2012; 100 Old Mammoth Rd; pizzas-
$11-27, slices $3; ☺11:30am-9pm) Family-run
casual pizzeria serving better-than-average
pies, handmade and cooked on the spot.
Sauce flavors include marinara chipotle,
creamy ranch, pesto, roasted pepper and
olive oil. Slices and Italian- and deli-style
sandwiches also available.

Base Camp Café AMERICAN **$**
(☑760-934-3900; www.basecampcafe.com; 3325
Main St; mains $7-15; ☺7:30am-4pm in winter,
longer hours in summer; 🛜🍴) Fuel up with a
bracing dose of organic tea or coffee and a
filling breakfast (pancakes, eggs, burritos
and omelets), or comfort food such as Tex-
Mex jalapeño-onion straws or turkey chili in
a bread bowl. The dining room is decorated
with various backpacking gear, ice picks,
wooden skis and beer mats. Meanwhile, the
bathroom has a comical photo display of
backcountry outhouses.

53 Kitchen & Cocktails AMERICAN **$$**
(☑760-934-0707; www.53mammoth.com; 6201
Minaret Rd; mains $16-33; ☺11am-late; 🍴)
Swanky for Mammoth, 53 is a modern
space recommended as much for its lengthy
cocktail menu as for its food, which includes braised short ribs and crispy brussels sprouts prepared with candied lardons,
homemade mustard and crispy quinoa. It
has a couple of vegetarian options too (cauli-
flower burger, and fresh butternut squash
salad). Worth visiting for cheap happy-hour
eats and drinks (3pm to 5pm).

Slocums AMERICAN **$$**
(www.slocums.com; 3221 Main St; mains $13-33;
☺4-9pm Mon-Sat) Slocums has a classic pub-
style bar and front room, and a large back
dining room furnished more elegantly with
red leatherette benches and a menu featuring mains such as filet mignon and surf and
turf. The popular happy hour (4pm to 6pm,
burgers only $4.75 and craft beers on tap
for $4) is fun, with a mix of locals, seasonal
workers and tourists.

Mammoth Tavern GASTROPUB **$$**
(☑760-934-3902; www.mammothtavern.com;
587 Old Mammoth Rd; mains $13-34; ☺5-9:30pm
Mon-Thu, until 10pm Fri & Sat) Mammoth Tavern
hits the spot with comfort food such as shepherd's pie, fondue and swordfish. Heaped
salads too. Warm lighting, wood-paneled
walls rising to a circular ceiling, and drop-
dead gorgeous views of the snow-capped
Sherwin Range mean the big-screen TVs are
an unnecessary distraction. Drinks include
tasty cocktails, draft beers, interesting whiskeys and over two dozen wines by the glass.
Walk-ins only.

★Skadi NORWEGIAN **$$$**
(☑760-914-0962; www.skadirestaurant.com; 94
Berner St; mains $30-38; ☺5-11pm Wed-Mon)
Considering its more-than-mundane location in an industrial strip, Skadi comes
as a surprise. Hip Swiss Alps decor and an
innovative menu are the creation of chef
Ian Algerøen, inspired by his Norwegian
heritage and European fine-dining techniques. On the menu you'll find pork belly confit and roast tenderloin, Canadian
duck breast with arctic lingonberries and
pan-seared day-boat scallops. Reservations
required.

Mammoth Rock Brasserie AMERICAN **$$$**
(☑760-934-4200; 3029 Chateau Rd; mains
$19-35; ☺5:30-9pm) The classically trained
French chef at this swanky brasserie on the
2nd floor of the Mammoth Rock 'n' Bowl
serves tasty small plates and meaty main
courses such as elk medallions and pork
mignon. Gaze at breathtaking views of the
Sherwin Range while you enjoy your meal.

Lakefront Restaurant AMERICAN **$$$**
(☑760-934-2442; www.lakefrontmammoth.com;
163 Twin Lakes Rd; mains $35-55; ☺5:30-9:30pm)
The most atmospheric and romantic (and
pricey) restaurant in Mammoth, this intimate dining room at Tamarack Lodge overlooks the lovely Twin Lakes. The chef crafts

delights such as slow-cooked steelhead rainbow trout, roasted sunchoke and puree, pickled mustard seed and watercress. The staff is superbly friendly. Menu changes each season. Reservations recommended.

Drinking & Nightlife

Clocktower Cellar
PUB

(☑ 760-934-2725; www.clocktowercellar.com; 6080 Minaret Rd; ⊙ 4-11pm) In winter especially, locals throng this dive bar pub in the basement of the Alpenhof Lodge. The ceiling is tiled with a swirl of bottle caps, and the bar has 160 whiskeys, 26 beers on tap and about 50 bottled varieties.

Mammoth Brewing Company
BREWERY

(☑ 760-934-7141; www.mammothbrewingco.com; 18 Lake Mary Rd; ⊙ bar 10am-9:30pm Sun-Thu, 10am-10:30pm Fri & Sat; kitchen from 3.30pm Sun-Thu, from 11.30am Fri & Sat) You be the judge whether beer is brewed best at high altitude. Boasting the highest West Coast brewery, at 8000ft, Mammoth Brewing Company offers more than a dozen brews on tap (flights around $7) – including special seasonal varieties not found elsewhere. Tasty bar food available (flatbreads, burgers and mac 'n' cheese).

Shopping

Wave Rave
SPORTS & OUTDOORS

(☑ 760-934-2471; www.waveravesnowboardshop. com; 3203 Main St; 3hr rental electric bike $50; ⊙ 7:30am-9pm Sun-Thu, to 10pm Fri & Sat) Snowboarders worship here. In summer it rents SUPs and electric bikes. Opening hours reduce in the low season.

Rick's Sports Center
SPORTS & OUTDOORS

(☑ 760-934-3416; 3241 Main St; per day ski rental from $24, snow shoes $10; ⊙ 7:30am-7pm) Rick's has been serving area fishers with advice and equipment for several decades now. It also does ski rental packages. It stays open longer in the summer.

Mammoth Mountaineering Supply
SPORTS & OUTDOORS

(☑ 760-934-4191; www.mammothgear.com; 361 Old Mammoth Rd; per day snow-shoe rental $10; ⊙ 8am-8pm) Offers friendly advice, maps and sells all-season equipment from winter sports to camping gear. Rentals available.

Information

Mammoth Lakes Welcome Center (☑ 760-924-5500, 888-466-2666; www.visitmammoth. com; 2510 Hwy 203; ⊙ 9am-5pm; in winter 8:30am-4:30pm) Full-service information desk sharing space with the ranger station. Also sells gifts and has an excellent selection of books on the Eastern Sierra. You can get local permits here, plus peruse a display of animal skins – from a black bear and marmot to a pine marten and weasel. All animals on display died of natural causes.

 Getting There & Away

AIR

Mammoth Yosemite Airport has nonstop flights to San Francisco and Denver, operating winter through to spring on **United** (www. united.com). Until November 2018 Alaska Airlines ran a year-round service to Los Angeles and ski-season service to San Diego, and at time of research a new airline partner was being sourced to cover these routes. All flights are about an hour.

From the airport, taxis meet incoming flights, while some lodgings provide free transfers. Otherwise Mammoth Express buses (run by Eastern Sierra Transit; one way $3.50) ply the route to Mammoth Lakes. **Mammoth Taxi** (☑ 760-934-8294; www.mammoth-taxi.com) does airport runs as well as hiker shuttles throughout the Sierra.

BUS

Mammoth is easy to navigate by public transportation year-round. YARTS runs buses to and from Yosemite Valley in summer. Eastern Sierra Transit Authority has a year-round service along Hwy 395, north to Reno, NV ($46, 4½ hours), and south to Lone Pine ($14.25, just over two hours). They run once a day in either direction from Monday to Friday, leaving Mammoth for Reno in the morning and Lone Pine in the afternoon.

Getting Around

Eastern Sierra Transit Authority operate a year-round system of free and frequent bus shuttles within Mammoth Lakes that connects the whole town with the Mammoth Mountain lodges; in summer, routes with bicycle trailers service the Lakes Basin Path and Mammoth Mountain Bike Park. Check the website for details on routes and schedules (usually they run every 15 to 30 minutes from around 7am to 5:30pm, with the town trolley running until 10pm).

Reds Meadow/Devils Postpile shuttle (www. nps.gov; adult/child $7/4; ⊙ approx 7am to 7pm, closed in winter) provides public transportation to Reds Meadow and the Devils Postpile National Monument. From 9am to 5pm it runs nearly every 20 minutes, departing from just under the base of the gondola in the **Village** (72 Canyon Blvd; ⊙ Village gondola open 8am-5pm daily Nov-Mar).

Convict Lake

One of the area's prettiest lakes, Convict Lake has emerald water embraced by massive peaks. A hike along the gentle trail skirting the lake, through aspen and cottonwood trees, is great if you're still adjusting to the altitude. A trailhead on the southeastern shore gives access to Genevieve, Edith, Dorothy and Mildred Lakes in the John Muir Wilderness. To reach the lake, turn south from Hwy 395 on Convict Lake Rd (across from the Mammoth airport) and go 2 miles.

Convict Lake got its name after a bloody shoot-out in 1871 between a band of escaped convicts and a posse that had given chase. The posse leader, Sheriff Robert Morrison, was killed during the gunfight and the tallest peak, Mt Morrison (12,268ft), was later named in his honor. The bad guys got away, only to be apprehended later near Bishop.

The **Convict Lake Resort** (☑760-934-3800; www.convictlake.com; 2000 Convict Lake Rd; cabins from $189-999, in winter $109-599; 🛜🐾) has houses and cabins with kitchens, sleeping from two to 34, and ranging from rustic to ritzy. There's horseback riding, hiking and fishing in the area, and Mammoth is a short 12-minute drive. The on-site **restaurant** (lunch $10-13, dinner $26-40; ⊗5:30-9pm daily, plus 11am-2:30pm Jul & Aug) is one of the best in the region.

McGee Creek Road

Eight miles south of Mammoth Lakes, off Hwy 395, McGee Creek Rd rises into the mountains and dead-ends in a dramatic aspen-lined canyon, a particularly beautiful spot for autumn foliage. From here, the McGee Pass Trail enters the John Muir Wilderness Area, with day hikes to **Steelhead Lake** (10 miles round-trip) via an easy walk to Horsetail Falls (4 miles round-trip). On the drive up, the McGee Creek Pack Station offers trail rides and spacious **McGee Creek campground** (www.fs.usda.gov; McGee Creek Rd; tent & RV sites $23; ⊗late Apr-Oct; 🐾) has 28 reservable sites at 7600ft, with campfire rings, drinking water, flush toilets and bear lockers. It also has sun-shaded picnic tables along the creek and stunning mountain vistas.

Rock Creek Road

South off Hwy 395 and roughly equidistant from Mammoth Lakes and Bishop, Rock Creek Rd travels 11 miles into some of the dreamiest landscapes in the Sierra. At road's end, the **Mosquito Flat trailhead** (Rock Creek Rd; ⊗road to trail is closed in winter) into the Little Lakes Valley (part of the John Muir Wilderness) clocks in at a whopping 10,300ft of elevation.

Mountaintops seem to be everywhere, with the 13,000ft peaks of Bear Creek Spire, Mt Dade, Mt Abbot and Mt Mills bursting out along the southwestern horizon and lush canyon meadows popping with scores of clear blue lakes. Ecstatic hikers and climbers fan out to explore, though most anglers and hikers just go as far as the first few lakes. An excellent day-hike destination is the second of the Gem Lakes (7 miles round-trip), a lovely aquamarine bowl and five-star lunch spot.

A dozen popular **USFS campgrounds** (☑877-444-6777; www.recreation.gov; off Rock Creek Rd; tent & RV sites from $22; ⊗late May-Sep; 🐾) line Rock Creek Rd; most are along Rock Creek and a few are reservable.

Just off Hwy 395, at the turnoff for Rock Creek Rd, is the classic **Tom's Place Resort Cafe** (☑760-935-4239; www.tomsplaceresort.com; 8180 Crowley Lake Dr; mains $7-22; ⊗7am-9pm; in winter 7.30am-8pm Thu-Mon). The decor is decidedly kitsch and brimming with Americana. Refuel in this friendly locals' joint with a stacked breakfast, or for dinner enjoy a country fried steak or burgers. A general store with food and other supplies is attached, as is a **resort** (☑760-935-4239; www.tomsplaceresort.com; 8180 Crowley Lake Dr; dm from $30-35, r $68-78, cabins $95-150) with basic, bare-bones cabins.

Bishop

☑442, 760 / POP 3800 / ELEV 4150FT

The second-largest town in the Eastern Sierra, Bishop is about two hours from Yosemite's Tioga Pass entrance. It's a major recreation hub, with dozens of motels and a funky little art and outdoor community. Bishop offers access to excellent fishing in nearby lakes, climbing in the Buttermilks just west of town, and hiking in the John Muir Wilderness via Bishop Creek Canyon and the Rock Creek drainage. The area is especially lovely in fall, when dropping temperatures cloak aspen, willow and cottonwood in myriad glowing shades.

The earliest inhabitants of the deep Owens Valley (which includes the towns of Independence, Big Pine, Bishop and Lone Pine) were Paiute and Shoshone Native

Americans, who today live on four reservations in the area. White settlers came on the scene in the 1860s and began raising cattle to sell to nearby mining settlements.

◉ Sights

★ Laws Railroad Museum
& Historic Site
MUSEUM

(☏760-873-5950; www.lawsmuseum.org; Silver Canyon Rd; donation $7; ☷10am-4pm Sep-May, 9.30am-4pm Jun-Aug; ⛟) This railroad and Old West museum recreates the village of Laws, an important stop on the route of the *Slim Princess,* a narrow-gauge train that hauled freight and passengers across the Owens Valley for nearly 80 years. You'll see the original 1883 train depot, a post office, a schoolhouse and other rickety old buildings. Many contain funky and eclectic displays (dolls, fire equipment, antique stoves, even stuffed conjoined twin lambs) from the pioneer days.

🏃 Activities

🧗 Climbing

Bishop is prime bouldering and rock-climbing territory, with terrain to match any level of experience and any climbing style. The main areas are the granite **Buttermilk Country**, nearly 8 miles west of town on Buttermilk Rd, and the stark **Volcanic Tablelands** and **Owens River Valley** (Happy and Sad Boulders) to the north. The tablelands are also a wellspring of Native American petroglyphs – tread lightly. For climbing advice pop into the visitors bureau or one of the many outdoor shops on Main St.

🏃 Hiking

Hikers will want to head to the high country by following Line St (Hwy 168) west along Bishop Creek Canyon, past Buttermilk Country and on to several lakes. Trailheads lead into the John Muir Wilderness and on into Kings Canyon National Park. Check with the White Mountain information station (p160) for suggestions, maps and wilderness permits for overnight stays.

🏃 Fishing

In the summer, fishing is good in the high-altitude lakes of **Bishop Creek Canyon** (west of town along Hwy 168). Other fine spots include the scenic, twisty and down-right magical **Owens River** (northeast) and the **Pleasant Valley Reservoir** (Pleasant Valley Rd, north of town).

✳ Festivals & Events

Mule Days RODEO

(www.muledays.org; Inyo County Fairgrounds; per show $15; ☷May; ⛟) Every Memorial Day weekend, Bishop hosts one of the more unique rodeo-like events in the US, celebrating and testing the skills of 'packers,' the cowboys running backcountry trips. One of the many shows and events is the Packer's Scramble, where 10-person teams have to unpack and repack their own mules in a chaos of hooves and saddles.

🛌 Sleeping

★ Keough's Hot Springs CABIN $

(☏760-872-4670; www.keoughshotsprings.com; 800 Keough Hot Springs Rd; tent/RV sites $28/33, cabins from $110; ⛟⛟) Head to this property southeast of Bishop, off Hwy 395, for a modest version of glamping in safari-like tents with their own front decks. Each of the four tent cabins has a small refrigerator and fire pit, perfect for nighttime barbecuing and stargazing. Ten campsites, two mobile homes for rent, and the pool and hot springs give it a basic resort feel.

Showers are $2 for guests and $4 for visitors.

★ Bishop Creekside Inn MOTEL $

(☏760-872-3044; www.bishopcreeksideinn.com; 725 N Main St; r from $130; ⛟⛟⛟⛟) Bishop's most upscale lodging underwent a full-scale renovation completed in summer 2017. Woodsy art and Western-style leather armchairs outfit rooms that come with marble bathrooms (with walk-in glass showers), roomy armchairs, Keurig coffee makers and thick duvet bedding. Bishop Creek runs right through the grounds; it can be crossed via a bridge.

PV Pit Campground CAMPGROUND $

(☏Bishop BLM field office 760-872-5008, reservations 877-444-6777; www.recreation.gov; off Pleasant Valley Dam Rd; tent sites $5) No water and no bathrooms, but this campground is especially popular with climbers for its backyard proximity to **Happy and Sad Boulders** and its dirt-cheap price. Take Hwy 395 north from Bishop and turn right onto Pleasant Valley Rd. After half a mile, turn left onto an unmarked gravel and dirt road; the campground is not far past this intersection.

Pleasant Valley Campground CAMPGROUND $

(☏760-873-5564; www.inyocountycamping.com; Pleasant Valley Dam Rd; tent & RV sites $14)

The narrow and twisty Owens River runs through this wide open campground not far northwest of Bishop. Ideal for those interested in fishing, or bouldering (or simply scampering up) the volcanic tableland towering over the sites and essentially right out front of your tent flap. Open year-round but hot in the middle of summer. Pay via the fee station on site.

USFS Campgrounds   CAMPGROUND $

(www.recreation.gov; tent & RV sites $26; ⊘ May-Sep; 🏕) For a scenic night, stretch out your sleeping bag beneath the stars. The closest USFS campgrounds, all but one first-come, first-served, are between 9 miles and 15 miles west of town on Bishop Creek along Hwy 168, at elevations between 7500ft and 9000ft.

Hostel California   HOSTEL $

(☏760-399-6316; www.thehostelcalifornia.com; 213 Academy Ave; dm from $25, private r from $60-100; ❉🐾) A rambling, historic Victorian house located in the center of town, this hostel packs in dusty long-distance backpackers during June and July, with a more varied mix of hikers, anglers, climbers and international travelers the rest of the year. There's a full kitchen, free coffee and bicycles for use, as well as a communal outdoors-loving atmosphere. Adults only.

Owner Matt Meyers, an avid climber, is an excellent source of information. Hostel showers are available for use for nonguests for $5.

Joseph House Inn
Bed & Breakfast   B&B $$

(☏760-872-3389; www.josephhouseinn.com; 376 W Yaney St; r incl breakfast $162-198; ❉🐾🅿) This beautifully restored ranch-style home with a patio overlooking a tranquil 3-acre garden has six nicely furnished rooms, some with fireplaces, all with TV. Guests enjoy a complimentary gourmet breakfast and afternoon wine.

✗ Eating

★ Erick Schat's Bakery   BAKERY $

(☏760-873-7156; www.erickschatsbakery.com; 763 N Main St; sandwiches $6-10; ⊘ 6am-6pm Sun-Thu, to 7pm Fri; 🐾) A deservedly hyped tourist mecca filled to the rafters with racks of fresh bread, dipping oil, jams and other goodies, Schat's has been making its baked goods since 1938. Some of the desserts, including the crispy cookies and bear claws, are ad-

dictive, and call for repeated trips while in town. Also has a popular sandwich bar and outdoor tables.

Holy Smoke Texas Style BBQ   BARBECUE $

(☏760-872-4227; www.holysmoketexasstylebbq. com; 772 N Main St; $7.50-18; ⊘ 11am-9pm Wed-Mon; 🅿🐾) Tasty barbecue food, flavorful smokey pulled pork and ridiculously cheesy baked mac 'n' cheese. The redneck taco comes with homemade cornbread piled with chopped brisket and outlaw coleslaw or potato salad on the side. Slather it in four different kinds of housemade sauces – ghost pepper, spicy, hot and regular. There's country apple crisp or banana pudding for desert.

Pupfish Café   CAFE $

(☏442-228-5100; www.pupfishcafe.com; 124 S Main St; mains $6-12; ⊘ 7am-2:30pm Mon-Fri, 8am-2pm Sat & Sun; 🐾) Named for a fish found in Death Valley, this small cafe at the back of Spellbinder Books (☏760-873-4511; www. spellbinderbookstore.com; 124 S Main St; ⊘ 10am-5:30pm Mon-Fri, 10am-5pm Sat, 10am-2pm Sun; 🐾) is an excellent place for breakfast or lunch or for whiling away a few hours with a coffee. The newspapers and board games help pass the time. Avocado toast and butter waffles are the specialties, but paninis and salads round out the menu.

Jack's Restaurant & Bakery   AMERICAN $

(☏760-872-7971; 437 N Main St; mains $8-20; ⊘ 6:30am-8.30pm) In business since 1946, old-school diner Jack's stocks a full menu of filling, inexpensive comfort food such as meatloaf and chicken fried steak, as well as hearty breakfasts. Its bread and pies are baked on site. The smaller portions are excellent value. Guess which of the wall-mounted fish are real.

Thai Thai   THAI $$

(☏760-872-2595; 703 Airport Rd; mains $14-16; ⊘ 11am-2pm & 5-8pm Tue-Sat) Thai food at the small Bishop airport seems fairly random, but locals rave about it. (Granted, it's the only Thai place in town.) Service can be slow, the portions relatively small and the furnishings 1970s-school-cafeteria chic, but it's a pleasant place to enjoy pad thai or a curry dish with a view of the White Mountains out the windows.

The entrance is inside the tiny terminal.

Back Alley   AMERICAN $$

(☏760-873-5777; www.thebackalleybowlandgrill. com; 649 N Main St; mains $10-24; ⊘ 11:30am-10pm

Sun-Thu, until midnight Fri & Sat) Tucked off the main drag, behind Yamatani's Restaurant, this busy bowling-alley bar and grill (with bowling-pin carpeting!) earns the locals' affection with huge portions of fresh fish, sirloin steak and burgers. Specials come with loads of sides and the homemade desserts are surprisingly good. Bowling is $4 per person, plus $2 shoe hire.

🍸 Drinking & Nightlife

Black Sheep Cafe   CAFE
(☑760-872-4142; www.blacksheepcoffeeroasters.com; 232 N Main St; ☺6:30am-6pm Mon-Thu, 6:30am-7pm Fri & Sat, 7am-6pm Sun) One for the coffee connoisseurs, this laid-back locals' hangout serves specialty java. Their aromatic Finca El Socorro is award-winning and has tropical notes of lemon, lime, mango and cacao. The cafe serves bagels, smoothies and lunch options; the housemade hummus, with avocado, fresh tomatoes and sprouts on whole-wheat toast is highly recommended. Serves craft beers on tap from 11.30am.

Mountain Rambler Brewery   MICROBREWERY
(☑760-258-1348; www.mountainramblerbrewery.com; 186 S Main St; ☺11:30am-10:30pm Sun-Thu, to 11:30pm Fri & Sat; 🐾) Rows of picnic tables and a high ceiling give this spot a beer-gardeny feel. Its own beers are mixed in with a rotating selection of artisan brews, and there's live music several nights a week. Worth visiting for lunch or dinner for classic pub fare like burgers and bratwurst or more sophisticated dishes such as flatbread pizza ($9) and lamb empanadas ($5).

Good Earth Yogurt   WINE BAR
(☑760-872-2020; www.goodearthyogurt.com; 251 N Main St; ☺11am-9pm Sun-Thu, to 10pm Fri & Sat; 🐾) Like its refreshing yogurt parfaits, this wine and craft-beer bar and dessert cafe is a pleasing departure from the more ubiquitous Old West–style places. Its whitewashed contemporary-farm aesthetic wouldn't be out of place in Malibu, where the owner is from. The hybrid menu mixes California wines, self-serve soft yogurt in flavors like blood orange or vegan coconut cream, and organic pies.

🛍 Shopping

★ Wilson's
Eastside Sports   SPORTS & OUTDOORS
(☑760-873-7520; www.eastsidesports.com; 224 N Main St; ☺9am-6pm Sun-Thu, 9am-9pm Fri & Sat

in winter, 9am-9pm daily other times of year) This large store is a one-stop shop for all your outdoor needs. Rents camping, climbing, backpacking and winter-trekking gear, and sells shoes, clothing and backpacks. The friendly staff will also help with info on the local area and have a range of maps for sale.

Gear Exchange   SPORTS & OUTDOORS
(☑760-873-4300; 298 N Main St; ☺9am-7pm) Like a thrift store for outdoor gear, this is the place to pick up cheap secondhand items such as climbing shoes, backpacks, hiking poles, sleeping bags and clothing.

Sage to Summit   SPORTS & OUTDOORS
(☑760-872-1756; www.sagetosummit.com; 312 N Main St; ☺9am-6pm Mon-Sat, 10am-6pm Sun) Top-quality outdoor gear with a focus on lightweight packs and trail running. Also rents different-sized crash pads (from $10 per day) for bouldering.

ℹ Information

Bishop Area Visitors Bureau (☑760-873-8405; www.bishopvisitor.com; 690 N Main St; ☺10am-5pm Mon-Sat; 🛜) Helpful staff with information on accommodations and activities in Bishop and the surrounding region.

Inyo National Forest Wilderness Permit Office (☑760-873-2483; www.fs.usda.gov/inyo; 351 Pacu Lane, Ste 200; ☺8:30am-4:30pm daily; 8:30am-4:30pm Mon-Fri in winter) Offices for Inyo National Forest staff and wilderness-permit office.

White Mountain Public Lands Information Station (☑760-873-2500; www.fs.usda.gov/inyo; 798 N Main St; ☺8am-noon & 1-5pm daily, 8am-noon & 1-4pm Mon-Fri in winter) Wilderness permits, trail and campground information for the entire area.

Ancient Bristlecone Pine Forest

For encounters with some of the earth's oldest living things, plan at least a half-day trip to the **Ancient Bristlecone Pine Forest** (☑760-873-2500; www.fs.usda.gov/inyo; White Mountain Rd; ☺trails open all year; visitor center Fri-Mon mid-May–early-Nov; 🅿🚻) 🍃. These gnarled, otherworldly looking trees thrive above 10,000ft on the slopes of the seemingly inhospitable White Mountains, a parched and stark range that once stood even higher than the Sierra Nevada. The oldest tree – called Methuselah – is estimated to be more than 4700 years old, beating even the Great Sphinx of Giza by about two centuries.

To reach the groves, take Hwy 168 east 12 miles from Big Pine to White Mountain Rd, then turn left (north) and climb the curvy road 10 miles to Schulman Grove, named for the scientist who first discovered the trees' age in the 1950s. The entire trip takes about one hour. There's access to self-guided trails, and a solar-powered visitor center (☏760-873-2500; www.fs.usda.gov/inyo; White Mountain Rd; per person/car $3/6; ⊙10am-4pm Fri-Mon late-May–Oct). White Mountain Rd is usually closed from November to April (if you're very fit it's possible to hike or snowshoe in). It's nicest in August, when wildflowers sneak out through the rough soil.

A second grove, the Patriarch Grove, is dramatically set within an open bowl and reached via a 12-mile, graded dirt road. Four miles further on you'll find a locked gate, which is the departure point for day hikes to White Mountain Peak – at 14,246ft, it's the third-highest mountain in California. The round trip is about 14 miles via an abandoned road, soon passing through the Barcroft High Altitude Research Station. Some ride the route on mountain bikes: the nontechnical and marmot-laden road winds above the tree line, though, so the high elevation makes the going tough. Allow plenty of time and bring at least two quarts of water per person. For maps and details, stop at the White Mountain ranger station in Bishop.

For altitude adjustment or some good stargazing, spend a night at the Grandview Campground, at 8600ft. It has awesome views, tables and vault toilets, but no water.

Big Pine

☏760, 442 / POP 1710 / ELEV 3990FT

This blink-and-you-missed-it town has a few motels and basic eateries. It mainly functions as a launchpad for the Ancient Bristlecone Pine Forest and to the granite Palisades in the John Muir Wilderness, a rugged cluster of peaks which include six above 14,000ft. Stretching beneath the pinnacles is Palisade Glacier (access trailhead at Glacier Lodge, Glacier Lodge Rd; ⊙May-Oct), the southernmost and the largest in the Sierra Nevada. A 20-mile hiking trip via the Palisade Glacier trail will get you there; pick up the info from Glacier Lodge. The total trip requires a night of wilderness camping.

Located on the way up into the mountains are three USFS campgrounds (www.recreation.gov; Glacier Lodge Rd; tent & RV sites $22-24; ⊙May–mid-Oct; ☏) – Big Pine Creek, Sage Flat and Upper Sage Flat – which line Glacier Lodge Rd alongside Big Pine Creek (west of Big Pine). For awesome stargazing and rustic car camping, spend a night at the Grandview Campground (☏877-444-6777; www.recreation.gov; White Mountain Rd; donation $5; ⊙road may be closed during winter; ☏), spread out on a plateau at 8600ft.

The roadside barbecue Copper Top BBQ (☏760-970-5577; www.coppertopbbq.com; 310 N Main St; mains $10-19; ⊙11am-6pm Wed-Sun) is a Big Pine classic, drawing fans from afar for its pulled pork sandwiches, Saint Louis-style ribs and sampler platters.

Independence

☏442, 760 / POP 670 / ELEV 3930FT

This sleepy highway town about 16 miles north of Lone Pine has been a county seat since 1866, but it's on the map because of its proximity to the Manzanar National Historic Site – the concentration camp in which Japanese people were held against their will by the US government during WWII. It's also home to the Eastern California Museum (☏760-878-0364; www.inyocounty.us/ecmsite; 155 N Grant St; donation requested; ⊙10am-5pm; ℗♿). It contains one of the most complete collections of Paiute and Shoshone baskets in the country, as well as artifacts from the Manzanar relocation camp and historic photographs of primitively equipped local rock climbers scaling Sierra peaks, including Mt Whitney.

About 15 miles west of town via Onion Valley Rd (Market St in town), pretty Onion Valley (elevation 9600ft) harbors the trailhead for Kearsarge Pass (p150; 9.5 miles round-trip), an old Paiute trade route. This is the quickest eastside access to the John Muir and Pacific Crest Trails, and Kings Canyon National Park.

There are three USFS campgrounds (www.fs.usda.gov; tent & RV sites $14-21; ⊙approx May-Sep; ☏) alongside Independence Creek, including one at the Kearsarge Pass trailhead. A low-key hiker favorite, the cute cabins of the Mt Williamson Motel & Base Camp (☏760-878-2121; www.mtwilliamsonmotel.com; 515 S Edwards St; r $85 -$135; ❋🛜☏) bask among fruit trees and feature flat-screen TVs, calico bedspreads, tea kettles and arresting prints of Sierra Nevada bighorn sheep. Ask about their hiker packages that include trailhead transportation.

The cafe in the **Owens Valley Growers Co-op** (☑760-915-0091; www.owensvalleygrowerscooperative.com; 149 S Edwards St; mains from $9; ☺5.30-8.30pm Fri-Sun for dinner, 10am-2pm Sat & Sun for brunch; supermarket hours from 8.30am-6pm; 🛜✍), serving locally grown produce and other products, is open for Friday, Saturday and Sunday-night dinners; an outdoor farmers market is held on Fridays during peak summer. Upscale and unexpected in such a flyspeck town, bright, artistic **Still Life Cafe** (☑760-878-2555; 135 S Edward St; lunch $9-16, dinner $16-29; ☺11am-1pm & 4-9pm Thu-Mon) prepares escargot, steak au poivre and other French bistro faves.

Manzanar National Historic Site

A stark wooden guard tower alerts drivers to one of US history's darkest chapters, which unfolded on a barren, windy sweep of land some 5 miles south of Independence. Little remains of the infamous war concentration camp, a dusty square mile where more than 10,000 people of Japanese ancestry were corralled during WWII. The camp's lone remaining building, the former high-school auditorium, houses a superb **interpretive center** (☑760-878-2194; www.nps.gov/manz; 5001 Hwy 395; ☺9am-4:30pm; P🚻) ✦FREE. A visit is one of California's historical highlights and should not be missed.

Watch the 20-minute documentary, then explore the thought-provoking exhibits chronicling the stories of the families who languished here yet built a vibrant community. A self-guided 3.2-mile driving tour around the grounds, usually includes a recreated mess hall and barracks, vestiges of buildings and gardens, and the haunting camp cemetery. Sites are all accessible by foot or an auto road tour.

Lone Pine

☑442, 760 / POP 2040 / ELEV 3730FT

Tiny Lone Pine is the gateway to big things, most notably Mt Whitney, the loftiest peak in the contiguous USA, and Hollywood. In the 1920s cinematographers discovered that the nearby Alabama Hills were a picture-perfect movie set for Westerns, and stars from Gary Cooper to Gregory Peck could often be spotted swaggering about town.

◉ Sights

★Alabama Hills   NATURAL FEATURE
(Movie Flat Rd/Whitney Portal Rd; P🚻) FREE
The warm colors and rounded contours of the Alabama Hills, located on Whitney Portal Rd/Movie Flat Rd, stand in contrast to the jagged, snowy Sierras just behind. The setting for countless ride-'em-out movies, the popular *Lone Ranger* TV series and, more recently, parts of *Iron Man* (Jon Favreau, 2008) and Quentin Tarantino's *Django Unchained* (2012), the stunning orange rock formations are a beautiful place to experience sunrise or sunset.

You can drive, walk or mountain bike along dirt roads rambling through the boulders, and along Tuttle and Lone Pine Creeks. A number of graceful rock arches are within easy hiking distance of the roads. Head west on Whitney Portal Rd and either turn left at Tuttle Creek Rd, after a half-mile, or north on Movie Flat Rd, after about 3 miles. Following the latter route, the road eventually turns into Moffat Ranch Rd and brings you back to Hwy 395, only 3½ miles south of Manzanar National Historic Site. The websites of the **Lone Pine Chamber of Commerce** (☑760-876-4444; www.lonepinechamber.org; 120 S Main St; ☺8:30am-4:30pm Mon-Fri) and the Museum of Western Film History have excellent movie-location maps.

Museum of Western Film History   MUSEUM
(☑760-876-9909; www.museumofwesternfilmhistory.org; 701 S Main St; adult/under 12yr $5/free; ☺10am-5pm Mon-Sat, to 4pm Sun; P🚻🚼)
More than 400 movies, not to mention numerous commercials (mostly for rugged SUVs and Jeeps), have been shot in the area. This fascinating museum contains paraphernalia from locally set films, not just Westerns (as the name of the museum suggests). One of the most fascinating pieces in the collection is the 1928 Lincoln camera car – mounted cameras caught the action while cars drove alongside galloping horses. See *Django Unchained, Gladiator, Star Trek, Superman* and other memorabilia in engaging exhibits.

The museum's theater screens a well-made film about the history of Westerns shot in the Alabama Hills. The museum hosts a film festival – geared to Westerns, of course – on the first weekend in October.

Sleeping

⭐ Alabama Hills

Bureau of Land Management CAMPGROUND
(www.blm.gov/visit/alabama-hills; Movie Flat Rd, Alabama Hills) `FREE` You can't go wrong with free camping amid some of the most striking scenery in the Sierras. Go along Movie Flat Rd, then pull off onto any of the dirt roads to find a private spot behind a rock formation with snowcapped mountains towering above. Of course, services are nonexistent, but for those you can head into Lone Pine, a short drive away.

⭐ Whitney Portal

Hostel & Hotel HOSTEL, MOTEL $
(☑760-876-0030; www.whitneyportalstore.com; 238 S Main St; dm/d from $32/100; ▩🛜▨) A popular launchpad for Mt Whitney trips and a locus of posthike washups (public showers are available), the Whitney has the cheapest beds in town – reserve dorms months ahead for July and August. There's no common space, just well-maintained single-sex bunk-bed rooms, though amenities include towels, TVs, in-room kitchenettes and stocked coffee makers.

The majority of the establishment consists of plush, modern motel rooms, and many look towards Whitney and its neighbors. The ground-floor general store is an excellent place to stock up on basic gear and food supplies. Showers for nonguests cost $7, include a free towel and are open until 7:30pm.

Tuttle Creek CAMPGROUND $
(www.blm.gov/visit/tuttle-creek-campground; off Horseshoe Meadows Rd; tent & RV sites $8; ▨) Off Whitney Portal Rd, this first-come, first-served Bureau of Land Management campground has 83 primitive sites at 5120ft with panoramic 'pinch-me!' views of the Sierras, the White Mountains and the rosy Alabama Hills. There's not much shade, though. It's near a small river, so occasionally can get mosquitos and is rather windy. Drop toilets on site.

Lone Pine Campground CAMPGROUND $
(www.fs.usda.gov; Whitney Portal Rd; tent & RV sites $22; ⏱mid-Apr–Oct; ▨) About midway between Lone Pine and Whitney Portal, this popular creekside USFS campground (elevation 6000ft) offers vault toilets and potable water. Also has a designated family section. Can get busy in peak summer, so pitch up early.

Dow Hotel & Dow Villa Motel HOTEL, MOTEL $
(☑760-876-5521; www.dowvillamotel.com; 310 S Main St; r $72-172; 🅿🛜▩@🛜▨▨) John Wayne and Errol Flynn are among the stars who have stayed at this venerable hotel. Built in 1922, the place has been restored but retains much of its rustic charm. The rooms in the newer motel section have air-con, but are also more generic. The cheaper rooms have shared bathrooms. Wi-fi in the historic wing is only available in the lobby.

🍴 Eating

Alabama Hills Cafe DINER $
(☑760-876-4675; www.alabamahillscafe.com; 111 W Post St; breakfast items $2.25-$14; ⏱7am-2pm; 🛜🚲▧) Just off the main streets, at everyone's favorite breakfast joint, the portions are big, the bread is freshly baked and the soups hearty. Sandwiches and fruit pies make lunch an attractive option too. You can also plan your drive through the Alabama Hills with the help of the map on the menu and rock formations painted on the walls.

Lone Pine Smokehouse BARBECUE $
(☑760-876-4433; www.lonepinesmokehouse.com; 325 S Main St; sandwiches & mains $7-23; ⏱noon-8pm Mon-Thu, to 9pm Fri-Sun; ▨) The quality at this friendly Texas-style-barbecue place seems to be hit or miss – the beef brisket and pulled pork are most consistent. Despite the Western-themed facade, the dining room is simple, unadorned and modern. It's best to grab an outdoor table on a sunny day (dogs allowed). Regular live music events; enquire inside.

Seasons AMERICAN $$
(☑760-876-8927; www.seasonslonepine.com; 206 N Main St; mains $18-33; ⏱5-9pm daily Apr-Oct; 5-9pm Tue-Sun Nov-Mar) Seasons has everything you fantasized about the last time you choked down freeze-dried hiking rations. Goats cheese pizza, steak eight ways, grilled lamb chops, roasted duck and plates of carb-replenishing pasta will revitalize your appetite. Meanwhile, the nice and naughty desserts will leave you purring. Reservations recommended.

🍸 Drinking & Nightlife

Jake's Saloon BAR
(☑760-876-5765; 119 N Main St; ⏱noon-2am) Proper small town honky-tonk with swing doors and a Wild West vibe, plus shuffleboard and pool tables. It serves Mammoth Brewery beers.

🛍 Shopping

Elevation SPORTS & OUTDOORS

(📞760-876-4560; www.sierraelevation.com; 150 S Main St, cnr Whitney Portal Rd; ⏰9am-6:30pm Sun-Thu, until 7pm Fri & Sat) Rents bear canisters and crampons, and sells hiking, backpacking and climbing gear.

❶ Information

Eastern Sierra Interagency Visitor Center

(📞760-876-6222; www.fs.fed.us/r5/inyo; cnr Hwys 395 & 136; ⏰8am-5pm, in winter 8am-4pm) USFS information center for the Sierra Nevada, Death Valley and Mt Whitney; about 1.5 miles south of town. The place to get trail info, plus self-issue wilderness permits (in the winter months) and pack out your poop packs.

Mt Whitney

The mystique of Mt Whitney (14,505ft) captures the imagination, and conquering its hulking bulk becomes a sort of obsession for many. The main **Mt Whitney Trail** (the easiest and busiest one) leaves from Whitney Portal, about 13 miles west of Lone Pine via Whitney Portal Rd (closed in winter), and climbs about 6000ft over 11 miles. It's a superstrenuous, really, *really* long walk that'll wear out even experienced mountaineers, but it doesn't require technical skills if attempted in summer or early fall. Earlier or later in the season, you'll likely need an ice axe and crampons, and to stay overnight.

Many people in good physical condition make it to the top, although only superbly conditioned, previously acclimatized hikers should attempt this as a day hike. Breathing becomes difficult at these elevations, and altitude sickness is a common problem. Rangers recommend spending a night camping at the trailhead and another at one of the two camps along the route: **Outpost Camp** at 3.5 miles or **Trail Camp** at 6 miles up the trail.

When you pick up your permit and packout kits (hikers must pack out their poop) at the Eastern Sierra Interagency Visitor Center (p164) in Lone Pine, get the latest info on weather and trail conditions. Near the trailhead, the **Whitney Portal Store** (📞760-876-0030; www.whitneyportalstore.com; ⏰hours vary May-Oct; 📶) sells groceries and snacks. It also has public showers ($7, including a towel) and a cafe with enormous burgers and pancakes. The message board on its website is a good starting point for Whitney research.

The biggest obstacle in getting to the peak may be obtaining a **wilderness permit**, which is required for all overnight trips and for day hikes past Lone Pine Lake (about 2.8 miles from the trailhead). A quota system limits daily access to 60 overnight and 100 day hikers from May to October. Because of the huge demand, permits are distributed via the online **Mt Whitney lottery** (📞760-873-2483; www.fs.usda.gov/inyo; admin fee $10, plus per person $15; ⏰8am-4:30pm), with applications accepted from February to mid-March ($15 per person reservation fee). To manage your expectations – around 18,000 people applied in 2017, with a 32% success rate.

Want to avoid the hassle of getting a permit for the main Mt Whitney Trail? Consider ascending this popular pinnacle from the west, using the **backdoor route** from Sequoia & Kings Canyon National Parks. It takes about six days from Crescent Meadow via the High Sierra Trail to the John Muir Trail – with no Whitney Zone permit required – and wilderness permits are much easier to secure.

AROUND YOSEMITE NATIONAL PARK MAMMOTH LAKES REGION

Sequoia & Kings Canyon National Parks

Best Hikes

➜ General Sherman Tree (p187)

➜ Tokopah Falls (p37)

➜ High Sierra Trail (p178)

➜ Moro Rock (p188)

➜ Mist Falls (p176)

➜ Rae Lakes Loop (p179)

Best Places to Stay

➜ Lodgepole Campground (p196)

➜ Three Rivers Hideaway (p205)

➜ Hume Lake Campground (p200)

➜ John Muir Lodge (p201)

➜ Bearpaw High Sierra Camp (p197)

Why Go?

The twin parks of Sequoia and Kings Canyon dazzle with superlatives, though they're often overshadowed by Yosemite, their smaller neighbor to the north (a three-hour drive away). With towering forests of giant sequoias containing some of the largest trees in the world and the mighty Kings River careening through the depths of Kings Canyon (one of the deepest chasms in the country), the parks are lesser-visited jewels where it's easier to find quiet and solitude. Throw in opportunities for caving, rock climbing and back-country hiking through granite-carved Sierra landscapes as well as backdoor access to 14,494ft Mt Whitney – the tallest peak in the lower 48 states – and you have all the ingredients for two of the best parks in the country.

Road Distances (Miles)

	Lodgepole Village	Three Rivers	Mineral King	Grant Grove Village
Three Rivers	25			
Mineral King	50	30		
Grant Grove Village	25	55	75	
Cedar Grove Village	55	80	100	30

Fast Facts

➡ Total area: 1353 sq miles (865,964 acres)

➡ Foothills (Sequoia) elevation: 1720ft

➡ Grant Grove (Kings Canyon) elevation: 6589ft

Reservations

DNC Parks & Resorts (☎801-559-4930, 866-807-3598; www.visitsequoia.com) Lodging in Sequoia and Kings Canyon National Parks.

NPS & USFS Campgrounds (☎518-885-3639, 877-444-6777; www.recreation.gov)

Sequoia-Kings Canyon Park Services Company (☎877-828-1440, 559-565-3388; www.sequoia-kings-canyon.com) Some Sequoia National Forest lodgings.

Resources

NPS (www.nps.gov/seki/planyourvisit/lodgingoutsideparks.htm) More area accommodations.

Sequoia National Forest (www.fs.usda.gov/sequoia) All about the Giant Sequoia National Monument.

Entrances

Both national parks are only accessible by car from the west and no roads cross the Sierra Nevada mountain range, only trails. Furthest south, Sequoia National Park's main entrance is at Ash Mountain (p182) in the foothills. Furthest north, Big Stump (Hwy 180; entry per car $30) is Kings Canyon National Park's only entrance.

All park entrances are open 24 hours a day year-round. Some roads – including Mineral King Rd beyond Three Rivers in Sequoia National Park, Hwy 180 past the Hume Lake turnoff in Kings Canyon National Park, and Big Meadows Rd in the Sequoia National Forest off the Generals Hwy – are closed during winter. Exact opening and closing dates vary by area of the park and on the weather from year to year. The most remote and hazardous roads may be inaccessible from autumn's first snowfall until the snow melts in late spring or early summer.

DON'T MISS

Although there's a lot to see just inside both national parks, Sequoia National Forest also has amazingly scenic spots, from ancient sequoia groves to alpine lakes. In fact, driving between the national parks on the Generals Hwy, or from Grant Grove to Cedar Grove via the Kings Canyon Scenic Byway, you'll pass right through the Sequoia National Forest and its Giant Sequoia National Monument, making it easy to stop off and see the sights, score a campsite or hike less-trammeled trails into the wilderness.

When You Arrive

➡ Although administered as a single unit by the National Park Service (NPS), Sequoia and Kings Canyon National Parks are actually two national parks.

➡ The two parks together are commonly referred to as 'SEKI.' The phrase 'Kings Canyon' may refer to the national park or may just mean the canyon itself.

➡ The seven-day entrance fee (per vehicle $30) covers both national parks and the nearby Hume Lake District of the Sequoia National Forest.

➡ If you arrive at night when park entrance stations are unstaffed, pay the entrance fee the next morning at the closest entrance station or upon exiting the park.

➡ The national parks' free seasonal newspaper, *The Visitor Guide,* is offered at either entrance station (Big Stump or Ash Mountain) and loaded with information on activities, campgrounds, lodging, shuttles, visitor services, safety tips and more.

⚡ DAY HIKES

Leave your car behind and go ramble around wildflower meadows and serene groves of giant sequoias, or hoof it to rushing waterfalls and up polished granite domes for epic views of Sierra Nevada peaks.

Sequoia National Park

The Giant Forest area has the biggest network of hiking routes, with a few wheelchair-accessible paved trails. The high-elevation Mineral King Valley steps you immediately into the Sierra Nevada backcountry.

⚡ Moro Rock

Duration 40 minutes

Distance 0.5 miles

Difficulty Easy

Start/Finish Moro Rock parking lot/ shuttle stop

Nearest Town Lodgepole Village

Transportation Shuttle, car

Summary After a quick ascent to the tippy-top of this granite dome, panoramic views are worth every ounce of effort. On clear days, open your eyes wide for views

up to 150 miles to the Coast Range, plus other skyscraping peaks and the foothills ever-so-far below.

Built by the Civilian Conservation Corps (CCC) in the 1930s, this trail features almost 400 steps, which shoot up over a quarter-mile to a railed-in viewpoint corridor atop Sequoia's iconic granite dome. Warning – you do *not* want to be anywhere on this trail during a lightning storm. From the summit, you can stare down at the Kaweah River's Middle Fork, across to Sawtooth Peak south in the Mineral King region and toward the peaks of the Great Western Divide to the east, including the spike of Black Kaweah, Lawson Peak, Kaweah Queen and Mt Stewart. It's sometimes possible to spot Sugarbowl Dome and Little Blue Dome, near Bearpaw Meadow in the distance. Near dusk, the monolith-like crags of Castle Rocks cast dramatic shadows over the dizzyingly deep river canyon. Beware that on hazy days (most common in summer), air pollution obscures the views.

The road to Moro Rock (Crescent Meadow Rd) is closed from late October until late May, but the hike is still accessible on foot. Walk the 1.7 miles from Giant Forest Museum along Crescent Meadow Rd (conditions may be snowy).

SEQUOIA & KINGS CANYON NATIONAL PARKS DAY HIKES

Sequoia National Park – Day Hikes

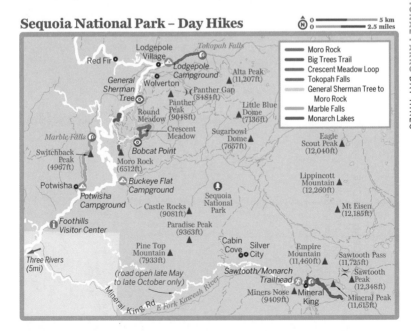

Sequoia & Kings Canyon National Parks

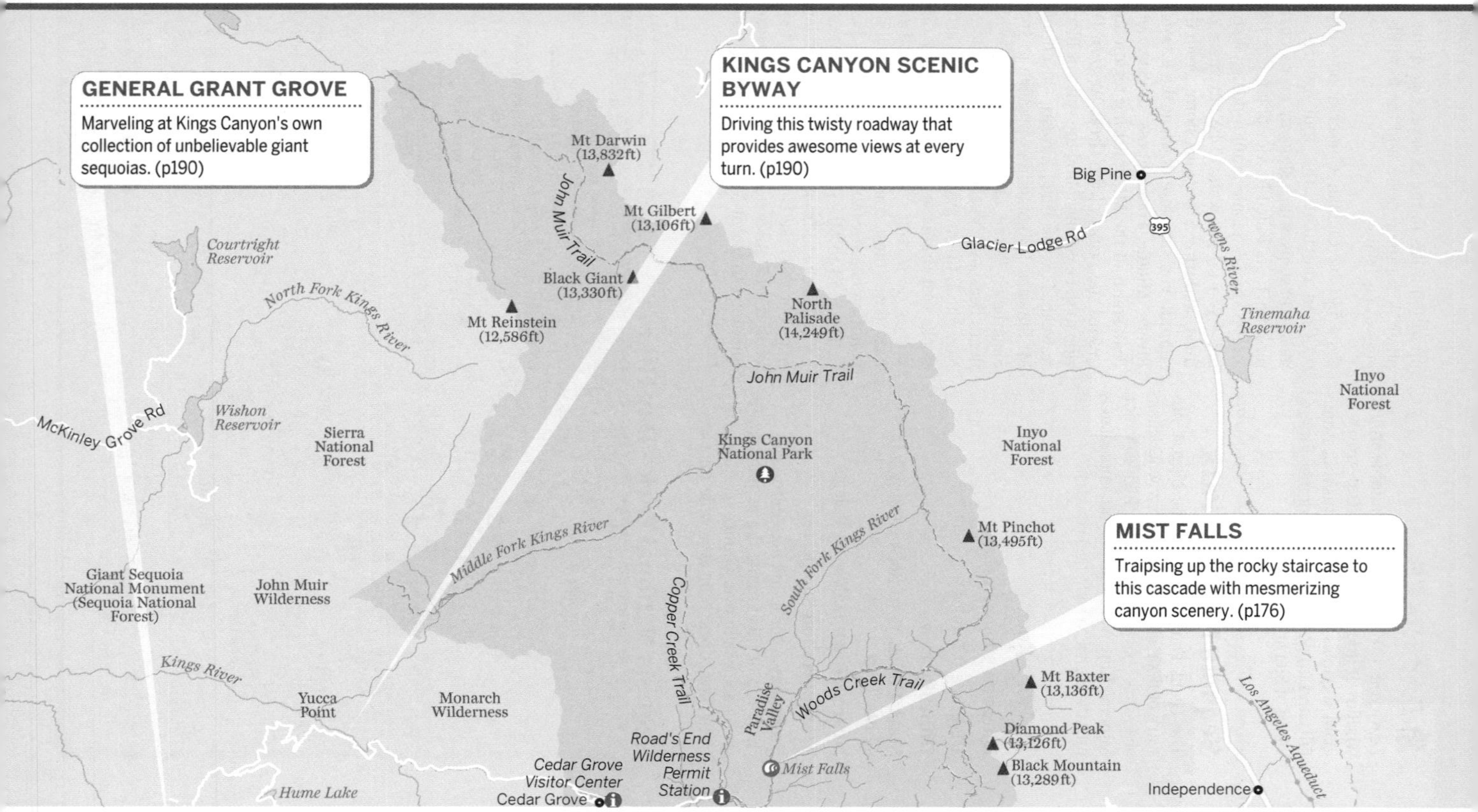

GENERAL GRANT GROVE

Marveling at Kings Canyon's own collection of unbelievable giant sequoias. (p190)

KINGS CANYON SCENIC BYWAY

Driving this twisty roadway that provides awesome views at every turn. (p190)

MIST FALLS

Traipsing up the rocky staircase to this cascade with mesmerizing canyon scenery. (p176)

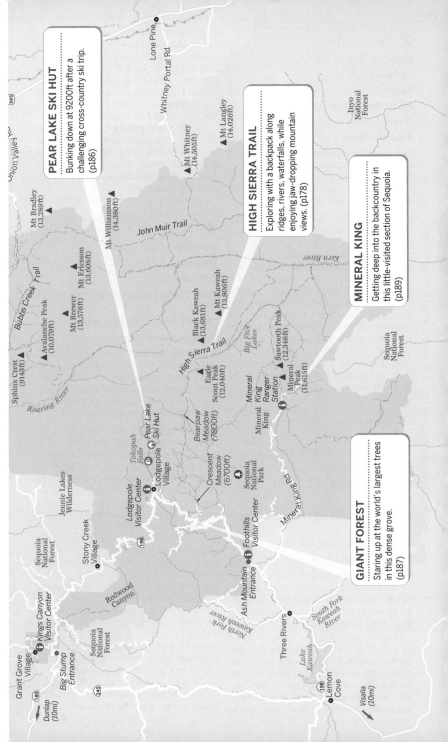

PEAR LAKE SKI HUT
Bunking down at 9200ft after a challenging cross-country ski trip. (p186)

HIGH SIERRA TRAIL
Exploring with a backpack along ridges, rivers, waterfalls, while enjoying jaw-dropping mountain views. (p178)

MINERAL KING
Getting deep into the backcountry in this little-visited section of Sequoia. (p189)

GIANT FOREST
Staring up at the world's largest trees in this dense grove. (p187)

Lone Pine

Whitney Portal Rd

395

Inyo National Forest

Mt Whitney (14,505ft)

Mt Langley (14,026ft)

Mt Bradley (13,289ft)

Mt Williamson (14,380ft)

John Muir Trail

Mt Ericsson (13,608ft)

Bubbs Creek Trail

Mt Brewer (13,576ft)

Avalanche Peak (10,079ft)

Sphinx Crest (9143ft)

Kern River

Black Kaweah (13,681ft)

Mt Kaweah (13,806ft)

High Sierra Trail

Big Five Lakes

Roaring River

Eagle Scout Peak (12,040ft)

Sawtooth Peak (12,348ft)

Sequoia National Forest

Mineral Peak (11,615ft)

Bearpaw Meadow (7800ft)

Pear Lake Ski Hut

Mineral King Ranger Station

Mineral King

Tokopah Falls

Lodgepole Village

Lodgepole Visitor Center

Jennie Lakes Wilderness

Crescent Meadow (6700ft)

Sequoia National Park

198

Mineral King Rd

Stony Creek Village

Sequoia National Forest

Redwood Canyon

Kings Canyon Visitor Center

Grant Grove Village

Big Stump Entrance

180

Dunlap (10mi)

245

Ash Mountain Entrance

Foothills Visitor Center

Sequoia National Forest

North Fork Kaweah River

Three Rivers

South Fork Kaweah River

Lake Kaweah

198

Lemon Cove

Visalia (10mi)

🚶 Big Trees Trail

Duration 45 minutes

Distance 1.2 miles

Difficulty Easy

Start/Finish Giant Forest Museum

Nearest Town Lodgepole Village

Transportation Shuttle, car

Summary On a paved trail circling a petite meadow embraced by giant sequoias, this family-friendly nature walk shows off some of the park's signature flora, all growing within one small area.

Starting from the 'Trail Center' outside the Giant Forest Museum, follow a well-marked path beside the Generals Hwy to join a paved and wooden-boardwalk loop around pretty Round Meadow. Giant sequoias over 250ft tall tower over the edge of the lush meadow, while interpretive panels give the lowdown on sequoia ecology, explaining how the western Sierra Nevada ecosystem supports these ginormous trees' growth. Wildflowers peak in early summer for kaleidoscopic bursts of color.

A wheelchair-accessible route starts from a specially designated parking lot (disabled-parking placard required) off the Generals Hwy, which shortens the total distance to 0.7 miles. The initial section is packed dirt and has a slight incline.

🚶 Crescent Meadow Loop

Duration 1 hour

Distance 1.6 miles

Difficulty Easy

Start/Finish Crescent Meadow parking lot/shuttle stop

Nearest Town Lodgepole Village

Transportation Shuttle, car

Summary At this beautiful and easily reached subalpine meadow, ringed by a canopy of firs and sequoias, early summer wildflowers turn up the color and black bears often forage nearby.

From the trailhead, stroll either clockwise or counter-clockwise around the peaceful, shady meadow loop. Downed logs make handy steps for peering over the high grass, but don't let your footfalls crunch and compact the fragile meadow itself. If you're quiet and stealthy, you may spy black bears ripping

apart logs as they look for tasty insects crawling around underneath the bark. Around the meadow's northeast corner, poke your head inside and look up the hollow fire-scarred Chimney Tree. It's a 0.3-mile detour east toward Log Meadow to inspect Tharp's Log, a fallen giant sequoia that a 19th-century settler converted into a rustic cabin.

During winter months (late October until late May), Crescent Meadow Rd is closed, but it's still accessible on foot. Walk the 2.6 miles from Giant Forest Museum along Crescent Meadow Rd (conditions may be icy – you may need snowshoes, which can be rented from Lodgepole Market) to reach the meadow.

🚶 Tokopah Falls

Duration 2 hours

Distance 3.6 miles

Difficulty Easy

Start/Finish Lodgepole Campground (p196)

Nearest Town Lodgepole Village

Transportation Shuttle, car

Summary Gradually rising over 500ft in elevation, this riverside stroll reaches one of the parks' most scenic waterfalls, tumbling down a boulder-lined canyon. Starting from the campground, it's a popular hike for families with children.

From the trailhead parking area next to the shuttle-bus stop inside Lodgepole Campground (open late May to late September), walk east along the access road. Cross the bridge to the north side of the Kaweah River's Marble Fork, where you'll spot a trailhead sign. The entire hike runs through a sun-dappled forest alongside the river, with exceptional views of the glacier-carved canyon and opportunities to watch mule deer, black bears and tiny pika.

As you near the falls, the severe 1800ft granite face of the Watchtower looms to the south. Now fully exposed to the sun, the rocky trail ascends through granite boulders and slabs before arriving at a viewing area. At 1200ft high, Tokopah Falls doesn't free fall but rather bounces off the granite canyon cliffs with all the noise it can muster, especially when snowmelt gushes in late spring and possibly early summer. When you're ready, return along the same route.

Note: the road up to the trailhead can be closed in winter months, but is still accessible by foot (roughly a half-mile walk from Lodgepole Market).

🏃 General Sherman Tree to Moro Rock

Duration 3–4 hours

Distance 6 miles one way

Difficulty Moderate

Start Wolverton Rd parking lot/shuttle stop

Finish Moro Rock parking lot/shuttle stop

Nearest Town Lodgepole Village

Transportation Shuttle, car

Summary A deviation from the popular Congress Trail loop, this rolling one-way hike takes in huge sequoias, green meadows and the pinnacle of Moro Rock. Expect stretches of blissful solitude and potential black bear sightings.

Keep in mind that hiking this route in one direction is possible only when the free seasonal park shuttle buses are running, usually from late May until September.

From the General Sherman parking lot and shuttle stop off Wolverton Rd, just east of the Generals Hwy, a paved trail quickly descends through towering sequoias. At an overlook on the way down, you'll get the best view of the General Sherman Tree. After walking up to the giant's trunk, turn around and walk downhill on the western branch of the Congress Trail loop. (If you end up on the eastern branch by mistake, jog right then left at two minor trail junctions that appear about 0.5 miles south of the General Sherman Tree.)

At a five-way junction by the McKinley Tree, continue straight ahead south on the dirt trail towards Cattle Cabin. Pass the hollow-bottom Room Tree and the pretty cluster of Founders Group as you walk through tufts of ferns and corn lilies. Approaching the bright green strip of 'C'-shaped Circle Meadow, there are no more crowds and all you can hear is the breeze and birdsong. Trace the eastern edge of the meadow toward another well-named tree group, the Pillars of Hercules. Stand between them and look up for a heroic view.

The trail then passes the huge charred maw of the Black Arch tree. Continue south, veering slightly right and then left at the next two trail junctions. At a three-way intersection, lush Crescent Meadow finally comes into view. Go straight at this junction and the next one to continue or make a 0.6-mile round-trip detour to the Squatters Cabin by going right on the trail marked 'Huckleberry Meadow.' On the north side of Crescent Meadow stands the hollow-bodied Chimney Tree. Continue east past Tharp's Log, which once was a pioneer cabin, then turn right (south) on a paved trail along the east side of Log Meadow.

Before reaching the Crescent Meadow parking lot, head left then right onto the signed High Sierra Trail, heading west for more marvelous ridge views. Stop at Bobcat Point overlook to take in the Great Western Divide and Kaweah Canyon. In 0.2 miles, cross Crescent Creek on a log to join the Sugar Pine Trail. Go left (west) and follow it for 0.9 miles to Moro Rock. Climb the granite dome for some of the park's best views, then return to your starting point via shuttle buses (the gray route leaves from Moro Rock and goes to Giant Forest Museum, from where the green route goes to General Sherman).

🏃 Marble Falls

Duration 3–4 hours

Distance 7.8 miles

Difficulty Moderate

Start/Finish Potwisha Campground

Nearest Town Three Rivers

Transportation Shuttle, car

Summary Climb over 1500ft as you follow the curves of chaparral-blanketed hills and parallel a river canyon to reach a tumbling cascade. Prime time is spring, when wildflowers bloom and it's not as hot.

Because of the extreme heat in the low-elevation foothills, get an early morning start in summer. There are a few parking spaces at the trailhead next to campsite number 14, but unless you are staying at Potwisha Campground you'll most likely have to park at the dumpsite opposite the campground. At the trail entrance, start walking on the dirt road, heading uphill and across a concrete viaduct. Look for a sign for the trail, which starts steeply to the right with a series of challenging switchbacks. The first five minutes of the trail is the steepest, but it evens out quickly, climbing slowly up 1450ft on the route.

Past the switchbacks, shady tree cover gives way to scrubby chaparral. The trail

NAME	REGION	DESCRIPTION	DIFFICULTY
Big Trees Trail (p170)	Giant Forest	paved, kid-friendly interpretive trail circling a sequoia-bordered forest meadow	easy
Crescent Meadow Loop (p170)	Giant Forest	beautiful subalpine meadow ringed by giant sequoias & summer wildflowers	easy
General Grant Tree Trail (p174)	Grant Grove	paved interpretive loop through a giant-sequoia grove	easy
General Sherman Tree to Moro Rock (p171)	Giant Forest	huge sequoias, peaceful meadows & the pinnacle of Moro Rock	moderate
High Sierra Trail to Lone Pine Creek (via Bearpaw High Sierra Camp; p178)	Giant Forest	gorgeous sequoia-grove & canyon-view hike, crossing mountain streams	difficult
Lakes Trail (p177)	Wolverton	forest climb to a string of gorgeous alpine lakes	moderate
Marble Falls (p171)	Foothills	lower-elevation hike parallels a river canyon to a thundering cascade	moderate
Mist Falls (p175)	Cedar Grove	partly shaded forest & granite hike to a gushing waterfall	moderate
Monarch Lakes (p172)	Mineral King	high-country hike to two alpine lakes at base of Sawtooth Peak	difficult
Moro Rock (p167)	Giant Forest	steep granite dome ascent for panoramic peak & canyon views	easy
Paradise Creek Trail (p196)	Three Rivers	riverside amble through moss-covered forest, with river crossings & pleated valley views	easy
Rae Lakes Loop (p179)	Cedar Grove	passes a chain of jewel-like lakes in the heart of the Sierra Nevada high country	difficult
River Trail (p175)	Roads End	mostly shaded woodland terrain, follows river, pretty meadow & a waterfall	easy
Tokopah Falls (p170)	Lodgepole	one of Sequoia's largest, most easily accessed scenic waterfalls	easy
Zumwalt Meadow Loop (p175)	Cedar Grove	flat, meadow boardwalk loop traces the Kings River beside canyon walls	easy

 Drinking Water   Restrooms   Waterfall   Transportation to Trailhead

continues north alongside a deep canyon, with carpeted valleys and views of the Kaweah River's Marble Fork. It crosses several streams and ducks into the woods, then veers towards the river and the booming falls, dead-ending in a heap of granite boulders – a lovely lunch spot.

Retrace your steps to return. Watch out for rattlesnakes, ticks and poison oak on the route.

🏃 Monarch Lakes

Duration 4–6 hours

Distance 8.4 miles

Difficulty Difficult

Start/Finish Sawtooth/Monarch trailhead parking area

Nearest Town Silver City

Transportation Car

DURATION	ROUND-TRIP DISTANCE (MILES)	ELEVATION CHANGE (FT)	FEATURES	FACILITIES
45min	1.2	+100	🦌 👪	🚰 🚻 🚌
1hr	1.6	+200	🦌 👪	🚰 🚻 🚌
30min	0.5	+100	🔭 👪	🚰 🚻
2½-4hr	6	+1600	🔭 🦌	🚰 🚻 🚌
3 days +	32	+2200	🔭 🦌	🚰 🚻 ▲ 👪
2 days	12.6	+2000	🔭 🦌	🚻 🚌
3-4hr	7	+2000	♨ 🔭	🚰 🚻
3-5hr	8	+800	♨ 🔭	🚰 🚻 👥
4-6hr	8.5	+2700	🔭 🦌	🚰 🚻 ▲
40min	0.5	+300	🔭 👪	🚌
2-2½hr	6	+520	🔭	🚰 🚻
5 days +	40	+7000	♨ 🔭 🦌	🚰 🚻 ▲ 👪
2-3hr	5.6	+100	♨	🚻
2hr	3.5	+500	♨ 🔭 🦌 👪	🚰 🚻 🚌
1hr	1.5	+100	🔭 🦌 👪	🚻

🔭 View   🦌 Wildlife Watching   ▲ Backcountry Campsite   👪 Great for Families   👥 Ranger Station

SEQUOIA & KINGS CANYON NATIONAL PARKS DAY HIKES

Summary A marmot-lover's paradise! This exceptionally scenic out-and-back high-country route reaches two alpine lakes below jagged Sawtooth Peak. Although it's not very long, the trail can be breathtakingly steep.

A steep climb kicks off this higher-altitude trek. At the Timber Gap Trail junction just over 0.5 miles in, you can see Mineral King Rd back below and snow-brushed peaks looking south. Turn right, following the signs for Sawtooth Pass. Corn lilies and paintbrush speckle Groundhog Meadow, named for the whistling marmots that scramble around the granite rocks seemingly everywhere you look during this hike.

Leaving the meadow, rock-hop across burbling Monarch Creek. On its far bank, a shady wooded spot is the perfect place for a picnic lunch. From there, begin ascending a stretch of loose and lazy switchbacks with goose-bump views. It's a slow, steady climb through red fir and pine forest that won't leave you too winded, though you'll feel the altitude the higher you climb. Blue grouse may be spotted on the hillsides.

At about 2.5 miles, there's a signed junction for the Crystal Lake Trail, which takes a hard and steep right. Bear left and continue straight up toward Sawtooth Pass instead. After flipping to the opposite side of the ridgeline, the trail rounds Chihuahua Bowl, an avalanche-prone granite basin named after a Mexican mining region. The tree line wavers and fades away, opening up gorgeous views of Monarch Creek canyon, Timber Gap and the peaks of the Great Western Divide.

The distinctive pitch of Sawtooth Peak (12,348ft) is visible ahead. A walk through a large talus field and some stream crossings brings you to Lower Monarch Lake (10,400ft), where round-topped Mineral Peak (11,615ft) points up directly south. The maintained trail stops here, but Upper Monarch Lake (10,640ft) can be reached by a steep trail heading up the hillside. Established backpacker campsites are by the lower lake; wilderness permit required for overnight camping.

When you're ready, retrace your steps to return. If you're looking for more challenging cross-country treks with some steep dropoffs and rock scrambling required, detour up scree-covered Sawtooth Pass (11,725ft) or make an alternate return route via Crystal Lake (10,900ft). Ask for route advice and safety tips at the Mineral King ranger station first.

Note: Mineral King Rd, the winding route up to the Sawtooth/Monarch trailhead, is closed during winter (usually between October and June). Hardcore hikers with snow gear may attempt to trek the snow-covered road from Three Rivers to the trailhead (around 25 miles), but it's not recommended.

Kings Canyon National Park

Towering stands of giant sequoias await in Grant Grove. Deep inside Kings Canyon is a meditative meadow walk and a day hike to a waterfall; start near Road's End.

🏃 General Grant Tree Trail

Duration 30 minutes

Distance 0.5 miles

Difficulty Easy

Start/Finish General Grant Grove parking lot

Nearest Town Grant Grove Village

Transportation Shuttle, car

Summary Meet the General Grant Tree, the second-largest living tree in the world, on a short, paved, self-guided interpretive loop through one of the park's most extraordinary giant sequoia groves. The trail is wheelchair accessible.

At the east end of the parking lot, you can see the cheerfully named tree cluster The Happy Family. Starting from the fenced main trailhead just west, bear right and begin a counter-clockwise loop. Many of the monster sequoias in General Grant Grove are named for US states, and the first you come across is the Pennsylvania Tree. Beyond stands the Lincoln Tree (it's the fourth-largest giant sequoia in the world, after General Sherman, General Grant and President). Look out for the submerged logs, which are actually exposed roots – the accumulated damage from more than a century of visitors' footsteps. Though it may be tempting not to, always stick to the trail (and make sure kids do too).

Further along is the Fallen Monarch, a toppled log so big that its hollow core has been used as a cabin, a hotel and saloon, and then as horse stables by the US Cavalry. Walk through a mix of young sequoias and other conifers, including sugar pine and white fir, until you reach the impressive General Grant Tree, measuring over 268ft high and more than 100ft around at its sturdy base.

Next is the one-room Gamlin Cabin, built from sugar pine in 1872 by the first white settlers in the Grant Grove area; it later served as the park's first ranger station. For another good view of the General Grant Tree, detour right here from the main loop and bear up and around to the left. The path leads to a peaceful overlook called North Grant View and, unlike the rest of the trail, there's rarely anyone here to share the scenery.

Continuing back along the main trail you'll see the California Tree, struck by lightning in 1967. The tree's top was incinerated and fire burned inside until rangers grew concerned that burning branches would hurt visitors. A nimble park employee strung a rope between two adjacent trees and extinguished the blaze with a hose.

Amble onward back to the parking lot.

Kings Canyon National Park – Day Hikes

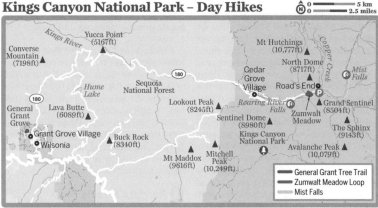

🥾 Zumwalt Meadow Loop

Duration 40 minutes–1 hour

Distance 1.5 miles

Difficulty Easy

Start/Finish Zumwalt Meadow parking lot

Nearest Town Cedar Grove Village

Transportation Car

Summary Beside the Kings River, this extremely scenic, mostly flat loop around a gorgeous meadow is a fun nature walk to do with kids. The trail flaunts knockout canyon views and excellent chances to spot wildlife.

A mile west of Road's End is Zumwalt Meadow, best in the early morning when mist floats above the meadow and birdsong echoes off the canyon's granite walls. Self-guided nature trail brochures ($1.50) are often available at the visitor center in Cedar Grove Village (open between late May and September).

From the parking lot, walk parallel to the river then across a suspension footbridge spanning the Kings River's South Fork. Behind you to the north is a view of North Dome, with a sheer cliff drop of more than 3600ft, higher than Yosemite's El Capitan. At the next junction, go left along the River Trail (Roads End, Hwy 180), then keep straight ahead to begin a counter-clockwise loop through a forest of cottonwood, willow, black oak, white fir and ponderosa pine trees. Early-morning hikers will be serenaded by birdsong.

Looking ahead, the granite cliffs of the Grand Sentinel cast shadows from more than a half-mile above the canyon floor. The trail ascends and continues over a talus slope with great views of canyon cliffs and the lush meadow. At the next signed junction, turn left and follow the Kings River bank through ferns and a carpet of soft pine needles, then traipse across boardwalks that afford panoramic meadow views (do you spy any black bears?) to close the loop. Turn right and retrace your steps across the footbridge to the parking lot.

🥾 Mist Falls

Duration 3–5 hours

Distance 9.2 miles

Difficulty Moderate

Start/Finish Road's End

Nearest Town Cedar Grove Village

Transportation Car

Summary A satisfying long walk along the riverside and up a natural granite staircase highlights the beauty of Kings Canyon. The waterfall is thunderous in late spring and possibly into early summer, depending on the previous winter's snowpack.

Bring plenty of water and sunscreen on this hike, which gains 600ft in elevation before reaching the falls. Get an early morning start because the return trip can be brutally hot on summer afternoons and also so you can beat the crowds of big families.

The trail begins just past the Road's End wilderness permit station (Hwy 180; ⊙ usually 7am-3:30pm late May-late Sep), crossing a small footbridge over Copper Creek. Walk along a sandy trail through sparse cedar and pine forest, where boulders rolled by avalanches are scattered on the canyon floor. Keep an eye out for black bears. Eventually the trail enters cooler, shady and low-lying areas of ferns and reeds before reaching a well-marked, three-way junction with the Woods Creek Trail, just shy of 2 miles from Road's End.

Turn left (north) toward Paradise Valley and begin a gradual climb that runs parallel to powerful cataracts in the boulder-saturated Kings River. Stone-framed stairs lead to a granite knob overlook, with wide southern views of Avalanche Peak and the oddly pointed Sphinx, another mountain peak, behind you. Follow cairns up the rock face and continue briefly through shady forest to reach Mist Falls, one of the parks' largest waterfalls, with a fine spray to cool down warm hikers. Warning: don't wade above the waterfall or swim below it due to the danger of rockfall and swift water currents, especially during snowmelt runoff. In late summer, the river downstream from the falls may be tame enough for a dip, but use your own best judgment.

Retrace your steps, around 2.5 miles downhill, to the three-way trail junction. Instead of returning directly to Road's End, you can bear left and cross the bridge over the Kings River, briefly joining the Bubbs Creek Trail. After less than a quarter-mile, turn right onto the untrammeled Kanawyer Loop Trail, which is mostly flat. After crossing Avalanche Creek (you may need to wade through or cross via a makeshift bridge), the tree canopy opens up to show off sprawling talus slopes along the Kings Canyon's southern walls.

Muir Rock and its late-summer swimming hole come into view across the river before you make a short climb to the River Trail junction. Turn right and walk across the red footbridge, below which is another favorite late-summer swimming hole. Follow the path back to the paved highway, turning right to walk back to the Road's End parking lot.

🚶 OVERNIGHT HIKES

More than 850 miles of maintained trails await your footsteps in both national parks. From sun-bleached granite peaks soaring above alpine lakes, to wildflower-strewn meadows and gushing waterfalls, it's backpacking heaven. Mineral King, Lodgepole and Cedar Grove offer the best backcountry trail access, while the Jennie Lakes Wilderness in the Sequoia National Forest boasts pristine meadows and lakes at lower elevations.

Park-approved, bear-proof food canisters, which are always recommended, are mandatory in some places, especially for wilderness trips (eg Rae Lakes Loop). Rent bear canisters at park visitor centers and trailhead ranger stations or at the Lodgepole, Grant Grove and Cedar Grove Village markets (from around $11 per three-day trip). To prevent wildfires, campfires are only allowed in existing campfire rings in some backcountry areas.

ℹ Permits & Fees

Wilderness permits, which are required for all overnight trips in the national parks, are usually issued at trailhead ranger stations or the nearest visitor center. Overnight trips in the national forest require only campfire permits (free), available at the Kings Canyon Visitor Center in Grant Grove Village and the USFS Hume Lake District Office (☑559-338-2251; www.fs.fed.us/r5/se quoia; 35860 E Kings Canyon Rd/Hwy 180, Dunlap; ⊙8am-4:30pm Mon-Fri) outside the parks.

For national park trips, there's a $15 nontransferable permit fee during the quota season (late May through late September). About 25% of all available permits are first-come, first-served, made available to walk-up visitors starting at 1pm *the day before* your trip. Permit reservations are held until 9am on the day of your trip, after which no-show vacancies can be claimed by walk-up visitors. Notify the Wilderness Office (Map p192; ☑559-565-3766; www.nps. gov/seki/planyourvisit/backpacking.htm; Generals Hwy behind Foothills Visitor Center; per trip $15, winter free; ⊙8am-4pm Mon-Fri) if you are going to be late. Outside the quota period, self-issue permits are free. Self-issue permit stations are located at some trailheads and visitor centers.

To reserve your wilderness permit ahead of time (essential for popular trails during the quota season), requests must be received two weeks in advance of your trip date, beginning on March 1 of that year. It's not unusual for permits for popular trails to sell out immediately for all summer weekend departures. Permit applications can be downloaded from the parks' website (www.nps. gov/seki), which also offers a comprehensive wilderness trip planner.

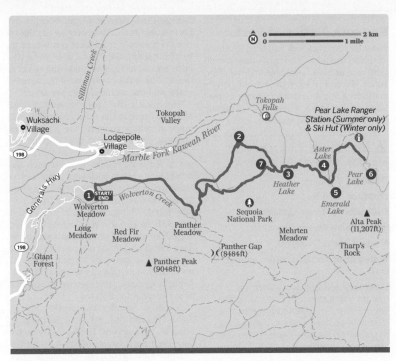

Overnight Hikes
Lakes Trails

START/FINISH WOLVERTON MEADOW
LENGTH 12.6 MILES

This popular overnight backpacking trip – or challenging day hike – winds upward more than 2000ft to a string of gorgeous alpine lakes, giving you a tantalizing taste of the Sierra Nevada high country.

At the north side of **1 Wolverton Meadow**, the trail commences by climbing through pine and red-fir forest, making an undulating traverse along a ridge to reach the **2 Alta Peak Trail junction** in less than 2 miles. At the next major junction, the Lakes Trail forks. Keep to the left and forge straight ahead on the Watchtower route (open when there's no ice and snow, which may last into early summer), then switchback up through the forest.

Where the trail emerges high above the canyon of the Kaweah River's Marble Fork, the sheer granite face of the Watchtower stands sentinel. Peer down at the tumbling Tokopah Falls far below. Mind your feet as the narrowing trail edges along a sheer cliff face

with dizzying drop-offs. After rejoining the shorter Hump route, the trail soon arrives on the shores of petite **3 Heather Lake**, just over 4 miles from the trailhead, surrounded by woods (no camping allowed). A few hikers picnic, fish or even take a swim here.

After a short rise, during which Alta Peak (11,207ft) comes into view, the trail rolls slowly downhill. Leveling out, it threads between **8 Aster Lake** (9230ft), where the backpacker campsites and a solar-powered outhouse appear. The last mile of the trail climbs out of the glacier-carved basin via steep and rocky switchbacks to **6 Pear Lake** (9550ft), sitting in a perfect glacial cirque. A seasonal ranger station, which doubles as a winter ski hut, is located down a spur trail that peels off east before reaching the lake, where more backpacker campsites await.

On the return trip, retrace your steps or shave off about 0.4 miles by taking the steeper, shadier **7 Hump** route (and soak up panoramic mountain views of the Tablelands from its crest) instead of going via the vertiginous Watchtower again.

Sequoia National Park

Shoulder your backpack and head for alpine lakes and meadows. The park's busiest trailheads are around Lodgepole and the Giant Forest. Protect your vehicle from hungry marmots if you're starting from the remote Mineral King Valley, where sculpted granite peaks and glacial cirques await.

🏃 High Sierra Trail (Crescent Meadow to Lone Pine Creek)

Duration 3–4 days

Distance 32 miles

Difficulty Moderate–difficult

Start/Finish Crescent Meadow

Nearest Town Lodgepole

Transportation Car, shuttle (summer only)

Summary A world-class wilderness hike on a trail that keeps on giving. The journey includes continuous spectacular mountain and valley views, plus roaring rivers, waterfalls, hair-raising ridges and picturesque camping spots.

During winter and spring, hikers need to park at the Giant Forest Museum and walk the extra 1.7 miles to Crescent Meadow, where the trailhead begins. In summer hikers can either leave their car at the Giant Forest Museum and get the shuttle to Crescent Meadow or nab one of the few parking spaces at Crescent Meadow (arrive early).

The trail begins passing Crescent Meadow to the left, through a mile or so of forest (sugar pines, giant sequoias and red and white fir can be seen here), before reaching a ridge and the spectacular Eagle View (Map p192; access via Crescent Meadow on the High Sierra Trail, Crescent Meadow Rd) vista, one of the most highly rated views in the park. From here, look right to Moro Rock, down to the Middle Fork of the Kaweah River and forward to snowcapped summits of the Great Western Divide.

The path continues on a warm ridge (pack a hat and sunscreen) and onto spring-fed streams, like Panther Gap. There may be half a dozen or more water crossings of various sizes in the spring. Some are trickier to negotiate than others, particularly Mehrten Creek, which rushes from snowmelt and has sheer drops over the cliff; the slippery rocks may cause you to lose your footing. Cross streams in the morning for lower water levels. Always err on the side of caution and only cross what you believe to be within your capabilities. Use poles for stability and do not rely on makeshift wooden beams. Check the conditions of the streams at the wilderness office before you set off.

The mostly flat path continues past Mehrten Creek to the Seven Mile Hill Trail junction, which connects the High Sierra and Alta Trails. The path hugs the cliff face as it goes along the valley. At sections there are a few switchbacks weaving into the mountain and then back onto ridges as you move towards Little Blue Dome – a large granite boulder that appears out of the alpine forest. The rocky trail is well carved out, with some narrower sections (and big cliffside drops), but exposed, although there are a few shaded forest sections for cover. At other parts of the trail, the path opens out on to killer mountain views, each with a different perspective, revealing other sections of the range in the distance.

A mile or so after the junction for the Seven Mile Hill Trail, potential flat camping areas begin to appear. The best spots to lay your head are a couple of miles before the Bearpaw Meadow turnoff – one sits before a stream with a small pool. The campground is shaded by forest canopy and has a bear box. Meanwhile, the other spot is after the same stream, positioned on a flat rock section overlooking a clearing and offering a staggering mountain view (choose the latter only when there is no wind).

Continuing on the ridge pathway, a bridge crosses a wider stream named Buck Creek with a rocky canyon (look out for marmots here), then the trail goes inland to a dense forest section climbing around 500ft. You'll spot a signpost marking the turning for Bearpaw Meadow and Bearpaw Meadow Camp; stay on the High Sierra Trail fork going towards Bearpaw High Sierra Camp. Those who book in advance can rest up here in cozy backcountry cabins with canvas roofs (June to September) overlooking scenes of the Great Western Divide (home-cooked meals in the dining room are included in the rate). There's a small ranger's office at the camp (also open only June to September). There's no potable water at the site in winter; you're better off filling up at one of the many streams (then boiling/filtering it). Those with no reservations are not permitted to camp at Bearpaw High Sierra Camp (instead, retrace your steps half a mile back to the Bearpaw Meadow camping spot). Walking straight through Bearpaw High Sierra Camp you join with the next section of the High Sierra Trail – arguably the most scenic so far.

The trail enters into a short section of forest before opening out onto stark looming walls of grey-and-silver mountain rock faces in the distance. Behind you are hypnotizing pleated valley views and green forest hillsides. As the path continues along the ridge, you get closer to a bowl-like cluster of granite rock where the valley ends – Hamilton Lake sits at the center right, although it's not visible from this angle. Entering a series of downward switchbacks leads to the charging Lone Pine Creek – it gushes in between a deep rock canyon (it's common to spot rainbows in the waterfall here). Those with strong legs should continue over the man-made bridge and on to a challenging section of intense switchbacks to reach the glistening Hamilton Lakes (it's only a few miles further, but a buttock-pounding path).

Retrace your steps to return to your car (factor in at least one overnight stop on your return).

Kings Canyon National Park

Myriad backcountry routes to granite peaks, alpine lakes and high-country meadows depart from Road's End, deep inside Kings Canyon, east of Cedar Grove Village.

🏃 Rae Lakes Loop

Duration 5 days

Distance 40 miles

Difficulty Difficult

Start/Finish Road's End

Nearest Town Cedar Grove Village

Transportation Car

Summary The best backpacking loop in Kings Canyon tours sun-blessed forests and meadows, crosses one mind-bending pass and skirts a chain of jewel-like lakes beneath the Sierra crest, joining the famous John Muir Trail partway along. Note: one of the bridges on this trail has washed out, making the trail impossible to complete unless you trek at the height of summer when the South Fork of the Kings River is at its lowest.

DAY 1: ROAD'S END TO MIDDLE PARADISE VALLEY
4–6 HOURS / 7 MILES

The Rae Lakes Loop kicks off with a 4.5-mile hike along the Woods Creek Trail from Road's End (5045ft) to Mist Falls (p176). Beyond the waterfall, a set of rocky switchbacks leads you up into the shadier forest above the river. The trail levels out as it enters Paradise Valley, less than 2 miles north of the falls. The Kings River's South Fork flows through forested meadows, inviting you to linger at the backpacker campsites in Lower Paradise Valley (6600ft). Continue up the beautiful river valley through mixed-conifer forest just over a mile further to Middle Paradise Valley (6700ft), with more open views and less crowded campsites.

DAY 2: MIDDLE PARADISE VALLEY TO WOODS CREEK
4–6 HOURS / 7 MILES

Among ponderosa pines, the trail gradually ascends alongside a grassy meadow before dropping back to the river in Upper Paradise Valley (6800ft). Forested campsites appear before the confluence of the Kings River's South Fork and Woods Creek, about 1.5 miles from Middle Paradise Valley.

At this point you would usually cross a footbridge, but the South Fork Kings River Bridge above Paradise Valley washed out during the winter of 2016–2017 and construction of a replacement bridge will not begin before 2019. It may be possible to cross this section of river in late summer, after a hot spell, when water levels are at their lowest. However, proceed with caution – crossing the South Fork of the Kings River can be extremely hazardous. On the other side of the river the trail steadily ascends sun-dappled switchbacks through a forested valley above Woods Creek. Less than 4 miles from the river crossing, the trail rolls into Castle Domes Meadow (8200ft), sitting beneath spectacular, polished granite domes.

The trail meanders across the meadow and re-enters pine forest. At the signposted John Muir Trail (JMT) junction (8500ft), turn right and cross Woods Creek on the wooden planks of a steel-cable suspension bridge. Backpacker campsites sprawl just south of the bridge.

DAY 3: WOODS CREEK TO MIDDLE RAE LAKE
4–6 HOURS / 6.5 MILES

Heading south, the JMT rolls easily on open slopes along the west side of Woods Creek's

SEQUOIA & KINGS CANYON NATIONAL PARKS OVERNIGHT HIKES

Rae Lakes Loop

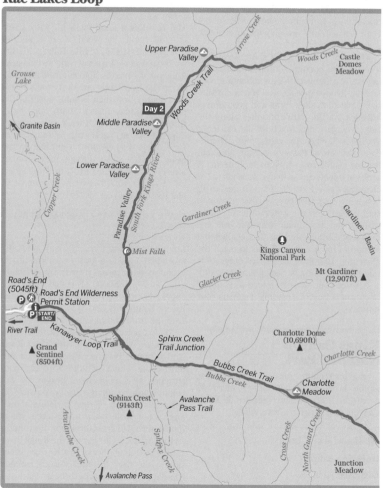

South Fork, with good views of the granite high country. Crossing a small stream, the trail continues up valley, rising over rocky terrain to reach a small meadow. At the next crossing, a bigger stream cascades over a cleft in the rock. Foxtail pines dot the dry slope above the trail as it continues up to Dollar Lake (10,220ft), about 3.5 miles from the Woods Creek crossing. The striking view of Fin Dome (11,693ft) above Dollar Lake (camping strictly prohibited) sets the theme of mountain splendor.

Skirting Dollar Lake's west shore, the JMT continues up to arrive at larger Ar-

rowhead Lake (10,300ft). It ascends more gradually to enchanting Lower Rae Lake (10,535ft). The gently rolling trail crosses several small side streams and passes a spur trail to a seasonal ranger station. Continue to the signed turnoff for campsites above the eastern shore of Middle Rae Lake (10,540ft).

DAY 4: MIDDLE RAE LAKE TO JUNCTION MEADOW
5–7 HOURS / 9 MILES

Get up early and eat a big breakfast, because this is game day.

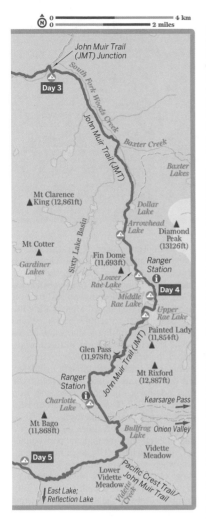

The trail passes several small mountain lakes, which glisten in the barren cirque to the west. Then it rises on a series of switchbacks up talus to the very narrow saddle of Glen Pass (11,978ft), almost 3 miles from Middle Rae Lake. From the pass, visible in the distance to the southwest, are massive Mt Brewer (13,576ft), with its often snowy northeast face, and other peaks along the Great Western Divide and Kings-Kern Divide. Mt Bago (11,868ft) is that distinctive reddish peak in the foreground.

Gravelly but well-graded switchbacks take you down from Glen Pass over a steep scree slope toward a pothole tarn at the tree line. Stop to filter water here – the next reliable water is not until the Bullfrog Lake outlet a few miles ahead. Head down the narrow canyon, passing above a snow-fed, talus-lined pool until the trail swings south, then contours high above Charlotte Lake. A connector trail to Kearsarge Pass appears about 2.5 miles from Glen Pass, after which you'll soon reach a four-way junction with the main Charlotte Lake (northwest) and Kearsarge Pass (northeast) trails. Continue straight (south).

At the head of Bubbs Creek, cross a low rise and then start descending, passing a junction with the trail heading northeast to Bullfrog Lake and Kearsarge Lakes. The scenic descent twice crosses the outlet from Bullfrog Lake to reach Lower Vidette Meadow (9480ft). Leaving the JMT, turn right (southwest) and follow the trail down Bubbs Creek past campsites at the forested edge of the meadow. Descending west along the tumbling creekside, the trail crosses several streams and a large rockslide to finally find some shade. Beneath soaring granite walls on either side of the canyon, the trail drops steadily down to narrower, rushing Bubbs Creek, continuing to aspen-filled Junction Meadow (8500ft). Past the signed junction with the East and Reflection Lakes Trails, you'll find grassy campsites.

DAY 5: JUNCTION MEADOW TO ROAD'S END

5–7 HOURS / 10.5 MILES

From the west end of Junction Meadow, the Bubbs Creek Trail meanders down the valley. Granite walls tower on both sides as you descend to Charlotte Creek, about 3.5 miles from Junction Meadow. After crossing the creek, the trail continues creekside downhill for three more miles to the Sphinx Creek Trail junction (6240ft).

Return to the JMT and turn right (south). Walk along the northern shore of Upper Rae Lake (10,545ft). Cross the connector stream between the lakes. At a signed trail junction, where a faint trail to Sixty Lake Basin peels off northwest, keep straight ahead on the JMT, which continues south up well-graded switchbacks above the west side of Upper Rae Lake. Heading higher, even more switchbacks take you up a talus slope to a tarn-filled basin, from where Glen Pass is visible ahead on the dark, rocky ridgeline.

Mineral King Road

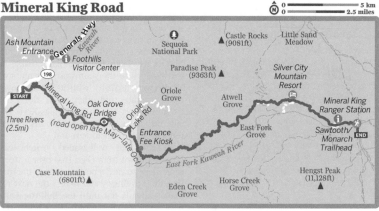

Continuing straight ahead, the Bubbs Creek Trail descends steeply on hot, open switchbacks, providing sweeping views into Kings Canyon and of the granite pinnacle of the Sphinx (9143ft) towering above you. At last reaching the canyon floor, the trail crosses braided Bubbs Creek over wooden footbridges. Just beyond the steel Bailey Bridge, which spans the Kings River's South Fork, is the Paradise Valley Trail junction. Turn left (west) and retrace your steps from day one for less than 2 miles to Road's End.

DRIVING

Mineral King Road

Duration 1½–2 hours

Distance 25 miles (one way)

Start/Finish Hwy 198/Eagle/Mosquito trailhead parking area

Nearest Town Three Rivers

Transportation Car (RVs and trailers prohibited)

Steel your nerves and take your time, because this twisting road will test your mettle. Skirting the canyon of the Kaweah River's East Fork, the road makes almost 700 sharp turns while ascending to 7500ft.

Usually only open late-May to late-October, this 25-mile road has sections that are hair-raisingly narrow and unpaved, but the grade is never too difficult – just remember that uphill vehicles have the right-of-way.

Outside Three Rivers town (last chance for gas), 2 miles south of the park's Ash Mountain Entrance (Generals Highway, via Sierra Drive; car/person (walk-in)/motorcycle $30/15/25), take a deep breath and turn off Hwy 198 onto well-signed Mineral King Rd. On the right you'll start to see long sections of water flume cutting a sharp line across the hillside. The metal flume you see now replaced the original sequoia-wood structure dating from 1899, which brought hydroelectric power to this remote region before the road was paved. To get a closer look, stop at the 1923 Oak Grove Bridge, around 6.5 miles from the start of the road.

Approximately 10.5 miles in, less than a mile after crossing the national park boundary, you'll reach the self-pay entrance fee kiosk, where there are pullovers and canyon views. Occasionally you'll see water troughs to the side of the road, built for horses pulling stagecoaches – the original users of this road in the late 19th century. Just over 16 miles from its start, the road passes a shady picnic area beside giant sequoias.

A little more than 5 miles further up the road is Silver City Mountain Resort, with a restaurant stop for fresh-baked pie and hot coffee. Your final destination, just over a mile past the Mineral King Ranger Station (☑ 559-565-3768; Mineral King Rd; ⊙ 8am-4pm late May-late Sep), is where the valley unfolds all of its hidden beauty and the high country beckons with granite peaks and alpine lakes. The Sawtooth/Monarch trailhead at the road's end is the start of some memorable hikes.

On the return trip, remember to downshift into lower gear to save your vehicle's brakes.

🏃 OTHER ACTIVITIES

🏃 Caving

The caves in Sequoia and Kings Canyon are so extensive that the parks could have been designated on the basis of their cave systems alone. Of all the California caves more than a mile long, half are found here, including Lilburn Cave – at 17 surveyed miles it's the longest known cave in the state. New caves are still being discovered, as are species of invertebrates, such as troglobites (animals that live in dark caves). Those identified in 2006 in Sequoia's Crystal Cave include translucent, eyeless insects and a tiny pseudoscorpion. Crystal Cave is currently the only cave open for public tours and even then, it's seasonal (late May to late September). Book your visit in advance to avoid disappointment.

🏃 Swimming, Canoeing & Kayaking

Swimming holes abound along the Middle Fork of the Kaweah River in the Foothills area of Sequoia National Park, especially on the opposite side of the Generals Hwy from Potwisha Campground and the Hospital Rock picnic area. Families also take dips in pools along the Marble Fork of the Kaweah River inside Lodgepole Campground near the Tokopah Falls trailhead. In Kings Canyon, Muir Rock and the Red Bridge by Road's End there are swimming holes. In the Sequoia National Forest, Hume Lake is dreamy on a hot summer day and you can rent canoes, kayaks and boats at the **Boathouse** (Map p192; 64144 Hume Lake Rd; rentals per hour $20; ⊙9am-4pm) by the beach at Hume Lake Christian Camp.

🏃 Horseback Riding & Pack Trips

Cedar Grove Pack Station   HORSEBACK RIDING
(Map p192; ☑559-565-3464; www.facebook.com/CedarGrovePackStation; Cedar Lane, Cedar Grove; 1/2hr ride $40/75, overnights (2-night minimum) from $350; ⊙late May–mid-Oct) Trail rides along the river deep in Kings Canyon and overnight pack trips (reservations required) to mountain lakes start from Cedar Grove.

Grant Grove Stables   HORSEBACK RIDING
(Map p192; ☑559-335-9292; Hwy 180; trail rides from $40; ⊙mid-Jun–early Sep) Just north of General Grant Grove in Kings Canyon, this pint-sized, summer-only operation offers one- and two-hour trail rides.

Horse Corral Pack Station   HORSEBACK RIDING
(Map p192; ☑559-565-3404, 559-564-6429; http://hcpacker.com/; off Big Meadows Rd, 12 miles east of Generals Hwy; horse/guide per day from $50/100; ⊙trip times vary; summer only) Offering half- and full-day rides through the Sequoia National park (summer only), plus extended pack trips (making it easy to get into the wilderness with all your gear). Trips are available for beginner riders, advanced riders and everything in between. Prices vary per route (call for details).

🏃 Rock Climbing

Both parks have rock-climbing spots, though it's not nearly as popular here as in Yosemite and many of the best places require a long backcountry hike before you even start climbing. The most spectacular climb is an 1800ft granite wall in the remote Valhalla Cirque called Angel Wings, nicknamed 'an alpine El Capitan' by renowned climber and photographer Galen Rowell.

In Kings Canyon, the backcountry Bubbs Creek Trail leads to multipitch climbs at Charlito and Charlotte Domes just before crossing Charlotte Creek, an 8-mile trek from Road's End, east of Cedar Grove Village. More accessible locations in Sequoia National Park include Moro Rock (closed during peregrine nesting season, usually April through mid-August) and Little Baldy, both off the Generals Hwy. In the Sequoia National Forest, west of the Generals Hwy via dirt road FR-14S29, Chimney Rocks has dozens of routes (all closed during peregrine nesting season; some will be inaccessible during winter months due to snowfall).

ⓘ WARNING!

Drownings in the Kings and Kaweah Rivers are the leading cause of death in the parks. Swift currents can be deadly, especially when rivers are swollen with snowmelt runoff in late spring and early summer. Never go in if you see any white water. When in doubt, stay out! Get smart advice about current swimming conditions at park visitor centers and ranger stations.

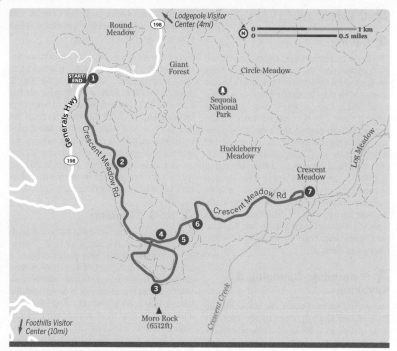

🚗 Driving Tour
Moro Rock–Crescent Meadow Road

START/FINISH GIANT FOREST MUSEUM
LENGTH 6 MILES

A narrow, winding and pockmarked road links some of the Giant Forest's popular roadside attractions, with giant sequoias lining the way. This road is closed to private vehicles on summer weekends and holidays, but you can take the free seasonal park shuttle, which usually runs between late May and late September. In winter the road closes to all traffic, but you can still hike (when snow levels are low), cross-country ski or snowshoe along it.

From the ❶ **Giant Forest Museum**, Moro Rock–Crescent Meadow Rd swoops into the southwestern section of the Giant Forest. Less than a mile in is the ❷ **Auto Log**, a hefty sequoia that fell in 1917. For early park visitors, a flat section was carved onto its top and the tree was actually used as part of the road. You can't drive on it anymore, but you can walk on it and imagine.

After more than another half-mile, turn into the super-small parking area (we told you to take the shuttle!) to gawk at the pale dome of ❸ **Moro Rock** (p188). Continuing on a half-mile, the mesmerizing flamelike roots of the 2300-year-old collapsed ❹ **Buttress Tree** face the road. On the opposite side of the road just a bit further along is the ❺ **Parker Group**, named for the eight-person family of US Cavalry Captain James Parker, who served as the park's superintendent during the 1890s.

In days gone by, the renown of Yosemite's Wawona Tunnel Tree prompted many visitors to inquire about Sequoia's drive-through tree, but the park didn't have one. So when a 275ft sequoia bit the dust and went splat across the road in 1937, the park took advantage of this gift and promptly cut a passageway for cars. This ❻ **Tunnel Log** has an 8ft-high, 17ft-wide opening, which larger vehicles can skirt using an adjacent bypass. From there, it's another mile to the road's end at verdant ❼ **Crescent Meadow**.

Return as you arrived, bypassing the side trip to Moro Rock.

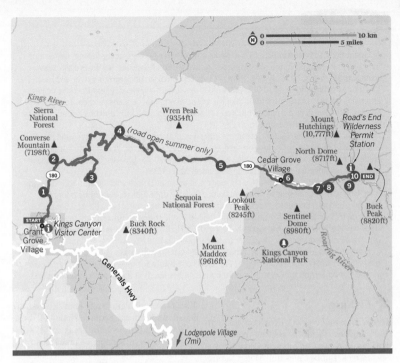

🚗 Driving Tour
Kings Canyon Scenic Byway

START GRANT GROVE
FINISH ROAD'S END
LENGTH 35 MILES (ONE WAY)

John Muir called Kings Canyon 'a rival of Yosemite.' This jaw-dropping scenic drive enters one of North America's deepest canyons, traversing the forested Giant Sequoia National Monument and shadowing the Kings River all the way to Road's End.

Fewer than 3 miles from **1 Grant Grove**, pull over to drink in the mountain panorama at **2 McGee Vista Point**. Then keep winding downhill through the Sequoia National Forest past the turnoff to **3 Converse Basin Grove**, a lonely testament to the 19th-century logging of giant sequoias, which turned out to be as economically unprofitable as it was environmentally unwise.

About 6 miles from Grant Grove is the turnoff to **4 Hume Lake** (p200), which offers sandy beaches and coves for summer swims. Keep heading downhill, ever deeper into the canyon. The road serpentines past

chiseled rock walls, some tinged by green moss and red-iron minerals, others laced by waterfalls. Roadside turnouts provide superb views, notably at Junction View, about 10.5 miles from Grant Grove, and beyond **5 Yucca Point**, another 3.5 miles further along.

After countless ear-popping curves, the road bottoms out and runs parallel to the Kings River, its roar ricocheting off granite cliffs soaring thousands of feet high above. Over 10 miles past Yucca Point is the picnic area by **6 Grizzly Falls**, often a torrent in late spring.

The scenic byway re-enters the national park just over 2.5 miles further along, quickly passing the Lewis Creek bridge and a riverside beach. It's less than 2 miles to Cedar Grove Village, where you can stop at the visitor center and **7 market** (p191) before pushing on. Over the next 6 miles, don't miss short walks to **8 Roaring River Falls** and pretty **9 Zumwalt Meadow** (p191). More hiking trails and swimming holes (like **10 Muir Rock**) await at Road's End – the only way to keep going across the Sierra Nevada is on foot!

DON'T MISS

CRYSTAL CAVE

Accidentally discovered in 1918 by two parks employees who were going fishing, this unique marble cave (Map p192; www.recreation.gov; Crystal Cave Rd, off Generals Hwy; tours adult/child/youth from $16/5/8; ☺ late May-Sep; [P] [♿]) ✒ was carved by an underground river and has formations estimated to be 10,000 years old. Stalactites hang like daggers from the ceiling, and milky white marble formations take the shape of ethereal curtains, domes, columns and shields. The cave is also a unique biodiverse habitat for spiders, bats and tiny aquatic insects that are found nowhere else on earth.

Beyond the historic Spider Gate at the entrance, underground passageways wind for more than 3 miles. To get inside the cave, you must buy a ticket for a 50-minute introductory guided tour. Teens and adults can take a more in-depth, 90-minute 'Discovery Tour' ($18) or sign up in advance for a full-day spelunking adventure ($135).

Tickets are only sold online up to six months in advance before your desired tour date and time. Online ticket sales close 48 hours before the tour date. Tickets cannot be bought at the cave. Tours fill up quickly, especially on weekends. Wheelchairs, baby backpacks, purses, strollers, tripods and walking sticks are prohibited inside the cave. Bring a light jacket, as chilly cave temperatures average only 50°F (10°C). No drinking water is available at the cave, which may close during rainy weather (refunds available).

From the Lodgepole or Foothills areas, allow at least 90 minutes to get to the cave, which is a half-mile walk from the parking lot at the end of a twisty 6.5-mile-long paved road. Look for the signed turnoff for Crystal Cave Rd about 2 miles south of the Giant Forest Museum.

🎣 Fishing

Rivers, lakes and creeks will delight amateur trout anglers. Tackle is sold at most park markets. In Kings Canyon near Cedar Grove, Lewis Creek, Bubbs Creek and Motor Nature Trail (River Rd) are popular places to fish. So is Hume Lake, where the US Forest Service (USFS) stocks trout. A fishing license, which can be obtained at Hume Lake and possibly some park markets, is required for anyone aged 16 and older. Visitor centers can provide a copy of park-specific regulations (eg lures, daily limits, mandatory catch-and-release of protected species).

🎿 Snow Sports

Winter is a memorable time to visit Sequoia and Kings Canyon. A thick blanket of snow drapes giant sequoia trees and meadows, the pace of activity slows and a hush falls over the roads and trails.

Dozens of miles of ungroomed trails for snowshoeing (Lodgepole Market, 63204 Lodgepole Rd; snowshoe rental per 24hr $22; ☺winter only (depending on snow fall)) and cross-country skiing criss-cross the Grant Grove and Giant Forest areas (trail maps sold at park visitor centers). There are more tree-marked trails in the Giant Sequoia National Monument (Map p192; www.fs.usda.gov; Sequoia National Park). Winter road closures also make for excellent cross-country skiing or snowshoeing on Sequoia's Moro Rock–Crescent Meadow Rd,

Kings Canyon's Panoramic Point Rd and Big Meadows Rd in the Sequoia National Forest. You'll find snow-play areas at Wolverton Meadow in Sequoia's Giant Forest; Big Stump (Hwy 180, just north of Big Stump Entrance) and Columbine in Kings Canyon's Grant Grove; and Big Meadows, Quail Flat and Cherry Gap in the Sequoia National Forest.

In the Sequoia National Forest, families head to the Montecito Sequoia Lodge (Map p192; ☏ 800-227-9900; www..mslodge.com; 63410 Generals Hwy) for cross-country skiing and snowboarding lessons, more than 30 miles of groomed terrain, and sledding and tubing hills. Rental snow-sports equipment available.

Backcountry experts who aren't intimidated by a steep 6-mile, cross-country ski or snowshoe trek climbing 2000ft can enter the lottery (held in early November) to bunk down overnight at the Pear Lake Ski Hut (Map p192; ☏ 559-565-4251; www.sequoiaparks conservancy.org; trailhead at Wolverton Meadow, hut located in Pear Lake Basin; per person $38-42; ☺usually mid-Dec–early Apr), a rustic back-country abode at 9200ft. The cozy hut sleeps 10 people and is warmed by a wood stove. It has a compost toilet. The trail begins at Wolverton Meadows.

Cross-country ski and snowshoe rentals are available at Grant Grove Village and Wuksachi Lodge, which sell limited winter clothing and snow-play gear. In winter, park rangers lead seasonal snowshoe walks (free snowshoe use included); check the online calendar (www.nps.gov/seki/planyourvisit/calendar.htm) for upcoming walks and activities. Ranger-led activities fill up fast, so reserve a spot in advance in person at park visitor centers or by calling the Giant Forest Museum.

⊙ SIGHTS

Giant sequoia groves, underground marble caves, sculpted granite domes, jagged high-altitude peaks and wildflower meadows where mule deer and black bears graze are just a small taste of what you'll see in both the national parks and nearby national forest lands. If the weather spoils your outdoor plans, the Giant Forest Museum, plus the educational exhibits and short nature films at park visitor centers, are welcome indoor diversions.

⊙ Sequoia National Park

Lodgepole & Wuksachi Villages

Lodgepole Village is the park's main hub. The market, deli, snack bar, ATM, pay showers and coin-op laundromat are usually open from April through October. Two miles further north along the Generals Hwy, Wuksachi boasts the park's highest-end hotel, restaurant and bar, all open year-round.

Lodgepole Visitor Center has exhibits on park history, covering buffalo soldiers, competing land uses from Native American dominion until the present and contemporary environmental challenges such as air pollution and wildfires. Entertaining and educational, the short movie *Bears of the Sierra* is screened upon request, or check out the video booth at the back to learn about black bears and the human history of the Giant Forest. The visitor center was being refurbished at the time of research, so exhibitions may be altered or updated on completion.

Giant Forest

During his travels in the Sierra Nevada, conservationist John Muir wandered into this cathedral-like grove of giant sequoias in 1875, baptizing it the 'Giant Forest.' Having escaped being logged in the late 19th century, today the Giant Forest (Map p192; off Generals Hwy) encompasses an amazing concentration of ancient sequoias, where the happy shouts of kids and trilling birdsong echo through the misty groves.

By the late 20th century, more than 300 buildings, including campgrounds and a lodge, which had been built in the Giant Forest, encroached upon the giant sequoias' delicate root systems, as did traffic jams. Tourist development had also made it necessary to suppress any wildfires, without which giant sequoias can't reproduce naturally.

Recognizing these adverse impacts, in 1997 the park began to remove structures, reposition parking lots and relocate visitor services further north. A convenient, free seasonal shuttle-bus system has significantly cut traffic congestion and reduced the potential harm to these majestic trees.

General Sherman Tree NATURAL FEATURE
By volume the largest living tree on earth, the massive General Sherman Tree rockets into the sky and *waaay* out of the camera frame. Pay your respects to this giant (which measures more than 100ft around at its base and 275ft tall) via a paved, wheelchair-accessible path from the upper parking lot off Wolverton Rd. The trail cleverly starts at the height of the tree's tip (14 stories high) and descends 0.5 miles to its base.

Then join the Congress Trail, a 2-mile paved loop that takes in General Sherman and other notable named trees, including the see-through Telescope Tree. Hint: take your time on the steep walk back up from the grove – it's 7000ft in elevation and the air is thin. If the idea of walking back to your car doesn't thrill you, catch the shuttle (summer only) from the lower parking lot (disabled-placard parking only) near the General Sherman Tree and ride it back to the main parking area, about 1.5 miles north of Lodgepole Village.

Giant Forest Museum MUSEUM
(Map p192; ☑ 559-565-4480; www.nps.gov/seki; 47050 Generals Hwy, cnr Crescent Meadow Rd; ⊙ 9am-4:30pm (winter), 9am-6pm (summer); Ⓟ ♿) ⌀ FREE For a primer on the intriguing ecology and history of giant sequoias, this tiny modern museum has hands-on exhibits about the life stages of these big trees, which can live for more than 3000 years, and the fire cycle that releases their seeds and allows them to sprout on bare soil. The museum is housed in an historic 1920s building designed by Gilbert Stanley Underwood, famed architect of the Majestic Yosemite (formerly Ahwahnee) Hotel.

The museum is crushed with visitors in summer. To avoid parking headaches, take the free in-park shuttle bus. You can also try the information desk here when the Lodgepole Visitor Center is closed in winter. During winter, the self-issue wilderness permit station (47050 Generals Hwy, at the Giant Forest Museum; ⊙ winter only) is located to the right of the main entrance.

Moro Rock   NATURAL FEATURE
(Map p192; One Way Rd, near Crescent Meadow Rd) A quarter-mile staircase climbs 350 steps (over 300ft) to the top of Sequoia's iconic granite dome at an elevation of 6725ft, offering mind-boggling views of the Great Western Divide, running north–south through the middle of the park and splitting the watersheds of the Kaweah River to the west from the Kern River to the east. Due to pollution drifting up from the Central Valley, this spectacular vantage point is sometimes obscured by thick haze, especially during summer.

Info boards along the route give facts about the geology and nature in the area, and map out the peaks in the distance (Mt Stewart, Lawson Peak, Kaweah Queen, Black Kaweah and Lippincott Mountain). Historical photos at the trailhead show the rock's original rickety wooden staircase, erected in 1917. You'll be grateful that the current staircase, built in 1931 by the Civilian Conservation Corps (CCC), has nearly 400 steps solidly carved into the granite and sturdy handrails for gripping.

From the Giant Forest Museum, the trailhead is 2 miles up narrow, twisty Moro Rock–Crescent Meadow Rd. The free seasonal shuttle bus (summer only) stops at the small parking lot, which is often full. Alternatively, park at Giant Forest Museum and walk the 1.7 miles along Crescent Meadow Rd to the trailhead.

Crescent Meadow   NATURAL FEATURE
(Map p192) Said to have been described by John Muir as the 'gem of the Sierra,' this lush meadow is buffered by a forest of firs and giant sequoias. High grass and summer wildflowers are a good excuse for a leisurely loop hike (1.3 miles), as is watching black bears snack on berries and rip apart logs to feast on insects. The meadow environment is fragile, so always stay on established trails.

Several short hikes surround the meadow, including spur trails to Tharp's Log (0.8 miles), where the area's first white settler, Hale Tharp, spent summers in a fallen sequoia. Next to Huckleberry Meadow you'll find the Squatters Cabin (0.4 miles), an 1880s log cabin that's a ghostly remnant of the failed utopian-socialist Kaweah Colony.

The meadow is almost 3 miles down Moro Rock–Crescent Meadow Rd, best accessed by the free seasonal shuttle bus. The road closes to all traffic after the first snowfall and doesn't reopen until spring, but you can still walk to it, snowshoes or cross-country skiing may be needed.

Foothills

From the Ash Mountain Entrance outside the town of Three Rivers, the Generals Hwy ascends steeply through the southwestern section of Sequoia National Park. At an elevation of less than 3500ft, the Foothills area is much drier and warmer than the rest of the park. Hiking here is best in spring, when the air is still cool and wildflowers peak early for a colorful show. Scorching-hot summers are buggy and muggy, but the area is still popular for swimming, particularly the Kaweah River (when waters are calm enough). Fall brings more moderate temperatures and colorful foliage.

The Foothills Visitor Center (⌨559-565-4212; 47050 Generals Hwy; ⊙8am-4:30pm) is open year-round. A mile north of the Ash Mountain Entrance, it has educational exhibits on the park's human history and ecology, focusing on Sierra Nevada wildlife across different life zones, as well as Native American heritage and 19th-century pioneers and conservationists.

Tunnel Rock   LANDMARK
(Map p192; Generals Hwy) In the 1930s, no one anticipated the development of monster SUVs. About 1.5 miles north of the Foothills Visitor Center (p188), a flat granite boulder on the western side of the Generals Hwy caps a tunnel dug by the Civilian Conservation Corps (CCC). Until the highway was widened in 1997, this narrow passageway was the only route through. It's closed to modern-day vehicles, which would have a tough time squeezing through side by side, but pedestrians can still stroll underneath it.

Hospital Rock   HISTORIC SITE
(Map p192; Generals Hwy) The Potwisha people, a band of Monache (also known as Western Mono), originally lived at this site. When the first white settler, Hale Tharp, arrived in 1858, it was home to about 500 villagers and had been inhabited for five centuries.

Pictographs (rock paintings) and grinding holes used by tribeswomen to make acorn meal can still be seen at the picnic area, about 5 miles northeast of the Foothills Visitor Center.

In the 1860s, diseases introduced by white settlers from Three Rivers quickly killed many of the Native Americans and within a decade the village had been abandoned.

In 1873, pioneer Alfred Everton injured his leg by getting it caught in his own bear trap. He lay down here to recuperate from his injury, hence the rock's name.

Mineral King

Perched at 7500ft, this giant, gorgeous and glacially sculpted valley ringed by massive mountains, including jagged Sawtooth Peak, is a supremely good place to find solitude. The Mineral King Preservation Society (www.mineralking.org) has all kinds of historical information about the area.

For two decades starting in the 1870s, Mineral King witnessed heavy silver mining and lumber activity. There are still remnants of old shafts and stamp mills around, though it takes some exploring to find them. After mining turned out to be a bust, Mineral King became a cool mountain retreat for families escaping the Central Valley's summer heat. A contentious proposal by the Walt Disney Company to develop the area into a ski resort was thwarted by a Sierra Club–led campaign. The issue was forever put to rest when Congress annexed Mineral King to Sequoia National Park in 1978.

Hiking anywhere from here involves a steep climb out of the valley along strenuous trails. Be aware of the high altitude, even on short hikes. Beautiful day hikes or overnight backpacking trips head up to Monarch, Crystal, Eagle, Mosquito, Franklin, Little Five and Big Five Lakes. If you're not up for the tough stuff, take a serene mile-long ramble along the nature trail from Cold Springs Campground to the Eagle/Mosquito trailhead parking area.

The valley is reached via narrow, twisting 25-mile Mineral King Rd, which heads east from Hwy 198 south of the park's Ash Mountain Entrance (p182). The road is usually open only from late May through late October. Scattered along the last 6 miles of road are two first-come, first-served park campgrounds, a ranger station and the private Silver City Mountain Resort, offering lodging, a restaurant and a tiny market.

Generals Highway

The Generals Hwy winds for almost 11 miles through the Sequoia National Forest, bridging the gap between Sequoia and Kings Canyon National Parks. A few accommodations and tourist services are right off the highway, while paved Big Meadows Rd (Forest Service road 14S11) burrows east into the Giant Sequoia National Monument near the Jennie Lakes Wilderness, a popular backpacking area.

The seasonal outpost (May to October) Stony Creek has a gas station (pumps available 24 hours for those with credit cards), ATM, pay phones, wi-fi, coin-op laundry and pay showers. It also has a lodge, a small market (Map p192; ☑559-565-3388; www.sequoia-kings-canyon.com; 65569 Generals Hwy; ☺8am-7pm Sun-Thu, to 8pm Fri & Sat mid-May–early Oct), restaurant and nearby campgrounds.

Four miles further north, Montecito Sequoia Lodge (p35) is primarily a summer family camp set around a small private lake, but it also offers groomed cross-country ski trails and other snow sports in winter.

Buck Rock Fire Lookout HISTORIC BUILDING
(Map p192; ☑559-901-8151; www.buckrock.org; FR-13S04; ☺10am-4pm mid–May-Oct) FREE Built in 1923 and staffed during the wildfire season, this fire lookout is one of the finest restored watchtowers you could ever hope to visit. A total of 172 stairs lead to a dollhouse-sized wooden cabin on a dramatic 8500ft granite rise. From the Generals Hwy, turn east onto Big Meadows Rd (FS 14S11). At approximately 2.5 miles, turn north on the signed dirt road (FS 13S04), then drive another 3 miles to the lookout parking area.

⊙ Kings Canyon National Park

Grant Grove Village

About 3 miles northeast of the park's Big Stump Entrance, Grant Grove Village is the park's main tourist hub year-round, with lodge and cabin accommodations, a restaurant, a market and free wi-fi. ATMs are located inside the lodge lobby and at the market. The closest gas is at Hume Lake or Stony Creek.

Grant Grove's busy visitor center has interesting exhibits on nature conservation, wildlife habitats and environmental issues, and also screens an introductory movie about Kings Canyon – all subtitled in both English and Spanish.

General Grant Grove
FOREST

(Map p192; N Grove Trail, off Hwy 180; P) This sequoia grove off Generals Hwy is astounding. The paved half-mile General Grant Tree Trail is an interpretive walk that visits a number of mature sequoias, including the 27-story General Grant Tree. This giant holds triple honors as the world's second-largest living tree, a memorial to US soldiers killed in war and the nation's official Christmas tree since 1926. The nearby Fallen Monarch, a massive, fire-hollowed trunk you can walk through, has been a cabin, hotel, saloon and stables.

To escape the bustling crowds, follow the more secluded 1.5-mile North Grove Loop, which passes wildflower patches and bubbling creeks as it gently winds underneath a canopy of stately sequoias, evergreen pines and aromatic incense cedars.

The magnificence of this ancient sequoia grove was nationally recognized in 1890 when Congress first designated it General Grant National Park. It took another half-century for this tiny parcel to be absorbed into the much larger Kings Canyon National Park, established in 1940 to prevent damming of the Kings River. Information booklets are available at the trail for $1.50 (use the honesty box), the main trail takes roughly 30 minutes, with plenty of time to read information boards.

Redwood Canyon
FOREST

(Map p192; unnamed road off Generals Hwy; road closed during winter) More than 15,000 sequoi-as cluster in Redwood Canyon, making it one of the world's largest groves of these giant trees. In an almost-forgotten corner of the park, this secluded forest lets you revel in the grandeur of the trees away from the crowds while you hike mostly moderate trails. What you won't find here, however, are any of the California coast's redwood trees – that's what early pioneers mistook these giant sequoias for, hence the erroneous name.

For the best view of this area, hike to the summit of Big Baldy (Generals Hwy). Alternatively, you can walk in the forest via trailheads at the end of a bumpy 2-mile dirt road (closed in winter) that starts across from the Hume Lake/Quail Flat signed intersection on the Generals Hwy, just over 5 miles southeast of Grant Grove Village. There's also a good spot for a picnic before heading out on a hike.

Kings Canyon Scenic Byway

The park's two main visitor areas, Grant Grove and Cedar Grove, are linked by narrow, twisting Hwy 180, which makes a dramatic descent into Kings Canyon, carved by glaciers and the mighty Kings River. The canyon itself, plunging over 8000ft when measured from the tip of Spanish Peak, is one of North America's deepest.

Expect spectacular views along this outstandingly scenic drive, where rugged peaks, sheer granite cliffs and a roaring river jostle for your attention. Hwy 180 all the way down to Cedar Grove is closed during winter (usually from mid-November until late April), but the stretch from Grant Grove to Hume Lake Rd is open year-round.

---

① MARMOT ALERT!

In late spring through midsummer, Mineral King's curious marmots come out of hibernation and anxiously await parked cars at trailheads. Besides such epicurean items as sweaty boots, backpack straps and hiking pole grips, these rodents also love to feast on the radiator hoses, belts and wiring of vehicles to get the salt they crave. They can chew through brake lines and completely disable your car. Toxic antifreeze tastes sweet, like dessert, to them.

Marmot-proofing one's vehicle has become a local art form. A few folks swear by wrapping the engine block in chicken wire, but most people swaddle the entire undercarriage with an enormous tarp and secure it with rope. You'll see how it's done just by looking at other cars parked at the trailheads. Vehicle tarps and rope can usually be bought (though not cheaply) before driving up to Mineral King at Three Rivers Mercantile (Map p192; 559-561-2378; 41152 Sierra Dr; 8am-6:30pm Mon-Fri, until 6pm Sat, 9am-5.30pm Sun) in the town of Three Rivers.

Always check under the hood before you drive off. Some marmots have ended up hitching as far as Southern California before they were finally discovered, still munching away.

PANORAMIC POINT

For a breathtaking view of Kings Canyon, head 2.3 miles up narrow, steep and winding Panoramic Point Rd (trailers and RVs aren't recommended), which branches off Hwy 180. Follow a short paved trail uphill from the parking lot to the **viewpoint** (Map p192; off Hwy 180; ☉ summer only), where precipitous canyons and the snowcapped peaks of the Great Western Divide unfold below you. Snow closes the road to vehicles during winter, when it becomes a cross-country ski and snowshoe route.

Hikers may access the road when snow levels are low. From Grant Grove's visitor center, follow the paved side road east, turning left after 0.1 miles, then right at the John Muir Lodge.

Converse Basin Grove   FOREST

(Map p192; off Hwy 180; ☉ the road up to Boole Tree may be closed in winter) Tragically, Converse Basin once contained the world's largest grove of mature sequoias, but it's now an unsettling cemetery for tree stumps. In the late 19th and early 20th centuries, the entire privately owned grove was felled by lumber companies. A financial boondoggle, in part because of high transportation costs, the trees ravaged in this grove were not even suitable for lumber and many shattered when they hit the ground. Most of the salvageable wood ended up as fence posts and matches.

The only survivor is a colossus called the **Boole Tree**. The sixth-largest known giant sequoia, it's ironically named for the lumber mill's foreman, and for reasons unknown it was allowed to live. A 2.5-mile loop hike reaches it from the dirt access road to the trailhead; bring plenty of water and insect repellant. On the way in, stop at **Stump Meadow** to see the oversized remains of 19th-century logging.

Off another dirt road further south, the 20ft-high **Chicago Stump** (road may be closed during winter, depending on weather) is all that's left of the 3200-year-old General Noble tree. The 285ft giant was cut into sections and transported to the 1893 World's Columbian Exposition in Chicago to demonstrate the unbelievable scale of the newly discovered giant sequoias. Dubious viewers soon nicknamed it the 'California hoax'!

The road to Boole Tree is unpaved and the turnoff sign is hard to spot. The turnoff for the Boole Tree road is along Hwy 180, on a dirt road that is often rough and slippery. The sandy conditions may require a 4WD. Alternatively, park at the turnout and hike around 2.5 miles in.

Hume Lake Recreation Area   LAKE

(Map p192; Hume Lake Rd; P) When it was dammed in 1908, this 87-acre artificial lake powered a huge log flume that whisked sequoias harvested in Converse Basin to a mill more than 70 miles away. Today it's a popular USFS campground, and sandy coves and beaches line the lakeshore. Restrooms are available in the parking area.

Cedar Grove

Cedar Grove, at the bottom of Kings Canyon, is the last outpost of civilization before you reach the rugged grandeur of the Sierra Nevada backcountry. The commercial area of Cedar Grove Village consists of a **market** (Map p192; Hwy 180, Cedar Grove Village; ☉ 8am-7pm mid-May–mid-Jun & mid-Sep–mid-Oct, 7am-8pm mid-Jun–mid-Sep), ATM, restaurant, lodge, pay showers and coin-operated laundry. Tourist services here are available from mid-May until mid-October. Hwy 180 beyond Hume Lake to Cedar Grove closes completely during winter, usually from mid-November through late April.

Six miles east of the village at Road's End, a seasonal ranger station issues wilderness permits, sells maps and hiking guides, and rents bear canisters. Hikes start out from here into the wilderness: it's the closest park trailhead to both the Pacific Crest National Scenic Trail (PCT) and the John Muir Trail (JMT).

Zumwalt Meadow   NATURAL FEATURE

(Map p192; off Hwy 108; 🚗) This verdant meadow, bordered by the Kings River and soaring granite walls, offers phenomenal views. In the early morning, the air hums with birdsong, the sun's rays light up the canyon and mule deer and black bears can often be spotted foraging in the meadow. Follow the partly shaded, easy loop nature trail (1.5 miles), with boardwalk sections and a few benches for resting, to get a quick snapshot of the canyon's beauty.

Roaring River Falls   WATERFALL

(Map p192; Hwy 180) A five-minute walk on a paved trail (0.3 miles) leads to this 40ft chute gushing into a granite bowl. In late

Sequoia & Kings Canyon National Parks Region

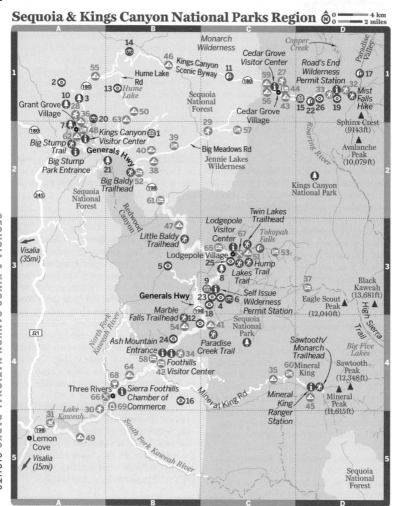

spring and sometimes in early summer the cascade flows strong. Look for the parking lot and trailhead on the south side of Hwy 180, about 3 miles east of Cedar Grove Village, slightly closer to Road's End. It's a great spot to stretch your legs after a long drive. You can dip your toes in the pool at the bottom of the falls, and there's access to the River Trail here, a pleasant walk along the riverbed reaching Zumwalt Meadow Loop (1.6 miles) and continuing a further mile onto Road's End.

Muir Rock   NATURAL FEATURE

(Map p192; Road's End, Off Hwy 180) On excursions to Kings Canyon, John Muir allegedly gave talks atop this large, flat river boulder, a short walk from the Road's End parking lot and less than a mile past Zumwalt Meadow. A sandy river beach here is taken over by swimmers in midsummer. Don't jump in when the raging waters, swollen with snowmelt, are dangerous. Ask at the Road's End ranger station if conditions are calm enough for a dip.

Sequoia & Kings Canyon National Parks Region

SEQUOIA & KINGS CANYON NATIONAL PARKS SIGHTS

Knapp's Cabin HISTORIC BUILDING
(Map p192; Hwy 180) During the 1920s, wealthy businessman George Knapp built this simple cabin to store gear in during his fishing and camping excursions in Kings Canyon. From a signed roadside pullout on Hwy 180, about 2 miles east of the village, a short trail leads to this hidden building, the oldest in Cedar Grove. Come around dusk, when the views of the glacier-carved canyon are glorious.

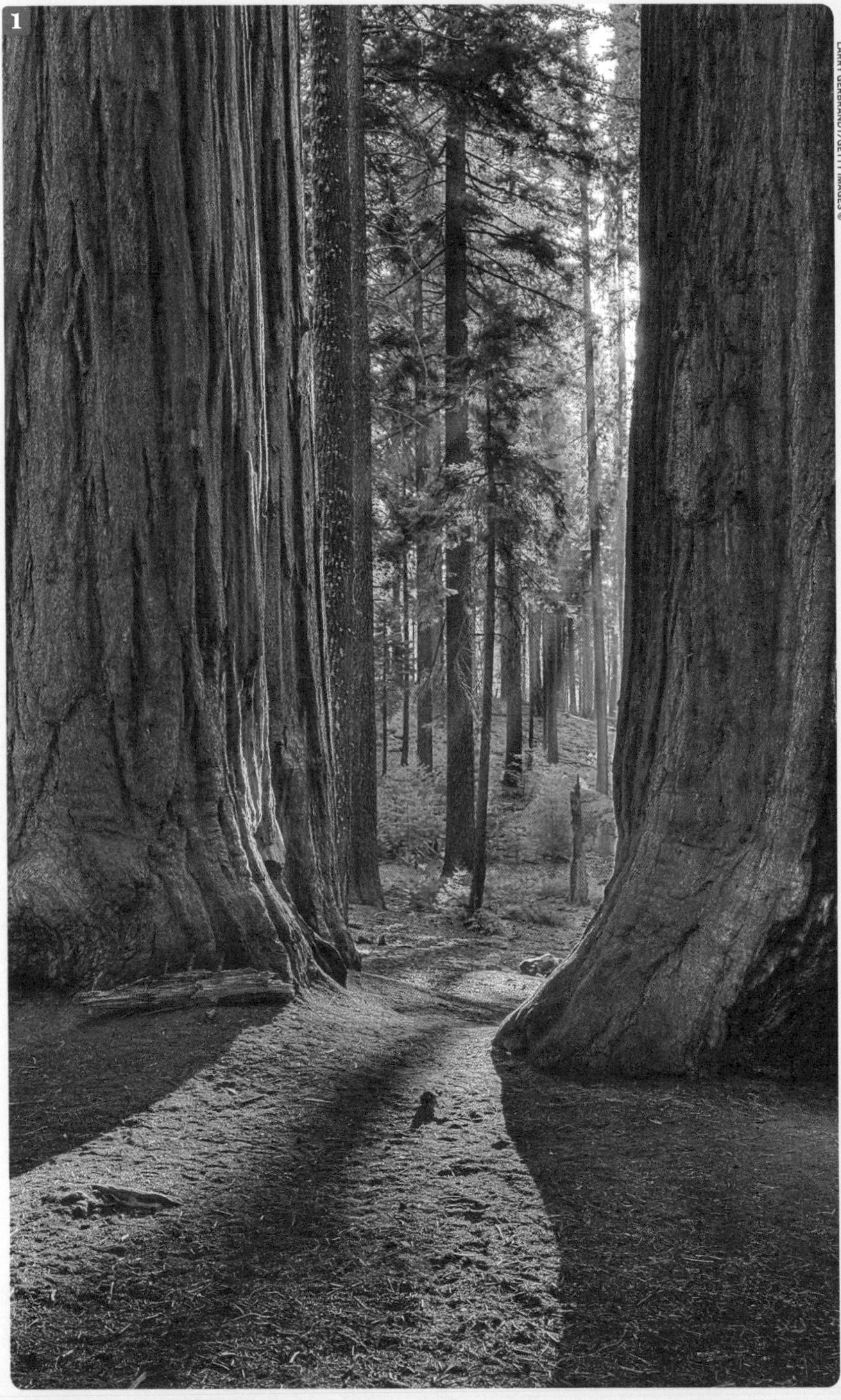
1

LARRY GEIHRANDT/GETTY IMAGES ©

1. General Grant Grove (p190)
This grove of giant sequoias is home to the General Grant, the world's second-largest living tree.

2. Roaring River Falls (p191)
This 40ft torrent gushes strongly in late spring and early summer.

3. Marmots (p190)
Cute, cheeky and problematic, marmots are common in Mineral King.

4. Rae Lakes (p179)
This multi-day hike through the lakes area gives the best backpacking loop in Kings Canyon.

🛏 SLEEPING

🛏 Sequoia National Park

Camping

Lodgepole, Potwisha and Buckeye Flat campgrounds in the national park and both Stony Creek campgrounds offer reservations (essential in summer); most other campgrounds are first-come, first-served.

Campfires are allowed only in existing fire rings. When the risk of wildfires is high, all campfires may be prohibited, especially in the lower-elevation Foothills area.

LODGEPOLE & WUKSACHI VILLAGES

Lodgepole Campground　　CAMPGROUND $
(Map p192; www.nps.gov/seki; Lodgepole Rd; tent & RV sites $22; ☉mid-Apr-late Nov; 🐾) Closest to the Giant Forest area, with more than 200 closely packed sites, this place fills quickly because of its proximity to Kaweah River swimming holes and Lodgepole Village amenities. The 16 walk-in sites are more private. Flush toilets, picnic tables, fire rings, drinking water and bear lockers are available.

Dorst Creek Campground　　CAMPGROUND $
(Map p192; www.recreation.gov; Generals Hwy; tent & RV sites $22; ☉late Jun-early Sep; 🐾) A big and busy campground with more than 200 sites. The quieter back sites are for tents only, while the front loops can fill with RVs. It's about 7 miles northwest of Wuksachi Village and is bookable online. It has picnic tables, fire rings, bear lockers and water (when water supply is low, the campsite may close).

FOOTHILLS

Lower-elevation campgrounds are very hot and dry, especially in summer. Potwisha and Buckeye Flat are often packed with groups and rowdy.

Potwisha Campground　　CAMPGROUND $
(Map p192; www.recreation.gov; Generals Hwy; tent & RV sites $22; ☉year-round; 🐾) Popular campground with shade near swimming spots on the Kaweah River. It's 3 miles northeast of the Ash Mountain Entrance, with 42 sites. There's flush toilets, bear lockers, picnic benches and fire pits. Reservations (highly recommended) taken May through September.

Buckeye Flat Campground　　CAMPGROUND $
(Map p192; www.nps.gov/seki; Buckeye Flat Campground Access Rd, off Generals Hwy; tent sites $22; ☉Apr-late Sep; 🐾) This well-maintained, well-shaded, tent-only campground is off Generals Hwy about 6 miles northeast of the Ash Mountain Entrance, down a winding road that's off-limits to RVs and trailers. It has water, fire rings and grills, bear lockers and clean flush toilets. There's access to the **Paradise Creek Trail**, with close passage to the rushing Paradise Creek river and falls.

Due to its lower elevation, it's a little warmer and one of the first campgrounds to open for the season. Reservations accepted (recommended) between late May and late September.

MINERAL KING

Two small campgrounds sit near the end of remote Mineral King Rd (no trailers or RVs allowed). Water taps are turned off in mid-October.

Cold Springs Campground　　CAMPGROUND $
(Map p192; www.nps.gov/seki; Mineral King Rd; tent sites $12; ☉late May-late Oct; 🐾) A short walk from the ranger station, Cold Springs has 40 sites (nine walk-in sites) and is a peaceful, creek-side location with ridge views and a gorgeous forest setting of conifers and aspens. If you spend the night here at 7500ft, you'll be well on your way to acclimatizing for high-altitude hikes. The campground often fills up on summer weekends.

Vault toilets and potable water are available until early October.

Atwell Mill Campground　　CAMPGROUND $
(Map p192; www.nps.gov/seki; Mineral King Rd; tent sites $12; ☉late May-late Oct; 🐾) Smaller and quieter than elsewhere, Atwell Mill has 21 sites scattered under a shaded forest canopy on the Kaweah River, inside a sequoia grove that was partly logged for timber. It has vault toilets, bear lockers, picnic benches and fire rings, plus water. Getting a site here is rarely a problem.

GENERALS HIGHWAY

Developed USFS campgrounds off the Generals Hwy in the Sequoia National Forest are open seasonally. Primitive campsites and dispersed camping off Big Meadows Rd may open earlier and shut down later in the year, depending on when snow closes the forest service roads.

Stony Creek Campground CAMPGROUND $
(Map p192; www.fs.usda.gov; Generals Hwy; tent & RV sites $25-29; ☺ mid-May–late Sep; 🐾) A mile north of the national park boundary near Stony Creek Lodge, this forest campground operated by California Land Management fills with families in summer. Its nearly 50 sites are spacious and shady. Flush toilets, drinking water, bear lockers, fire rings and an amphitheater are also on site.

Upper Stony Creek Campground CAMPGROUND $
(Map p192; www.fs.usda.gov; off Generals Hwy; tent & RV sites $23-25; ☺ late May-late Sep) With around 25 sites (11 reservable), this primitive campground, accessed off Generals Hwy via unpaved roads in Sequoia National Forest, feels less crowded than others. It has fire rings, vault toilets, picnic benches and bear lockers. It's under a mile from Stony Creek Lodge.

Buck Rock Campground CAMPGROUND
(Map p192; www.fs.usda.gov; FR-13S04, off Big Meadows Rd; tent sites free; ☺ usually Jun-Oct (weather depending)) 𝗙𝗥𝗘𝗘 A handful of primitive first-come, first-serve campsites (no water) are hidden near a fire lookout at an elevation of 7600ft, deep in the forest in the Sequoia National Monument, off Big Meadows Rd. Not bookable.

Horse Camp CAMPGROUND
(Map p192; Big Meadows Rd/FR-14S11; ☺ usually Jun-Oct) 𝗙𝗥𝗘𝗘 Primitive forest campground (no water) used exclusively for horse camping. It's situated at around 7000ft elevation and has half a dozen horse corrals for overnight stock use, plus fire rings.

Big Meadows Campground CAMPGROUND $
(Map p192; www.fs.usda.gov; Big Meadows Rd/ FR-14S11; tent & RV sites $21-50; ☺ end May-Sep (weather permitting)) Over 40 primitive campsites here are spacious, shady and often peaceful. Though there's no potable water, a creek is nearby. The campground is less than 5 miles east of the Generals Hwy. Vault toilets, picnic tables and campfire rings are avilable.

Lodging

LODGEPOLE & WUKSACHI VILLAGES

Bearpaw High Sierra Camp CABIN $$
(Map p192; ☑ reservations 866-807-3598; www. visitsequoia.com/bearpaw.aspx; per person per tent

(sleeps 2) incl breakfast & dinner $350; ☺ usually mid-Jun–mid-Sep) An 11.3-mile hike east of Crescent Meadow on the High Sierra Trail, this canvas-tent village at 7800ft is ideal for exploring the backcountry without lugging your own gear. Rates for each of the six tents include showers, dinner and breakfast, as well as bedding and towels. Bookings start at 7am PST every January 2 and places sell out almost immediately.

Though you can always check for last-minute cancellations, call the reservations line too, as they often know about cancellations first. Two-night minimum stay.

Wuksachi Lodge LODGE $$$
(Map p192; ☑ information 866-807-3598, reservations 317-324-0753; www.visitsequoia.com; 64740 Wuksachi Way; r $220-325; 🅿☺🛜📶🐾) Built in 1999, Wuksachi Lodge is the park's most upscale option. But don't get too excited: the wood-paneled atrium lobby has an inviting stone fireplace and forest views, but the motel-style rooms are fairly generic, with coffeemakers, minifridges, oak furniture and thin walls. The location near Lodgepole Village, however, can't be beat and staff members are friendly and accommodating.

The superior rooms have been recently renovated and sleep between two and six people. They are spread out over three three-story buildings a short walk from the lobby and restaurant and from each building's respective parking lot. If you have a lot of gear, it's best to ask for help lugging things to your room. At the time of research, a new pizza terrace was being planned. Wi-fi can be very patchy.

MINERAL KING

Silver City Mountain Resort CABIN $$
(Map p192; ☑ 559-561-3223; www.silvercityresort. com; Mineral King Rd; cabins with/without bath from $205/165, largest cabin from $495; ☺ late May-late Oct; 🛜) The only food-and-lodging option anywhere near these parts, this rustic, old-fashioned place rents everything from cute and cozy 1950s-era cabins to modern chalets sleeping up to eight. Bring your own sheets and towels for some of the cabins (or rent linens for $45 per cabin). It's 3.5 miles west of the ranger station. Minimum two-night booking may be required.

There's a Ping-Pong table, an outdoor playground and a small pond. Some cabins don't have electricity and the property's generator usually shuts off in the evenings.

SEQUOIA NATIONAL PARK CAMPGROUNDS

CAMPGROUND	LOCATION	DESCRIPTION	NO OF SITES	ELEVATION
Buckeye Flat (p196)	Foothills	Hot, part exposed, next to river and Paradise Creek Trail; sometimes noisy; tent only	28	2800ft
Potwisha (p196)	Foothills	Hot in summer, often noisy; near the Kaweah River and Marble Falls trail	40	2100ft
Big Meadows (p197)	Generals Hwy	Spacious but primitive forest campsites	45	7600ft
Buck Rock (p197)	Generals Hwy	Remote primitive campsites near a fire lookout	11	7600ft
Horse Camp (p197)	Generals Hwy	Primitive wooded campsites; metal horse corral	5	7600ft
Stony Creek (p197)	Generals Hwy	Woodsy campsites, including some creekside	49	6400ft
Upper Stony Creek (p197)	Generals Hwy	Primitive, mostly quiet sites near Stony Creek Lodge	18	6400ft
Dorst Creek (p196)	Lodgepole & Wuksachi Villages	Sprawling forest campground; quieter tent-only sites in back	203	6800ft
Lodgepole (p196)	Lodgepole & Wuksachi Villages	Busy family campground; some sites and features available summer only	205	6700ft
Atwell Mill (p196)	Mineral King	Shady, often damp sites under forest canopy; tent only	21	6650ft
Cold Springs (p196)	Mineral King	Pretty creekside setting in high-elevation valley; tent only (some walk-in sites)	40	7500ft

All of the above campgrounds have bear-proof boxes, picnic tables, fire pits and trash cans.

 Drinking Water   Flush Toilets   Ranger Station Nearby   Wheelchair Accessible   Dogs Allowed (On Leash)

GENERALS HIGHWAY

Big Meadows Guard Station — CABIN **$**

(Map p192; ☑reservations 518-885-3639; www.recreation.gov; Big Meadows Rd/FR-14S11; cabin $125; ⊘usually late Jun–mid-Oct) This restored 1930s USFS patrol station built by the Civilian Conservation Corps (CCC) sleeps six people and offers a rustic stay. Around 4 miles east of the Generals Hwy between the parks, the one-bedroom cabin sits at an elevation of 7600ft. It has hot water, electricity and a full kitchen (with utensils), but you'll need to bring bedding and towels.

★ **Sequoia High Sierra Camp** — CABIN **$$**

(Map p192; ☑866-654-2877; www.sequoiahighsierracamp.com; off Forest Route 13S12; tent cabins without bath incl all meals (price based on 2 people per tent) $500; ⊘early Jun–mid-Sep) A mile's hike deep into the Sequoia National Forest, this off-the-grid, all-inclusive resort is nirvana for those who don't think luxury camping is an oxymoron. Canvas bungalows are spiffed up with pillow-top mattresses, feather pillows and cozy wool rugs. Restrooms and a shower house are shared. Reservations are required and there's usually a two-night minimum stay.

Stony Creek Lodge — LODGE **$$**

(Map p192; ☑877-828-1440, reservations 559-565-3388; www.sequoia-kingscanyon.com; 65569 Generals Hwy; r $149-318; ⊘mid-May–early Oct; P🐾🛜) About halfway between Grant Grove Village and Giant Forest, this wood-and-stone lodge has a big river-rock fireplace in its lobby and 11 aging motel rooms with private bathrooms, telephones and TVs.

OPEN (APPROX)	RESERVATION AVAILABLE?	DAILY FEE	FACILITIES
Apr–late Sep	yes (late May–late Sep)	$22	
year-round	yes (May–Sep)	$22	
May–Sep	no	$21+	
Jun–Oct	no	free	
Jun–Oct	no	free	
mid-May–late Sep	yes	$25+	
mid-May–late Sep	yes	$23+	
mid-Jun–early Sep	yes	$22	
mid-Apr–late Oct	yes (late May–Sep)	$22	
late May–late Oct	no	$12	
late May–late Oct	no	$12	

 Grocery Store Nearby

 Restaurant Nearby

 Payphone

 RV Dump Station

SEQUOIA & KINGS CANYON NATIONAL PARKS SLEEPING

🛏 Kings Canyon National Park

Camping

Unless otherwise stated, all campsites are first-come, first-served. Apart from the campsites, facilities in Cedar Grove Village don't start operating until mid-May.

Campfires are allowed only in existing fire rings. When the risk of wildfires is high, all campfires may be prohibited.

GRANT GROVE

Sunset Campground CAMPGROUND $
(Map p192; www.nps.gov/seki; Hwy 180, near Grant Grove Village; tent & RV sites $22; ☺ late May-early Sep; 🐾) Grant Grove's biggest campground has 157 sites and is a short five-minute walk from the village. Sites are set among evergreen trees. Ranger campfire programs run in summer. Two large group sites are also available (with space for 15 to 30 people). Flush toilets, water, bear lockers, fire rings and picnic benches are available.

Azalea Campground CAMPGROUND $
(Map p192; www.nps.gov/seki; off Hwy180/Generals Hwy; tent & RV sites $18; ☺ year-round; 🐾) Among stands of evergreens, the nicest of the 110 sites at this busy campground border a green meadow. It's off Generals Hwy; General Grant Grove (p190) is a short walk downhill. Offers flush toilets, bear lockers and fire rings.

Crystal Springs Campground CAMPGROUND $

(Map p192; www.recreation.gov; Crystal Springs Rd, off Hwy 180; tent & RV sites $18-40; ☺ mid-May–Sep; 🐾) At the smallest campground in the Grant Grove area, off Generals Hwy, 14 mid-sized group sites and 36 standard camp sites are available. It also has picnic tables, fire rings, bear boxes, flush toilets and potable water. Online booking is possible.

KINGS CANYON SCENIC BYWAY

Developed USFS campgrounds in the Sequoia National Forest off Hwy 180 (Kings Canyon Scenic Byway) and Hume Lake Rd are open seasonally.

Hume Lake Campground CAMPGROUND $

(Map p192; www.fs.usda.gov; Hume Lake Rd; tent & RV sites $27; ☺ mid-May–mid-Sep; 🐾) Almost always full yet still managing a laid-back atmosphere, this campground operated by California Land Management offers almost 65 relatively uncrowded, shady campsites at 5250ft. A handful come with lake views. It's on the lake's northern shore and has picnic tables, campfire rings, flush toilets and drinking water. Reservations are highly recommended. Bookable online at www.recreation.gov.

Princess Campground CAMPGROUND $

(Map p192; www.fs.usda.gov; Hwy 180; tent & RV sites $27-29; ☺ late May-late Sep; 🐾) Just off the scenic byway and only a few miles from Hume Lake, almost 90 reservable sites border a pretty meadow, with sequoia stumps at the registration area. It's especially popular with RVs. Vault toilets, drinking water, picnic tables, fire rings and bear lockers are available. Reservations are essential.

Landslide Campground CAMPGROUND $

(Map p192; www.fs.usda.gov; Forest Rd 13S09/Ten Mile Rd, off Hume Lake Rd; campsites $18; ☺ usually May-Nov, road closed in winter until snow clears) Nine primitive but spacious woody campsites (only six tent sites) are a few miles uphill from Hume Lake in the Giant Sequoia National Monument (elevation 5800ft). Reservations are recommended. Vault toilets and water are available on site. Find it 3 miles south of Hume Lake.

Convict Flat Campground CAMPGROUND

(Map p192; www.fs.usda.gov; Hwy 180; tent sites free; ☺ late Apr–mid-Nov) FREE Five secluded, primitive sites near Yucca Point in the Sequoia National Forest with tree-sheltered views of cliffs deep inside Kings Canyon. Offers vault toilets, picnic benches, fire rings, but no water.

Tenmile Campground CAMPGROUND $

(Map p192; www.fs.usda.gov; Ten Mile Road; campsites $23; ☺ usually mid-May–mid-Sep) A forested campground another 1.5 miles uphill from Landslide Campground (p200) in the Sequoia National Forest with 11 sites. Reservations may be available in peak summer season. Campfire rings, vault toilets, picnic tables and bear lockers are available, but there is no potable water. The campground road is closed during winter.

CEDAR GROVE

Cedar Grove's Sentinel Campground, next to the village area, is open whenever Hwy 180 is open; Sheep Creek, Canyon View (tent only) and Moraine are opened for overflow when needed. These campgrounds are usually the last to fill up on busy summer weekends and are also good bets early and late in the season, thanks to their comparatively low elevation (4600ft). All have flush toilets.

Sheep Creek Campground CAMPGROUND $

(Map p192; www.nps.gov/seki; Hwy 180, Cedar Grove Village; tent & RV sites $18; ☺ late May–mid-Sep) Just a short walk west of the visitor center and village, Cedar Grove's second-biggest campground, with 111 sites, has shady waterfront loops that are especially popular with RVers. Flush toilets, water, bear lockers and restrooms are available.

Sentinel Campground CAMPGROUND $

(Map p192; www.nps.gov/seki; Hwy 180, Cedar Grove Village; tent & RV sites $22; ☺ late Apr-early Nov; 🅿🐾) Sentinel is Cedar Grove's busiest and most centrally located campground, near the visitor center and campfire ranger programs (open in summer only). Premier riverside sites at the beginning of the first loop fill fastest. Facilities include bear lockers, water, fire rings and picnic benches. Also bookable at www.recreation.gov.

Moraine Campground CAMPGROUND $

(Map p192; www.nps.gov/seki; Hwy 180; tent & RV sites $18; ☺ late May-early Sep) The 121 well-spaced, but often sunny and exposed, sites open intermittently as overflow space is needed near Cedar Grove (eg on summer weekends and holidays). Because it's further east of Cedar Grove Village, you can often find a last-minute site here. Has picnic tables, bear lockers, fire rings and water.

Canyon View Campground CAMPGROUND $
(Map p192; www.nps.gov/seki; Hwy 180; tent sites $40-60; ☺late May-Sep) East of Cedar Grove Village, Canyon View has a fair amount of shade and 16 spacious group-only sites (available by reservation only most of the year; walk-ins between late May and June). Has picnic tables, fire rings and bear lockers, plus drinking water.

Lodging

GRANT GROVE

Grant Grove Cabins CABIN $
(Map p192; ☎866-807-3598; www.visitsequoia. com; 86728 Highway 180, Grant Grove Village; cabins $70-149; ☺some cabins Apr-Oct only) Set amid towering sugar pines, the accommodations here include aging tent-top shacks, rustic camp cabins with electricity and outdoor wood-burning stoves, and heated duplexes (a few wheelchair accessible) with private bathrooms and double beds. Number 9 is the lone hard-sided, free-standing 'Honeymoon Cabin' with a queen bed, and it books up fast. Guest registration takes place at John Muir Lodge.

John Muir Lodge LODGE $$
(Map p192; ☎866-807-3598; www.visitsequoia. com; 86728 Highway 180, Grant Grove Village; r from $210; P☺☎) An atmospheric building hung with historical black-and-white photographs, this is a place to lay your head and still feel like you're in the forest. Wide porches have rocking chairs, and homespun rooms, renovated in 2014, contain rough-hewn wooden furniture and patchwork bedspreads. On chilly nights, cozy up to the big stone fireplace with a board game.

CEDAR GROVE

Cedar Grove Lodge LODGE $
(Map p192; ☎559-565-3096; www.visitsequoia. com; 86724 Hwy 180, Cedar Grove Village; r from $147; ☺mid-May–mid-Oct; P☺✳☎) The only indoor sleeping option in the canyon, this riverside lodge offers 21 motel-style rooms. Three ground-floor rooms with shady furnished patios have spiffy river views and kitchenettes. All rooms have phone and TV.

✗ EATING & DRINKING

✗ Sequoia National Park

Lodgepole & Wuksachi Village

Peaks Restaurant AMERICAN $$
(Map p192; ☎559-565-4070; www.visitsequoia. com; Wuksachi Lodge, 64740 Wuksachi Way; mains lunch $8-18, dinner $13-35; ☺breakfast 7-10am, lunch 11:30am-3pm, dinner 5-10pm, lounge 3-10pm, shorter hours low season; ☎☺) The lodge's dining room has an excellent breakfast buffet and soup-and-salad lunch fare, but dinners aim somewhat successfully to be more gourmet, with mains like panseared trout, lamb shank and pork loin. In the lounge, nosh on appetizers and swill cocktails, beer and wine. Non-hotel-guests are welcome.

Lodgepole Market Center FOOD & DRINKS
(Map p192; ☎559-565-3301; www.visitsequoia. com; Lodgepole Rd, Lodgepole Village; ☺9am-5pm Thu-Mon late Oct-early Apr, 8am-9pm early May to late Oct) The park's biggest general store sells groceries, camping supplies, snacks and hot drinks. It's recently refurbished snack bar also serves various hot foods (like burgers and chicken tenders). The market also rents snowshoes in winter ($22 for 24 hours).

General's Highway

Stony Creek Lodge Restaurant AMERICAN $
(Map p192; ☎559-565-3909; www.sequoia-kings canyon.com; 65569 Generals Hwy; pizzas & mains $10-20; ☺4-7:30pm Sun-Thu, 4-7:30pm Fri & Sat mid-May–early Oct; ☺) The lodge's basic restaurant serves decent pizzas and salads.

Mineral King

Silver City Mountain Resort Restaurant AMERICAN $
(Map p192; ☎559-561-3223; www.silvercityresort. com; Silver City Mountain Resort, Mineral King Rd; pie from $5, mains $10-20; ☺usually 8am-8pm) This little country store serves simple fare – usually one or two choices like salmon or pasta – on wooden picnic tables. Try the dreamy thick slabs of homemade pie and French-press coffee. It's 3.5 miles west of the ranger station.

SEQUOIA & KINGS CANYON NATIONAL PARKS EATING & DRINKING

KINGS CANYON NATIONAL PARK CAMPGROUNDS

CAMPGROUND	LOCATION	DESCRIPTION	NO OF SITES	ELEVATION
Moraine (p200)	Cedar Grove	Large, well-spaced but only partly shaded; used as overflow	120	4600ft
Sentinel (p200)	Cedar Grove	Centrally located at Cedar Grove Village; fills up fast	83	4600ft
Sheep Creek (p200)	Cedar Grove	Pretty riverside loops; almost as crowded as Sentinel	111	4600ft
Canyon View (p201)	Cedar Grove	Shady group-only sites	16	4600ft
Azalea (p199)	Grant Grove	Shady forest sites near giant sequoia trees	110	6500ft
Crystal Springs (p200)	Grant Grove	Quieter campsites are wooded and well-spaced	36	6500ft
Sunset (p199)	Grant Grove	Huge evergreen-shaded forest campground near the village	157	6500ft
Hume Lake (p200)	Hume Lake	Lakeside campsites popular with families and anglers	74	5200ft
Landslide (p200)	Hume Lake	Primitive forested sites are fairly spacious	9	5800ft
Princess (p200)	Hume Lake	Meadow-edged sites off scenic byway, convenient for RVs	88	5900ft
Tenmile (p200)	Hume Lake	Bigger but still primitive woodsy campground	13	5800ft
Convict Flat (p200)	Kings Canyon Scenic Byway	Secluded primitive sites with tree-sheltered canyon views	5	3000ft

All of the above campgrounds have bear-proof boxes, picnic tables, fire pits and trash cans.

 Drinking Water   Flush Toilets   Ranger Station Nearby   Wheelchair Accessible   Dogs Allowed (On Leash)

✗ Kings Canyon National Park

Grant Grove Restaurant
AMERICAN $$

(Map p192; Hwy 180, Grant Grove Village; mains $8-30; ⊙ 7-10am, 11:30am-3:30pm & 5-9pm late May-early Sep, until 8pm Apr-late May & early Sep-Oct; 🖥🖉👶) 🍴 After undergoing a top-to-bottom renovation in 2017, this is the best place for a meal (albeit competition is limited) in Grant Grove Village. The new menu focuses on local produce and highlights seasonal dishes. Choose fresh local berries, organic granola, fair-trade coffee, San Joaquin Valley–raised eggs for breakfast, and California grass-fed beef for dinner. Service can be slow.

Cedar Grove Snack Bar
AMERICAN $

(Map p192; Hwy 180, Cedar Grove Village; breakfast $3.50-10, lunch & dinner mains $7-11; ⊙ 8am-10am, 11:30am-2.30pm & 5-9pm mid-May–mid-Oct; 🖥👶) This basic counter-service grill dishes up hot meals (burgers/hot dogs/burritos) and cold deli sandwiches. Dine outside on the riverside deck. In summer there's an occasional barbecue and the smoky smell is too tempting to resist after a long hike.

ℹ Orientation

Most of the star attractions are off the Generals Hwy, the main road that starts in the Foothills area and continues north to Grant Grove, traversing both parks and parts of the Giant Sequoia National Monument in the Sequoia National Forest.

OPEN (APPROX)	RESERVATION AVAILABLE?	DAILY FEE	FACILITIES
late May & early Jul–early Sep	no	$18	
late Apr–early Nov	no	$18	
mid-May–mid-Oct	no	$18	
late-May–late Sep	yes	$40–60	
year-round	no	$18	
mid-May–Sep	no	$18	
mid-May–early Sep	no	$18	
mid-May–mid-Sep	yes	$24–26	
May–Nov	yes (mid-May–late Sep)	$20	
late May–late Sep	yes	$24–26	
May–Nov	maybe	$20	
late Apr–mid-Nov	no	free	

Legend:

- Grocery Store Nearby
- Restaurant Nearby
- Payphone
- RV Dump Station

Visitor activity concentrates around the Giant Forest area and Lodgepole Village, which has the most tourist facilities. Just outside the gateway town of Three Rivers, south of Sequoia's Ash Mountain Entrance, the switchbacking road to remote Mineral King Valley veers east of Hwy 198.

Hwy 180 passes the Big Stump Entrance before reaching Grant Grove Village, which has tourist amenities. Continuing northeast, the Kings Canyon Scenic Byway winds through a section of the Giant Sequoia National Monument and bisects the stunning Monarch Wilderness Area, then descends to Cedar Grove, where it dead-ends at aptly named Road's End.

❶ Information

BOOKS & MAPS

Books and topographic recreational maps are sold at the Giant Forest Museum and all park visitor centers (Lodgepole has the biggest selection).

The nonprofit **Sequoia Parks Conservancy** (p248) publishes an excellent series of fold-out trail map brochures covering the Cedar Grove, Grant Grove, Giant Forest, Lodgepole and Mineral King areas (each $3.50 to $11) for day hikes. Plus, they do topographic trail maps for overnight trips, available at park visitor centers and wilderness permit–issuing stations. Highly recommended are the conservancy's Rae Lakes Loop Trail Map ($8.95) and the Tom Harrison Maps series, all printed on waterproof, tear-resistant paper. These, plus other brands of hiking maps and books, are sold at Foothills visitor center and at the Giant Forest Museum bookstore.

INTERNET ACCESS

Look for free wi-fi in the lobby of Wuksachi Lodge, near the lodging check-in desk in Grant Grove Village and at Stony Cedar Grove Creek Lodge in the Sequoia National Forest.

LAUNDRY

Coin-operated laundries are available seasonally at Lodgepole Village, Grant Grove Village and Stony Creek (from $1.50 per load).

MONEY

Find ATMs at Lodgepole Village, Grant Grove Village, Cedar Grove Village and Stony Creek.

No foreign-currency exchange is available in the parks.

POST

Grant Grove Post Office (Hwy 180; ⊗ usually 9am-4pm Mon-Fri) Next to the village market.

SHOWERS

Pay showers are available seasonally at Lodgepole Village, Grant Grove Village, Cedar Grove Village, Stony Creek Lodge and Silver City Mountain Resort (from $1 for three minutes).

TELEPHONE

Cell-phone coverage is practically nonexistent, except for limited reception at Grant Grove.

Pay phones are found in all village areas and at all visitor centers and some campgrounds; many accept only credit cards or prepaid phonecards.

TOURIST INFORMATION

Cedar Grove Visitor Center (☑ 559-565-3793; Hwy 180, Cedar Grove Village; ⊗ 9am-5pm late May-late Sep) Near the end of the road in Kings Canyon.

Foothills Visitor Center (p188) Just beyond the Ash Mountain Entrance to Sequoia.

Kings Canyon Visitor Center (☑ 559-565-4307; Hwy 180, Grant Grove Village; ⊗ 9am-5pm) In the Grant Grove Village of Kings Canyon.

Lodgepole Visitor Center (☑ 559-565-4436; 63100 Lodgepole Rd, Lodgepole Village; ⊗ 7am-4:30pm late May-early Oct) Located in the heart of Sequoia.

USFS Hume Lake District Office (p176) Stop here for recreation information, maps and campfire and wilderness permits for the Sequoia National Forest. The office is more than 20 miles west of the Big Stump Entrance.

❶ Getting There & Away

Sequoia and Kings Canyon are both accessible by car only from the west, via Hwy 99 from Fresno or Visalia. It's 46 miles east on Hwy 198 from Visalia into Sequoia National Park – you pass through the gateway town of Three Rivers before entering the park. From Fresno, it's 57 miles east on Hwy 180 to Kings Canyon. The two roads are connected by the Generals Hwy, inside Sequoia. There is no access to either park from the east.

BUS

During peak summer season (8am to 6.30pm late May to early September only), **Sequoia Shuttle** (☑ 877-287-4453; www.sequoiashuttle. com; round-trip incl park entry $15; ⊗ 6am-6:30pm late May-late Sep) runs buses five or six times daily between Visalia, Three Rivers and the Giant Forest Museum in Sequoia National Park (two hours, $15 round-trip, including park fee); advance reservations required. All shuttles are wheelchair-accessible and equipped with bicycle racks.

❶ Getting Around

Sequoia National Park has four free shuttle routes within the park (operating between 8am and 6.30pm late May to early September); Kings Canyon has no shuttles. Routes include Gray Route Giant Forest Museum to Moro Rock and Crescent Meadow (every 20 minutes); Green Route General Sherman Tree parking areas and Lodgepole Village (every 15 minutes); Orange Route General Sherman Tree parking areas and Wolverton Rd picnic area and trailhead (every 15 minutes); Purple Route Lodgepole, Wuksachi Lodge and Dorst Campground (every 20 minutes).

The nearest gas stations to Sequoia and Kings Canyon are at Stony Creek Lodge (open mid-May to mid-October only) and **Hume Lake** (☑ 559-305-7770; 64144 Hume Lake Rd; ⊗ pumps 24hr (credit card only after hours), market 8am-noon & 1-5pm), and both carry diesel. It's best to enter the park with a full tank.

AROUND SEQUOIA & KINGS CANYON NATIONAL PARKS

Three Rivers

Named for the nearby convergence of three Kaweah River forks, Three Rivers is a friendly small town populated mostly by retirees and artsy newcomers. For those who have a limited amount of time in the park, there are a number of hikes that border the park (meaning you can avoid paying the entrance fee again). While they're not as epic, they're still very enjoyable. Want to slough off the heat in summertime? Just west of Three Rivers, at the mouth of **Lake Kaweah** (☑559-597-2526; http://kaweahmarina.com; 34467 Sierra Dr, Lemon Cove; kayak & paddleboard rental from $20, 5-passenger boat from $50; ⊙8am-4:30pm winter, 8am-7pm summer), the Slick Rock Recreation Area has pools amid big boulders that make for cool swimming spots. And **Kaweah White Water Adventures** (Map p192; ☑559-740-8251; Mtn Rd 349, near Sierra Dr; rafting trips per person from $50, full river trips with lunch per person $120; ⊙trips leave at 9am & 3pm daily) runs trips on the river through class III to V rapids.

The town's main drag, Sierra Dr (Hwy 198), is sparsely lined with small motels (many with riverfront views), eateries and shops. Day trippers in need of supplies should fill up here before entering the park.

🛌 Sleeping

A few chains and a number of independently owned motels line Sierra Dr all the way to just short of the Ash Mountain Entrance (p182) to Sequoia National Park. All are less expensive than the few lodging options available in Sequoia or Kings Canyon.

Three Rivers Hideaway CAMPGROUND $
(Map p192; ☑559-561-4413; http://threerivers hideaway.com/; 43365 Sierra Dr; tents per 1/2 guests $15/30, per extra guest (up to 6 per site) $7, RVs/cabins from $44/99; ℗🐾🛜) This friendly campground, right outside the Ash Mountain Entrance (p182) to Sequoia park, is one of the best options in the area. It has free showers, clothes-washing facilities ($1.50 per load) and wi-fi in the main check-in area. All sites have picnic tables and fire rings. Three cabins include AC, hot showers, cable TV and linen. RV hookups are available.

Horse Creek Campground CAMPGROUND $
(Map p192; ☑518-885-3639, info 559-597-2301, reservations 877-444-6777; www.recreation.gov; Hwy 198, Lemon Cove; tent & RV sites $20-25) At Lake Kaweah, about 20-minutes' drive from Sequoia National Park, this developed family campground has all the amenities, including warm showers, water points and flush toilets. The views of the lake and mountains are magnificent. There's birdsong in the morning, but you may also hear the distant sound of cars, due to the campsite's close proximity to the road.

Sequoia Village Inn CABIN, COTTAGE $$
(Map p192; ☑559-561-3652; www.sequoia villageinn.com; 45971 Sierra Dr; d $145-309; ✳🛜🏊🐾) These nine cottages, cabins and chalets (most with kitchens and the rest with kitchenettes) border the park and are great for families or groups. Most have outdoor woody decks and BBQs. The largest can sleep 10 people. Guests can also arrange access to the Kaweah River beach, across the street at their sister property Buckeye Tree Lodge.

Buckeye Tree Lodge MOTEL $$
(Map p192; ☑559-561-5900; www.buckeyetree lodge.com; 46000 Sierra Dr; d $162; ✳🛜🏊🐾) 🍃 Sit out on your grassy back patio or perch on the balcony and watch the river ease through a maze of boulders. Fairly generic motel rooms, one with a kitchenette, feel airy. The outdoor picnic area has BBQ grills. One cabin named 'River House' sleeps up to 10 people. Breakfast includes muffins, fruit and juice.

🍴 Eating & Drinking

Sierra Subs & Salads SANDWICHES $
(Map p192; ☑559-561-4810; www.sierrasubs andsalads.com; 41717 Sierra Dr; mains $6-16; ⊙10:30am-6pm Tue-Sat, to 5pm Sun; 🌱) Friendly roadside sandwich and salad shop with a riverside back deck. There's a choice of fresh breads along with healthy wraps, freshly baked pizzas, burgers, hot dogs, salads and fruit smoothies. There's a small sheltered dining hut where you can eat when the weather is bad. Vegetarian, vegan and gluten-free options are available.

Buckaroo Diner AMERICAN $$
(Map p192; ☑559-465-5088; www.olbuckaroo. com; 41695 Sierra Dr; brunch $9-14, dinner $14-22; ⊙5-9pm Thu, Fri & Mon, 10:30am-2:30pm & 5-9pm Sat & Sun) Bay Area transplants started with the Ol' Buckaroo food truck next door before opening this permanent, contemporary restaurant serving modern American cuisine. Simple, local, creative dishes come in the form of small plates of feta faro salad or escarole spicy bean soup, and entrees of organic buttermilk fried chicken. The menu changes frequently to accommodate what's seasonal – it's always good.

Three Rivers Brewing MICROBREWERY
(Map p192; ☑ 559-909-5483; www.threerivers
brewingco.com; 41763 Sierra Dr; ⊙ 11am-9pm
Thu & Sun, to 11pm Fri & Sat) Awesome new
microbrewery run by award-winning craft
beer-maker and Pismo Beach implant Matt
McWilliams. There's usually a couple of
beers on tap at a time, which vary from stout
and reds to honey wheats, blondes and IPAs.
The tiny tasting room is a good chance to
meet the friendly locals.

River View Restaurant & Lounge BAR
(Map p192; ☑ 559-561-2211; 42323 Sierra Dr;
⊙ 11am-9pm Mon-Thu, to 10pm Fri & Sat, bar to
midnight or later) River-view honky-tonk with
live music some nights. The food is medio-
cre and overpriced, but the raucous and fun
bar stays busy in summer. There's karaoke
on Friday nights, and usually a band on Saturday nights.

Visalia

Its agricultural prosperity and well-
maintained downtown make Visalia one of
the valley's convenient stops en route to Sequoia and Kings Canyon National Parks or
the Sierra Peaks. Bypassed a century ago by
the railroad, the city is 5 miles east of Hwy
99, along Hwy 198. Its downtown has old-
town charm and makes for a nice stroll, with
plenty of restaurants and shops.

The main draw in the area is the **Kaweah Oak Preserve** (www.sequoiariverlands.
org; 29979 Rd 182, Exeter; donation adult/child
$3/1; ⊙ sunrise-sunset), about 7 miles east of
town. With 324 acres of majestic oak trees,
it is a gorgeous setting for easy hikes. From
Hwy 198, turn north onto Rd 182; the park is
about a half-mile along on your left.

There's no shortage of chain hotels, most
along CA198. Or try the **Spalding House**
(☑ 559-739-7877; www.thespaldinghouse.com; 631
N Encina St; s/d $85/95; ⊛ ⧡), an atmospheric
Colonial Revival–style home with three cozy
guest suites featuring gorgeous details, such
as mosaic-tiled bathrooms, a stained-glass
ceiling or a sleigh bed.

If you stay for a bite there are plenty of
options, including classic American eats

and international offerings. Restaurants are
mainly clustered along Main St between Flo-
ral and Bridge Sts. **Char-Cu-Te-Rie** (☑ 559-
733-7902; www.char-cu-te-rie.com; 211 W Main St;
mains $7-9; ⊙ 8am-2pm Wed-Mon), a downtown
cafe with artisan sandwiches and egg dishes
and always jam-packed **Brewbakers Brewing Company** (☑ 559-627-2739; www.brew-
bakersbrewingco.com; 219 E Main St; mains $12-22;
⊙ 11:30am-10pm Mon-Thu, 11am-10pm Fri-Sun; ⧡)
are good places to refuel after a few days in
the mountains.

Visalia punches above its weight when it
comes to nightlife, with a brewery, good live
venue and other entertainment options.

❶ Getting There & Away

Visalia's transit options, including direct access
to Sequoia National Park, all funnel through the
Visalia Transit Center (www.ci.visalia.ca.us;
425 E Oak Ave). **Amtrak** (☑ 800-872-7245;
www.amtrak.com; 425 East Oak Street) shuttles
run between the Transit Center and Hanford
station a half hour away by reservation only (use
local buses as an alternative). From Hanford,
you can connect to all other Amtrak routes in the
state, including the San Joaquin, which travels
north to Sacramento ($32, four hours, two
direct daily) or south to Bakersfield ($22.50, 1½
hours, six daily).

Hwy 198 runs north from Visalia through Three
Rivers to Sequoia National Park's Ash Mountain
Entrance. Beyond here, the road continues as
the narrow and windy Generals Hwy, snaking all
the way into Kings Canyon National Park.

The road to remote Mineral King veers off Hwy
198 at the northern end of town, just south of the
park's Ash Mountain Entrance.

The convenient, bike-rack equipped Sequoia
Shuttle buses run five to six times daily (May to
September) between Visalia and the Giant Forest Museum ($15 round-trip, 2½ hours, including
park entry fees) via Three Rivers; reservations
required and pickups from major hotels. From
Sierra Foothills Chamber of Commerce
(Three Rivers Historical Museum; ☑ 559-561-
3300; www.threerivers.com; 42268 Sierra Dr;
⊙ 9am-5pm May-Sep, hours vary low season;
⧡) in Three Rivers, the journey to Foothills Visitor Center (inside Sequoia National Park) takes
roughly 20 minutes; to Giant Forest Museum it's
around one hour.

Understand Yosemite, Sequoia & Kings Canyon National Parks

Yosemite, Sequoia & Kings Canyon Today

The Sierra Nevada has experienced extraordinary conditions over the last several years. An extended drought stressed natural resources and altered the rhythm of the seasons, then in 2017 snow covered the mountains to a degree not seen in decades, providing momentary respite from lack of precipitation. Yosemite has made progress on plans to restore its river corridors and forests, following through with major projects to preserve Mariposa Grove and the Merced and Tuolumne River areas.

Snippets

Best in Print

The Last Season (Eric Blehm; 2007) Gripping investigation into the disappearance of park ranger and passionate conservationist and mountaineer Randy Morgenson.

The Wild Muir: Twenty-Two of John Muir's Greatest Adventures (2013) Essential collection of Muir's writings on Yosemite and the Sierra.

An Uncertain Path: A Search for the Future of National Parks (Bill Tweed; 2010) Retired Sequoia park planner hikes and ponders park management in an era of climate change.

A Way Across the Mountain: Joseph Walker's 1833 Trans-Sierran Passage and the Myth of Yosemite's Discovery (Scott Stine; 2015) A reevaluation of how white explorers first encountered Yosemite.

Best on Film

Valley Uprising (2014) Fast-paced documentary on Yosemite's Camp 4 rock-climbing revolution.

The National Parks: America's Best Idea (2009) Documentary series on US park history.

Yosemite (2017) PBS documentary exploring the extraordinary impact of climate change on the park.

Climate Change

The 2013 Rim Fire scorched 402 sq miles of the Stanislaus National Forest and the northwestern periphery of Yosemite. It was the largest recorded wildfire in the Sierra Nevada (and the third largest in California history) and many viewed its rapid acceleration as an unsettling portent. If severe climate change became the new normal for California, would drought convert its forests to kindling stockpiles?

Other shifts reinforce these concerns. Small, upper-elevation mammals such as the beloved little pika (a tiny relative of the rabbit) have moved to higher, previously uninhabitable elevations and abandoned their lower stomping grounds. Remaining glaciers such as the Lyell Glacier are rapidly receding as temperatures rise. In 2015 scientists determined that the glacier had only 10% of its original volume and 20% of its surface area remaining and that it could vanish completely within several years.

Most of the Sierra, including the majority of Yosemite, is above the snow line, which in the latter averages 5700ft. This means, or at least used to mean, that when precipitation falls in the mountains in the winter it does so as snow. If the snow line recedes, and there's some evidence of this, heavy rain at high altitudes results in heavy and dangerous flooding in the valleys below. It also leads to a reduced snow pack, which has severe consequences on the entire ecosystem, not to mention drinking-water supplies for California cities.

Tourism & Development

The parks continue the tricky footwork of facilitating preservation while accommodating high levels of tourism. After considerable public comment – and an equal amount of litigation – Yosemite continues to carry out comprehensive management plans along the Tuolumne and Merced River corridors. Tuolumne Meadows has shrunk its development footprint with the closure of its gas station and stables, as well as a reconfiguration of parking areas and the restoration of native riparian habitat and vegetation. In Yosemite Valley, which teeters on the edge of being loved to pieces, the comprehensive Merced plan is meant to spearhead riverbank restoration coupled with improved traffic patterns and additional campsite capacity (Camp 4, famous for its connection to rock-climbing history, is set to double in size).

A two-year restoration project to remove development in Mariposa Grove was completed in early summer 2018, revitalizing the long-term health of the stately trees and the awesome experience of visiting them. With a pared-down parking area and the introduction of a new shuttle system from the South Entrance, visitors will reach the grove via public transportation and new trails. Yosemite has also continued the free shuttle services along Glacier Point Rd and between the Valley and Tuolumne Meadows that were first trialed in summer 2015.

Visitor Responsibilities

There is a perpetual conversation about the parks' duty to warn visitors about dangers in the natural world and the responsibility that people must take for their own actions. Near-drownings and slip-and-fall injuries are commonplace along waterways in the national parks. There have been so many injuries from hikers rock hopping or scrambling off trail at Yosemite Falls that the park has posted a warning sign illustrated by an X-ray of broken bones. And with the popularity of personal locator beacons, an increasing number of people are counting on search-and-rescue teams to extricate them in the case of an emergency – or sometimes mere inconvenience. Connectivity is no substitute for knowing your abilities and using good judgment.

Backcountry use continues to rise steadily throughout the Sierra Nevada, highlighting the importance of minimizing human impact and practicing Leave No Trace principles. There are time-tested reasons for all the regulations. Campfire and stove restrictions prevent accidental blazes. Wilderness permits regulate the use of popular trails and campsites. Bear canisters protect bears from habituating to human presence, becoming a danger and being destroyed. And no one wants to accidentally discover what someone else saw fit to leave behind: pack out your trash and toilet paper and keep the wilderness pristine for generations to come.

AREA: **YOSEMITE 1169 SQ MILES, SEQUOIA & KINGS CANYON 1353 SQ MILES**

MILES OF TRAILS:
YOSEMITE 800, SEQUOIA & KINGS CANYON 866

ANNUAL VISITATION (2017):
YOSEMITE 4.3 MILLION, SEQUOIA & KINGS CANYON 1.98 MILLION

if 100 people visited Yosemite, where they would enter

30 South Entrance   12 Tioga Pass
30 Arch Rock   **1** Hetch Hetchy
27 Big Oak Flat

seasonal visitation – Yosemite
(% of annual visitors)

45 summer   26 fall   20 spring   9 winter

visitors per sq mile

YOSEMITE   SEQUOIA   KINGS CANYON

≈ 960 people

History

History unfolds here at varying rates of speed. The timelessness of the physical land-scape, the presence of its first people – Native American tribes who still call the Sierra Nevada home – the decomposing ghost towns left behind by California's early settlers and miners, and the record-setting feats of modern rock climbers and mountaineers have all left their mark. The names you'll encounter as you explore – Tenaya, Ahwahnee, Whitney, Olmsted, Degnan, Muir, Adams – tell the story of the parks' peopled past.

Native Americans

Archeologists believe indigenous people were living in the Sierra Nevada – and Yosemite Valley, with its abundance of natural resources – for several thousand years before Spanish explorers and, later, American pioneers first arrived.

Most Sierra Nevada tribes migrated with the seasons, and though they established warm-weather hunting sites in the High Sierra, they generally kept to lower elevations. Heavy snow cover on the range's western slopes discouraged year-round habitation above 5000ft, but the oak forests of the lower western foothills and piñon-juniper forests on the eastern escarpments were hospitable year-round.

Both sides of the mountain range were occupied by distinct linguistic groups. The western slopes of today's Yosemite region were home to the Sierra Miwok. To the south, the Western Mono (or Monache) and the Tubatulabal inhabited the western slopes of what is now Sequoia and Kings Canyon National Parks, with the Yokut residing in the lowest foothills and across the central valley. Meanwhile, the Eastern Sierra was home to the Paiute.

While most tribal groups traveled only when hunting and gathering or migrating, trading and warring parties regularly crossed the Sierra on foot to exchange goods and fight battles. Obsidian and pine nuts from the Eastern Sierra were in great demand from western-slope and coastal people, who traded them for acorns and seashells. Early Euro-American explorers making their way over the Sierra often followed these ancient trade routes – as do hikers and backpackers today.

The Sierra Club's online John Muir Exhibit (http://vault.sierraclub.org/john_muir_exhibit) is a storehouse of everything Muir, featuring the author's complete books, as well as historical photos, essays and documentaries.

TIMELINE	AD 1400	1848	1851
	The Ahwahneechee ('people of the gaping mouth'), a subtribe of the Sierra Miwok, settle in Yosemite Valley and become its first known permanent residents.	Mexico cedes California to the US under the Treaty of Guadalupe Hidalgo; gold is discovered at Sutter's Mill, starting California's epic gold rush.	Members of the Mariposa Battalion, led by James Savage in paramilitary pursuit of Native Americans, become the first white people to enter Yosemite Valley.

Early Explorers

As early as the 18th century, Spanish explorers described a great *sierra nevada* – a snow-covered mountain range – glimpsed from the San Joaquin Valley. In 1805 a Spanish military expedition stumbled across a great canyon in the southern Sierra and named the river El Río de los Santos Reyes, having discovered it on the Christian Feast of Epiphany.

Even before California became a US state in 1850, American trappers and explorers started arriving from the east. Trailblazer Jedediah Smith became the first European to cross the Sierra Nevada in 1827. In 1833 frontiersman Joseph Walker led the first party of American emigrants across the range. Even if he was indeed the first nonindigenous person to gaze down into Yosemite Valley, he was probably too exhausted to appreciate the extraordinary sight.

Over the next decade, rumors of rich farmlands in Alta California (a province of Mexico) reached emigrants on the Oregon Trail. Several emigrant groups made the difficult trans-Sierra trek, which inevitably ended at the region's only pioneer settlement: Sutter's Fort, a nascent utopian community on the Sacramento River founded by Swiss immigrant John Sutter.

Mariposa Battalion

In February 1848, during construction of John Sutter's sawmill in the Sierra Nevada foothills, foreman James Marshall found flecks of gold in the water. News of Marshall's discovery immediately spread around the world. As many as 200,000 people poured into the Sierra Nevada over the next decade alone. The newly minted state of California sanctioned the creation of militias to settle any conflicts the new arrivals had with indigenous inhabitants.

During the gold rush, prospector James Savage began mining on the Merced River. After clashes with local tribes culminated in the burning of his trading post, Savage sought revenge by forming a militia called the Mariposa Battalion. When Savage learned that the raiding tribespeople might belong to a holdout group of Sierra Miwok from a valley upriver, the militia hastily marched to root them out.

On March 27, 1851, after a brief encounter with Ahwahneechee chief Tenaya, the battalion entered Yosemite Valley. Determined to drive out the valley's indigenous inhabitants, it burned Native American camps and provisions, but it failed to find many tribespeople on its first expedition. (A young recruit named Lafayette Bunnell gave the valley the name Yosemite, a corruption of the Miwok word *oo-soo'-ma-te,* meaning 'grizzly bear.')

....
Yosemite Museum & Indian Village of Ahwahnee (Yosemite Valley)
....
Manzanar National Historic Site (Independence)
....
Laws Railroad Museum & Historic Site (Bishop)
....
Bodie State Historic Park (near Bridgeport)

1853	1858	1864	1868
Chief Tenaya, the last chief of the Ahwahneechee, is killed under still-mysterious circumstances, and the last of his people disperse from Yosemite Valley.	Homesteader Hale Tharp becomes the first white person to enter the grove of giant sequoias that would later be named the Giant Forest in Sequoia National Park.	President Lincoln signs the Yosemite Grant, establishing the Yosemite Valley and Mariposa Grove as a state park, the first such park in the world.	Hired to watch over a flock of sheep and its wayward herder, naturalist John Muir makes his first visit to the Sierra Nevada mountains and Yosemite Valley.

Written while exploring with Josiah Whitney and the California Geological Survey between 1860 and 1864, botanist William Brewer's entertaining journal *Up and Down California* makes scaling a mountain sound like a Sunday picnic.

The Mariposa Battalion made several forays into the Yosemite region that spring, forcing Tenaya and most of his people from their Yosemite Valley home to a reservation near Fresno. The following winter, the chief and some of his people were allowed to return to Yosemite. But hostilities continued and, in circumstances that are still debated, Chief Tenaya was killed in Yosemite Valley, allegedly by Mono Lake Paiute tribespeople angered by the theft of some horses.

Entrepreneurs & Homesteaders

Tales of cascading waterfalls and towering stone columns followed the Mariposa Battalion out of Yosemite and soon raised public awareness. In 1855 an entrepreneurial Englishman named James Hutchings led the first tourist party into Yosemite Valley. Another visitor that same summer was Galen Clark, who returned the following year to establish a homestead near the Mariposa Grove of giant sequoias, where he lived for several decades. Clark took on the role of Yosemite guardian, a title that became official when the area became public land in 1864.

As word got around, entrepreneurs and homesteaders began arriving to divvy up the real estate of Yosemite Valley, creating ramshackle residences and roads, cutting down forests and planting the meadows with gardens and orchards. They brought in livestock and started running sheep into high mountain meadows, where trampling hooves destroyed wildflowers and delicate grasses.

Despite a flurry of silver-mining claims that were filed in relation to the optimistically named Mineral King Valley of present-day Sequoia National Park, the area failed to turn up much of value. Instead it was ranching that brought the first homesteader, Hale Tharp, to the southern Sierra. In 1858, led by a Native American guide, Tharp became the first nonindigenous man to enter the Giant Forest, where he famously fashioned a cabin inside a fallen giant sequoia.

The First State Park

First published in 1966, Francis P Farquhar's *History of the Sierra Nevada* is still one of the region's definitive books. It's an enjoyable read for armchair travelers.

In 1860 Thomas Starr King, a Unitarian minister, orator and respected nature writer, helped rescue Yosemite from runaway commercialism. King wrote a series of widely read letters to the *Boston Evening Transcript* describing his trip to the region. Shortly after the publication of King's letters, an exhibition opened in New York featuring photographs of Yosemite by Carleton E Watkins. The exhibition was a critical success, and Watkins' work caught the attention of California senator John Conness.

Meanwhile Frederick Law Olmsted, the landscape architect who designed New York's Central Park, brought his ideals to bear on Yosemite. He believed government should play a role in preserving natural spaces

1890	1892	1899	1900
In late September President Harrison authorizes the creation of Sequoia National Park; one week later, Congress passes the Yosemite Act, establishing Yosemite National Park.	The Sierra Club is founded with 182 charter members, and John Muir is elected its first president; its first task is to defeat proposed reductions in Yosemite's boundaries.	Led by Colonel Charles Young, a regiment of 'Buffalo Soldiers' – the African American cavalry and infantry regiments of the US Army – arrive for duty in Sequoia National Park.	The first automobile sputters into Yosemite Valley, but a ban on cars inside the park is immediately established by park rangers, citing vehicular disturbance to livestock and tourists.

that nourished the human spirit. Olmsted met with San Francisco businessman Israel Ward Raymond, who had become concerned about the fate of Yosemite's giant sequoias.

In 1864 Raymond wrote a letter to Senator Conness, proposing a bill that would grant Yosemite Valley and the Mariposa Grove to the state of California. Conness presented the bill to Congress, and on June 30, 1864, in the midst of the Civil War, President Abraham Lincoln signed the Yosemite Grant into law. This marked the first time the US federal government had ever mandated the preservation and protection of a natural area for public use, making Yosemite the first state park.

Whitney Versus Muir

As the gold rush waned (the equivalent of $2 billion was extracted by 1852) by 1860, the newly appointed California state geologist, Josiah Whitney, assembled a crew of scientists, surveyors and cartographers to map out the state's natural resources. Officially the California Geological Survey, Whitney's team explored Yosemite in 1863, and the Kings Canyon and Mt Whitney regions the following year. During their expeditions they surveyed and named lakes, passes and peaks, including titling some after themselves – Mt Dana in Yosemite National Park and Mt Whitney in Sequoia National Park, for example.

As Whitney's survey assembled its theories on Yosemite's formation, a naturalist named John Muir, who first visited Yosemite Valley in 1869, began to put forth his own ideas. Muir attributed the valley's formation to glaciers, a theory Whitney vehemently shot down, but one that would later prove correct. Meanwhile the Scottish-born Muir, a prolific writer and indefatigable advocate for conservation, would become Yosemite's most adamant and successful defender.

New National Parks

In 1889 John Muir took Robert Underwood Johnson, publisher of the national magazine *Century,* on a camping trip to Tuolumne Meadows. Under the stars the two men hammered out a plan to save the area from 'hoofed locusts' (what Muir infamously called sheep) and commercial interests. Their plan drew upon the precedent set by Yellowstone, established as the country's first national park in 1872. Muir agreed to write some articles promoting the concept, and these were published in *Century* the following summer, while Johnson exercised his considerable political influence in Washington, DC.

Around the same time, the groves of giant sequoias south of Yosemite were falling at an alarming rate beneath the saws of lumber companies that were acquiring enormous tracts of old-growth forest through government loopholes. Visionary Visalia newspaper editor George Stewart

Thousands of pages of digital books fill the Yosemite Online Library (www.yosemite.ca.us/library), including century-old newspaper articles and the complete text of books by John Muir, Galen Clark and others.

Part history and part adventure tale, Clarence King's *Mountaineering in the Sierra Nevada* (1872) is a dramatic account of his exploits in the mountains and a gripping read to boot.

HW Brand's *The Age of Gold: The California Gold Rush and the New American Dream* (2003) tells the story of the discovery of the precious metal and helps explain why dreamers are still panning for instant wealth to this day.

1916	1923	1927	1935
Congress authorizes establishment of the National Park Service (NPS), and Stephen T Mather becomes its first director; Tioga Rd and John Muir Trail under construction.	Construction of O'Shaughnessy Dam finished, costing $100 million and 68 lives, damming the Tuolumne River and flooding Hetch Hetchy Valley, which John Muir likened to a holy temple.	Yosemite's luxurious Ahwahnee Hotel (now the Majestic Yosemite Hotel), which was dreamed up to promote tourism by NPS director Stephen T Mather, opens on the site of a former Native American tribal village.	After years of work, the Generals Hwy is extended from the Giant Forest to General Grant National Park; it's immediately declared one of the nation's most scenic roads.

Chinese Camp, a town on Hwy 120 west of Groveland and the entrance to Yosemite, was home to 5000 Chinese immigrant miners in the 1850s. No descendants of these miners live here today.

began pushing for federal protection of a sequoia grove that Muir had christened the Giant Forest. Muir, Johnson and others quickly joined Stewart's fight.

On September 25, 1890 President Benjamin Harrison signed a bill into law that protected the Giant Forest, thus creating Sequoia National Park, California's first national park. A week later Congress passed the Yosemite Act, creating Yosemite National Park (although Yosemite Valley and Mariposa Grove remained under state control) *and* General Grant National Park, which encompassed Grant Grove and would later be incorporated into Kings Canyon National Park. In 1906, after lobbying by John Muir and the Sierra Club that Muir had co-founded, California finally ceded Yosemite Valley and the Mariposa Grove to Yosemite National Park.

The Beginning of Tourism

William C Tweed's *King Sequoia* (2016) is a biography of the world's largest tree species and traces the fascinating history of the battle to protect or log them.

Hotels came and went in Yosemite Valley's early years. Hastily erected of wood and canvas to house the ever-increasing hordes of tourists, many of the early hotels burned down when sparks escaped from stoves, or lanterns got too close to curtains. Tourism started off more slowly in Sequoia National Park, where in 1898 a horse-and-mule packing service started bringing visitors to Giant Forest, housing them in a simple tent hotel.

In 1899, when a night in Yosemite's popular Sentinel Hotel cost $4, David and Jennie Curry established a tourist camp at the base of Glacier Point in Yosemite Valley. At Camp Curry, campers were provided with a bed in a large canvas tent, shared bathroom facilities and home-cooked meals for a mere $2 a day. What's more, Camp Curry offered an evening program of music, stunts, nature talks and views of the nightly 'firefall' (p106).

The year 2016 marked the centennial of the National Park Service (NPS), a time of reflection, assessment and celebration for the nation's 400-plus national parks and monuments.

The first automobile sputtered into Yosemite Valley in the summer of 1900, but cars were quickly prohibited in the park, on the grounds that they spooked livestock and ruined tourists' experience (those were the days!). A few years after the ban was lifted in 1913, a serviceable dirt road opened through Tioga Pass. By 1922 annual visitation surpassed 100,000.

In Sequoia National Park, the first automobile arrived in 1904. The Generals Hwy opened in 1926 between the park's foothills and the Giant Forest. It took almost another decade to push the highway through to Grant Grove, in what would later become Kings Canyon National Park. Though the Generals Hwy was one of the country's most scenic (and expensive) roads, the park still received less than a quarter of the visitors at Yosemite.

The automobile increased visitation to all three parks, but it was the enthusiastic – and sometimes extreme – policies of Stephen T Mather,

1940	1978	1984	1996
Congress creates Kings Canyon National Park, encompassing General Grant National Park and including a large part of the namesake canyon that John Muir once called 'a rival to the Yosemite.'	Mineral King Valley, a glacially formed canyon of vast natural beauty, is added to Sequoia National Park, preventing the Walt Disney Company from building a ski resort there.	Unesco declares Yosemite National Park a World Heritage Site; Congress passes the sweeping California Wilderness Act, designating almost 90% of Yosemite as specially protected wilderness.	Annual visitation to Yosemite National Park peaks at over four million people, then abruptly declines over the next decade before beginning to recover.

the first director of the National Park Service (NPS), established in 1916, that sent the numbers climbing. During his tenure (1917 to 1929), Mather oversaw the development of Yosemite's Wawona Golf Course (now Big Trees Golf Course), Ahwahnee Hotel (now the Majestic Yosemite Hotel), Yosemite Museum, and Camp Curry (now Half Dome Village) ice rink, and he initiated nature walks and educational programs at all three parks.

George Anderson, who was the first man to reach the summit of Half Dome in 1875, is buried in Yosemite Valley's pioneer cemetery.

From WWII to Modern Park Management

In 1940, just before the US entered WWII, Congress passed a law creating Kings Canyon National Park, which absorbed General Grant National Park into its much larger boundaries. As the national war effort gobbled up federal funds, Sequoia and Kings Canyon National Parks were merged into a single administrative body in 1943.

In Yosemite the Ahwahnee Hotel (now the Majestic Yosemite Hotel) became a wartime naval hospital and the US Army set up camps at Wawona and Badger Pass. The California National Guard was stationed at Hetch Hetchy to protect the public water supply, while 90,000 troops occupied Yosemite Valley. At the height of the war, public visitation plummeted to just 116,000 people a year.

After WWII families taking vacations in shiny new cars started rolling into Yosemite in record numbers. Tensions over crowding came to a head on July 4, 1970, during the Stoneman Meadow Riot, when park rangers on horseback forcefully removed partying youths who were illegally camped out. Rangers were pulled from their horses and beaten, dozens of revelers suffered injuries, and by morning 135 people had been arrested and the National Guard called in.

In 1980 Yosemite adopted its first General Management Plan, calling for restrictions on private cars, increases in public transportation, changes to Merced River campgrounds and the relocation of many commercial services to outside the park. Mired in political and public opposition, the plan foundered until a major flood in 1997 forced it into its final revision. The restoration plans for Yosemite's Mariposa Grove and the Tuolumne River share the same goal: restoring health to the park's natural environment while minimizing the impact of human visitation.

To immerse yourself in the yesteryear world of the Sierra Nevada, you can do no better than dive into John Muir's many books and essay collections, including *My First Summer in the Sierra* (1911) and *The Yosemite* (1912).

Pick up the historical novel *Gloryland* (2009) by Yosemite ranger Shelton Johnson, a well-known historian of the African American 'Buffalo Soldiers' who served as the Sierra Nevada's first national-park rangers.

1998	2006	2013	2017
A 7in-tall specimen of crystallized gold, called 'the dragon' for its unusual shape, is discovered in the Colorado Quartz Mine in Mariposa County. It now resides in the Houston Museum of Natural Science.	In August four amateur cave researchers discover Ursa Minor cave in Sequoia National Park, one of the most significant cave discoveries in recent history.	The Rim Fire, the third-largest wildfire in Sierra Nevada history, burns 402 sq miles of the Stanislaus National Forest on the northwestern edge of Yosemite.	Northern Sierra Nevada receives record winter precipitation, ending a five-year drought.

Geology

Poetically nicknamed the 'Range of Light' by conservationist John Muir, the 400-mile-long Sierra Nevada mountain range gives California much of its astonishing geological diversity. With peaks over 14,000ft high, it creates a towering wall that captures clouds and douses the western slopes in water, while shutting off the supply of rain to the eastern slopes into the Great Basin desert beyond. Stretching ever skyward, the Sierra Nevada provides living, earth-shaking evidence of the irresistible geological forces still shaping the landscape today.

The Lay of the Land

Geologists call the Sierra Nevada a tilted fault-block range – and it's a particularly impressive example at that, spreading 40 to 60 miles wide, with hundreds of peaks over 10,000ft. Picture a tilted fault block as an iceberg listing to one side while floating in the earth's crust. In the Sierra Nevada, that imaginary 'iceberg' is actually an immense body of granite known as a batholith that formed deep within the earth's crust, then 'floated' up and became exposed on the surface over millions of years. Today visitors can see the tip of this batholith, though it's obscured in places where older rocks (mostly metamorphic) still cling, like pieces of a torn cloak, or where newer rocks (mostly volcanic) have been added on top, like icing.

Drifting on Ancient Seas

California claims both the highest point in the contiguous US (Mt Whitney, 14,505ft) and the lowest elevation in North America (Badwater, Death Valley, 282ft below sea level) – and they're only 90 miles apart, as the eagle flies.

Around 225 million years ago, the area that is now the Sierra Nevada was actually a shallow sea lying off the coast of a young North American continent. Material from island volcanoes exploding offshore, plus tons of debris that were eroding from the continental landmass, gradually began filling in this sea with weighty layers of sediment.

At the same time, the continental North American Plate started drifting westward and riding over the leading edge of the oceanic Pacific Plate. With almost unimaginable force, this movement drove the edge of the Pacific Plate down to depths where it melted into magma, later cooling to form the Sierra Nevada batholith (a term derived from the Greek words for 'deep rock').

Today's Sierra Nevada and Cascade mountain chains mark the edge of this submerged, melting plate. The force of the continental and oceanic plates colliding and crushing together also generated such enormous heat and pressure that old sedimentary and volcanic rocks turned into the metamorphic rocks now found throughout the Sierra Nevada range.

Building Mountains: Batholiths & Plutons

As it made its huge, continual push over the Pacific Plate, the North American Plate buckled so strongly that it formed a proto–Sierra Nevada mountain range of folded rock that may have reached as high as 15,000ft. This initial phase of building the Sierra Nevada ceased about 130 million years ago, when the older mountains began a long erosional phase that, by 50 million years ago, had reduced them to gently rolling uplands, leaving the batholith exposed on the earth's surface.

Between 80 and 210 million years ago, the Sierra Nevada batholith began as magma deep in the earth's crust, cooling to form giant blocks of rock more than 100 different times. Each magma event formed a discrete body of granitic rock known as a pluton (from Pluto, the Roman god of the underworld), each with a characteristic composition and appearance. Hikers today can trace the layout of these well-mapped plutons by examining the mix of minerals and the size of the crystals within rocks alongside park trails.

Pushing Up, Sliding Down

About 10 million years ago the Sierra Nevada's granite batholith began to lift and bulge upward between parallel sets of faults (that is, cracks in the earth's crust). Regions of much older rocks were uplifted on the newly forming crest of the Sierra Nevada. Remnants of old rocks perched on top of granite ridges are today called roof pendants, of which Yosemite's Mt Dana is an outstanding example.

The Sierra Nevada batholith has continued to lift, reaching its current height an estimated two million years ago. Since then, the counterbalancing forces of uplift and erosion have created an equilibrium that keeps the Sierra Nevada at more or less the same size, although the range continues to slowly grow at a minuscule, yet measurable, rate.

From two million years ago until about 10,000 years ago, Ice Age glaciers covered portions of the Sierra Nevada with snow and ice. The largest ice field was a giant cap of ice that covered an area 275 miles long and 40 miles wide between Lake Tahoe and Yosemite. From high-elevation ice fields, rivers of ice (glaciers) flowed down and scoured out rugged canyons, simply enlarging some or beautifully sculpting others such as Yosemite Valley, Mineral King Valley in Sequoia National Park and the upper portions of Kings Canyon.

After the Ice Age came a warm period when there were no glaciers in the Sierra, but during the last 1000 years or so, about 99 glaciers and 398 glacierets (small glaciers or pockets of ice) reformed during the Little Ice Age. The largest remaining glaciers are on Mt Lyell and Mt Maclure in the Yosemite region, and on the Palisades in the John Muir Wilderness in the Eastern Sierra further south. However, due to global warming, these glaciers are all melting rapidly and are in danger of disappearing entirely within decades. Maclure Glacier is only half the size it was when John Muir visited it in the mid-19th century, and Lyell Glacier is so thin it has completely stopped moving downhill.

The Forces at Work

The dramatic tale of how the Sierra Nevada range first formed is only the beginning of the geologic story – as soon as its rocks were exposed on the earth's surface, a host of new forces shaped them into the impressively varied landscape you see today. Hugely powerful glaciers have played a dramatic role, but erosion and weathering have also done their part, as have volcanic lava and ash eruptions.

Glaciers

Most of the Sierra Nevada's landscape has been substantially shaped by glaciers. In fact, of all the forces that have contributed to the landscape, none has had greater impact than the relentless grinding caused by millions of tons of ice over a period of two million years. Evidence of this dramatic grinding process is often right at your feet in areas of the Sierra Nevada where glaciers have worn granite surfaces down to a smooth, shiny finish. Along the road at Tenaya Lake, for example, flat granite

---

GEOLOGY THE FORCES AT WORK

The vast wilderness of the High Sierra (lying mostly above 9000ft) presents an astounding landscape of glaciers, sculpted granite peaks and remote canyons, beautiful to look at but difficult to access on foot or horseback. It presented one of the greatest challenges for 19th-century settlers attempting to reach California.

The highest single-tier waterfall in North America is not Yosemite Falls – it's Ribbon Fall, which plummets 1612ft from a precipice west of El Capitan. Because it has three distinct falls, Yosemite Falls gets disqualified – despite measuring an astonishing 2425ft from top to bottom.

THE EASTERN SIERRA'S SHAKY GROUND

Uplift of the Sierra's batholith continues to occur along its eastern face, where a zone of geologic activity keeps life exciting for folks living along Hwy 395 between Mammoth Lakes and Lone Pine.

In 1872 the Eastern Sierra jerked upward 13ft in a single earthquake (the town of Lone Pine was destroyed), while over the past two decades Mammoth has endured a nerve-wracking series of minor earthquakes and tremors. The Sierra crest is estimated to lift as much as 1.5in per century and, as a result of this skewed tilting, the eastern face of the Sierra is now an abrupt wall rising up to 11,000ft high, while the western face is a long, gentle incline.

Due to uplift along the eastern face, rivers flowing down the range's western slopes have picked up speed and cut progressively deeper canyons into the formerly flat, rolling landscape. Today, over a dozen major river canyons mark the western slope, and the rock that formerly filled those canyons now buries the Central Valley under 9.5 miles of sediment. Talk about rolling stones!

shelves are so polished they glisten in the early morning light. In contrast hikers to high-alpine nunataks (peaks and plateaus that were too high to be glaciated) such as Mt Conness will find rough-textured, sharp-edged and jagged granite formations. For a living geology lesson, hike the gentle, half-mile Nunatak Nature Trail in the Inyo National Forest, off Hwy 120 just east of Tioga Lake and Yosemite's Tioga Pass entrance.

Glaciers arise where snowfields fail to melt completely by summer's end. Over time, delicate snow crystals dissolve into tiny spheres that connect and fuse into solid ice. True glacial ice forms after hundreds of years, with the original snowflakes becoming nine times heavier and 500 times stronger in the process. These ice fields develop in high mountain valleys where snowdrifts readily accumulate, and from there they flow downhill at the rate of inches or yards per day. The longest-known glacier in the Sierra Nevada was a 60-mile tongue that flowed down the Tuolumne River canyon about 20,000 years ago.

In some Sierra Nevada valleys, the ice field once measured 500ft to 4000ft thick. Hundreds of thousands of cubic feet of ice thus created an unbelievable amount of pressure and shearing strength that completely altered the landscape. Massive boulders were plucked up and dragged along like giant rasping teeth on a file's edge. Smaller rocks and sand carried along the glacier's bottom acted like sandpaper that polished underlying bedrock. Every rock that was loose or could be pried loose was caught up and transported for miles.

Glaciers have the funny effect of rounding out landscape features that lie below the ice while sharpening features that rise above the ice. The same grinding force that smooths out valleys also quarries rocks from the base of peaks, resulting in undercutting that forms towering spikes. In Tuolumne Meadows this effect is particularly dramatic – compare the smooth domes on the valley floor, such as Lembert Dome and Pothole Dome, with the sheer spires of Cathedral and Unicorn Peaks visible nearby.

Can't see yourself backpacking for days into the Sierra Nevada to glimpse a glacier, or hanging around for weeks in Yosemite Valley to witness a rockfall? Download the free video-podcast series 'Yosemite Nature Notes,' available on iTunes and from www.nps.gov/yose/photos multimedia/ynn.htm.

Rocks: Cracking, Fracturing & Weathering

The distinctive granite of the Sierra Nevada owes its appearance not only to the tremendous sculpting power of glaciers but also to something far more subtle: the internal properties of the rock itself and how it behaves in its natural environment. The first rule of thumb is that granite tends to crack and separate along regular planes, often parallel to the surface of the rocks. Everywhere you travel in the High Sierra, you'll easily be able to see evidence of this ongoing cracking.

At Olmsted Point along Tioga Pass Rd, visitors can see a surrealistic view of vast granite walls peeling off like onion layers below Clouds Rest. This exfoliation is the result of massive rock formations expanding and cracking in shell-like layers as the pressure of overlying materials erodes away. Over time, sharp angles and corners give way to increasingly rounded curves that leave us with distinctive landmarks such as Yosemite Valley's Half Dome, Moro Rock in Sequoia National Park and Charlotte Dome in the backcountry of Kings Canyon National Park.

Weathering breaks granite down through a process different from glacial erosion or internal cracking, yet its effects are equally profound. Joints in the granite allow water to seep into deep cracks where the liquid expands during winter's freezing temperatures. This pushes open cracks with pressures up to 1000lb per square inch and eventually forces square-angled blocks to break off from the parent formation.

Granite-rock edges and corners are further weathered over time to create rounded boulders. Rain and exposure to the elements wear down granite's weaker minerals, leaving an unstable matrix of hard, pale minerals (quartz and feldspar) that crumble into fine-grained rubble called grus. Hikers walking on granite slabs might experience the unnerving sensation of slipping on tiny pebbles of grus that roll underfoot like ball bearings. In the presence of water, grus eventually break down into crumbly soil.

On the western slopes of the Sierra Nevada, granites are mostly fine grained, with joints spaced fairly widely. As a result, rock formations tend to be massive structures shaped by exfoliation, such as Yosemite's Half Dome. Further east, granites are more likely to be coarse grained and to have closely spaced joints. There the process of water seeping into cracks and pushing rocks apart results in characteristically jagged, sawtooth ridges such as those in the Cathedral Range of Yosemite's high country and aptly named Sawtooth Peak looming above Mineral King Valley in Sequoia National Park.

SIERRA NEVADA ROCKS: A PRIMER

The Sierra Nevada is one of the world's premier granite landscapes, yet these mountains include much more than just granite!

Metamorphic rocks Older volcanic and sedimentary rocks whose structure has been dramatically altered by intense heat and pressure deep within the earth's crust. These rocks predate the Sierra Nevada batholith, and their reddish, purplish or greenish hues are a distinctive change from the speckled grays of granite. The dark, exposed, high-altitude crests of the Sierras are formed from metamorphic rocks, and in Sequoia and Kings Canyon National Parks vast cave systems have been formed by limestone metamorphized into marble.

Granite Describes a broad category of rocks formed when molten magma cools within the earth's crust (called lava when it erupts or flows onto the earth's surface). Sierra Nevada granite is actually composed of five separate minerals occurring in complex combinations that produce a characteristic salt-and-pepper appearance.

Volcanic rocks In the Sierra Nevada these rocks have mostly weathered away except for high, uplifted pockets. Chemically identical to rocks that form deep within the earth's crust, volcanic rocks change as they erupt on the surface as lava. Gases injected into the liquid rock give it a pockmarked or bubbled appearance. Rocks that cool deep underground do so very slowly, forming large, visible crystals, while liquid rock exposed to air cools so quickly that crystals can't form.

So what causes those dramatic rockfalls? Once a chunk of the granite is primed to break off and fall, a final precipitating factor could be a tree whose roots pry the rock apart, extreme temperature changes or perhaps water that seeps into the rock and freezes, then thaws. Earthquakes can also trigger rockfall. Sometimes the reason for a rockfall is a mystery, which makes future events difficult to predict and prevent.

Around 1000 rockfalls have happened in Yosemite Valley alone since the mid-19th century (around 60 a year), as is clearly evidenced by the jumble of talus sitting at the base of the valley's tall, weathered cliffs. A 2500-ton slab sloughed off of Half Dome sometime in early July, 2015. It was neither seen nor heard and was only discovered by climbers who noticed the missing chunk on their way up the cliff face.

Volcanoes

Between five and 20 million years ago, a series of lava and mud flows covered about 12,000 sq miles of the Sierra Nevada region north of Yosemite, with some volcanic activity extending south to the area now enclosed by the national park. While much of this violent geological history has since eroded away, caps of old volcanic material still exist along Hwy 108 at Sonora Pass, an otherworldly landscape of eroding debris.

About three million years ago, the zone of volcanic activity shifted from the region north of Yosemite to the slopes east of the Sierra Nevada crest. Massive eruptions between Mammoth Lakes and Mono Lake created a series of calderas and volcanic mountains, including Mammoth Mountain itself. Mono Lake gained two islands and a small chain of hills on its southern side during this period of activity, which is still ongoing. Over time the volcanic landscape at Mono Lake has undergone dramatic changes, with the last eruption at the lake's Paoha Island taking place less than 700 years ago.

The most familiar and popular landmark formed in the current (geologically speaking) era of volcanic activity is Devils Postpile, a national monument located west of Mammoth Lakes. About 80,000 to 100,000 years ago, a violent volcanic vent filled a river canyon and a natural lake with lava 400ft deep. The lava cooled so quickly that it formed one of the world's most spectacular examples of columnar basalt, today reaching up to 60ft high. These multisided columns are virtually perfect in their symmetry, and the iconic formation can be viewed by taking just a short hike.

The rawness and relative newness of all these volcanic formations reminds us how active and ongoing is the Sierra Nevada's evolution. For example, just consider how the Ice Age glaciers retreated a mere 10,000 years ago – there hasn't been enough time even for soil to develop in most places! This is a remarkably young range, still jagged and sharp, still rising – and yes, still shaking.

Take a virtual field trip into the Sierra Nevada, courtesy of the myriad links put together online by the California Geological Survey (www.conservation.ca.gov/cgs/Pages/Geotours.aspx).

Roadside Geology

Glacier Point
(Yosemite National Park)

Tunnel View
(Yosemite National Park)

Olmsted Point
(Yosemite National Park)

Moro Rock
(Sequoia National Park)

Junction View
(Kings Canyon Scenic Byway)

Wildlife

Sierra Nevada's wildlife – lumbering bears, whistling marmots, soaring birds, scurrying lizards and flitting butterflies – is scattered across vast, untamed terrain. Only in a few places do animals congregate in conspicuous numbers, but if you remain patient and alert in the parks, you'll be rewarded with lifelong memories of wildlife spotting. An especially good time to visit is during late spring or early summer, when the foothills and mountains are abloom with wildflowers.

Mammals

Black Bears

Arguably the animal that visitors would most like to see is the black bear. (Though a grizzly is on the California state flag, the last one was killed around 1920.) They come in a variety of shades and colors and weigh in at around 300lb. These bears can be formidable fighters, but they generally shy away from human contact. There's an estimated 30,000 black bears in California alone (around 300 to 500 in Yosemite), so sightings aren't unlikely.

Whether climbing trees, poking under logs and rocks or crossing rivers, bears are basically big noses in search of food – they'll eat almost anything. Bears may spend a considerable amount of time grazing like cows on meadow plants. Later in summer, they switch over to berries and acorns, with insects (including ants, beetles, termites and wasps) making up about 10% of their diet.

Bighorn Sheep

A high-elevation dweller, although rarely seen, is the endangered Sierra Nevada bighorn sheep. Although they once numbered in the thousands, their wild population declined to around 100 by the year 2000 due to hunting and exposure to diseases from domesticated livestock. Thanks to interagency conservation efforts, especially from the Sierra Nevada Bighorn Sheep Foundation (www.sierrabighorn.org), that number has rebounded to nearly 400 – gains, however, have been slow now for several years. Your best chance of spotting bighorns is during summer as they scale granite slopes and peaks above 10,000ft in the Eastern Sierra to graze on alpine plants and escape predators.

California's mountain forests are home to an estimated 25,000 to 30,000 black bears, whose fur actually ranges in color from black to dark brown, cinnamon or even blond.

Mule Deer

The most common large mammals in the Sierra Nevada, mule deer dwell in all forest habitats below the timberline. In parks they have become remarkably unconcerned about human observers and tend to frequent meadows. White-spotted fawns first appear in July, while tannish adults with big floppy ears become numerous in early winter, when deep snows push them out of the high country to forage at lower elevations. Deer favor leaves and young twigs as a source of food; in late fall, they feed heavily on acorns.

Mountain Lions & Bobcats

You'll rarely glimpse a mountain lion bounding into the woods. Reaching up to 8ft from nose to tail tip and weighing as much as 150lb, this solitary and highly elusive creature is a formidable predator. In the Sierra Nevada mountain lions roam all forested habitats below the timberline in search of mule deer and, occasionally, bighorn sheep. Humans are rarely more than a curiosity or a nuisance to be avoided, although a few attacks have occurred.

Hikers are more likely to see the handsome bobcat, looking like a scaled-up version of the domestic tabby, with a brown-spotted, yellowish-tan coat and a cropped tail.

Coyotes & Foxes

The ubiquitous coyote and its much smaller cousin, the gray fox, share the same grayish-brown coat. Both have adapted to human habitats, becoming altogether too comfortable around roads, campgrounds and any food left unguarded. You stand a good chance of seeing a coyote during the daytime, especially in meadows, where they hunt rodents.

Foxes mainly come out at night, when you might spy one crossing a road. One of the rarest (there are no more than 50 in North America), most elusive mammals, the Sierra Nevada red fox, was spotted in 2015. Confirmed sightings happen only a few times a decade at most.

Rodents

That odd little 'bleating' call coming from jumbles of rocks and boulders is likely a pika. A careful search will reveal the hamster-like vocalist peering from under a rock with small beady eyes. Pikas typically live on talus slopes above 8000ft, especially in the alpine realm of mountain hemlock, whitebark pine and heather plants.

The golden-mantled ground squirrel is often mistaken for a chubby chipmunk. However, ground squirrels have no stripes on their heads and shoulders, while chipmunks are striped all the way to the tip of their noses. Ground squirrels spend the winter hibernating, so in late summer they start gaining an extreme amount of weight.

A large cousin of the chipmunk, the western gray squirrel, with its long, fluffy tail trailing behind, tends to live at low to mid-elevations in the Western Sierra. The smaller Douglas squirrel, recognizable by its slender tail and rusty tone, inhabits conifer forests up to the timberline.

Among the most curious mammals in the Sierra high country, the yellow-bellied marmot inhabits rocky outcrops and boulder fields at or above 7500ft. Sprawled lazily on sun-warmed rocks, marmots scarcely attract any notice until they're closely approached, when they jolt upright and send out shrieks of alarm to the entire marmot neighborhood. Marmots have a great appetite – they spend four to five months putting on weight (incredibly, up to 50% of their body weight can be fat) before starting a long, deep hibernation through winter until the following spring.

Birds

Whether you enjoy the aerial acrobatics of swifts and falcons over Yosemite Valley's waterfalls, the flash of brilliant warblers in oak woodlands, or the bright presence of the more than 250 other bird species found in the Sierra Nevada, it goes without question that birding is a highlight here.

No other bird commands attention quite like the ubiquitous Steller's jay, found in virtually every forested habitat and around campgrounds. With a shimmering cloak of blue feathers and an equally jaunty attitude, these noisy birds wander fearlessly among picnic tables and parked cars in pursuit of overlooked crumbs.

Enjoy the 2800 hand-drawn watercolor illustrations and easy-to-understand descriptions of more than 1700 species of plants and animals found in *The Laws Field Guide to the Sierra Nevada* by John Muir Laws.

The Yosemite Conservancy (www.yosemite conservancy.org) is a nonprofit group that publishes books and teaches a wide variety of natural-history classes about the Sierra Nevada, including family-friendly outings, day hikes, wilderness backpacking trips and art workshops.

Top Great gray owl

Bottom Black bear,
Yosemite National Park

BJORN BAKSTAD/GETTY IMAGES/ISTOCKPHOTO ©

WILDLIFE AMPHIBIANS

While almost a dozen species of owl live in the Yosemite region, none of them evoke the mystery of the nocturnal realm quite like that rare phantom, the great gray owl. Easily the most famous and sought-after bird in Yosemite, this distinctive owl stands 2ft tall and has a wingspan of 5ft. A small population (less than 200 individuals) of these birds survives in the park. These majestic owls have been spotted at Crane Flat, where they hunt around large meadows in the early morning and late afternoon.

You'll also be fortunate if you see the peregrine falcon, a species that has climbed back from the brink of extinction and is now present in healthy numbers. This streamlined, fierce hunter with long, pointed wings and a black 'moustache' mark on its cheek nests in cliffs in the Yosemite Valley, where seasonal rock-climbing-route closures protect chicks until they've fledged, usually by late summer.

Another conspicuous bird, the small mountain chickadee, with its distinctive black cap, is a perennial favorite with children because its merry song sounds like 'cheese-bur-ger.' You'll hear this song often in forested areas at middle elevations.

Hikers at higher elevations are greeted by the raucous and inquisitive Clark's nutcracker, a hardy resident of subalpine forests recognizable by its black wings and white tail. A flock of nutcrackers will survive the winter by gathering and storing up to four million pine nuts each fall, burying the nuts in thousands of small caches.

John Muir favored the American dipper (also known as the water ouzel) for its ceaseless energy and good cheer even in the depths of winter. This 'singularly joyous and lovable little fellow' rarely leaves the cascading torrents of cold, clear mountain streams, where it dives to capture underwater insects and larvae.

Amphibians

Among the region's several unique amphibians is the Yosemite toad. This endemic, high-elevation toad used to abound, but in recent years it has mysteriously disappeared from many of its former haunts. At lower elevations the western toad is still quite common and often observed moving along trails or through campgrounds at night. To identify a toad, look for a slow, plodding walk and dry, warty skin, which easily distinguishes it from a smooth-skinned, quickly hopping frog.

Another unusual amphibian of the High Sierra is the scarce mountain yellow-legged frog, whose numbers have declined sharply around alpine lakes stocked with trout. The abundant Pacific tree frog, by contrast, is extremely widespread and diverse in its habitat preferences. Tree frogs have the familiar 'ri-bet' call that nearly everyone associates with singing frogs.

Oddest among amphibians is the rare Mt Lyell salamander, first discovered in Yosemite in 1915 when it was accidentally captured in a trap. This brownish-grey salamander resides on domed rocks and talus slopes from 4000ft to over 11,000ft, where it uses its webbed toes and strong tail to climb sheer cliffs and boulders in search of food.

Located in the stunning southern Sierra, the Sequoia Parks Conservancy (www.sequoiapark sconservancy.org) has one of the best outdoor classrooms in the region, offering guided hikes, underground cave tours, campfire programs, stargazing and other family fun.

Reptiles

The most abundant and widespread reptile is the western fence lizard, a 6in-long creature you're likely to see perched on rocks and logs or scampering across the forest floor. During breeding season you'll notice males bobbing energetically (doing 'push-ups') as they conspicuously display their iridescent-blue throats and bellies.

Found in forest-floor debris, southern alligator lizards wriggle away noisily like clumsy snakes when disturbed. These 10in-long yellow-tan lizards with crossbars on their backs reside from the lower foothills up into the mixed-conifer zone.

The region has over a dozen snake species, including garter snakes, which live in the widest diversity of habitats and are the snakes you're most likely to see. Two kinds of garter snake sport mainly black skin, with yellow or orange stripes running the length of their bodies.

No other snake elicits as much fear as the western rattlesnake. Even if they're not rattling, you can quickly recognize rattlers by their bluntly triangular heads perched on remarkably slender necks. Rocky or brushy areas below 8000ft are the preferred haunts of this venomous though generally docile snake.

Often confused with the deadly coral snake (which doesn't live in California), the mountain king snake – with bright-orange, black and white bands around its body – is harmless to humans and lives throughout the Sierra Nevada.

Fish

The most widely distributed fish in the Western Sierra is the rainbow trout. Formerly limited to the lower reaches of streams below insurmountable barriers (eg waterfalls), rainbow trout have been introduced into countless alpine and eastern creeks and lakes for sportfishing. Now threatened with extinction, the California golden trout – the state's official fish – inhabits the Kern River drainage of Sequoia and Kings Canyon National Parks.

Further complicating the natural order of things, non-native species such as brook trout, lake trout, brown trout and kokanee salmon have been successfully introduced throughout the Sierra Nevada. Introduced fish have had a devastating impact on aquatic ecosystems, especially in formerly fish-less alpine areas, where fragile nutrient cycles and invertebrate populations have changed dramatically as a result.

Insects

There's an amazing variety of insects in the Sierra Nevada, but – except for a handful of conspicuous butterflies and other charismatic creatures – they're hard to spot. Foremost among the large, showy butterflies are the five swallowtail species. The Western tiger swallowtail, yellow in color with bold black bars and beautiful blue and orange spots near its 'tail,' follows stream banks from the lower foothills up to subalpine forest. The stunning, iridescent-blue pipevine swallowtail flits in large numbers along foothill canyons and slopes almost year-round.

Plants

The Sierra Nevada boasts one of the most varied selections of plants found anywhere in North America. Yosemite National Park alone is home to over 20% of California's 7000 plant species, even though it encompasses less than 1% of the state's total land.

Wildflowers

You can see flowering plants from early March until late August, and taking time to find them will enrich your park experience.

At low elevations in early spring, when wildflowers carpet low-elevation hillsides, you can't miss the brilliant-orange native California poppy, each one with four floppy, silken petals. At night and on cloudy days, poppy petals fold up and become inconspicuous.

At least a dozen species of Indian paintbrush of varying colors and shapes can be found in the region. Most are red or orange in color and

WILDLIFE FISH

Wildlife Spotting

Yosemite Valley (Yosemite National Park)
....
Tuolumne Meadows (Yosemite National Park)
....
Giant Forest (Sequoia National Park)
....
Kings River (Kings Canyon National Park)
....
Mono Lake (Eastern Sierra)

Wildflower Blooms

Tuolumne Meadows (Yosemite National Park)
....
McGurk Meadow (Yosemite National Park)
....
Wawona Meadow (Yosemite National Park)
....
Crescent Meadow (Sequoia National Park)
....
Zumwalt Meadow (Kings Canyon National Park)
....
Lundy Lake (Mono Lake Region)
....
Little Lakes Valley (Mammoth Lakes Region)

THE SMALL KINGDOM OF GIANT SEQUOIAS

The Sierra Nevada's most famous tree, the giant sequoia *(Sequoiadendron giganteum)*, is also the source of much legend and ballyhoo. Even information as basic as the trees' maximum height and width remains uncertain because loggers and claim-seekers who cut down many of the original giants found it beneficial to exaggerate records. Today the General Sherman tree in Sequoia National Park, which measures 274.9ft tall and 102.6ft in circumference, is recognized as the largest-known living specimen (and it's still growing!).

Giant sequoias cluster in fairly discrete groves on the western slopes of the Sierra Nevada. You can recognize them by their spongy, cinnamon-red bark and juniper-like needles – it's this bark, strong disease resistance and lack of low branches that means they rarely die from fire. Despite claims that these are the world's oldest trees, it's now thought that the longest they can live is just over 3000 years, far short of the age reached by ancient bristlecone pines.

Between five and 25 million years ago, the giant sequoias' arboreal ancestors covered a vast area between the Sierra Nevada and the Rocky Mountains. Migrating westward, possibly through low mountain passes, these trees got a foothold on the western slope of the Sierra Nevada just as the range began to reach its current height. The formation of the Sierra Nevada isolated those sequoias on the western slope while at the same time creating a rain shadow that killed off the main population of sequoias to the east.

Giant sequoias survive today in about 75 scattered groves. In Yosemite National Park, the Tuolumne Grove and Merced Grove along Hwy 120 and the Mariposa Grove along Hwy 41 are relatively small groves, while the 20-plus groves in Sequoia and Kings Canyon National Parks are generally more extensive because the soil is deeper and better developed in areas that weren't covered by glaciers.

appear somewhat hairy. Surprisingly the flowers themselves are hidden and accessible only to hummingbirds (the plants' pollinators), while a set of specialized colored leaves takes on the appearance of petals. Paintbrushes are semiparasitic, often tapping into the roots of their neighbors to draw nourishment. So are snow plants, which feed on fungi in the soil and shoot up fleshy stems with brilliant red flowers that bloom early and often at the edges of melting snow banks.

Mountaineers climb into a rarified realm rich in unique flowers, and if you need a single target flower to hunt for – one that's rare and mysterious like a distant peak – you couldn't make a better choice than the Sierra primrose. Confined to a handful of high subalpine slopes and peaks, this brilliant magenta beauty is a real find for the lucky hiker. Arising from clumps of toothed, succulent leaves, primroses sometimes grow in large patches sprawling across rocky slopes.

Highest and showiest of all is the aptly named sky pilot. Usually found only above 11,000ft, this plant erupts into flagrant displays of violet-blue flowers arranged in dense, ball-like clusters. After a long and grueling ascent, hikers to the highest peaks will better understand its name, which is a slang term for a military chaplain or priest said to lead others to heaven.

Trees

While flowers rise and fade with ephemeral beauty, trees hold their majesty for centuries. Given a few simple tips, you can easily learn to identify many of the region's prominent species and appreciate the full sweep of trees cloaking the parks' landscape.

Pines are conifers whose needles appear in tight clusters, with two, three or five needles per cluster. Named for its straight, slender trunk, the abundant lodgepole pine has two-needled clusters and globular cones that are less than 2in long. Lodgepoles are the most common tree around mountain meadows because they have adapted to survive in waterlogged soils and in basins where cold air sits at night (so-called frost pockets).

The ponderosa pine, with some examples of the Jeffrey pine mixed in, covers vast tracts of low to mid-elevation Sierra Nevada slopes. Three-needled clusters characterize both trees. Virtually identical in appearance, the two species do have distinct cones: on ponderosa cones the barbs protrude outward, and on Jeffrey pines they curve inward. If you're unsure of the identification, simply hold a cone in your hand and remember the adage: 'Gentle Jeffrey, prickly ponderosa.'

Bristlecone pines, some thousands of years old, can be found in several groves in the barren White Mountains east of Big Pine above 10,000ft.

The wide variety of deciduous trees in the region includes the quaking aspen, with its smooth, white bark and oval leaves. Every brief gust sets these leaves quivering on their flattened stems. Aspens consist of genetically identical trunks arising from a single root system that may grow to be more than 100 acres in size. By sprouting repeatedly from this root system, aspens have what has been called 'theoretical immortality,' and some aspens are thought to be over 80,000 years old.

Magnificent black oaks grow up to 80ft high at mountain elevations between 2000ft and 7000ft, where their immense crops of acorns are a food source for many animals, including bears, deer and woodpeckers. Native Americans ground the acorns into flour in order to make nutritious soup, porridge and bread.

Want to learn more about the local ecosystem? For an explanation of just about everything, check out *Sierra Nevada Natural History* (University of California Press) by Tracy Storer, Robert Usinger and David Lukas.

WILDLIFE PLANTS

Shrubs

No other shrub may be as worthy of note as poison oak, which can trigger an inflammatory skin reaction in people who come into contact with it. The shrub is distinguished by shiny, oak-like leaves that occur in groups of three. Clusters of white berries appear by late summer. If you'll be exploring the western slopes of the Sierra Nevada, learn how to identify this common trailside plant.

At higher elevations, huckleberry oak and greenleaf manzanita form a dense, nearly impenetrable habitat known as montane chaparral, which carpets the high country around granite boulders and outcrops. There bears, deer, rabbits and many other animals find food and shelter not provided by nearby forests.

At lower elevations you'll find foothill chaparral, characterized by whiteleaf manzanita. Greenleaf and whiteleaf manzanita feature the same smooth, reddish bark and small, red, apple-like berries (*manzanita* is Spanish for 'little apple'), but they differ in the color of their leaves. During late summer the scat of animals such as black bears, coyotes and foxes is chock-full of partly digested manzanita berries.

Conservation

The discovery of gold in 1848 forever altered the Sierra Nevada's natural world: the resulting human stampede had a devastating impact on Native Americans and the landscape. Today California is the most populous US state, with the nation's highest projected growth rate, which strains the region's precious natural resources. Tourism also has an impact: more than five million people visit the parks each year. Ongoing drought, interrupted by a record wet 2017, and invasive species also threaten the parks' delicate ecosystems.

Known as the little organization that triumphed over Los Angeles, the Mono Lake Committee (www. monolake.org) has matured into an environmental powerhouse in the Eastern Sierra, offering field seminars and naturalist-guided walks, talks and kayak tours.

Water

Without doubt the greatest benefit that the Sierra Nevada provides to the state of California is a (dwindling, until the record wet winter of 2017) supply of fresh, clean water. Ironically the greatest harm to the Sierra Nevada has come from using, managing and collecting this essential resource.

During the mid-19th century, rivers were diverted, rocks moved and entire hillsides washed away to reveal gold deposits north of Yosemite. More than 1.5 billion tons of debris and incalculable amounts of poisonous mercury flowed downstream, with harsh consequences for aquatic ecosystems and watershed health that are still felt today in both the Sierra Nevada and the Central Valley.

Early 20th-century construction of a dam in Yosemite's Hetch Hetchy Valley to provide the city of San Francisco with water apparently broke conservationist John Muir's heart. In the Eastern Sierra the diversion of

JOHN MUIR: A MAN OF THE MOUNTAINS

Arriving in San Francisco in the spring of 1868, John Muir started out to walk across California's Central Valley to the then scarcely known Yosemite Valley, where his wanderings and writings later earned him lasting worldwide fame.

This Scotsman's many treks led him into the highest realms of Yosemite's backcountry. He took with him little more than a wool overcoat, dry crusts of bread and a bit of tea. Though not a trained scientist, Muir looked at the natural world with a keen curiosity, investigating glaciers, trees, earthquakes, bees and even the most plain-coated of Sierra Nevada birds, recording them in great detail.

Muir's prolific and poetic writings spanned the gap between literature and science. His popular magazine articles and lobbying efforts became the foundation of the campaign that established Yosemite as a national park in 1890. Despite that success and his other accomplishments with the Sierra Club, Muir was unable to save Hetch Hetchy Valley, which he said rivaled Yosemite Valley for beauty and grandeur. Muir lost that final battle in 1913, when Hetch Hetchy was sacrificed to the water and power needs of a growing San Francisco.

Today you can visit the farm where Muir once lived with his family, and view the writing desk where he penned those famous words, at the John Muir National Historic Site in the San Francisco Bay Area. You can learn more about the man, his writings and his politics at the Sierra Club's online John Muir Exhibit (http://vault.sierraclub.org/john_muir_exhibit).

Yosemite Falls (p102), Yosemite National Park

water for the city of Los Angeles contributed to the destruction of Owens Lake and its fertile wetlands, and the degradation of Mono Lake.

Throughout the 20th century, dams drawn across the Sierra Nevada severely altered aquatic habitats and eliminated spawning habitats for fish such as salmon. Native fish populations and aquatic ecosystems have been further decimated by the introduction of dozens of non-native fish species, mostly through sportfishing.

But there's good news, too. The 2004 removal of the Cascades Diversion Dam west of Yosemite Valley has helped to restore the wild and scenic Merced River. In the Eastern Sierra the ongoing restoration of Mono Lake is another water-conservation success story: lake levels have risen over 10ft, after reaching their lowest point in 1982.

California's five-year drought ended with a historic snowfall in 2017 – the snowpack was 190% of the average. Concerns immediately turned to worries over flooding. However, a lack of precipitation, shrinking rivers and lakes, bigger wildfires and the decimation of millions of pine trees by bark beetles are threats that are likely to persist over the long term.

Air Quality & Pollution

After drought, perhaps the most pernicious environmental issue in the parks today is air pollution. In 2004 Yosemite joined a growing list of national parks that violate federal smog standards, and the situation in Sequoia and Kings Canyon is much worse. Monitoring stations in Sequoia's Foothills area detect high ozone levels more than 50 times per year, and it's not uncommon for higher-elevation park views to be obscured by haze all summer long. Tighter regulations are slowly making California's air cleaner, but plenty of pollution still drifts up from the Central Valley.

Tourism also has a detrimental effect on air quality, as every visitor arriving by car or bus contributes to the overall impact of vehicle emissions and worsens traffic jams. You can help the parks' air quality by leaving your car parked and riding shuttle buses, or renting or bringing bicycles. Always turn the car engine off rather than letting it idle at roadside viewpoints.

Co-founded by John Muir in 1892, the Sierra Club (www.sierra club.org) was the USA's first conservation group and it remains the nation's most active, offering educational programs, group hikes, organized trips and volunteer vacations.

ONNES/SHUTTERSTOCK ©

Hiking near Half Dome (p102), Yosemite National Park

Livestock, Logging & Fire

Following the mid-19th-century gold rush, ranchers began driving millions of sheep into the Sierra Nevada's mountain meadows, where they wreaked havoc. Sheep turned meadows into choking dust bowls by devouring fragile plants before they could flower and produce seeds. Even now, over 100 years later, the pattern of vegetation in the high mountains largely reflects this grazing history, with many hillsides still dry, barren or choked with species that the 'hoofed locusts' (to use John Muir's term) didn't like.

Fortunately the Sierra Nevada's mountain environments can be so extreme that few weed species ever took hold. The opposite is true of its foothill slopes, where weed species introduced by humans and their livestock now dominate and choke out native plants. Global climate change has further imperiled native plants across the Sierra Nevada.

John Muir's concern over destructive logging practices, especially those that felled giant sequoias, played an important role in establishing Yosemite National Park, but Muir didn't live long enough to see the worst of what could happen. Industrial-scale logging took off after WWII, when gasoline-powered chainsaws, logging trucks and heavy equipment were brought into national forests surrounding the parks, causing lasting soil and watershed damage and devastating forest fires.

Since the 1960s national forest-management directives have begun to reverse this course, aiming to better balance conservation and public recreation with big-business tree 'harvesting.' Toward the end of the 20th century, both national forests and parks also changed their approach to wildfire management. In the past all park fires, whether initiated by lightning or irresponsibly managed campfires, were considered bad and extinguished as quickly as possible.

However, it's now known that fires create the conditions for forests to regenerate and are part of an ecosystem's healthy life cycle. (Controlled and otherwise, nearly 49% of Yosemite alone has experienced fire since 1930.) They're now often allowed to burn naturally, so long as they don't threaten lives and important infrastructure, and prescribed, deliberate fires are commonplace in the parks – there will be signs to let visitors know.

Survival Guide

Clothing & Equipment

Clothing

Layering

For comfortable hiking, wear several layers of light clothing, which you can easily take off or put on as you warm up or cool down. Most hikers use three main layers: a base layer next to the skin, an insulating layer and an outer, shell layer for protection from wind, rain and snow.

➡ For the upper body, the base layer is typically a shirt (long or short sleeves depending on temperatures) of synthetic material (nylon or polyester) for wicking moisture away from the body. Merino wool is an option for cooler climes.

➡ The insulating layer retains heat next to your body and is often a synthetic fleece or lightweight down or synthetic-filled jacket.

➡ The outer shell should be a waterproof jacket that protects against cold winds.

➡ For the lower body, the layers generally consist of either shorts or loose-fitting pants, Capilene 'long-john' underwear, and waterproof rain pants.

Waterproof Shell

The ideal specifications for a rain jacket are:

➡ breathable, waterproof fabric (Gore-Tex Active, Columbia Outdry Extreme and Sierra Designs

Airflow Rainwear are recommended); often, the more breathable a jacket is, the less waterproof it is.

➡ a hood that's roomy enough to cover headwear but still allow peripheral vision

➡ a capacious map pocket

➡ a heavy-gauge zipper protected by a storm flap. If heavy rain is unlikely, a poncho is a lightweight option.

Footwear, Socks & Gaiters

Trail-running shoes are fine over easy terrain, but for more difficult trails and across rocks and scree, try hiking shoes or boots for more ankle support.

➡ Hiking shoes are lighter than boots (and generally don't need to be broken in) and more structured than trail-running shoes, which make them the preferred choice, especially outside of winter conditions. Nonslip soles (such as Vibram) provide the best grip.

➡ Buy boots in warm conditions or go for a walk before trying them on so that your feet can expand slightly as they would on a walk.

➡ Many hikers carry a pair of river sandals to wear at night, at rest stops and/or when fording waterways.

➡ For longer hikes, synthetic socks wick away moisture better than cotton and wool

ones. Also consider wearing lightweight liner socks for comfort and to avoid blisters.

➡ If you'll be hiking through snow, deep mud or scratchy vegetation, gaiters will protect your legs and help keep your socks dry. Choose gaiters made of strong fabric, with a robust zip protected by a flap, that secure snugly around your hiking boots.

➡ Bring sandals if you'll be lounging around a campsite in warm weather.

Navigation

Maps

Carry a good map of the area in which you're hiking, and know how to read it.

➡ Before setting off, ensure that you understand the contours and map symbols, plus the main ridge and river systems in the area.

➡ Familiarize yourself with the true north–south directions and the general direction in which you are heading.

➡ On the trail try to identify major landforms (eg mountain peaks) and locate them on your map. This will give you a better grasp of the region's geography.

Compass

Buy a magnetic baseplate compass and learn how to use it. The attraction of magnetic north varies in different parts of the world, so compasses need to be balanced accordingly. Make sure your compass is balanced for your destination zone. There are also 'universal' compasses with 'global needles' on the market that can be used anywhere in the world.

GPS

GPS receivers are small, computer-driven devices that can give an extremely accurate reading of their location – to within 15m, anywhere on the planet, any time, in almost any weather. Many are now wrist-worn de-vices, though the screen size and resolution make them generally inferior to stand-alone units. GPS apps, such as BackCountry Navigator, AllTrails or Gaia GPS, are also popular, but they're limited by your phone's battery life.

➡ The cheapest good-quality handheld GPS receivers cost less than $150 (although these may not have a built-in averaging system that minimizes signal errors). Other important factors to consider are the receiver's weight and battery life.

➡ Remember that a GPS receiver is of little use to hikers unless it's used with an accurate topographic map. The receiver simply gives your position, which you must then locate on the map.

➡ GPS receivers will only work properly in the open. The signals from a crucial satellite may be blocked (or bounce off rock or water) directly below high cliffs, near large bodies of water or in dense tree cover, giving inaccurate readings.

➡ Many top-end receivers also have built-in barometric altimeters, eliminating the need for another device.

➡ GPS receivers are more vulnerable to breakdowns (including dead batteries) than a magnetic compass, so don't rely on them entirely for your navigational needs. And always bring extra batteries!

Altimeter

Altimeters determine altitude by measuring air pressure. Because pressure is affected by temperature, altimeters are calibrated to take lower temperatures at higher altitudes into account. How-ever, discrepancies can still occur, especially in unsettled weather, so it's wise to take a few precautions:

➡ Reset your altimeter regularly at known elevations such as spot heights and passes. Do not take spot heights from villages, where there may be a large difference in elevation from one end of the settlement to another.

➡ Use your altimeter in conjunction with other navigation techniques to fix your position. For instance, taking a back bearing to a known peak or river confluence, determining the general direction of the track and obtaining your elevation will usually give you a pretty good fix on your position.

➡ Altimeters are also barometers and are useful for indicating changing weather conditions. If the altimeter shows increasing elevation while you are not climbing, it means the air pressure is dropping and a low-pressure weather system may be approaching. The best altimeters for hiking are wrist-worn devices (rang-ing from $30 to $300), fea-tures of high-tech watches, or GPS units. Apps such as Gaia and Accurate Altimeter are good alternatives.

Equipment
Backpacks & Daypacks

➡ For day hikes, a daypack (1800 to 2450 cu inches, or 30L to 40L) usually suffices; these can be frameless (comfortable enough if the carrying weight is minimal) or framed. Those with built-in hydration systems are convenient.

➡ For multiday hikes you will need a backpack of between 2750 and 5500 cu inches (45L and 90L) capacity; try

ROUTE FINDING

Good-quality maps are accurate but not perfect. Inaccuracies in altitudes are commonly caused by air-temperature anomalies. Natural features such as river confluences and mountain peaks will be in their true position, but sometimes the location of a trail may not be. This could be because the size of the map does not allow for the detail of the trail's twists and turns. How-ever, by using several basic route-finding techniques, you should have few problems following most hiking maps and descriptions:

➡ Be aware of whether the trail should be climbing or descending.

➡ Check the north-point arrow on the map and determine the general direction of the trail.

➡ Time your progress over a known distance and calculate the speed at which you travel in the given terrain. From then on, you can determine with reasonable accuracy how far you have traveled.

➡ Watch the path – look for boot prints, broken branches, cut logs, cairns and other signs of previous passage.

EQUIPMENT CHECKLIST

Your list will depend on the kind of hiking you do, whether you're car camping or back-packing, and the weather. Light and durable are the two key qualities. Stuff sacks, travel-size supplies and container bags help keep you organized.

Clothing

- ☐ broad-brimmed sun hat
- ☐ hiking boots, socks, gaiters and spare laces
- ☐ jacket (waterproof) and rain pants
- ☐ shorts and lightweight nylon trousers
- ☐ sweater or fleece jacket
- ☐ thermal underwear
- ☐ T-shirt and collared long-sleeved shirt
- ☐ warm hat and gloves

Equipment

- ☐ backpack with waterproof liner or cover
- ☐ first-aid kit, including foot-care equipment
- ☐ insect repellent
- ☐ map, compass and guidebook
- ☐ pocketknife

- ☐ sunglasses, sunscreen and lip balm
- ☐ survival blanket or bivvy bag
- ☐ toilet paper and trowel
- ☐ flashlight or headlamp and spare batteries
- ☐ watch
- ☐ water containers
- ☐ whistle
- ☐ small bag for garbage

Overnight Hikes

- ☐ bear canister
- ☐ cooking, eating and drinking utensils
- ☐ sleeping bag and liner
- ☐ sleeping mat (and, if mat is inflatable, patch kit)
- ☐ spare cord, duct tape and sewing/repair kit
- ☐ stove, fuel and lighter/matches/flammable food wrapper

- ☐ tent
- ☐ quick-dry towel
- ☐ water-purification system
- ☐ hand sanitizer

Optional Items

- ☐ camera and spare batteries
- ☐ cell phone and external portable charger
- ☐ emergency distress beacon
- ☐ GPS receiver and spare batteries
- ☐ groundsheet
- ☐ mosquito net
- ☐ swimsuit
- ☐ hiking poles
- ☐ small dry sack for electronics
- ☐ hand lens for wildflower enthusiasts

---

wearing it before purchasing to ensure it correctly matches your torso length and body type.

➡ A good backpack should be made of strong fabric, have a lightweight internal frame and an adjustable, well-padded harness that evenly distributes weight (external-frame packs distribute weight less evenly and are bulkier).

➡ Look for backpacks with robust, easily adjustable waist belts that can support the entire load; shoulder straps should serve only to steady the pack.

➡ Even if the manufacturer claims your pack is waterproof, use heavy-duty liners or a pack cover.

Tents

➡ A three-season tent will usually suffice, except during winter, when you'll need a sturdy four-season tent to combat windy, wet and freezing conditions, especially in the backcountry.

➡ Regardless of the season, the tent's floor and outer shell, or fly, should have taped or sealed seams and covered zips to stop leaks.

➡ Dome- and tunnel-shaped tents handle windy conditions better than flat-sided tents.

➡ Ultralight backpackers can ditch the tent and opt for using the fly and ground tarp, or even a hammock system during warm, dry weather.

Sleeping Bags & Mats

➡ Mummy bags are the best shape for warmth and reducing draft; top bags have a bottom layer of fabric that attaches to a sleeping pad, which means you're less likely to roll off.

➡ Down fillings are warmer than synthetic for the same weight and bulk, but unlike synthetic fillings they do not retain warmth when wet.

➡ The given figure (eg 10°F/-12°C) is the coldest temperature at which a person should feel comfortable in the bag.

➡ An inner liner helps keep your sleeping bag clean, as well as adding an insulating layer. Silk liners are lightest, but liners are also made with less expensive synthetics.

➜ Air mats, which you inflate like a balloon, are the best in terms of warmth, packability and thickness. However, they're pricier than other options and prone to leaks. Self-inflating sleeping mats work like a thin air cushion between you and the ground and insulate you from the cold. Foam mats are a low-cost, but less comfortable, alternative.

Stoves & Fuel

Cooking systems, excluding open fires and wood stoves, fall roughly into four categories: solid fuel, alcohol, liquid fuel and canister stoves. The latter two are most popular.

➜ Bulky car-camping liquid-fuel stoves (think Coleman) run on a variety of petroleum-based products. This fuel is inexpensive and available everywhere. Good for groups, but they are heavy and produce noxious fumes.

➜ Canister stoves (remote, upright or integrated systems) are small, efficient and ideal for extended use; the 'pot holder' is part of the stove itself. Fuel canisters of pressurized liquid propane plus n-butane or isobutane can, however, add weight to a pack and are a potential hazardous-waste problem.

➜ Solid-fuel stoves are favored by solo backpackers for their simple and fast assembly. They are slow to boil and the fuel (cubes of hexamethylenetetramine) is expensive and can be challenging to find.

➜ Alcohol stoves are mostly DIY setups preferred by long-distance backpackers. They're cheap, reliable, and easy-to-use, but fuel weight adds up and the flame they produce is relatively weak.

➜ Propane and butane stove performance decreases in below-freezing temperatures.

Bear Canisters

Most backcountry hikes require a bear-resistant container for storing all scented items (eg food and toiletries).

➜ If you have your own canister, confirm that the model is approved for the Sierra Nevada, where black bears have learned how to open some types of canisters. Ursack bear bags ($80) are lighter and more flexible than hard-sided canisters. They're approved for use everywhere in the Sierra Nevada, except Yosemite National Park, Rae Lakes, Dusy Basin and Rock Creek.

➜ All-black Garcia canisters can be rented cheaply in the parks and at USFS ranger stations.

➜ Canisters cost anywhere from $75 for a heavier Garcia to $350 for the Wild Ideas 'Bearikade' expedition model (John Muir Trail hikers might want to invest).

Buying & Renting Locally

Yosemite National Park

Yosemite Mountain Shop (☎209-372-8396; Half Dome Village; ◷8am-8pm summer, shorter hours rest of year) Sells clothing, maps, books and climbing, hiking, backpacking and camping gear.

Around Yosemite

Bear Valley Cross Country Adventure Company (☎209-753-2834; www.bearvalleyxc.com; 1 Bear Valley Rd, Bear Valley; snow shoes/sleds/mountain bikes/kayaks from $22/25/30/35; ◷9am-5pm; ♿) Maps, supplies, inside info and every kind of rental, no matter the season.

Beaver's Sporting Goods (☎760-647-6406; 51328 Hwy 395; ◷9am-6pm) One-stop shop in Lee Vining for everything fishers need.

Elevation (☎760-876-4560; www.sierraelevation.com; 150 S Main St, cnr Whitney Portal Rd; ◷9am-6:30pm Sun-Thu, until 7pm Fri & Sat) Rents bear canisters and crampons; sells hiking, backpacking and camping gear.

Lone Pine Sporting Goods (☎760-876-5365; www.facebook.com/lonepinesportinggoods; 220 S Main St; ◷8am-8pm; winter hours shorter) Sells camping gear, clothing, fishing licenses and maps.

Mammoth Mountaineering Supply (☎760-934-4191; www.mammothgear.com; 361 Old Mammoth Rd; per day snowshoe rental $10; ◷8am-8pm) Hiking, backpacking and snow-sports gear rentals and sales, plus topo maps and shoes.

Wilson's Eastside Sports (☎760-873-7520; www.eastsidesports.com; 224 N Main St; ◷9am-6pm Sun-Thu, 9am-9pm Fri & Sat in winter, 9am-9pm daily other times of year) Rents camping, climbing, backpacking and winter-trekking gear; sells shoes, clothing and backpacks.

Yosemite Adventure Supplies (☎209-962-0923; www.facebook.com/YosemiteAdventureSupplies/; 18911 Ferretti Rd, Bldg A; ◷9am-5pm) Has a large selection and bike rentals.

Yosemite Bicycle & Sport (☎559-641-2453; www.yosemitebicycle.com; 40680 Hwy 41; rentals per day from $50; ◷11am-6pm Mon-Fri (summer), 11am-6pm Tue-Fri Feb-Nov, 10am-5pm Sat) Oakhurst shop with quality rentals for off-road cycling trails.

Sequoia & Kings Canyon

Big 5 Sporting Goods (☎559-625-5934; www.big5sportinggoods.com; 1430 S Mooney Blvd; ◷10am-9pm Mon-Thu, 9:30am-9:30pm Fri, 9am-9pm Sat, 9:30am-8pm Sun) Basic camping, fishing and outdoor-sports equipment.

Three Rivers Mercantile (☎559-561-2378; 41152 Sierra Dr; ◷8am-6:30pm Mon-Fri, until 6pm Sat, 9am-5.30pm Sun) Limited camping, fishing and outdoor-sports equipment sales.

Directory A–Z

Accessible Travel

➡ Yosemite publishes an accessibility brochure (www.nps.gov/yose/planyourvisit/upload/access.pdf) and Sequoia and Kings Canyon have an online link with helpful information (www.nps.gov/seki/planyourvisit/accessibility.htm). Both are excellent sources of information on everything from hotels and campgrounds to visitor sites and ranger-led activities. If you need to make arrangements in advance, call any park visitor center or contact the accessibility coordinator prior to your arrival.

➡ Most sights and campgrounds within the parks are wheelchair accessible; for a complete and detailed list, download the accessibility brochure. All Yosemite campgrounds have accessible sites, except for Camp 4, Bridalveil Creek and Hodgdon Meadow.

➡ All lodging options within Yosemite have wheelchair-accessible rooms.

➡ Shuttle buses in Yosemite all have wheelchair lifts and tie-downs, and the drivers can assist disabled passengers on and off. The **Yosemite Valley Lodge Bike Stand** (per hr/day $12/33.50; ⊘8am-7pm) and the **Half Dome Village Bike Stand** (per hr/day $12.50/30.50; ⊘8am-6pm Mar-Oct) both have wheelchairs for rent, as well as hand-crank bicycles; call 209-372-8319 for reservations. In Sequoia and Kings Canyon, free wheelchairs can be borrowed from the Kings Canyon Visitor Center (p203), the Lodgepole Visitor Center (p203) and the Giant Forest Museum (p188).

➡ For hearing-impaired visitors, a ranger may be available during the summer months for American Sign Language (ASL) interpretation during park-led walks and talks. For information contact one of the visitor centers or call 209-372-4726 (TTY). For paid tours, ASL interpretation can be arranged through the Yosemite Valley Lodge tour desk (p96).

➡ Based in Mammoth Lakes the nonprofit organization **Disabled Sports Eastern Sierra** (✆760-934-0791; www.disabledsportseasternsierra.org) offers a variety of educational opportunities for travelers with disabilities, including skiing and climbing courses.

➡ Discount passes (p239) to the parks and national forests are available for people with disabilities.

➡ Download Lonely Planet's free Accessible Travel guides from http://lptravel.to/AccessibleTravel.

PRACTICALITIES

➡ **Newspapers** US newspapers (*San Francisco Chronicle, Fresno Bee, Modesto Bee* and *Merced Star*) are available from coin-operated newspaper boxes in Yosemite and Sequoia and Kings Canyon National Parks.

➡ **Radio** Local FM and AM radio stations can be picked up within Yosemite Valley. In the Eastern Sierra, 92.5 FM broadcasts news and regional information.

➡ **Smoking** Prohibited in restaurants and bars throughout California. Most accommodations are completely nonsmoking and will charge a hefty cleaning fee if you smoke indoors.

➡ **Weather Services** National Weather Service forecasts are available at www.forecast.weather.gov.

Accommodations

High-end park lodges provide comfort and convenience, and sometimes a sense of history. Camping offers unrivaled scenery and unbeatable value. Campgrounds, while thick on the ground, fill up, especially in the parks, in high season. Gateway towns – that is, those near park entrances – tend to offer less-than-stellar value. Mammoth Lakes and Bishop are your best bets as base camps for exploring the eastern side of the Sierra.

Reservations

➜ If you want to stay within Yosemite or Kings Canyon and Sequoia National Parks, make a reservation no matter what time of the year you plan to visit. Anyone hoping to sleep in Yosemite during the peak months of May through September should try to reserve *far* in advance.

➜ If you don't have a reservation, don't write off your trip – you might get lucky, especially if you're camping in May, early June or September and you turn up before noon.

➜ All reservable park and USFS campgrounds are bookable through www.recreation.gov. It's always worth checking for last-minute cancellations.

Campgrounds
TYPES OF CAMPGROUNDS

➜ **Backpacker** Yosemite has four of these (there are none in Sequoia or Kings Canyon) to accommodate people heading into or out of the backcountry. You must have a wilderness permit to stay in them.

➜ **Car** Most of the parks' sites and those elsewhere in the region are designated for car camping, meaning you pull up, unload your car and pitch your tent or park your RV.

➜ **Walk-in** You have to park your vehicle in a designated lot and carry your camping equipment and supplies to the campsite. The advantage of walk-in sites is the lack of cars and RVs, which

makes for a more 'natural' experience.

➜ **Wilderness** Also called 'backcountry camping' or 'dispersed camping.' Provided you meet certain requirements, you can camp wherever you want. Along popular trails there are often established wilderness campsites, as well as trailhead quotas and even lottery systems.

INSIDE THE PARKS
Camping inside the parks offers the distinct advantage of putting you closest to what you came to see. You likely won't have to drive to the trailhead nor (and this pertains primarily to Yosemite) deal with the day-parking nightmare that day trippers face. On the other hand, park campgrounds generally fill up the fastest.

OUTSIDE THE PARKS
➜ The advantage of staying outside the park is that reservations are often easier to make closer to the date you wish to camp. You'll likely pay a little less as well, but the difference is almost negligible.

➜ Though some are privately owned, most campgrounds outside the national parks are operated by the US Forest Service (USFS). A few are run by other local- or federal-government entities.

➜ Campgrounds at lower elevations are open year-round, while upper-elevation campgrounds usually open only seasonally.

➜ There are also many free, car-accessible campgrounds within the national forests surrounding the parks, though they generally lie at the end of long dirt roads and don't offer access to the parks or potable water.

➜ Bureau of Land Management (BLM) campgrounds are primitive but also free or very cheap. The one in the Alabama Hills (p163) just outside Lone Pine is especially recommended.

➜ Free wilderness permits for overnight camping are required year-round in the Ansel Adams, John Muir, Golden Trout and Hoover Wilderness Areas.

➜ The forums on High Sierra Topix (www.highsierratopix.com) are an excellent resource for planning camping trips in the region.

FIRST COME, FIRST SERVED
Some campgrounds, both within and around the parks, operate on a first-come, first-served basis. For folks without reservations (especially those heading to Yosemite), these generally offer the only hope. The key to scoring a first-come, first-served campsite is arriving between 8am and noon. Arrive too early and the previous night's guests haven't left; arrive too late and sites are full with new campers.

In Yosemite seven campgrounds operate on a first-come, first-served basis. In Sequoia and Kings Canyon most of the 14 campgrounds are first come, first served.

Even in the heat of summer, getting a first-come, first-served campsite isn't that difficult if you arrive early enough. Yosemite recommends mid-morning, but on weekdays you'll probably be fine before noon. Drive or walk around the campground loops until you see an unoccupied site – that means no tents, equipment or hired bodyguards there to hold it, and no receipt hanging from the site's little signpost. If it's free take it, because if you're too picky it might be gone the next time you drive by. Remember that check-out time is not until noon at most campgrounds, so late risers may not clear out until close to lunchtime. Take a look at the check-out date printed on the campsite receipt for some guidance. And be patient.

Once you have claimed a site, head back to the campground entrance and follow instructions listed there for paying and properly displaying your receipt. If you extend your stay, just pay again in the morning before check-out time.

Tent Cabins

Tent cabins are a sort of in-between option: not quite camping, not quite a hotel. Generally they consist of cement walls with canvas roofs, and amenities mean a light bulb, an electrical outlet and camp beds. Bedding usually costs extra, so you're better off (and will be more comfortable) bringing your own. All parks have tent cabins, most notably Yosemite Valley's vast array in Housekeeping Camp (p117) and Half Dome Village (p117). Sleeping up to four (sometimes more) and costing anywhere from $80 in low season to $175 in summer, they're generally a more affordable alternative to lodges. Some, such as Sequoia High Sierra Camp (p200) in Kings Canyon and those in Yosemite's backcountry network, are in spectacular

high-altitude settings only reachable after long hikes. If you've got the tent-cabin bug, you can check out a few other places outside the parks, including Yosemite Bug Rustic Mountain Resort (p136; Midpines), Keough's Hot Springs (p158; Bishop) and Virginia Creek Settlement (p147; Bridgeport). If you're staying in a tent cabin in spring or winter, remember that those lacking heating can get very cold.

Lodges

The word 'lodge' usually connotes a stately structure with stone fireplaces, beamed ceilings and rustic but well-kept rooms. Lodges in and around Yosemite, including Rush Creek (p122) and Evergreen Lodge (p124) just outside the park's confines, Kings Canyon and

Sequoia National Parks, and a few around Mammoth Lakes, including ski lodges at Mammoth Mountain Inn (p153), often fit the stereotype. Most offer a choice between rooms in the main lodge (which sometimes have shared bathrooms) and cabins (with private bathrooms). Rates can start at just $80 in low season and climb to as much as $600 for a cabin in July and August at the grand and historic Majestic Yosemite Hotel (p118). The latter may seem high, but when you consider that some cabins can hold several families, the price is more manageable.

Hotels

You'll find national chains and small mom-and-pop roadside motels, many with Western-themed decor. Some

Climate

Yosemite Village

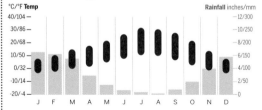

Lodgepole Village

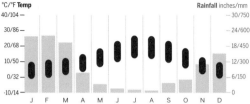

Mammoth Lakes

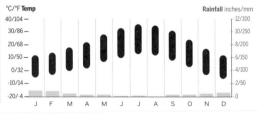

are chintzy, some atmospheric. In-park lodging comes at a premium. There is more variation in gateway towns, though value and quality isn't always up to snuff and pricing reflects proximity. Rooms are often priced by size, view and number of beds, rather than number of guests – children under a certain age may be free. Many nonpark hotels offer free continental breakfast. The largest selection and most luxurious options in the Eastern Sierra are in Mammoth Lakes, while Bishop has a good number of ordinary motels to choose from.

Hostels

There is a handful of hostels in the area. In addition to the hostel-lodge of Yosemite Bug Rustic Mountain Resort, on Hwy 140 outside Yosemite National Park in Midpines, there are options in the Eastern Sierra towns of Mammoth Lakes, Bishop and Lone Pine.

Discount Cards

➡ All National Park Service (NPS) passes cover the cardholder and up to three adult occupants of their vehicle and can be purchased at park entrances. An annual pass for Yosemite costs $70; for Sequoia and Kings Canyon it's $50.

➡ An Interagency Annual Pass costs $80 and grants the holder (and everyone in his or her vehicle) entrance to any national park or federal recreation area for one year.

➡ Current US military members and their dependents can obtain the yearly pass for free.

➡ US fourth-graders can also get a free pass for the duration of the school year. You must apply in advance at www.everykidinapark.gov.

➡ Two 'America the Beautiful' passes are valid for life and available to US citizens and permanent residents: the $80 Senior Pass (for those

aged 62 or over) and the free Access Pass for people with permanent disabilities. These passes cover free entry to all US national parks and federal recreation areas, plus deep discounts on some campgrounds and services.

➡ The parks offer no student or youth discount cards. Children under 16 years enter the parks free of charge with a paying adult.

Electricity

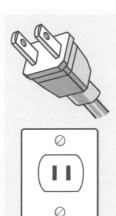

120V/60Hz

120V/60Hz

Etiquette

➡ **Mind your manners** Keep noise levels low and cell-phone usage to a minimum.

➡ **On the trail** Stay on the trail. Greet others you meet. Horses and pack trains have right of way.

➡ **Be courteous** Provide assistance if someone needs help.

➡ **Proper preparation** Prepare yourself for challenging and emergency situations.

➡ **In the campground** Respect private property and never leave fires unattended.

➡ **Respect nature** Don't break branches from bushes or trees. Don't remove any fossils, plant (such as pine cones) or animal products from where you find them.

➡ **Be mindful of animals** Don't feed wild animals and never leave food unattended.

➡ **Clean up after yourself** Dispose of waste, human and otherwise, properly.

Food

Much of the region is rugged wilderness – store-bought granola and fruit are meals fit for the trail. Towns on the eastern side of the Sierra, such as Mammoth Lakes and Bishop, have the best dining scenes; the former is certainly the most cosmopolitan. Diner-style restaurants and burger joints aren't in short supply. Often the highest-quality fare, and the highest prices, can be found in park lodges. Yosemite Valley is your best bet in terms of quantity and quality.

Bear Proofing

➡ Most campsites, most trailheads and many parking lots, including all of those in Yosemite, Sequoia and Kings Canyon National Parks, have bear-proof metal storage boxes. You are required by law to store all your food (including canned goods, beverages and coolers) and all scented products (toothpaste, shampoo, sunscreen etc) in these boxes at all times.

→ Never leave food unattended in your car, especially in Yosemite, whether you're taking a multiday backpacking trip or just spending a few hours meandering through the museum. It may seem like a hassle to put your picnic lunch in a locker, but having a bear break your window, ransack your car and tear up your upholstery is even more hassle. What's more, you can be fined for leaving anything in your car (or in your bike's panniers).

→ Proper storage helps keep bears from becoming 'problems,' which can mean a bad end for the bear.

→ Backcountry hikers must use bear-proof canisters, which can be rented inexpensively when you pick up your wilderness permit, or bought at stores in and near the parks. Popular backcountry campgrounds in Sequoia and Kings Canyon have bear-proof lockers.

Self-Catering

→ Grocery stores inside the parks, including several attached to gas stations, stock items such as packaged foods, ice, beer, s'more fixings, sandwiches and other staples, as well as junk food, but they charge top dollar.

→ The Village Store in Yosemite Valley is the best option in any of the parks and

has the equivalent offerings of any large chain store.

→ You can stock en route to the parks at large groceries in Oakhurst, Mariposa and Groveland; Lee Vining's store is smaller.

→ Bishop and Mammoth Lakes on the eastern side of the Sierra have the largest grocery stores.

→ Most campsites have fire pits (you can grill your food if you bring a grill) and picnic tables.

Insurance

If you're traveling very far to get here (and especially if you're flying), it's a good idea to get some travel insurance to cover baggage theft, trip cancellation and, most importantly, medical emergency. When choosing a policy, read the fine print; some policies will not cover 'extreme' activities, which could include anything from river rafting to rock climbing. Domestic rental and homeowners' insurance policies often cover theft while you're on the road.

Worldwide travel insurance is available at www.lonelyplanet.com/travel-insurance. You can buy, extend and claim online anytime – even if you're already on the road.

Internet Access

Most lodgings in and outside the parks offer free wi-fi for their guests. Reception is spotty at best in most corners of the parks and wilderness areas. Free internet

access can be found in most public libraries.

Legal Matters

→ Feeding bears or taking insufficient food safety measures (p239) is a felony. Tickets are common.

→ No hunting inside national parks. It is generally allowed within national forests with a proper hunting license.

→ Carrying concealed firearms, with proper California permitting (California doesn't recognize concealed weapons permits from any other state), is allowed, even in national parks. However, no firearms are allowed inside federal and some national-park facilities such as visitor centers.

→ Possession of up to 1oz of marijuana (if you are 21 years or older) for recreational use is not a crime in California, but it is still illegal to use marijuana in public (subject to fines up to $250, as well as mandatory community-service hours and drug-education classes).

→ It's illegal to transport marijuana of any amount by plane, even if medicinal. This includes trips within state borders and to other states that have legalized marijuana.

→ Consuming alcohol anywhere other than at a private residence or licensed premises is a no-no, which puts most parks off-limits (although many campgrounds legally allow it).

→ It's also illegal to carry open containers of alcohol inside a vehicle, even if they're empty. Unless full and still sealed, best to store in the trunk.

LGBT+ Travelers

Same-sex marriage is legal in California, and northern California, especially San

Francisco, one of the gateways to the region, is a magnet for lesbian, gay, bisexual and transgender travelers. Despite widespread tolerance, homophobic bigotry still exists. In small towns tolerance often means 'don't ask, don't tell.'

Maps

For multiday hikes, purchase an appropriately detailed topographic map. GPS navigation can be helpful but isn't 100% reliable for drivers in remote areas. Recommended maps:

DeLorme California Atlas and Gazetteer (www.delorme.com) Excellent driving atlas.

Eastern Sierra: Bridgeport to Lone Pine Produced and sold locally by Sierra Maps (www.sierra maps.com); detailed recreation information.

National Geographic (www.nationalgeographic.com) Has one Sequoia/Kings Canyon and five hiking maps for Yosemite in its 'Trails Illustrated' series.

Tom Harrison (www.tomharris onmaps.com) Waterproof topo maps of the Sierra Nevada; the John Muir Trail map pack is the gold standard.

Money

If you're arriving from abroad and need to change money, do so at the airport or at an exchange bureau or bank in a major city. It's nearly impossible to exchange money in most small towns throughout the Sierra.

ATMs

Yosemite:
➜ Yosemite Valley
➜ Crane Flat gas station
➜ Wawona

Sequoia and Kings Canyon:
➜ Lodgepole
➜ Grant Grove
➜ Cedar Grove
➜ Stony Creek

Credit Cards

➜ Major credit cards (Visa, MasterCard, Amex) are widely accepted throughout the region and are almost always required as deposits when renting a car or reserving a hotel room.

➜ Debit cards are accepted everywhere.

Opening Hours

Businesses and services maintain opening hours based on a wide range of factors: some close for the winter, and 'winter' can begin and end on different dates each year. Others stay open year-round but maintain shorter hours in winter and their longest hours in summer.

Note that even when opening hours are listed, they're still subject to change based on weather, demand and budgetary constraints.

Bars In the parks, usually open approximately 5pm to 10pm. Outside the parks they may close as late as 2am.

Cafes and restaurants Generally serve breakfast 7am to 10:30am, lunch 11am to 2:30pm and dinner about 5pm to 9pm.

Shops and services About 9:30am to 5:30pm.

Post

Nearly every town around the national parks has a post office. Yosemite National Park has four and there's one at Grant Grove in Kings Canyon.

Public Holidays

The parks (and the areas surrounding the parks) are at their absolute busiest during the summertime school-holiday period, which runs roughly from mid-June through August. During this period, *everything* is packed and reservations are a must. The greatest numbers of

visitors also hit the parks during the following public holidays.

New Year's Day January 1

Martin Luther King Jr Day Third Monday in January

Presidents Day Third Monday in February

Easter A Friday through Sunday in March or April

Memorial Day Last Monday in May

Independence Day July 4

Labor Day First Monday in September

Columbus Day Second Monday in October

Veterans Day November 11

Thanksgiving Day Fourth Thursday in November

Christmas December 25

Safe Travel

The area is not immune from crime, especially in the national parks – and it's no wonder, considering they see millions of visitors each year. However, the majority of crimes are small-time theft, vandalism and public drunkenness.

➜ Though weapons and unpiloted aircraft (eg drones) are strictly prohibited in the parks, beware of visitors who flout the law and use them. Better yet, report illegal activity to the nearest park ranger.

➜ Car break-ins are more often the work of opportunistic bears than burglars.

➜ Carry money and valuables with you at all times – if you leave anything in the car, store it out of sight in the trunk.

➜ When possible avoid parking your vehicle at an isolated trailhead. Instead, park in a more heavily used area within walking distance of the trail, or ride park shuttle buses.

Solo Travelers

➡ Group hikes and other park programs are good options for meeting other travelers.

➡ It is common (and considered safe) for both men and women to backpack alone in the Sierra Nevada. However, always let someone know where you're going.

➡ Hiking long routes such as the John Muir Trail means having to shoulder all of your equipment and supplies, rather than splitting the weight.

Telephone

In the parks you'll find payphones at almost every developed location.

Mobile Phones

➡ Cell-phone reception, including your carrier's wi-fi, is patchy through the Sierra region, depending on your carrier. In Yosemite National Park, Yosemite Valley, Tuolumne Meadows, Crane Flat and Wawona generally have good to fair reception; AT&T and Verizon have the best coverage. In Sequoia and Kings Canyon, Grant Grove is the only option.

➡ When breaking out that cell phone, consider the reality of noise pollution. Hearing someone's cell phone ring in a neighboring campsite or at a scenic lookout is annoying at best, while being subjected to a loud and

lengthy phone conversation is grounds for launching a pine-coning.

Toilets

Public toilets are available at all national-park facilities. Trailheads for popular hikes and important sites often have public toilets. All car-camping sites in the national parks, and most in the state parks and wilderness areas, have toilet facilities – some in the latter are primitive enclosed pit-style toilets.

Tourist Information

Tourist-information offices (known as visitor centers) are found throughout Yosemite and Sequoia and Kings Canyon, and in nearly every town in the Sierra.

Bishop Area Visitors Bureau (☑760-873-8405; www. bishopvisitor.com; 690 N Main St; ☺10am-5pm Mon-Sat; 🖥) Tips, itineraries and outdoor info on the city and region.

Mammoth Lakes Welcome Center (☑760-924-5500, 888-466-2666; www.visit mammoth.com; 2510 Hwy 203; ☺9am-5pm; in winter 8:30am-4:30pm) The largest Eastern Sierra visitor center, with excellent regional information, maps and brochures.

Sequoia & Kings Canyon National Parks (www.nps.gov/ seki) Official website.

Visit California (www.visitcali fornia.com) The official state tourism website.

Yosemite National Park (www. nps.gov/yose) Official Yosemite National Park website, with the most comprehensive and current information. News and road closures/openings are often posted first on its Facebook page (www. facebook.com/YosemiteNPS).

Useful sources for areas around the national parks:

Eastern Sierra Interagency Visitor Center (☑760-876-6222; www.fs.fed.us/r5/inyo; cnr Hwys 395 & 136; ☺8am-5pm, in winter 8am-4pm) Trail conditions, weather and permits for Mt Whitney and other area info around Lone Pine.

Inyo National Forest (www. fs.usda.gov/inyo)

Sierra National Forest (www. fs.usda.gov/sierra)

Stanislaus National Forest (www.fs.usda.gov/stanislaus)

White Mountain Public Lands Information Station (☑760-873-2500; www.fs.usda.gov/ inyo; 798 N Main St; ☺8am-noon & 1-5pm daily, 8am-noon & 1-4pm Mon-Fri in winter) Wilderness permits, trail and campground information for the entire area.

Yosemite Sierra Visitors Bureau Located in Oakhurst; has information about Yosemite and Madera County.

Visas

Visa information is highly subject to change. Depending on your country of origin, the rules for entering the USA keep changing. Double-check current visa requirements before coming to the USA.

For up-to-date information about entry requirements and eligibility, check the visa section of the US Department of State website (http://travel.state.gov/content/visas/en.html).

LOST & FOUND

➡ **Yosemite** For anything left or recovered in restaurants, hotels or gift shops or on buses, call 209-372-4357. For items astray elsewhere, call the NPS (209-379-1001). In Yosemite Valley you can also go to the information desk at the **Yosemite Valley Visitor Center** (☑209-372-0200; 9035 Village Dr, Yosemite Village; ☺9am-5pm; ♿), where rangers keep a stash of things found.

➡ **Sequoia & Kings Canyon** Each visitor center maintains its own lost and found.

Volunteering

Besides helping the national parks, volunteering is a great way to see a side of Yosemite and Sequoia and Kings Canyon that most tourists never experience. It's also a great way to meet locals and fellow volunteers – contacts that can last a lifetime. As a volunteer you can do everything from weeding and sweeping to working on restoration projects, monitoring bears and leading educational walks. Most volunteer positions require advance applications and background checks.

➡ The extensive **Yosemite Park Volunteer Program** (☑209-379-1850; www. nps.gov/yose/getinvolved/ volunteer.htm) has a number of sought-after long-term positions (some include housing), as well as shorter projects for individuals and groups, and a weekly drop-in program that does hands-in-the-dirt activities such as removing invasive plants in some of the most scenic areas of the park.

➡ The **Volunteer.gov** website maintains a comprehensive database on positions available at all national parks and federal recreation areas, allowing you to browse openings by category, eg backcountry, fish and wildlife or historical preservation.

➡ The **Yosemite Conservancy** (☑209-379-3217; www.yosemiteconservancy.org) runs an established volunteer program for its members that includes restoration and revegetation projects as well as staffing information stations. Long-term volunteers receive free camping and bookstore discounts.

➡ Earth Day (April 22) celebrations in Yosemite feature chances to help out the park and include cleanup projects and tree planting as well as kids' educational events, a vendors' fair and live music and poetry.

➡ The **Yosemite Conservation Heritage Center** (☑209-372-4542; www.sierraclub.org/education/ leconte; ⏱10am-4pm Wed-Sun & evenings Fri & Sat May-Sep; 🚭; 🚌shuttle stop 12) puts Sierra Club members to work in the operation of the former LeConte Memorial Lodge for one-week stints between May 1 and mid-September.

➡ The huge week-long Yosemite Facelift (p23) event picks up tons of trash throughout the park, with free campsites for volunteers and fun evening activities. Check its Facebook page for info.

Work

➡ Most workers inside the parks are employed either by the NPS or by park concessionaires. Most employment opportunities within the parks are seasonal – roughly Memorial Day (the last Monday in May) through Labor Day (the first Monday in September). Applications are almost always due at least six months in advance.

➡ Seasonal and year-round positions with the NPS are posted at www.usajobs.gov. Only US citizens are eligible for NPS employment.

➡ **NatureBridge** (☑209-379-9511; www.naturebridge.org/yosemite) hires seasonal environmental-science educators for its programs in Yosemite.

➡ Yosemite's concessionaire, **Aramark/Yosemite Hospitality** (☑888-413-8869; www.travelyosemite.com), runs nearly all of the park's businesses and transportation and is your best bet – about 1800 employees are needed per summer. If you're already in Yosemite Valley and are struck by the need to stay and work, drop by the human-resources department in the administration offices in Yosemite Village.

➡ **DNC** (☑801-559-4930, 866-807-3598; www.visitsequoia.com) is the park concessionaire for Sequoia and Kings Canyon.

➡ The chambers of commerce websites for various Sierra counties might provide leads on area jobs.

Transportation

GETTING THERE & AWAY

Getting to the Sierra Nevada by car or public transportation is easy. Flights, cars and tours can be booked online at lonelyplanet.com/bookings.

Entering the Country/Region

For up-to-date information on travel to the US, as well as current procedures, visit the websites of the US Department of State (www.travel.state.gov) and US Customs and Border Protection (www.cbp.gov). It is highly recommended that you check and confirm all entry requirements with a US consulate in your home country before leaving.

Air

A number of airports have good public transportation connections to Yosemite and Sequoia and Kings Canyon National Parks; **YARTS** (☑877-989-2787; www.yarts.com) buses run directly from the Fresno airport. When booking flights, keep in mind rush hour and traffic patterns in the arrival city if hoping for as quick a commute as possible to your destination in the mountains.

Backpackers should look over Transportation Security Administration (TSA) guidelines for flying with equipment at www.tsa.gov/blog/2014/05/13/tsa-travel-tips-travel-tips-backpackers-campers-and-fishers. Camp stoves and empty fuel containers are OK; fuel fumes are not.

Airports

Major international airports three to five hours' driving time from Yosemite and Sequoia and Kings Canyon National Parks are as follows:

Los Angeles International (LAX; www.lawa.org/welcome LAX.aspx; 1 World Way) California's largest and busiest airport.

McCarran International (LAS; ☑702-261-5211; www.mccarran.com; 5757 Wayne Newton Blvd; ☎) In Las Vegas.

Mineta San Jose International (SJC;☑408-392-3600; www.flysanjose.com; 1701 Airport Blvd) Around 45 miles south of San Francisco, near Silicon Valley.

Oakland International (OAK; www.oaklandairport.com; 1 Airport Dr; ☎; Ⓑ Oakland International Airport) In San Francisco's East Bay.

Reno-Tahoe International (RNO; www.renoairport.com; ☎) About 5 miles southeast of Reno.

Sacramento International (SMF; www.sacramento.aero/smf; 6900 Airport Blvd) Midway between the San Francisco Bay Area and Lake Tahoe.

San Francisco International (SFO; www.flysfo.com; S McDonnell Rd) Northern California's major hub.

Two smaller, closer airports are:

Fresno Yosemite International (FAT; www.flyfresno.com; 5175 E Clinton Way) Approximately 70 miles southwest of Yosemite and 60 miles west of Sequoia and Kings Canyon.

Mammoth Yosemite (MMH; www.visitmammoth.com/fly-mammoth-lakes; 1300 Airport Rd) Closest airport to the eastern side of Yosemite, 2½ hours' drive from Yosemite Valley.

Land

Maybe the most important feature to keep in mind is the scarcity of east-west mountain crossings. An indicator of the region's ruggedness is that none exist between Sherman Pass Rd in the far south and Tioga Pass in Yosemite National Park. CA 88 (Carson Pass), I 80 (Donner Pass) and Hwy 50 (Echo Summit) remain open through the winter.

Bicycle

Cycling is a great way to get to the national parks, but roads are narrow, grades are steep and summer temperatures can climb well over 90°F (32°C).

➡ Long-distance cyclists can overnight in Yosemite's backpacker campgrounds.

CLIMATE CHANGE & TRAVEL

Every form of transport that relies on carbon-based fuel generates CO_2, the main cause of human-induced climate change. Modern travel is dependent on airplanes, which might use less fuel per kilometer per person than most cars but travel much greater distances. The altitude at which aircraft emit gases (including CO_2) and particles also contributes to their climate change impact. Many websites offer 'carbon calculators' that allow people to estimate the carbon emissions generated by their journey and, for those who wish to do so, to offset the impact of the greenhouse gases emitted with contributions to portfolios of climate-friendly initiatives throughout the world. Lonely Planet offsets the carbon footprint of all staff and author travel.

➡ All trails within the national parks are off-limits to mountain bikes – head to **Mammoth Lakes** (☎800-626-6684; www.mammothmountain.com; day pass adult/7-12yr $45/24; ⏱9am-6pm Jun-Sep) instead.

➡ **Better World Club** (☎866-238-1137; www.betterworldclub.com) offers emergency roadside assistance for cyclists for an annual membership fee of about $40.

➡ If you need a lift, YARTS buses can stash bikes in their storage areas if there's enough space, and Eastern Sierra Transit Hwy 395 buses have bike racks.

Bus

Greyhound (☎800-231-2222; www.greyhound.com) runs to the parks' hub cities – Merced for Yosemite, Visalia for Sequoia and Kings Canyon, and Fresno for all.

There is no direct public transportation between any of the parks. However, you can use Fresno to connect between Yosemite, via YARTS, and Sequoia and Kings Canyon. Big Trees Transit service connecting Fresno and Grant Grove in Kings Canyon is no longer operating.

Eastern Sierra Transit Authority (☎760-872-1901; www.estransit.com) buses make a round trip between Lone Pine and Reno ($59, six hours) on Monday, Tuesday, Thursday and Friday, stopping at all Hwy 395 towns in between. Fares depend on distance, and reservations

are recommended. There's also an express bus between Mammoth and Bishop ($7, one hour, around three times daily) that operates Monday to Friday.

Car & Motorcycle

Driving is by far the most popular way to get to and around the Sierra Nevada. In Yosemite National Park this means traffic, smog and sometimes frustrating battles for parking spaces during peak summer months.

Outside the parks lies an endless network of fire and forest-service roads, many leading to remote campgrounds and lakes. While many of these roads are drivable with a standard-clearance vehicle, potential explorers would be better off with above-average clearance and 4WD.

For current state of road conditions call:

California Department of Transportation (http://quickmap.dot.ca.gov) Current road conditions for highways throughout California.

Sequoia and Kings Canyon Road information ☎559-565-3341.

Yosemite Road information ☎209-372-0200.

AUTOMOBILE ASSOCIATIONS

American Automobile Association (AAA; ☎800-222-8252, emergency roadside assistance 800-222-4357; www.aaa.com) Has free maps and discounts on accommodations, theme parks and other services.

Better World Club has imilar services to AAA and donates 1% of its revenue to environmental cleanup and advocacy.

DRIVER'S LICENSE

➡ Non-US residents can legally drive in the US for up to a year with only their home driver's license and passport, though proffering an international driver's license if you get pulled over can make things easier on everyone.

➡ Most car-rental companies don't require an international driver's license, but having one makes the rental process easier.

INSURANCE

➡ California requires liability insurance for all vehicles; proof must be carried in the car at all times.

➡ Credit cards or your own auto insurance policy (be sure to check both) often cover insurance for rentals. If not, you can purchase optional liability insurance that adds between $10 and $20 per day to the rental rate.

➡ If you're driving a friend's car, you'll be insured under their policy (assuming they have one).

CAR RENTAL

Carefully read rental policies regarding snow tires. Mountain roads in winter are often open only to cars fitted with these and most rental-car companies restrict their usage. City locations, even for big agencies such as Hertz or Budget, sometimes offer much cheaper rates than airport offices – often cheaper than the most-no-frills, budget-minded company. If arriving at LAX for example, it makes economic sense to take a taxi to a close off-site location. This is less applicable at SAF, where the rental-car agencies are easier to reach via the AirTrain.

Avis (800-633-3469; www.avis.com)

Budget (800-218-7992; www.budget.com)

Dollar (800-800-5252; www.dollar.com)

Enterprise (855-266-9289; www.enterprise.com)

Fox (855-571-8410; www.foxrentacar.com)

Hertz (800-654-3131; www.hertz.com)

National (877-222-9058; www.nationalcar.com)

Rent-a-Wreck (877-877-0700; www.rentawreck.com) Minimum rental age and under-25 driver surcharges vary at a dozen locations, mostly around LA and the San Francisco Bay Area.

Super Cheap! Car Rental (in Los Angeles 310-645-3993, in San Francisco 650-777-9993; www.supercheapcar.com) Locations in Los Angeles International Airport, Orange County and the San Francisco Bay Area. No surcharge for drivers aged 21 to 24 years; a nominal daily fee for drivers under age 21 with full-coverage insurance.

Thrifty (800-847-4389; www.thrifty.com)

RV RENTAL

Most campgrounds in the Sierra Nevada don't have electricity or water hookups for RVs. RVs are cumbersome to drive and they burn fuel at an alarming rate. That said, they do solve transportation, accommodations and cooking needs in one fell swoop. Note that there are many places in the national parks and in the mountains that RVs can't go.

Book RV rentals as far in advance as possible. Rental costs vary by size and model, but you can expect to pay over $100 per day. Rates often don't include mileage, taxes, vehicle prep fees and bedding or kitchen kits. If pets are even allowed, a surcharge may apply.

Apollo RV Rentals (800-370-1262; www.apollorv.com) Camper-van rentals in the San Francisco Bay Area, LA and Las Vegas.

El Monte (888-337-2228; www.elmonterv.com) With 15 locations across California, this national RV rental agency offers AAA discounts.

Escape Campervans (877-270-8267, 310-672-9909; www.escapecampervans.com) Awesomely painted camper vans at economical rates in LA, Las Vegas and San Francisco. No extra charges for young drivers or multiple renters.

Jucy Rentals (800-650-4180; www.jucyusa.com) Camper-van rentals in San Francisco, LA and Las Vegas.

ROAD RULES

➡ Cars drive on the right-hand side of the road.

➡ Unless signed otherwise, it's legal to make a right turn on a red light after coming to a complete stop.

➡ Distances and speed limits are shown in miles.

➡ On a two-lane highway, you can pass cars on the left-hand side if the center line is broken (not solid yellow).

➡ Talking on a handheld cell phone or texting while driving is illegal.

➡ Drive extra cautiously along roads marked with animal crossing signs.

➡ It's illegal to operate a motor vehicle with a blood alcohol content of 0.08% or higher.

WINTER DRIVING

➡ Snow and ice present hazards and road closures; many of the latter are predictable, occuring every year in the winter.

➡ During snowy months motorists will encounter 'chain controls' on many mountain roads. Continuing past these without snow tires or four- or all-wheel drive is illegal. Unless you're properly equipped, your only option is to buy or rent chains or turn back. If you plan to drive to the parks when there's any chance of snow, the easiest solution is to bring your own chains, as renting or purchasing at or near chain controls is expensive. (Depending on your type of car, it costs from $55 to $125 to purchase.) Permitted workers along the roadside will fit the chains for about $20, saving your knuckles

DRIVING DISTANCES & TIMES

FROM	DISTANCE/TIME TO YOSEMITE VALLEY	DISTANCE/TIME TO SEQUOIA	DISTANCE/TIME TO BISHOP
Fresno	65 miles/1½hr	83 miles/1½hr	225 miles/5¼hr
Las Vegas	400-475 miles/8-8½hr	400 miles/6½hr	266 miles/4½hr
Los Angeles	276 miles/6hr	225 miles/4hr	267 miles/4½hr
Reno	213 miles/4hr	379 mile/5¾hr	205 miles/3½hr
San Francisco	210 miles/4hr	280 miles/5½hr	297 miles/6¼hr

in the process. If you plan to put your chains on yourself, bring gloves.

➡ A smart precaution in winter is to pack emergency food and water and a sleeping bag for each person in the car. If you're on a remote road and get stuck or lose control and slide off the road, assistance could be hours or days away. Provisions and warmth in the car can literally save your life.

FUEL & ELECTRIC-CAR CHARGING

➡ Fuel becomes more expensive the closer you are to the national parks, with gas stations just outside the parks' borders charging almost comical rates. In the Eastern Sierra, Bishop is your best bet and Bridgeport may be the worst.

➡ The nearest place to Yosemite Valley for fuel is El Portal, about 14 miles west of Yosemite Village on Hwy 140.

➡ Diesel fuel is available at Yosemite's Wawona and **Crane Flat** (Big Oak Flat Rd; ⏲8am-7pm Mar-Oct) stations.

➡ There are no gas stations in Sequoia and Kings Canyon; the nearest ones are at Stony Creek Lodge (p198; open mid-May to mid-October only) and Hume Lake (p191), and both carry diesel.

➡ There are two electrical charging stations in Yosemite Valley: the Village Garage (p131) in the valley and the Majestic Yosemite (p100 parking lot, which has two chargers (one for Teslas).

➡ The town of Groveland, Tenaya Lodge (p140) in Fish Camp and Hounds Tooth Inn (p141) in Oakhurst also have charging stations. There is no fee.

Train

No trains serve the parks directly, but **Amtrak** (☎800-872-7245; www.amtrak.com) offers daily service to the transport hubs of Merced and Fresno for Yosemite, and Fresno and Visalia (via Han-

ford) for Sequoia and Kings Canyon, where bus service is available into the parks. From most major airports the first leg of Amtrak service is often by bus to the nearest train station. The earlier you book your Amtrak ticket, the cheaper the fare.

From Hanford you can connect to all other Amtrak routes in the state, including the San Joaquin, which travels north to Sacramento ($32, four hours, two direct daily) or south to Bakersfield ($22.50, 1½ hours, six daily).

TO YOSEMITE

From San Francisco you can book an Amtrak ticket all the way to Yosemite Valley (6½ hours) or Tuolumne Meadows. Quick Amtrak Thruway buses connect San Francisco to Emeryville, where San Joaquin trains run to Merced. At Merced station transfer directly to the YARTS bus. Connections to Tuolumne Meadows (daily July and

August, weekends June and September) can be difficult to book without calling. Park entry is included in the fare, and you're guaranteed a seat on the YARTS bus.

TO SEQUOIA & KINGS CANYON

Take a San Joaquin train to Hanford (20 miles west of Visalia), where an Amtrak bus picks you up and takes you to Visalia. From there, transfer to the summer-only **Sequoia Shuttle** (☎877-287-4453; www.sequoiashuttle.com; round-trip incl park entry fee $15; ⏲late May-late Sep).

TO EASTERN SIERRA

From Los Angeles' Union Station frequent **Metrolink** (☎800-371-5465; www.metrolinktrains.com) trains service Lancaster (two hours), which has ESTA bus service to Mammoth Lakes. From Mammoth onward bus connections run to Yosemite when Tioga Pass is open.

ROUTES INTO THE PARKS

Yosemite National Park

Yosemite operates three entrance stations on the western side of the Sierra Nevada: the South Entrance on Hwy 41 (Wawona Rd) north of Fresno (convenient from southern California), the Arch Rock Entrance on Hwy 140 (El Portal Rd) east of Merced (convenient from northern California) and the Big Oak Flat Entrance on Hwy 120 W (Big Oak Flat Rd) east of Manteca (the quickest route from the Bay Area). Roads are generally kept open all year, though in winter (usually November to April) drivers may be required to carry tire chains.

The Tioga Pass Entrance, along Hwy 120 E (Tioga Rd) on the eastern side of the park, is open from about June to October, depending on when the snow is cleared. From Tioga Pass drivers connect with Hwy 395 and points such as Reno and Death Valley National Park.

Sequoia & Kings Canyon National Parks

The two routes into Sequoia and Kings Canyon approach from the west, departing Hwy 99 from Fresno or Visalia. From Visalia, Hwy 198 leads 46 miles east into Sequoia National Park. From Fresno, Hwy 180 E leads 57 miles east to Kings Canyon. The two roads are connected by the Generals Hwy, inside Sequoia. There is no access to either park from the east, and no internal roads between the parks.

GETTING AROUND

Bicycle

Hwy 395 along the eastern spine of the Sierras is mostly flat and traffic is usually not heavy, though it's completely exposed. Roads heading up and into the mountains from this side quickly gain elevation, so they're challenging to say the least. Cycling is limited in the national parks.

Bus

YARTS buses travel all the way from Fresno Yosemite airport to Yosemite Valley along Hwy 140 several times daily year-round, with a variety of stops at hotels and post offices in Midpines and El Portal along the way. In summer (roughly June through September), another YARTS bus route, called the Trans-Sierra connection, runs from Mammoth Lakes along Hwy 395 to Yosemite Valley via Hwy 120.

Eastern Sierra Transit Authority has year-round service along Hwy 395, running between Reno, NV, and Lone Pine, with numerous stops in between. Check the website for updated timetables.

During peak summer season (8am to 6.30pm late May to early September only), Sequoia Shuttle runs buses five or six times daily between Visalia, Three Rivers and the Giant Forest Museum in Sequoia National Park (two hours, $15 round-trip, including park fee); advance reservations required. All shuttles are wheelchair-accessible and equipped with bicycle racks.

Car & Motorcycle

Traffic can get extremely heavy in the national parks in the summer. Bumper-to-bumper standstills aren't uncommon. Pay attention to speed limits, especial-ly in parks. Many spur roads into the mountains from Hwy 395, including most of the passes, close in the winter. Driving conditions can deteriorate quickly in winter storms on mountain roads, and chains are often required.

Hitchhiking

Hitchhiking is never entirely safe anywhere in the world, and it's not necessarily recommended. Travelers who hitch should understand that they are taking a small but potentially serious risk. That said, hitching is quite common in Yosemite and the Eastern Sierra and is sometimes necessary to get to or from a trailhead. While hitchers are generally viewed with suspicion in the US, Sierra backpackers often get a break.

➡ If you're trying to get home from Yosemite, check the bulletin board at Camp 4 for rides offered and needed, or just stick out your thumb at the parking-lot entrance.

➡ To get a ride to the parks, check out the ride-share forums on Craigslist (www.craigslist.org).

➡ For Eastern Sierra trailheads, try the 'Transportation To & From' board of High Sierra Topix (www.highsierratopix.com/community).

Tours

Aramark/Yosemite Hospitality (☎888-413-8869; www.travelyosemite.com) The park's main concessionaire runs private and group guided hikes and overnight backpacking trips, including for beginners.

Discover Yosemite Tours (☎559-642-4400; www.discoveryosemite.com; full-day tours adult/child $152/76) Operates bus tours year-round from Oakhurst, Fish Camp and Bass Lake.

Green Tortoise (☎415-956-7500, 800-867-8647; www. greentortoise.com) ✈ Runs backpacker-friendly two-day ($300) and three-day ($360) trips to Yosemite from San Francisco where travelers sleep in the converted bus or in campgrounds, cook collectively and choose from activities like hiking, swimming or just hanging out (and there's always some great hanging out). Prices (which change annually) include most meals and the park entry fee.

Incredible Adventures (☎800-777-8464, 415-642-7378; www.incadventures.com) ✈ This outfit uses biodiesel vans for its San Francisco–based tours to Yosemite, from one-day sightseeing tours ($159) to three-day camping tours ($489). Park entry fees and most meals are included, and it provides all cooking and camping gear except sleeping bags.

Road Scholar (p29) Outdoors-oriented 'learning adventures' and hiking trips for those aged 50 and over.

Sequoia Parks Conservancy (p29) Easy guided, group day hikes along the Big Stump Trail or through the Giant Forest, plus custom private naturalist-guided hikes and outdoor-skills instruction in anything from birding to caving. Phone ahead to check prices for custom tours.

Sierra Club (p29) The national environmental nonprofit has both paid trips and free activity outings sponsored by local chapters.

Southern Yosemite Mountain Guides (p29) Long-established outfitter offering guided hiking, backpacking and packhorse-supported trips.

Tenaya Lodge (p140) Large family-friendly resort in Fish Camp operates full-day park tours in luxurious Mercedes-Benz buses with retractable roofs that allow you to experience the natural sights a little more naturally. Guests of the lodge have priority.

Yosemite Conservancy (p29) Park-affiliated nonprofit offers multiday courses, custom trips and seminars that are great alternatives to tours.

Health & Safety

Keeping safe while visiting the parks depends on your predeparture preparations, daily routines and how you handle any dangerous situations that develop. While the potential problems can seem quite frightening, in reality most park visitors don't experience anything worse than mosquito bites or a skinned knee.

BEFORE YOU GO

Insurance

Review the terms of your health-insurance policy before your trip. Some policies won't cover injuries sustained, or emergency evacuation required, as a result of 'dangerous' activities such as backpacking, rock climbing or mountaineering. Some policies require you to get pre-authorization for medical treatment from a call center. Be sure to keep all receipts and documentation.

Websites

Sequoia & Kings Canyon National Park – Safety (www.nps.gov/seki/planyourvisit/yoursafety.htm)

Wilderness Medicine Institute (www.nols.edu/wmi) Classes, case studies and articles.

Yosemite National Park – Safety (www.nps.gov/yose/planyourvisit/yoursafety.htm)

Further Reading

Backcountry First Aid and Extended Care (Buck Tilton, 2007) Inexpensive, pocket-sized wilderness-survival manual.

NOLS Wilderness Medicine (Tod Schimelpfenig, 2016) Comprehensive wilderness first-aid curriculum.

IN YOSEMITE & THE SIERRA NEVADA

Availability of Health Care

For emergencies call 911. Inside the parks, cell phones often won't work. Carrying a satellite phone or personal locator beacon is an option for backcountry trips. Park rangers with medical training can provide basic first aid, free of charge. For serious ailments, drive to the nearest hospital emergency room (ER). Hospital costs can be astronomical, especially if providers are 'out of network,' which they're bound to be. Search-and-rescue (SAR) and helicopter evacuations are *only* for life-threatening emergencies; they are very costly for the parks and put employees' lives at risk.

Yosemite Area

In Yosemite Valley, **Yosemite Medical Clinic** (☑209-372-4637; 9000 Ahwahnee Dr, Yosemite Village; ☉9am-7pm daily late May-late Sep, to 5pm Mon-Fri late Sep-late May) is just east of Yosemite Village.

Hospitals near Yosemite:

Doctors Medical Center (☑209-578-1211; www.dmc-modesto.com; 1441 Florida Ave; ☉24hr) The nearest Level II trauma center, in the Central Valley.

John C Fremont Hospital (☑209-966-3631; www.jcf-hospital.com; 5189 Hospital Rd; ☉24hr) A 24-hour emergency room, west of Yosemite.

Mammoth Hospital (☑760-934-3311; www.mammothhospital.org; 85 Sierra Park Rd; ☉24hr) A 24-hour emergency room in the Eastern Sierra.

Sequoia & Kings Canyon Area

First aid is available at visitor centers and ranger stations. Hospitals nearby:

Adventist Medical Center (☑559-638-8155; www.adventisthealth.org; 372 W Cypress Ave, Reedley; ☉24hr) Limited emergency services, closer to Kings Canyon.

Community Regional Medical Center (☑559-459-6000; www.communitymedical.org; 2823 Fresno St; ☉24hr) The region's Level I trauma center, west of Kings Canyon.

Kaweah Delta Medical Center (☑559-624-2000; www.kaweahdelta.org; 400 W Mineral King Ave; ☉24hr) A 24-hour emergency room near Sequoia's south entrance.

Infectious Diseases

Amebic Dysentery

Serious diarrhea caused by contaminated water is an increasing problem in heavily used backcountry areas. If diarrhea occurs, fluid replacement is key: drink weak black tea with a little sugar, or a soft drink allowed to go flat and 50% diluted by water.

With severe diarrhea a rehydrating solution is necessary to replace minerals and salts. Commercially available oral-rehydration salts are useful. Gut-paralyzing drugs such as diphenoxylate or loperamide can be used to bring relief from the symptoms but do not actually cure the problem.

Giardiasis

If you drink snowmelt, stream, lake or groundwater, you risk being infected by waterborne parasites. Giardiasis is an intestinal disease marked by chronic diarrhea, abdominal cramps, bloating, fatigue and weight loss; symptoms can last for weeks. Though not usually dangerous, giardiasis requires treatment with antibiotics. To protect yourself, always boil, filter or chemically treat water before drinking. Do not even brush your teeth or rinse dirty dishes with untreated water.

Hantavirus & Plague

Hantavirus and plague are rare but serious diseases endemic to the Sierra Nevada. Hantavirus is transmitted by infected rodents through droppings, urine, saliva or blood. Plague is most commonly transmitted by the bite of infected fleas who live on plague-carrying rodents. Initial flu-like symptoms usually manifest within a week of exposure to the plague, and up to seven weeks afterward

for hantavirus. If you show symptoms or suspect you were exposed, seek medical attention immediately.

Rare cases of both diseases have occurred in the parks, most recently in Yosemite. In 2012 several visitors were infected with hantavirus after staying in tent cabins in Yosemite Valley and the high country. In 2015 two visitors to the Yosemite region were diagnosed with plague. To protect yourself from infection, store all food in animal-proof containers, avoid pitching your tent near rodent habitat (eg woodpiles), use insect repellent with DEET, check for rodent droppings and avoid stirring up dust in park lodgings, and never feed or touch (alive or dead) a wild animal.

Environmental Hazards

Altitude

Most people adjust to altitude within a few hours or days. Occasionally acute mountain sickness (AMS) occurs, usually at elevations greater than 8000ft. Being physically fit offers no protection, and the risk increases with faster ascents, higher altitudes and greater exertion. When traveling to high elevations, avoid overexertion, eat light meals, hydrate and abstain from alcohol and sedatives.

Initial symptoms of AMS, which is essentially the result of insufficient oxygen in the blood, may include headaches, nausea, vomiting, dizziness, weakness, shortness of breath and loss of appetite. The best treatment

MEDICAL CHECKLIST

In addition to any prescription or over-the-counter medications you typically take, consider adding these to your first-aid kit:

- ☐ acetaminophen/paracetamol (eg Tylenol) or aspirin
- ☐ adhesive or paper tape
- ☐ antibacterial ointment for cuts and abrasions
- ☐ antidiarrhea and antinausea drugs
- ☐ antifungal cream or powder
- ☐ antihistamines (for hay fever and allergic reactions)
- ☐ anti-inflammatory drugs (eg ibuprofen)
- ☐ bandages, gauze pads and rolls
- ☐ calamine lotion, sting-relief spray or aloe vera
- ☐ cortisone (steroid) cream for allergic rashes
- ☐ elasticized support bandage for knees, ankles etc
- ☐ eye drops
- ☐ insect repellent
- ☐ moleskin (for blisters)
- ☐ nonadhesive dressings
- ☐ oral rehydration mix
- ☐ pocketknife
- ☐ poison-oak skin cleanser
- ☐ scissors, safety pins, tweezers
- ☐ sunscreen and lip balm

BLACK BEAR ENCOUNTERS

Black bears are the only species of bear that live in California. They're active day and night throughout the Sierra Nevada. While wild black bears often flee at the sight, sound or smell of people, many park bears have lost their natural fear of humans. In 2015, the last reported full-year analysis, there were 76 'incidents' involving bears 'stealing' and exhibiting aggressive behavior – this marked a 40-year low. It was also the fourth year in a row without an injury or death from a bear attack.

Bears that associate people with food become increasingly bold about approaching humans, to the point where they become dangerously aggressive. Habituated bears regularly break into vehicles and raid campgrounds and backcountry campsites in search of food. You must remove all scented items from your car, including any food, trash (scour the car for empty potato-chip bags, soda cans, recyclables etc) and products such as gum, toothpaste and sunscreen. Cover up anything in your car that even resembles food or a cooler. Place all food and scented items in bear boxes – large metal storage lockers found in most parking lots and at every park campsite.

When camping think of the bear box as your refrigerator: keep it shut and latched when you are not actively using it. Keep all food within arm's reach at all times. Bears can sneak up and steal food from picnic tables or campsites when your back is turned, even for just a second. Failure to use bear boxes may result in a fine (law-enforcement rangers do regular campground and parking-lot monitoring).

Backpackers without a park-approved bear-resistant food container must usually rent one from a wilderness-permit-issuing station, visitor center or park store. Hanging your food in a tree (the counterbalancing method) no longer works, as too many black bears have figured out that trick.

Bear Encounters: Dos & Don'ts

For many visitors, black bears represent a mix of the fascinating and the frightening. It's not often we get to see such powerful, majestic animals in the wild – at the same time, some visitors would just as soon not see one while in the park. Bears entering developed areas in search of human food should be treated differently from wild bears observed in their natural environment.

➡ If you spot a bear, do not drop your food and run. Gather others together and wave your arms to look big and intimidating. Make noise by banging pots and pans, clapping your hands and yelling.

➡ Do not attempt to retrieve food from a bear, and don't corner the bear – give it plenty of room to escape.

➡ Never throw rocks, which can seriously injure or kill a bear.

➡ Do not drop your pack or run, which may trigger the bear's instinct to chase – you can't outrun a bear!

➡ Stay together and keep small children next to you, picking up little ones. Give the bear lots of room (150ft or more). If a bear chuffs (ie huffs and puffs), stamps its feet and paws the ground, you're way too close.

➡ Never get between a sow and her cubs. If you spot a lone cub, its mother and siblings are likely nearby.

➡ Stand still and watch the bear (nonflash photos are OK), but don't linger. If a bear starts moving toward you, step far off the trail and let it pass by, making sure not to block its escape routes.

➡ A bear may 'bluff charge' to test your dominance. Stand your ground by making yourself look as big as possible (eg wave your arms above your head) and shouting menacingly.

➡ It's extremely rare for a black bear to attack humans, but if one does, fight back using any means available.

is descent. If symptoms are severe or don't resolve promptly, seek medical help. AMS can be life-threatening.

Cold
HYPOTHERMIA
Temperatures in the mountains can quickly drop from balmy to below freezing. A sudden downpour and high winds can also rapidly lower your body temperature.

Seek shelter when bad weather is unavoidable. Woolen clothing and synthetics, which retain warmth even when wet, are superior to cotton. Always carry waterproof layers and high-energy, easily digestible snacks such as chocolate or dried fruit.

Symptoms of hypothermia include exhaustion, numbness (especially in fingers and toes), shivering, stumbling, slurred speech, disorientation or confusion, dizzy spells, muscle cramps and irrational or even violent behavior.

To treat the early stages of hypothermia, get victims out of the wind or rain, remove any wet clothing and replace it with dry, insulating clothing. Give victims warm liquids (no alcohol or caffeine) and high-calorie, easily digestible food.

In advanced stages, gently place victims in warm sleeping bags with heat packs or hot-water bottles (insulated to prevent burns) cocooned inside a waterproof outer wrapping. Do not rub a victim's skin.

FROSTBITE
Frostbite refers to the freezing of extremities, including fingers, toes and nose. Signs and symptoms include a whitish or waxy cast to the skin, as well as itching, numbness and pain.

Warm the affected areas by immersion in warm (not hot) water, only until the skin becomes flushed. Frostbitten body parts should not be rubbed, and blisters should not be broken. Pain and swelling are inevitable. Seek medical attention immediately.

Heat
DEHYDRATION
To prevent dehydration drink plenty of fluids (minimum one gallon per day). Eat enough salty foods – when you sweat, you lose electrolytes, too. Avoid diuretics such as caffeine and alcohol.

Because your body can only absorb about a quart (1L) of water per hour, prehydrate before starting a long hike.

HEAT EXHAUSTION
It's easy to forget how much fluid you are losing through perspiration while you are hiking, particularly at cooler, higher elevations or if a strong breeze is drying your skin quickly.

Symptoms of heat exhaustion include feeling weak, headache, irritability, nausea or vomiting, dizziness, muscle cramps, heavy sweating and/or cool, clammy skin and a fast, weak pulse.

Treatment involves getting out of the heat and/or sun to rest, removing clothing that retains heat (cotton is OK), cooling skin with a wet cloth and fanning continuously. Rehydrate with water, sugar drinks with a teaspoon of salt, or sports drinks. Recovery is usually rapid, though you may feel weak for days afterward.

HEATSTROKE
Heatstroke is a serious, life-threatening condition that occurs when body temperature rises to dangerous levels. Symptoms come on suddenly and include weakness, nausea, hot, flushed and dry skin (sweating stops), elevated body temperature, dizziness, confusion, headaches, hyperventilation, loss of coordination and, eventually, seizures, collapse and loss of consciousness.

Seek medical help immediately. Meanwhile rapidly cool the person by getting them into the shade, removing clothes, spraying with water, covering them with a wet cloth or towel, fanning vigorously and applying ice or cold packs to the neck, armpits and groin. Give fluids if they're conscious.

SUNBURN
You face a greater risk from sun exposure at high elevations. Sunburn is possible on hazy or cloudy days, and even when it snows. Use sunscreen and lip moisturizer with UVA and UVB protection and an SPF of 30 or greater, and reapply throughout the day. Wear a wide-brimmed hat and sunglasses, and consider tying a bandanna around your neck for extra protection.

Bites & Stings
Do not attempt to pet, handle or feed any wild animal, including squirrels and deer, that may bite humans. Any animal bite or scratch should be promptly and thoroughly cleansed with soap and water, followed by application of an antiseptic (eg iodine, alcohol) to prevent infection. Ask local health authorities about the advisability of rabies treatments.

SNAKES
Snakes frequent areas below 8000ft, so keep your eyes on the trail, wear hiking boots and don't stick your hands into any places you can't see (eg under rocks).

Rattlesnakes, the only venomous snakes in the Sierra Nevada, usually give warning of their presence and are most often found near streams in tall grasses and underneath rocks. Backing away (slowly!) from rattlers usually prevents confrontation. Most rattlesnake bites are caused by people intentionally picking up the snake or poking it with a stick. Rattlesnake bites are seldom fatal and adult rattlers don't always inject venom when they bite.

If bitten, remove any constricting jewelry and clothing, splint the extremity, keep the wounded part below the level of the heart and move it as little as possible. Stay calm and get to a medical facility as soon as possible. Depending on the bite, antivenom, available only in a few area hospitals, is usually the only cure. If there is no sign of bruising, swelling or other symptoms after 30 minutes, envenomation is unlikely. Bring the dead snake for identification if you can, but don't risk being bitten again.

The use of tourniquets and sucking out the venom have been comprehensively discredited.

INSECTS & SPIDERS

Much of the Sierra Nevada teems with annoying mosquitoes, especially at high elevations in midsummer. You're more likely to get bitten near standing water or snowmelt. Apply insect repellent and wear long-sleeved shirts and long pants when hiking, especially in late spring and early summer.

Present in brush, forest and grassland, ticks may carry Lyme disease. Early symptoms are similar to the flu (eg chills, high fever, headache, digestive problems, general aches). Also look for an expanding red rash. Check your clothes, hair and skin after hiking, and your sleeping bag if it has been outside. If you find unattached ticks, simply brush them off. Otherwise, carefully grab the tick's head with tweezers, then gently pull upwards – do not twist or force it.

Some spider bites (eg from black widows or brown recluses) contain toxic venom, to which children are more vulnerable. Clean the bite site and apply ice or cold compress to the affected area, then seek medical help immediately.

Safe Hiking
Poison Oak

Watch out for western poison oak on the western slopes of the Sierra Nevada below elevations of 5000ft. This poisonous shrub is most easily identified by its shiny, reddish-green tripartite leaves, which turn crimson in the fall, and its clusters of green or white berries. In winter, when the plant has no leaves, it looks brown and twiggy, but it can still cause a serious allergic reaction if it touches your skin. If you accidentally brush against poison oak, scrub the area immediately with soap and water or an over-the-counter remedy such as Tecnu, a soap specially formulated to remove the plant's itchy urushiol oils.

Waterfalls, Cliffs & Rockfall

Smooth granite beside rivers, streams and waterfalls is often slippery, even when dry. Approach any waterfall with caution and, above all, don't get into the water. If you slip, the current will drag you over the top of the fall, likely killing you. Despite warning signs in several languages and protective railings in many places (eg Yosemite's Mist Trail), people do die after wading above waterfalls.

Use caution when hiking around cliff edges and precarious viewpoints. Some park overlooks have railings, but plenty don't.

Always be alert to the danger of rockfall, especially after heavy rain. If you accidentally let loose a rock on a trail, loudly warn other hikers below. Moss- and lichen-covered rocks mean the rockfall is an old one. Rockfall is second only to drownings as the most common cause of fatalities to hikers in the Sierra Nevada. In Yosemite at least, 2018 saw the first rockfall fatality since 1999 (16 in all of the park's history).

Crossing Streams & Rivers

On some backcountry trails you may have to ford a river or stream swollen with snow-melt that is fast flowing and cold enough to be a potential risk. Before stepping out from the bank, ease one arm out of the shoulder strap of your pack and unclip the belt buckle – should you lose your balance and be swept downstream, it will be easier to slip off your backpack.

If you're linking hands with others, grasp at the wrist or cross arms at the waist, both of which are tighter grips than a simple handhold. If you're fording alone, plant a stick or your hiking poles upstream to give you greater stability and to help you lean against the current.

Walk side on to the direction of flow so that your body presents less of an obstacle to rushing water.

Lightning & Storms

Before starting your hike, especially if you're heading up an exposed peak or dome, check the weather forecast first at a visitor center or ranger station. Regardless of the forecast, if you're planning a long hike you should carry rain gear and be prepared for the worst. Changeable weather is a given in the mountains.

When a storm is brewing avoid exposed ridges, summits and granite domes (eg Yosemite's Half Dome), as well as shorelines and bodies of water. Lightning has a penchant for crests, lone trees, small depressions, gullies and cave entrances, as well as wet ground.

If you are caught out in the open during a lightning storm, crouch or squat on dry ground with your feet together, keep a layer of metallic-free insulation (eg sleeping pad) between you and the ground, and place all metal objects (eg metal-frame backpacks and hiking poles) far away from you.

Behind the Scenes

SEND US YOUR FEEDBACK

We love to hear from travelers – your comments keep us on our toes and help make our books better. Our well-traveled team reads every word on what you loved or loathed about this book. Although we cannot reply individually to your submissions, we always guarantee that your feedback goes straight to the appropriate authors, in time for the next edition. Each person who sends us information is thanked in the next edition – the most useful submissions are rewarded with a selection of digital PDF chapters.

Visit **lonelyplanet.com/contact** to submit your updates and suggestions or to ask for help. Our award-winning website also features inspirational travel stories, news and discussions.

Note: We may edit, reproduce and incorporate your comments in Lonely Planet products such as guidebooks, websites and digital products, so let us know if you don't want your comments reproduced or your name acknowledged. For a copy of our privacy policy visit lonelyplanet.com/privacy.

WRITER THANKS

Michael Grosberg

Thanks to the following for their hospitality, advice and insight: Steve Bumgardner of Yosemite Notes; Lisa Cesaro and Anna Williams from Aramark; Brooke Smith in Fish Camp; Terri Marshall; Jenn Edwards in Groveland; Scott Gediman and Jamie Richards from the National Park Service; and baby Rosie and Carly for sharing the trip and trails.

Jade Bremner

Thanks to destination editor Sarah Stocking for her support and quick-fire responses on Yosemite, Kings Canyon and Sequoia. Plus, everyone working behind the scenes on this project – Cheree Broughton, Dianne, Jane, Neill Coen, Evan Godt and Helen Elfer. Last but not least, thanks to my fearless hiking companion Jo Walton, who didn't even flinch when we encountered black bears, and helped me in crossing some treacherous rivers to bring Lonely Planet readers the most up-to-date trail information.

ACKNOWLEDGMENTS

Climate map data adapted from Peel MC, Finlayson BL & McMahon TA (2007) 'Updated World Map of the Köppen-Geiger Climate Classification', Hydrology and Earth System Sciences, 11, 163344.

Cover photograph: Bridalveil Fall and Yosemite Valley shrouded in cloud, Michael Hutchinson/Robert Harding ©

THIS BOOK

This 5th edition of Lonely Planet's *Yosemite, Sequoia & Kings Canyon National Parks* guide was curated by Michael Grosberg, and researched and written by Michael and Jade Bremner. The 3rd and 4th editions were written by Beth Kohn and Sara Benson. This guidebook was produced by the following:

Destination Editor Sarah Stocking

Senior Product Editors Grace Dobell, Kate Mathews, Victoria Smith

Product Editor Bruce Evans

Senior Cartographer Alison Lyall

Book Designer Jessica Rose

Assisting Editors Melanie Dankel, Andrea Dobbin, Shona Gray, Carly Hall, Trent Holden, Anne Mulvaney, Maja Vatrić

Cartographer Corey Hutchison

Cover Researcher Naomi Parker

Thanks to Ben Buckner, Evan Godt, Trisha Ping, Isla Ratcliff

Index

NIGEL HEANEY

LONELY PLANET IN THE WILD